Pastoral Deities in Western India

Pastoral Deities in Western India

Günther-Dietz Sontheimer

Translated by
Anne Feldhaus

New York Oxford
OXFORD UNIVERSITY PRESS
1989

Oxford University Press

Oxford New York Toronto
Delhi Bombay Calcutta Madras Karachi
Petaling Jaya Singapore Hong Kong Tokyo
Nairobi Dar es Salaam Cape Town
Melbourne Auckland

and associated companies in
Berlin Ibadan

Published by Oxford University Press, Inc.,
200 Madison Avenue, New York, New York 10016

Library of Congress Cataloging-in-Publication Data
Sontheimer, Günther-Dietz.
[Birobā, Mhaskobā und Khaṇḍobā. English]
Pastoral deities in western India/by Günther-Dietz Sontheimer:
translated by Anne Feldhaus.
p. cm.
Translation of: Birobā, Mhaskobā und Khandobā.
Bibliography: p. Includes index.
ISBN 0-19-505500-4
1. Cults—India—Maharashtra.
2. Maharashtra (India)—Religion. I. Title.
BL2016.M33S66 1989 294.5'0954'792—dc19 88-16872 CIP

Map of Southwestern Maharashtra
from the original German version, Birobā, Mhaskobā und
Khaṇḍobā, © 1976 South Asia Institute.
Reprinted by permission of the Institute.

Map of the monsoon camps
from Pastoralists and Nomads in South Asia, L. S. Leshnik
and G. D. Sontheimer, eds., © 1975 South Asian
Institute of the University of Heidelberg.
Reprinted by permission of the Institute.

9 8 7 6 5 4 3 2 1

Printed in the United States of America
on acid-free paper

Preface

This book is based primarily on oral texts collected during field work carried out in Maharashtra and Karnatak between 1967 and 1972. Rather than concentrating on the usual Indological study of written sources, the book is devoted to the context in which the sources were composed. The danger of losing valuable materials for the historical study of Indian culture and religion is not the most immediate with respect to Sanskrit texts, although many of these have not yet been published. The danger is rather that scholars of the texts will lose awareness of the texts' presuppositions, and hence of their full meaning.

Much in the Sanskrit texts is but allusion and hint based on traditional thought and ways, self-evident to a reader or listener who retains the traditional consciousness. Today these ways are disappearing, or they are adapting to westernized or new Indian middle-class conceptions. Such conceptions are in many respects the result of a spiritual and cultural evolution; they emphasize only certain components of traditional behavior and thought. For this reason, much in the classical scriptural sources remains unexplained, or receives an idiosyncratic, selective, or modernistic interpretation.

If one wants to understand the background, function, and genesis of the Sanskrit texts, one must remember that, however abstract and "philosophical" the texts may be, their substance, their "raw material," did not arise on its own in the mind of the Brahman. One can almost postulate a continuity from the notions of the forest tribes to the highest thought in the Sanskrit texts. The life and conceptual universe of many castes and groups, including pastoralist groups and forest tribes, contributed to the formation of the texts. At some point, in any case, the Brahman scholar was compelled to take into account the customs and thought of these groups, whether he had to "codify" extremely heterogeneous, even "shocking," forms of marriage in the Dharmaśāstras or to confront the more popular forms of worship that he attempted to refute in the *Pūrvamīmāṃsāsūtras.*[1]

The compartmentalization of Indian social life and the persistent preservation of tradition within a group in spite of innovations resulting from symbiosis with other groups (''Sanskritization'' or ''Kṣatriyaization,'' for example) have meant that old, even prehistoric, ideas and patterns of behavior have been retained.[2] In the villages, among pastoralist groups and forest tribes, it is still possible to examine the multiple manifestations of culture, religion, and history, as well as the customs and oral materials reflected in the written texts. Except for attempts like Ruben's somewhat diffuse one in *Eisenschmiede und Dämonen in Indien* [Blacksmiths and demons in India] (Leiden, 1931), Indologists have until very recently neglected to take account of these sources. Among historians, D. D. Kosambi was perhaps the first to make a serious attempt to combine armchair philology with archeological, ethnological, linguistic, and other investigations.[3]

If, as an Indologist, a historian, or a student of religion, one wants to free oneself from purely ethnocentric ideas rooted in Western presuppositions, then one must also put aside or modify certain important assumptions that influence the European study of history. Louis Dumont has pointed out how wrong it is to take the individual as the starting point for the study of Indian social phenomena.[4] The group is of primary importance; the individual is subordinated to it. Kingship, for example, is as important in India as in Europe, but the Hindu king is essentially a fairly anonymous *arbiter* among various groups; his kingdom has fluctuating borders and he tends to be involved in endless feuds. Thus modern historical accounts of Hindu dynasties remain, in the last analysis, conventional, uninformative, and anemic. Indian history should also be considered from the point of view of the historical development of groups; the present work attempts to make a start in this direction.

---

1. The folk conception, expressed in the thesis of the *pūrvapakṣin,* is that the deity is embodied, that he receives food in the form of sacrificial offerings, that he accepts gifts and can be their ''owner,'' and that he rewards the sacrificer for his actions by giving him what he wants (Śabara on Jaimini's *Pūrvamīmāṃsāsūtras,* IX.1.6–9). See Günther-Dietz Sontheimer, ''Religious Endowments in India: the Juristic Personality of Hindu Deities,'' *Zeitschrift für vergleichende Rechtswissenschaft,* 67 (1964) 45–100.

2. D. D. Kosambi, ''Living Pre-History in India,'' *Scientific American,* 216/12 (1967) 112ff.

3. D. D. Kosambi, ''Combined Methods in Indology,'' *Indo Iranian Journal,* 6 (1963) 177–202.

4. Louis Dumont, ''The Individual as an Impediment to Sociological Comparison and Indian History,'' in *Social and Economic Change (Essays in Honour of Professor D. P. Mukerji),* Baljit Singh and V. B. Singh, eds. (Bombay, 1967), pp. 226–48.

The multilayered character and simultaneous juxtaposition of religious conceptions are found not only in Sanskrit texts but also in the great folk cults and their centers. The different layers consist in large part of the traditional notions of the different groups. What, then, could be more appropriate than a precise investigation of each group's notions?

To be sure, the notions characteristic of the various groups have become mixed together, and an individual or group may borrow ideas from other layers and groups: thus, Dhangars believe in the individuality of their special god Birobā in a particular place, and on the other hand they believe—a notion more typical of other castes—that Birobā is but an *avatār* of one aspect of Śiva. With Hultkrantz we can speak of religious "configurations."[5]

The same complexity and "contradictoriness" mark the Sanskrit texts as well. But for traditional Indians this does not involve a cleavage in religious consciousness. Rather, all religious phenomena have their meaning and function in relation to each group, individual, time, and place, and are only to this extent mutually exclusive. The "persistence" of older layers rests in part upon the fact that the ideas correspond to the natural and social environment.[6] Taking the three deities Birobā, Mhaskobā, and Khaṇḍobā as an example, this work will attempt to say something about the religious conceptions of the groups behind the cults, and at the same time about the history of these groups, bearing in mind their social and ecological environment.

The term "ecological environment" brings us to another postulate for the understanding of history. Until the most recent times, ecology—the alternation of the seasons, the monsoon, and the characteristics of the soil—has had a greater influence on the course of Indian history than a scholar thinking in Western terms is inclined to believe. Economic forms, religion, myths—the landscape has made its impression on all of them. In Caṅkam literature the land was divided into five regions: the mountain land or impenetrable forest; the forest/pastureland; the river landscape, with irrigated rice cultivation; the seashore; and the wasteland. Each of these regions was characterized by particular economic forms, social groups, and cults—even when, if the regions became incorporated into a kingdom, they entered into symbiosis with one another and their cults merged.

Although the division into five landscapes in ancient Tamil literature takes external reality more fully into account, and the differentiation between mountainland/jungle and forest/pasture is especially valuable, in Sanskrit

5. A. Hultkrantz, "Configurations of Religious Belief among the Wind River Shoshoni," *Ethnos,* 21 (1956) 194–215.

6. See K. Jettmar, "Fruchtbarkeitsrituale und Verdienstfeste im Umkreis der Kafiren," *Mitteilungen der Anthropologischen Gesellschaft in Wien,* 95 (1965) 109–16.

literature a major role is played by the opposition between, on the one side, the established settlement/regularly ordered land/established social system, and, on the other side, the jungle/forest, where there lives the ascetic who has left society. Louis Dumont is again the one who has pointed out this spatial dichotomy and its possible implications.[7] To Dumont's ideas it can be added that the Buddhist monk, the Śaiva or Vaiṣṇava Gosāvī, the Liṅgāyat priest, the immigrant Brahman, and others, did not merely live as ascetic renouncers in the forest area. They also brought with them the religion of the established settlement, and thus contributed to the transformation of the "uncivilized" area (*vanam*) into a "civilized" *kṣetra* or *tīrtha*.

In his outstanding work *Trilogie altindischer Vegetationsmächte* (Zurich/Leipzig, 1937), J. J. Meyer has described especially the religion of farmers and sedentary peoples, with a profound understanding of their ways of thought. There are also numerous studies of castes and villages by social anthropologists, and, at the other end of the scale, numerous ethnographic and ethnological works on forest tribes.

Here my primary effort has been to gather material in a particular region about the Dhangars, a group situated between these two poles. Until recently, the Dhangars were mostly nomadic herdsmen and herdsmen-farmers. For the sake of simplicity, I have used the term "pastoralist groups" to refer to both of these divisions of the Dhangars, as long as the context does not require a distinction.

The description rests principally on the oral traditions of the Dhangars—that is, on myths and legends (in *ovī* meter and in prose), on the recollections of old Dhangars, and on temple and village traditions. But I have also included the oral traditions and statements of members of other groups who live in the area of my research and who play a role in the history of the cults. In addition I have used written sources in Marāṭhī, Kannaḍa, and Tamil, ethnographic and iconographic observations, and occasionally archeological finds.

In contrast to Purāṇic mythology, the myths of the Dhangars are relatively concrete in their setting and contents, and often correspond to verifiable occurrences. If one makes a systematic collection of oral literature in a particular region, there emerges almost spontaneously a history of the Dhangars and their cults. Many of the situations referred to in the legends and stories, but also in casual statements (such as Text 24), reflect typical events that have

7. *Homo Hierarchicus,* translated into English by Mark Sainsbury (London, 1970), p. 195 and n. 96c: "A major implication remains to be studied: the concept of space. . . . In particular, a clear dichotomy can be seen between cultivated or inhabited space and wild space, 'forest' or jungle, the village and the hermitage (*āśrama*) in which dwells the man who has left society, the renouncer."

occurred again and again in the history of the Dhangars and of many groups related to them—and perhaps also generally in the history of the Deccan. The arrival of the Dhangars in an established settlement of other groups, for instance, may be reflected in the story of the Dhangars' gods' arrival in the place.

The texts cited are extracts from a collection of about two hundred tape recordings lasting 90 to 120 minutes each. The language of most of these oral statements is a rural dialect of Marāṭhī found in the southern districts of Maharashtra, including Poona District. Several Kannaḍa texts have also been included. All of the tapes have been transcribed.

In citing these texts, I have preserved their integrity as far as possible, even though some parts are not needed as documentation. Certain key terms are reproduced in parentheses in the original language. Words needed to elucidate the contents or the meaning are enclosed in square brackets. In order to protect the narrators' anonymity, at least to some extent, usually only the place of origin of the text is given, and sometimes the caste of the narrator or singer as well. A list of 250 names, caste designations, and addresses of the narrators and informants was appended to the original manuscript but has been omitted from the published version.

The multilayered character of a group's or even an individual informant's religious conceptions necessitated long and frequent stays among the Dhangars. The boundaries of the "focal area of research" referred to frequently below are roughly those of Map 3.

The Appendix, below, is a translation of "The Biography of God Śrī Nāth Mhaskobā"[8] from Vīr (Purandar Taluka, Poona District). In a sense, this account of the god Mhaskobā can be considered a final chapter, because it vividly illustrates the last stage in the development of a pastoralist god: his arrival in a permanent settlement of agriculturalists and his adoption by all castes.

The field work I carried out in Maharashtra and Karnatak from 1967 to 1972 was made possible by the generous financial support of the German Research Council (DFG) and the South Asia Institute of the University of Heidelberg. I owe great thanks to Professor Dr. H. Berger for his unending encouragement. He fully supported the idea that Indology need not be conceived exclusively as the study of written texts. In his lectures and in conver-

---

8. Hari Bālakṛṣṇa Ārole, *Śrīnāth Mhaskobā Devācem̐ Caritra* (Puṇem, 1889; second printing, 1926; third printing, 1972; slightly revised edition, Vīr, 1972). TRANSLATOR'S NOTE: The translation of this *Caritra* in the German version of this book was based on the third and fourth printings of the *Caritra,* but the present translation, in the Appendix of this English version, has been made directly from the Marāṭhī of a later, but undated, printing. The footnotes in the Appendix are for the most part translated from the German.

sation he has also contributed substantially to my understanding of India, and he has enriched my work with valuable suggestions and advice. In addition I am grateful to many colleagues at the South Asia Institute for a number of stimulating discussions.

From 1958 to 1961, Professor D.D. Kosambi introduced me to the history and religion of Maharashtra; for this I owe him deep thanks. Mr . R. P. Nene and Dr. S. N. Bhavsar, both of Poona, accompanied me at the beginning of my field work; I am grateful for their help. For assistance in transcribing the tapes I thank Mr. Rajaram Zagade as well as Mr. Ramdas Atkar, who also distinguished himself as a jeep driver. I am grateful to the scholars of Deccan College, especially to the late Professor Iravati Karvé, for much advice and assistance. I should like to thank my informants and friends, especially the Dhangars, for their readiness to help and their interest in my work. I might mention here, standing for all of them, Mr. Sakharam B. Lakade, a nomadic Dhangar, who helped me greatly both by putting me in contact with informants and by sharing with me his own rich knowledge of the Dhangars' traditions.

Finally I should like to thank Mrs. H. Werny and others for their patient assistance in typing the manuscript.

New Delhi
May 1974

G. D. S.

Translator's Note

Except for the Appendix, which has been retranslated from the Marāṭhī, this book is a translation of Günther-Dietz Sontheimer's *Birobā, Mhaskobā und Khaṇḍobā: Ursprung, Geschichte und Umwelt von Pastoralen Gottheiten in Mahārāṣṭra* (Schriftenreihe des Südasien-Instituts der Universität Heidelberg, vol. 21 [Wiesbaden: Franz Steiner Verlag, 1976]). Slight changes have been made, principally in order to make the book accessible to a wider readership than that for which the original German version was intended. Some of the paragraphs have been rearranged, for example, and several Marāṭhī and Sanskrit terms that occur in the original have been translated into English (the Marāṭhī or Sanskrit is usually given in parentheses after the English). In addition, Professor Sontheimer has made some minor changes and additions to the contents, and has added to the bibliography a number of works that have appeared since the book was first published in German.

I am grateful to Mr. Tilmann Waldraff of the Max Mueller Bhavan, Poona, for his generosity in checking parts of the translation; to Bonnie Kline, Lisa Lyons, and others of the Arizona State University Word Processing Center for typing the manuscript and the many revisions; and to the South Asia Institute of the University of Heidelberg for permission to publish the translation. I am grateful to Professor Sontheimer not only for his tolerance of my attempt to translate his work for English readers, but especially for his painstaking field research and the astonishingly fresh glimpses he has given us of the religious life and oral literature of pastoralists in the western Deccan.

Poona A. F.
September 1988

Notes on Transliteration

Citations of individual terms, phrases, or sentences from the original texts have been transcribed according to the dialect in which they were spoken. Occasionally these citations have been elucidated by giving their written Marāṭhī form. In transcribing the written language, which essentially corresponds to careful pronunciation of the Marāṭhī spoken in Poona, the inherent *a* is omitted: Bhairav, rather than Bhairava, for example. Certain written forms deriving from Sanskrit have been retained: Śiva and *vāhana,* for example, instead of Śiv and *vāhan.* Names of states, districts, and major cities, as well as certain terms rather widely used in English, have been given in their English forms, without diacritical marks: Maharashtra, Sholapur District, Poona, Brahman, and Taluka, for example, rather than Mahārāṣṭra, Śolāpūr District, Puṇeṃ, Brāhmaṇ, and Tālukā. Otherwise, geographical names have been transcribed according to their local pronunciation, which often allows for etymological inferences. An *anusvāra* occurring in the written form of a word has been represented here by the corresponding nasal: Khaṇḍobā rather than Khaṃḍobā.

For written sources, the author, title, and publication data have been transliterated according to customary Indological usage, and the *anusvāra* has been represented by *ṃ*.

Contents

1. Ecology and the Distribution of Pastoralist Groups in the Deccan, 3

1. Ecological conditions in the area under study: rainfall, vegetation, and soil, 3
2. Ecological conditions and the distribution of traditional pastoralist groups elsewhere in the Deccan, 8

2. The Landscapes in Ancient Tamil Literature, 11

1. The five landscapes in Caṅkam literature, 11
   - 1.1. The theory of five landscapes, 11
   - 1.2. The mountain landscape (*kuṟiñci*), 12
   - 1.3. The pastureland (*mullai*), 13
   - 1.4. The river valley (*marutam*), 15
   - 1.5. The desert region (*pālai*), 15
2. The deities of the various landscapes, 16

3. The Landscapes in the Period of the "Great Empires": The Example of Mhasvaḍ and Kharsuṇḍī, 19

1. The period of the "great empires," 19
2. Mhasvaḍ and Kharsuṇḍī as an example of the origin and development of cults in the forest and pastoral area, 22
   - 2.1. Mhasvaḍ, 22
   - 2.2. Kharsuṇḍī, 30

4. Forest and Pastoral Goddesses: Independence and Assimilation, 34

1. The "seven" goddesses, 34
2. The "mothers" and "sisters": protection, help, and magical power, 40
3. Mhākubāī—the Dhangar goddess, 43
4. M(h)asā—Rukmiṇī—Padubāī, 45
5. The quarrel between Kāḷbhairav and Yeḷammā, 50
6. Tukāī/Durgāmahiṣāsuramardinī, 56
7. The marriage to the goddess of the forest and the tribe: Bhairav/Mhaskobā/Khaṇḍobā and Bāḷāī ~ Bāṇāī ~ Bāḷubāī, 58

5. Forest and Pastoral Peoples: Hunters, Robbers, Traders, Ascetics, 69

1. The Koḷīs, 69
   - 1.1. Traditional occupations and gods, 69
   - 1.2. The encounter with Birobā, 77
   - 1.3. The assimilation of the Koḷīs, 83
2. The Rāmośīs: professional robbers and devotees of Khaṇḍobā, 84
3. The Liṅgāyats: ascetics, priests, and merchants, 88
   - 3.1. The Liṅgāyats as a link between nuclear agricultural regions, 88
   - 3.2. The Liṅgāyat merchants and Khaṇḍobā and Mhāḷsā, 91
   - 3.3. The Liṅgāyat gurus, 92
4. The Gosāvīs and the cult of Bhairav, 95
   - 4.1. The groups of Gosāvīs, 95
   - 4.2. The Gosāvīs and Kāḷbhairav of Sonārī, 97

6. Forest and Pastoral Peoples: Pastoralist Groups, 100

1. Gollas/Gavḷīs, 100
2. Kurubas, 105
3. Dhangars, 122
   - 3.1. The groups of Dhangars, 122
   - 3.2. Hāṭkar Dhangars, 123

7. The Religious Milieu of Two Camps of Nomadic Dhangars, 131

1. Description of the camps, 131
2. The religious year, 133
3. The Dhangars' *jatrās*: the change to vegetarianism, 135
4. *Kheḷ*: the festival for the gods and ancestors before the beginning of the migration; the importance of the ancestors, 137
5. Birobā comes to the camp, 141
6. The *devṛṣī,* 142
7. The roles of the Jaṅgama and the Brahman, 146

8. Integration of the Landscapes of Maharashtra: The Spread of Agriculture, 151

1. The period of the Yādavas of Devgiri, 151
2. The period of the local Rājās, Nāīks, and Marāṭhās, 155
3. The spread of agriculture; historical evidence from the Nirā and Karhā valleys, 166
   - 3.1. The expulsion of the Gavḷīs, 166
   - 3.2. Herdsmen (Dhangars) and farmers (Kuṇbīs, Marāṭhās, and Māḷīs), 173
   - 3.3. The transformation of herdsmen's gods into gods of all castes, 180

9. The Origin, Structure, and Transformation of the Cults of Birobā, Mhaskobā, and Khaṇḍobā, 185

1. Origin in the world of nature spirits, 185
2. The *vāhanas,* 195
3. The emergence of iconographic form; attributes and cult objects: the "fifty-two" *birudeṃ,* 198
4. Dominion over lower gods and spirits, 200
5. The marriage of the god; the scriptural definition of the god's "history," 203
6. Conclusion, 205

Appendix. The Biography of God Śrī Nāth Mhaskobā (*Śrīnāth Mhaskobā Devāceṃ Caritra*), 207

Part 1. The Origin of Śrī Kāḷbhairav, 207
Part 2. Why He Became Incarnated in Vīr, 210

Part 3. Description of the Festival, 225
Part 4. Devotees' Experiences, and the Things the God Likes Best, 231
Part 5. Who Built the Temple and When, and Present Arrangements, 235

Bibliography, 239

Index, 249

List of Illustrations

Map 1. Southwestern Maharashtra xviii

Map 2. Modern states and districts of South India 2

Map 3. The main area of the monsoon camps of the nomadic Hāṭkar Dhangars, including *vāḍīs* A and B 130

Illustrations follow page 122

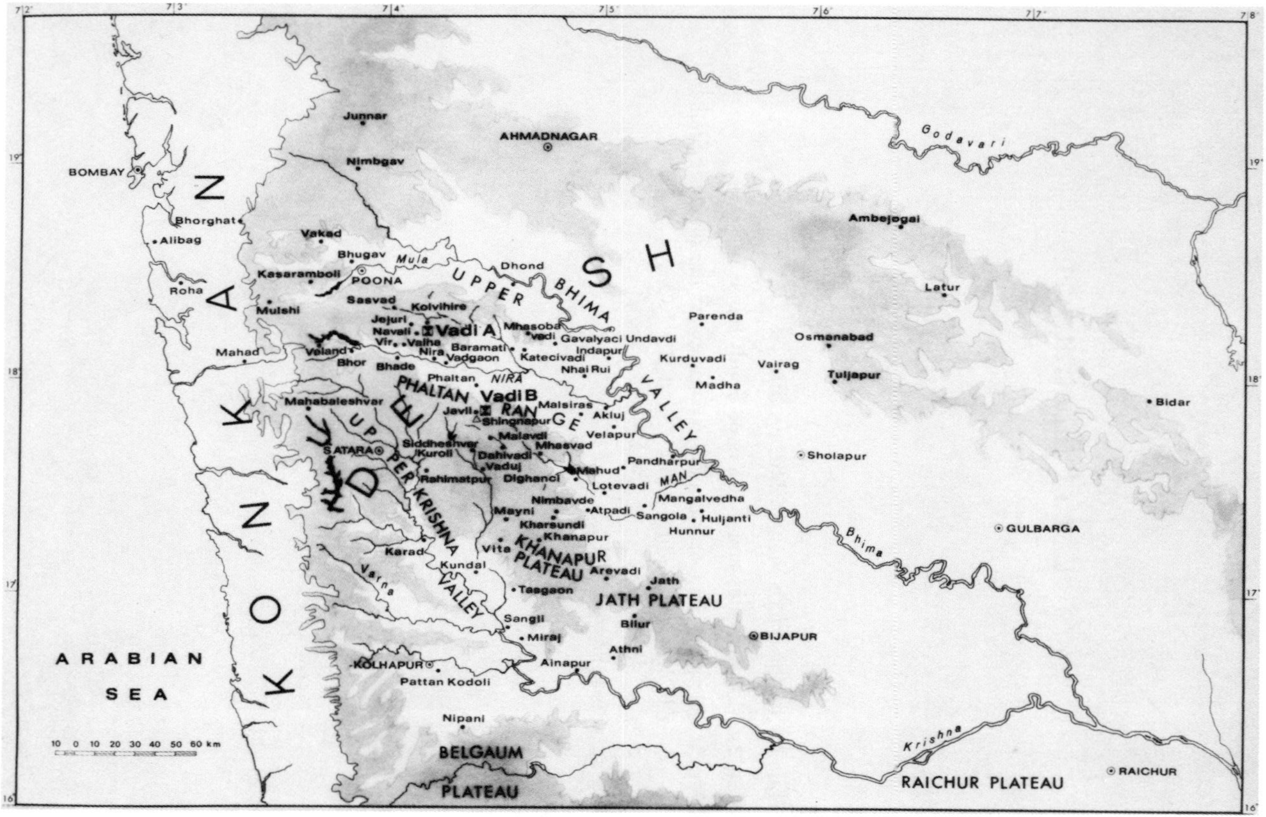

Southwestern Majarashtra.

Pastoral Deities in Western India

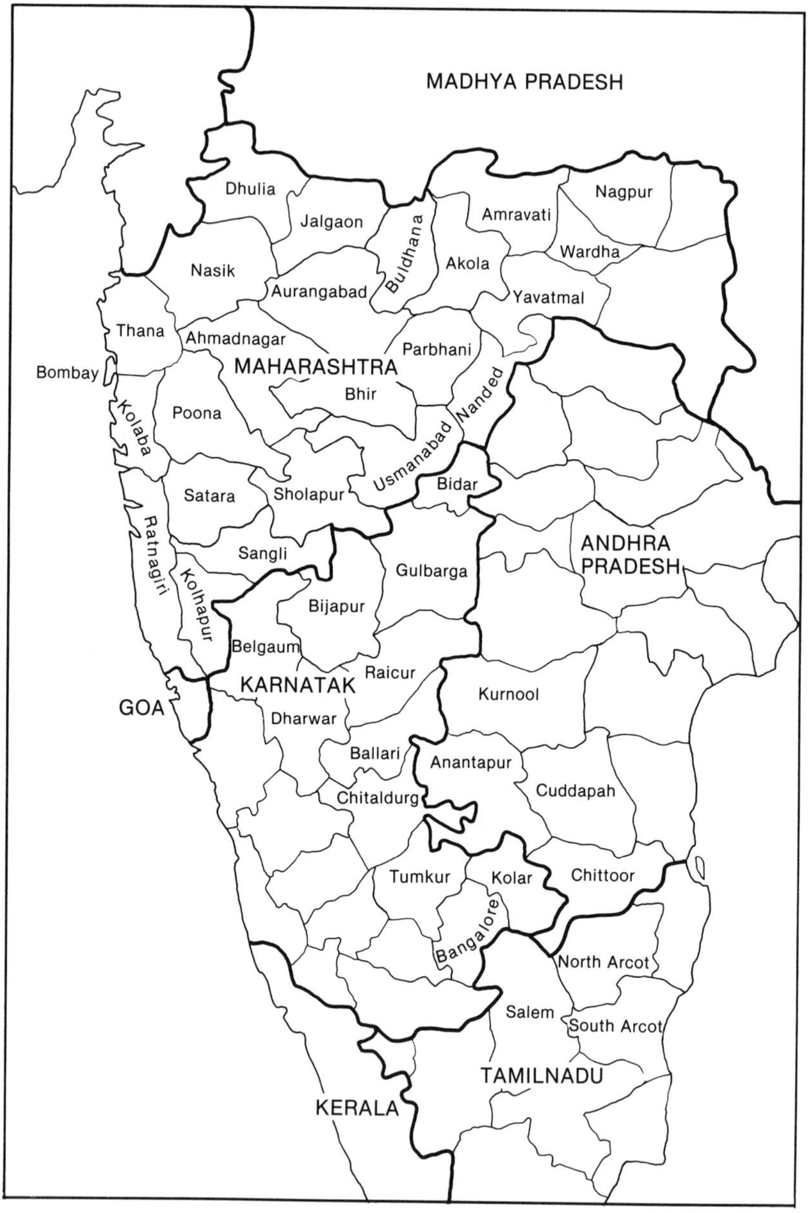

Modern states and districts of South India.

1

Ecology and the Distribution of Pastoralist Groups in the Deccan

1. Ecological Conditions in the Area under Study: Rainfall, Vegetation, and Soil

The field investigations for this study centered on western and southern Maharashtra, in the Deccan plateau (Marāṭhī, *deś*). The focus was on the districts of Poona, Satara, Kolhapur, and Sangli, the northern part of Belgaum District (in Karnatak State), the western part of Sholapur District, the southwestern edge of Usmanabad District, and the southern part of Ahmadnagar District. Without an understanding of the ecology of this region, an account of the history of its pastoral cults cannot be complete or even intelligible. For this reason, I begin by sketching the ecological conditions in the specific area under study as well as in the Deccan as a whole.[1]

Kolhapur District and the western parts of Poona, Ahmadnagar, Satara, Sangli, and Belgaum districts receive sufficient rain from the summer (June to September), southwest monsoon. In the eastern parts of these districts, east of a line drawn eastward from Poona and then bending southeast along the Mahādev mountain range, the frequency and amount of precipitation is much lower. In the coastal rice-growing area west of the Western Ghāṭs (the Koṅkaṇ), there are an average of twenty-five days of rain per month during the summer monsoon,[2] and at the highest point in the Ghāṭs, in Mahābaḷeśvar, the average annual rainfall reaches 6,000 millimeters. The amount of

1. These remarks on ecological conditions are based inter alia on the district handbooks of Maharashtra (census of 1961), on old and revised gazetteers, and on my own observations.

2. M. Domrös, "Zur Frage der Niederschlagshäufigkeit auf dem Indisch-Pakistanischen Subkontinent nach Jahresabschnitten," *Meteorologische Rundschau,* 21/2 (1968) 35–43.

precipitation declines rapidly in the so-called Māvaḷ,[3] the area between the Western Ghāṭs and Poona. In the thick forests of the Ghāṭs and the Māvaḷ, where rain is plentiful, there is still a scattering of exclusively pastoralist cattle-raising groups (e.g., the Mhaske Dhangars in the Koynā Valley), as well as the remnants of such tribes as the Koḷīs and Kātkarīs. The Māvaḷ is also an area characterized by the cultivation of rice. The soil is often reddish and dries out quickly, in stark contrast to the moist black soil to be seen farther east, in the valleys of the eastward-flowing rivers.

The amount of precipitation in the Māvaḷ is far greater than that in the area east of Poona. Accordingly, the *District Census Handbook* of 1961 divides Poona District into three zones:

1. the western zone (the Ghāṭs and the Māvaḷ), including Lonāvlā, a town on the Bombay-Poona railway line with an average annual rainfall of 4,500 millimeters;
2. the central zone, including Poona, which has an average annual rainfall of 750 millimeters; and
3. the eastern zone, which has an average annual rainfall of less than 500 millimeters. In this zone are included Havelī, Junnar, Śirūr, and Purandar Talukas.

Whereas the rains of the southwest monsoon fall heavily in Poona, they often do not reach the eastern zone; and the northeast monsoon can also sometimes fail here. A government inquiry commission appointed to determine where in Maharashtra scarcity conditions are regularly brought on by drought and insufficient irrigation concluded in 1960 that such conditions occur once every three years in the eastern talukas of Poona District, and once every six years in the other talukas. It is thus no coincidence that in the eastern talukas there are numerous settlements of nomadic Dhangars inhabited only seasonally. The Dhangars generally stay here from the middle of June to the middle of October—only as long, that is, as the monsoon brings enough rain to revive the pastures.

---

3. "The region along the eastern side of the *sahyādri* range. It is viewed as commencing at the termination of the *murheṃ*, and as extending forty or fifty miles eastward" (Molesworth, *Dictionary*). "*Murheṃ* = 1. mist; 2. (because it is, through the monsoon-months, enveloped in mists) the region along the summit and the levels of the waist and the immediate base of the Sahyādri-range. It is considered as extending five or six miles eastward, and as then lost in the *māvaḷ*" (Molesworth, *Dictionary*). See also D. D. Kosambi, *Myth and Reality* (Bombay, 1962), p. 61, who traces the name *māvaḷ* to *mavaḷā-devī*, mother goddesses who are found primarily in the Māvaḷ region, and who have also given their name to the region referred to as *māmāla-hāra* in Sātavāhana inscriptions. The *mavaḷā-devī* are generally identified with the seven *apsarases* (Marāṭhī, *sātī āsarā*) (Kosambi, ibid.), who are also found as sixteen water goddesses.

Satara District, which adjoins Poona District to the south, has the same three distinct rainfall zones. Khaṭāv, Māṇ, and Phalṭaṇ talukas—that is, the eastern part of the district—have an average annual rainfall of less than 600 millimeters; in the middle zone the rainfall varies from 600 to 1,200 millimeters. In Phalṭaṇ Taluka the soil near the hills is stony and not very fertile, but there is black soil along the Nirā River and its tributaries. In Khaṭāv Taluka the fertile soil is fairly deep and extends farther from the rivers than in Māṇ Taluka, but it is not as productive as that in Koregāv Taluka, to the west. In Māṇ Taluka the soil is poorer and less deep, with good soil to be found only in narrow strips along the rivers. Between these rivers, which generally dry up after the monsoon season, there lie broad tracts of *māḷ*—high, rocky terrain with not very fertile soil, suitable only for grazing and for the sparse cultivation of millet (Marāṭhī, *bājrī; Holcus spicatus*). With their pastures, Khaṭāv, Phalṭaṇ, and Māṇ talukas are, and have long been, a classic region of cattle herders. Besides raising cattle, the herders also cultivate millet, or lease land to farmers—particularly to members of the Māḷī caste—for half the harvest. Luckily for the present rapid development of agriculture, in the two eastern talukas of Khaṭāv and Māṇ one can strike underground water at relatively shallow levels, despite the unreliability of the rains.

In Kolhapur District also, the amount of precipitation decreases from west to east. In the western part of the district, the average annual rainfall is 6,000 millimeters near the Western Ghāṭs; in the region of Kurundvāḍ-Śiroḷ the annual average is 500 millimeters. Yet from the 1940s to the 1970s this district was not afflicted by a period of scarcity brought on by drought. Kolhapur has developed into a flourishing agricultural district, and exclusively pastoralist groups are now found only in the forests of the Ghāṭs.

In Sangli District the lowest annual rainfall is to be found in the northeast, in Khānapūr and Jath talukas, which have an average rainfall of 500 millimeters per year. This is another region that is stricken by drought one year out of every six, and is characterized for the most part by rocky and relatively infertile soil (*māḷ*).

To the south, Belgaum District in northern Karnatak adjoins both Kolhapur and Sangli districts. In contrast to the lava rock of Maharashtra, Karnatak has primarily archaic gneiss and granite. But although Maharashtra and Karnatak differ geologically—and are supposed for this reason to differ historically, culturally, and linguistically as well—in terms of precipitation there is no significant difference between Maharashtra and northern Karnatak up to the Tuṅgabhadrā River. Belgaum, in the west, has an average rainfall of 1,250 millimeters. The rainfall diminishes progressively toward the east: 500 to 620 millimeters per year in the area from the confluence of the Bhimā and Kṛṣṇā rivers to the Tuṅgabhadrā. South of the Tuṅgabhadrā the amount of precipitation rises: 750 to 1,000 millimeters per year. In this connection Raymond Allchin refers to the concentration of neolithic pastoralist centers in this area, which, with its scanty vegetation and low rainfall but good pastures, provided a suitable area for neolithic cattle herders.[4] For the same reason, northern Karnatak has also traditionally been a region of cattle herders.

Iron and regular plow-based agriculture seem to have advanced the development of the area south of the Tuṅgabhadrā River, whereas the northern part was unable to recover from the effects of deforestation, overgrazing, and dehydration. Here agriculture has been made possible only by irrigation provided by reservoirs and modern projects like the Tuṅgabhadrā dam.

In the eastern part of the focal area of study is Sholapur District, whose western part, comprising Sāṅgolā and Karmāḷā talukas, receives a fairly meager amount of rain. The average annual rainfall of the district amounts to 620 millimeters, but in Bārśī Taluka, near the Bālāghāṭ range, the annual rainfall reaches 720 millimeters. Sholapur District is known for its cotton. O. H. K. Spate characterizes the town of Śolāpūr as follows:

> . . . an isolated phenomenon, a predominantly industrial town, with no *raison d'être* save its position in a cotton tract. Originally a strategic centre commanding the Bhima route into or out of Maharashtra, it is now one of the few predominantly industrial towns of India, and perhaps the most homogenous, since its life revolves around its cotton mills.[5]

In this district as well there have time and again been periods of scarcity brought on by drought.

Large parts of Usmanabad District, in the northeastern part of the region under study, lie in the area affected by the northeast monsoon. This is true of Lāṭūr, Udgīr, Ahmadpur, Tuḷjāpūr, and Usmānābād talukas, which have an average rainfall of 900 millimeters per year. But in the northwestern part of the district, Parendā Taluka and Bhūm Mahāl, both of which lie on the lee side of the southwest monsoon, have an average annual rainfall of only 600 millimeters.

In the northern part of the region lies Ahmadnagar District. A rather large part of this district has a similarly scanty rainfall: 508 to 638 millimeters per year. Only six of its thirteen talukas are not subject to drought, and these lie in the west (Akolā Taluka) and in the north, in the valley of the Godāvarī River. Of the other talukas, Śrīgonda Taluka and a part of Karjat Taluka (= Rashin Circle) are affected by drought one year out of every three on the average, and Saṅgamner, Pātharḍī, and Jāmkheḍ talukas one year out of ten.

---

4. F. R. Allchin, *Neolithic Cattle-Keepers of South India* (Cambridge, 1963), pp. 6f.
5. O. H. K. Spate, *India and Pakistan* (London, 3rd edition, 1967), p. 697.

Similarly, in Aurangabad District there is a medium to low amount of rain east of Aurangabad: 625 to 750 millimeters per year in Auraṅgābād, Sillоḍ, Bhokardhan, Paiṭhaṇ, and Khuldābād Mahāl talukas. Parts of Gaṅgāpūr Taluka and Vaijāpūr Taluka have an average annual rainfall of less than 625 millimeters.

In northeastern Maharashtra there is a transition to regular and sufficient rainfall, such as is found, for example, in the districts of Buldhana, with 898 millimeters per year, and Nagpur, with 1,237 millimeters. The two districts of Dhulia and Jalgaon (West and East Khandesh) are in the transitional zone. These form an ecologically and historically important transition between central India and the Deccan. Jalgaon District and a part of Dhulia District lie in the dry zone, where there is a moderate annual rainfall of 625 millimeters.

Thus through the length of Maharashtra there stretches from north to south a strip of land that lies on the lee side of the southwest monsoon and is characterized by an average yearly rainfall of approximately 500 to 800 millimeters. But even beyond this central strip, to the northeast—that is, in Usmanabad, Bhir, and Parbhani districts—sufficient rainfall is not assured. This is also true of the area to the east. Thus, O. H. K. Spate aptly describes the site of the city of Bijapur: "Bijapur indeed is an extraordinary misfit; the capital of the Adil Shahi kingdom (15th–17th centuries), its immense domes look out over a poor and precarious countryside."[6]

This central north-south stretch of Maharashtra is crossed by the valley of the Taptī River, and by the valley of each of the rivers that flow toward the southeast. It is crossed by the Godāvarī River, and then, in the focal area of our study, by the Muṭhā and Mūlā rivers, tributaries of the Bhimā, and by the Karhā River in the high Sāsvaḍ basin (600 meters); it is crossed by the Māṇ, Yerlā, Pañcgaṅgā, and Dudhgaṅgā rivers, all of which flow into the Kṛṣṇā; and finally by the Bhimā itself, north of Raicūr. The river valleys are framed by mountain ranges, which fall away gradually to the east (like the Purandar hills) or southeast (like the Phalṭaṇ range), and by high plateaus: the Ahmadnagar plateau, the Rājurī plateau, the high river valleys of the Sāsvaḍ basin, Māṇdeś, the Khānapūr plateau, and the Jath plateau.

Generally, the soil in the river valleys is *regur*, the famous black earth that retains moisture and is often so dense that ten or twelve oxen are required to plow it. In the higher plateaus there is black or brown soil suitable for *rabi* crops of *jovārī (Holcus sorghum), bājrī,* and sugarcane, as long as there are canals, reservoirs, or wells to provide irrigation. Otherwise this central zone is characterized by high, rocky land, by mountain ranges and rocky foothills. In Marāṭhī such terrain is called *māḷ,* a term that also plays an important role

6. Ibid., pp. 704f.

in the realm of religious ideas.[7] This zone, which reaches from Khāndeś to the Tuṅgabhadrā River in Karnatak, has been a preferred area for herdsmen-farmers and nomadic herdsmen from the earliest—indeed, prehistoric—times.

2. Ecological Conditions and the Distribution of Traditional Pastoralist Groups Elsewhere in the Deccan

Andhra Pradesh, which borders the area of our study on the east and south-east, can also be characterized as basically a region of cattle herders, or at least a region preferred by cattle herders. This region—essentially the Telaṅgaṇa plateau—stretches from Hyderabad to the Tuṅgabhadrā and Kṛṣṇā rivers, including the districts of Kurnool, Anantapur, Cuddapah, and Chittoor. The mountains to the east, the Eastern Ghāṭs, separate this region from the fertile coastal rice-growing region of the state of Andhra Pradesh. On the plateau the annual rainfall varies from 635 to 1,016 millimeters. Except in the north, which is primarily jungle, the landscape is characterized by barren hills and reddish-brown plains scattered with isolated clusters of bushes. The rivers in the plains dry up for six months each year. Irrigation is provided by reservoirs created by damming water in the valleys. Most of the rice cultivation depends on irrigation made available in this way. The area looks like a savanna, with secondary shrubbery growing on soil that has long been exposed to overgrazing by goats. Much of it was formerly agricultural land.

Cuddapah, Kurnool, and Anantapur districts in southern Andhra Pradesh and Ballari District in Karnatak—which are also grouped together under the name Rāyalasīma—belong, along with the Rai doab, to the driest area of the Deccan (annual rainfall, 500 to 700 millimeters). Before the Tuṅgabhadrā dam was built, artificial irrigation played only a minor role in this entire region. Despite their dense population, even the plains of Anantapur and Chittoor districts are an agriculturally underdeveloped area, with *jovārī* and *bājrī* as the principal crops.

A large part of the population is composed of pastoralist groups and groups that traditionally followed pastoralist occupations. The principal group is the Gollas, a large, heterogeneous group consisting of numerous endogamous subcastes. Syed ul Hassan counted eighteen subcastes, but, as he himself discovered, this number is not exhaustive—a fact already suggested by the

7. For example, the god Birobā lives outside the village on high pasture land or on a hill (see 9.1, below). There is also Mhāliṅgrāya Māḷāppā, "the father on the high pasture."

number eighteen, a classic number that occurs as a stereotype in other contexts as well.[8]

Contemporary Gollas are cattle herders by tradition, but they often have other occupations as well. Their name is derived from Sanskrit *gopālā,* Prakrit *goālā,* as are the caste names of the Gvālas (in Bengal and Bihar), the Govārīs (in the eastern Sātpuḍā plateau and the Vaingaṅgā basin), and the Gavḷīs (in Maharashtra).

Another large group is the Kurumas, whose traditional occupation is herding sheep and goats or weaving woolen blankets (*kāmbḷī*). Corresponding to the Kurumas of Andhra Pradesh are the Kurubas in Karnatak.

Despite several minor regional differences, the present state of Karnatak can be divided into three areas: northern Karnatak (the former Bombay Karnatak), the Malnāḍ (which means "mountain land"), and the Maidān (here meaning "park land"). The Malnāḍ is a zone of woods along the Western Ghāṭs; the Maidān is generally the high plateaus that rise in the east (between Tumkur and Kolar) to granite hills. The *Mysore Gazetteer* sums up the general appearance of the Maidān region:

> The means of water-supply and the prevailing cultivation give the character to the various parts of the open country. The level plains of alluvial black soil, as in the north, growing cotton or millet; the districts irrigated by channels drawn from rivers, as in the south and west, displaying the bright hues of sugar-cane and rice-fields; the lands under tanks, filled with gardens of cocoa and areca palms; the higher-lying undulating tracts of red soil, as in the east, yielding ragi and the common associated crops; the stony and wide-spreading pasture grounds, as in the central parts, covered with coarse grass and relieved by shady groves of trees.[9]

In this region there live the traditional herding castes of Kurubas and Gollas.

To the north, northern Karnatak forms the transition zone between Maharashtra and Mysore. The Kuruba caste is especially typical of the Belgaum and Hublī-Dhārvāḍ area of northern Karnatak, cast of Kolhāpūr. Today this caste is divided into two principal groups. The more agriculturalist group is the Hattikaṅkaṇ Kurubas; in their weddings, cotton bracelets are tied on the bride and the bridegroom (*hatti* = cotton; *kaṅkaṇ* = bracelet). Among the Uṇṇikaṅkaṇ Kurubas, who specialize in raising sheep and goats, the wedding bracelet is made of wool (*uṇṇi* = wool).

The present state of Karnatak (Mysore) is renowned for its cattle raising—

---

8. Syed Siraj ul Hassan, *The Castes and Tribes of H.E.H. The Nizam's Dominions* (Bombay, 1920), p. 196.

9. B. Lewis Rice, *Mysore: A Gazetteer Compiled for Government* (London, revised edition, 1897), vol. 1, p. 3. See Spate, *India,* p. 702.

for example, for the Amrit Mahal breed of oxen from Hansur. These are used primarily as pack oxen and draft oxen, and they contributed to the speed and mobility of Haider Ali's military leadership. In the southeastern hill land of Mysore, up to the forested hills of Salem District in Tamilnadu (Pennagaram), is found the famous Ālambādī breed. Oxen of this breed are preferred as draft animals.[10]

Besides the Gollas and the Kurubas, there are also other pastoralist groups in this region, such as the Badagas in the Nilgiris. Finally, the Todas are also found here, representatives of a pastoral tradition of particular interest because of its great isolation. In Tamilnadu the principal pastoralist group is the Idaiyan (or *iṭaiyar*), who claim to be descended from the Yādavas; this group is to be found in the western districts of the coastal region (North and South Arcot), as well as farther inland in the basins of Salem and Chittoor.

---

10. *Madras District Gazetteer,* vol. 1, Salem (Madras, 1913), part 1, pp. 34f. R. W. Littlewood, "Alambady Cattle," *The Journal of the Madras Geographical Association,* 2/2 (1936) 126–29.

2

The Landscapes in Ancient Tamil Literature

1. The Five Landscapes in Caṅkam Literature

1.1 The Theory of Five Landscapes

The theory of five landscapes (*tiṇai*) is a motif of classical Tamil literature of the Caṅkam period.[1] The two types of Caṅkam poetry, *puṟam* and *akam,* are classified according to this principle. *Akam* has to do with domestic life, with people's inner lives, and especially with love: with the most personal aspect of people's lives. *Puṟam,* by contrast, represents everything about external, active life in the open, including a good deal about warlike activities. Thus, *akam* means love poetry and *puṟam* war poetry. On the basis of precise observations, certain situations, especially such romantic situations as separation, waiting, and union, were assigned, as themes of *akam* poetry, to certain physiographical regions, as were also certain activities of a chieftain—cattle theft, for instance—as themes of *puṟam* poetry. Thus the word *tiṇai* designates not only a region marked by certain ecological features, but also at the same time a romantic situation. Observation of the countryside, the landscape, the seasons, the fauna, the flora, the inhabitants, and so on, of a region formed an indispensable prerequisite for poetic creativity.

Although the description of the five landscapes became a matter of poetic convention, it is nevertheless based on an observation of nature that reflects actual conditions and occurrences in the five landscapes. If one speaks of "petrifications of old customs developed in objective reality,"[2] one easily

1. Ca. the 2nd century A.D. The grammar text *Tolkāppiyam* is supposed to have been composed in its principal features before the Caṅkam period, the *Cilappatikāram* around the 4th or 5th century (dating according to Kamil V. Zvelebil and A. Dhamotharan).

2. P. T. Srinivasa Iyengar, *History of the Tamils from the Earliest Times to 600 A.D.* (Madras, 1929), p. 60.

overlooks the fact that this division of the land into five regions with their physiographical, social, cultural, and religious peculiarities remains essentially valid in India, and particularly in the Deccan. Each of these five regions represents a world that is relatively independent, but nevertheless in symbiosis with the other four. Moreover, later regional development in the Deccan took place according to this pattern of five regions. An approach that recognizes this also permits us better to understand the historical significance and contemporary vestiges of the culture of pastoralist groups and forest tribes.

Unfortunately, Caṅkam literature, which is linguistically quite difficult, has not yet been exhaustively studied from the point of view of its significance for history, ethnology, and the study of religion; nor can such a study be carried out here in detail. Hence only a few of the basic features will be set forth and clarified by examples. Because the fifth landscape, the seashore (*neytal*), has no particular importance for our topic, it will be omitted.

1.2 The Mountain Landscape (*kuṟiñci*)

Kuṟiñci is the name of a flower (*Strobilanthus kunthianus*) that blooms once every twelve years in the mountains of South India. The *kuṟiñci* or mountain landscape described in the poems can still be recognized today in the sparsely populated parts of the Palani hills, in the Nilgiris, and in the Western Ghāṭs. *Akam* poems of the *kuṟiñci* landscape are connected with night, the cold season, and early frost. Typical birds are the peacock and the parrot; typical beasts are the monkey, the elephant, the horse, and the bull. The most important trees and plants are jackfruit trees, *vēṅkai* trees, and bamboo. The *vēṅkai* tree dominates the region.

The impenetrable forests of this region are the home of the mountain tribes of the Kāṉavar and Kuṟavar,[3] who live in the shelter of the jungle.[4] Bamboo provides them with "rice."[5] They trade ivory for salt, which comes from the coast. They cultivate millet (*cāmai; panicum*), which is watched over by young women in small fields, and watered by mountain streams. When the millet is pounded, depressions in the rocky ground serve as mortars.[6] In addition, the mountain tribes nourish themselves on tubers and wild honey.

3. *Malaipaṭukaṭām*, 318 and 320. (This and other references to Caṅkam texts are from the edition of S. Vaiyapurippillai, *Caṅka Ilakkiyam* [Madras, 2nd edition, 1967].)

4. *Malaipaṭukaṭām*, 279: *kāṭu kāttu uṟaiyum kāṉavar*.

5. Ibid., 121: *tōrai;* 133: *untūḻ*.

6. *Perumpāṇāṟṟuppaṭai*, 96f.

1.3 The Pastureland (*mullai*)

The pastoral region has less rich vegetation than does the mountain land. Rockier soil and thornbushes are typical.[7] The region takes its name from the jasmine creeper (*mullai; Jasminum sambac* or *Jasminum auriculatum*).

Scattered groups of trees or small groves provide diversion for the eye. Typical animals are gazelles, jungle fowls, cows, bulls, sheep, and goats.[8] The time of the "situation" is late evening and the beginning of the rainy season. So herdsmen keep their flocks near the villages; they are bringing them back to their pens. There are three types of herdsmen: those who keep cows,[9] those who keep buffaloes,[10] and those who keep sheep.[11]

In *Akam,* 94.1–8, we find the description of a shepherd (*iṭaiyaṉ*). In his hair he wears jasmine flowers (*mullai*), which shine like stars. It is midnight. With a long, drawn-out cry, the shepherd protects the herd and the young rams (*maṟitturu*) against the fox (*kuṟunari*). He has made his blanket into a hood and drawn it over his head, and he warms his hands at the fire.

In *Naṟṟiṇai,* 364.8–10, we read of herdsmen who have brought their herd back into the village. We hear how the muffled sound of the cowbells spreads through the village. Flutes sound in the village square. The herdsmen are called *kallākkōvalar*—occupants of the forest region who follow exclusively pastoralist occupations. *Perumpāṇāṟruppaṭai* describes a herdsmen's village (*varaippu*) where cows and sheep are kept in corrals made of thorn hedges and filled with cow dung.[12]

Outside the settlement (*pāṭi*) are the fields of the *mullai* region. In them is grown not rice, as in the fluvial plain, but only millet of the types *varaku* and *cāmai*. The fields belong to the farmers of the pastoral region. Huge plow oxen stand in their courtyards.[13] Thus, although cattle-raising predominates, the pastoral region is not defined by that alone, but supplements it with the cultivation of millet.[14]

---

7. Xavier S. Thaninayagam, *Landscape and Poetry* (London, 2nd edition, 1966), p. 99.

8. Kamil V. Zvelebil, "Pastoralism as Reflected in the Classical Tamil Theory of Landscapes," in L. S. Leshnik and G. D. Sontheimer, eds., *Pastoralists and Nomads in South Asia* (Wiesbaden, 1975), pp. 30ff.

9. *Kalittokai,* 103,37: *kōviṉattāyar.*

10. Ibid., 103,33: *kōṭṭiṉattāyar.*

11. Ibid., 103, 47; 113, 7: *pulliṉattāyaṉ.*

12. *Perumpāṇāṟruppaṭai,* 153ff.

13. Ibid., translation, p. 117, lines 226ff.; text, lines 195ff.

14. This mixed economy in the pastoral region of the Deccan and South India (the "tribal belt") is also attested to in L. S. Leshnik, *Burials of the Early Iron Age in South India* (Wiesbaden, 1974).

The inhabitants of the *mullai* region are called *āyar* (m.), *āycciyar* (f.), and *iṭaiyar* (m.), *iṭaicciyar* (f.). In the land of the Cholas, the Āyars seem to have had their own princes, but these were conquered.[15] A connection has been made between the Āyars and the Ābhīras.[16] They worshiped *yakṣas.*[17] Like the Ābhīras, the Āyars had bullfights, which mainly consisted in baiting or grappling the bulls.[18] After the fight, the young men and women would dance the *kuravai* dance.[19] The Āyars are mentioned by Ptolemy, who calls them Arioi. The next-largest herding group of the *mullai* region are the *Iṭaiyar.* They still live in Tamilnadu today, and follow pastoralist occupations.

The *mullai* and *kuṟiñci* regions were much less isolated from each other than are the other regions; there was a symbiosis between the two regions and they blended into each other.[20] At the bullfight, the herdsmen (*kōvalar*) of the *mullai* region and the residents of the *kuṟiñci* region (*kuṟavar*) rejoice at the victory. The noise of the fighting bull is so loud that the flowers of the *mullai* and *kuṟiñci* regions wither.[21] *Malaipaṭukaṭām* contains a description of a herdsmen's forest camp: the herdsmen have blankets made of sheepskin and move near the fire, which is supposed to keep away wild animals.[22] Cattle were often kept in the forests of the *kuṟiñci* region—perhaps a matter of transhumance. According to poetic convention, the first phase of war was cattle theft.[23] The word for cattle theft was *veṭci,* after the red flowers of that name of the *kuṟiñci* region; warriors setting off to steal cattle would decorate themselves with these flowers. Here again one cannot speak of a custom that has become fossilized into a poetical convention. Until the most recent times, cattle theft remained the principal cause of feuds between minor princes, villages, and tribes. The Maḻavars (section 1.5, below) provide an illustration of this.

---

15. V. Kanakasabhai, *The Tamils Eighteen Hundred Years Ago* (Madras, 1956), p. 57.

16. Ibid. Suryavanshi, *The Abhiras, Their History and Culture* (Baroda, 1962), pp. 16–18.

17. *Cilappatikāram,* Kaliyanasuntaraiyer, ed. (Madras, 1950), XV.116: *iyakki.*

18. *Kalittokai,* 102–6. Kanakasabhai, *Tamils,* p. 57. Suryavanshi, *Abhiras,* p. 63. Kamil V. Zvelebil, "Bull-baiting festival in Tamil India," *Annals of the Náprstek Museum in Prague* (Prague, 1962), pp. 191–99. *Bhāgavatapurāṇa,* X.36.1–10.

19. *Kalittokai,* 106.

20. This "mixing" was based on the observation of actual phenomena, and could be employed as a stylistic device: *tiṇai-mayakkam*—"mixing of *tiṇai.*" A. K. Ramanujan, *The Interior Landscape* (Bloomington, 1967), p. 108.

21. *Malaipaṭukaṭām,* 330–35.

22. Ibid., 414f.

23. *Tolkāppiyam, Poruḷatikāram,* 60. Cattle theft as an invitation to feud or war still survives in the oral traditions of Saurashtra as well (information from S. Doshi). See chap. 5, below.

1.4 The River Valley (*marutam*)

Typical examples of the *marutam* region are the broad fields around Tanjore and the fields watered by the Kāvēri and its anicuts. This is a region of fresh water, in contrast to the coastal region with the salt water of the ocean. Rice fields and sugarcane are characteristic of the fluvial plain. Sugarcane is supposed to have been domesticated in South India, by an ancestor of the prince of the Maḻavar tribe, the ruler of Takaṭūr (that is, Dharmapuri in Salem District).[24] The region is inhabited by farmers, who form a solid foundation for the state. Under the peaceful rule of a king, the subjects know no bow but the rainbow, and no weapon but the plowshare.[25] Many of the inhabitants also follow pastoral occupations.

Storks, herons, buffaloes, freshwater fish, mango trees, and ponds are found in this region.[26]

1.5 The Desert Region (*pālai*)

This "region" comes into existence only under certain conditions—namely, when the summer changes parts of the *mullai* and *kuṟiñci* regions into a dry desert.[27] The reservoirs and lakes become so dry that animals suffer. Elephants, tigers, and wolves become exhausted. Typical fauna and flora of this region are lizards and cactuses. Highway robbers and bandits, especially the tribe of the Maḻavars, make the region unsafe; they attack merchants and their caravans. After a raid, the robbers drive the cows far off into the desert, kill a fat cow, sprinkle her blood under a margosa tree (*vēmpu*), and cook and eat the meat.[28] At many crossroads, places where enemies of the king typically live, there are stones with inscriptions commemorating fallen heroes and Maḻavar robbers.[29]

This is the region that forces herdsmen and herdsmen-farmers to move around in search of pastures. That famines occurred in the time of classical Tamil literature is clear from the account of Kallāṭaṉār (ca. A.D. 100–130),

24. *Puṟanāṉūṟu,* 230. Kanakasabhai, *Tamils,* p. 107.

25. *Puṟanāṉūṟu,* 20, 10–11. Thaninayagam, *Landscape,* p. 111.

26. Ramanujan, *Landscape,* p. 107 (see the table).

27. *Akanāṉūṟu,* 11.1–3: *mullai* turns into *pālai*. *Kalittokai,* 2.6–8: *kuṟiñci* turns into *pālai*. See *Cilappatikāram,* XI.62–66.

28. *Akanāṉūṟu,* 309, 1–6; 129, 12.

29. *Malaipaṭukaṭām,* 387ff. On the survival of old traditions having to do with the worship of heroes through hero stones and the personification of heroes in ecstatic dances, see K. K. N. Kurup, *The Cult of Theyyam and Hero Worship in Kerala* (Calcutta, 1973), pp. 17ff.

who left his town because of a famine and traveled south with his family to the fertile region of the Kāvēri River.[30]

2. The Deities of the Various Landscapes

Cēyōṉ is the god of the *kuriñci* region, Māyōṉ the god of the *mullai* region.[31] The name Cēyōṉ is derived from *cēy,* which means either "red" or "young." Cēyōṉ or Murukaṉ is a god of the hills (*malaikiḻavōṉ*), and he lives on a hill.[32] He loves to dance there.[33] Murukaṉ is the *kaṭampu* tree, or he lives in it.[34] He lives in its shade,[35] and comes from heaven to live in the *kaṭampu* tree on the hill in order to help people.[36] His garland is made of fresh flowers from this tree.[37] Murukaṉ is also at home in forests, groves, creeks, rivers, and ponds, at crossroads, and in the gathering places of villages.[38] He carries a spear,[39] like the chieftains of the *kuriñci* region.[40] His priests, who also act as oracles, are called *vēlaṉ* (spearmen),[41] a name also used for Murukaṉ himself. The vēlaṉ perform an ecstatic dance.[42] Murukaṉ receives offerings of millet, flowers, and the flesh of rams.[43] He is represented by a flag depicting a rooster,[44] or sometimes a peacock.

Murukaṉ's favorite wife, Vaḷḷi, comes from the hill tribe of the Kuṟavars.[45] His first wife is Teyvayāṉai, the pure,[46] who comes from the higher classes. The god with two wives is a widespread phenomenon in South India: he is found as Mallikārjuna at Śrīśailam in Andhra Pradesh; as Mallanna at several places in Andhra Pradesh; as Mailāra at Haḍagali and Devaraguḍḍa (near Rānebennūr) in Karnatak; and as Khaṇḍobā at many places in Maharashtra.

30. *Puṟanāṉūṟu,* 391. Kanakasabhai, *Tamils,* pp. 198f.
31. *Tolkāppiyam, Poruḷatikāram,* 5 and 60.
32. *Tirumurukāṟṟuppaṭai,* 317; 77.
33. Ibid., 217: *kuṉṟu tōṟaṭal.*
34. *Paripāṭal,* 8, 126; *Perumpāṇāṟṟuppaṭai,* 75: *kaṭampu amar neṭu vēḷ.*
35. *Tirumurukāṟṟuppaṭai,* 225.
36. *Paripāṭal,* 19, 2; 104.
37. *Tirumurukāṟṟuppaṭai,* 5; 81. *Maturaikkāñci,* 613–14.
38. *Tirumurukāṟṟuppaṭai,* 223–25.
39. Ibid., 265.
40. *Malaipaṭukaṭām,* 319: *tiruntuvēl aṇṇal.*
41. *Tirumurukāṟṟuppaṭai,* 222.
42. Ibid.
43. Ibid., 221.
44. Ibid., 220, 210, 211, 121.
45. Ibid., 101–2.
46. Ibid., 175.

His first wife comes from the upper class of society, is light-skinned, and is properly married to him. The second wife is dark, and comes from the tribes; their union does not conform to Brahmanical conceptions or rules. Aiyan̲ār, the god of Tamil villages, also has two wives: a fair one from the upper castes and a dark one from the lower.[47] In this way the god binds together heterogeneous tribes and groups, and castes of unequal rank. Thus he also has the function of a king, rides on an elephant,[48] and wears a crown[49] and dangling golden earrings.[50]

Gradually Cēyōn̲ acquires demons whom he conquers with a spear and a drum.[51] Finally, he is identified with the six-headed Skanda,[52] and thus becomes the offspring of the god under the banyan tree (that is, Śiva), as well as a son of the six women (the *kṛttikās*), and a son of the daughter of the king of the mountain (Pārvatī).[53]

The god of the pastoral region is Māyōn̲. His name means literally "the dark one," and can also denote the color dark green or dark blue.[54] Whereas the hill tribe Kān̲avars dedicate their dance[55] to Murukan̲ and Vaḷḷi, the wives of the herdsmen (*āycciyar*) dance the *kuravai* in honor of Māyōn̲ and his herdswoman wife Nappin̲n̲ai.[56] Neṭumāl and Tirumāl are names of Māyōn̲ in later texts. He is a shepherd who plays the flute and sports with the herdswomen.[57] The transformation of the herdsmen's god and his identification with Kṛṣṇa, as well as the identification of Viṣṇu with the Kṛṣṇa of the epic and of the Vaiṣṇavas, are later developments. The earlier Māyōn̲ is perhaps Cēyōn̲ of the *kur̲iñci* region, who changes himself in the *mullai* region to fit in with it. Two gods of the tribes, who arose from tribal notions, became identified with Skanda/Kārttikeya and Kṛṣṇa. In addition, these two gods exhibit numerous analogies and connections to each other. Still today, popular regional cults and tribal and lower caste conceptions reflect the early stages of Murukan̲/Subramaṇyan̲/Skanda/Kārttikeya and Māyōn̲/Kṛṣṇa/Vāsudeva/Tirumāl/Neṭiyōn̲.

---

47. Louis Dumont, "A Structural Definition of a Folk Deity of Tamilnad: Aiyanar, the Lord," *Contributions to Indian Sociology,* 3 (1959) 75ff.

48. *Tirumurukār̲r̲uppaṭai,* 82.

49. Ibid., 84 (*muṭi*).

50. Ibid. (*polaṅkuḷai*).

51. *Kur̲iñcippāṭṭu,* 51. *Tirumurukār̲r̲uppaṭai,* 46.

52. *Tirumurukār̲r̲uppaṭai,* 103.

53. Ibid., 155ff.

54. Zvelebil, "Pastoralism." *Dravidian Etymological Dictionary,* 3918: *mā* = "black"; *māyam* = "blackness"; Māyavan̲, Māyan̲ = "the dark-complexioned one, Vishnu, Krishna."

55. *Tirumurukār̲r̲uppaṭai,* 194–97: *kuravai.*

56. *Cilapattikāram,* XVII.

57. Zvelebil, "Pastoralism."

The goddess of the *pālai* region is Korravai. In her case too, many analogies to the other goddesses of the Deccan and South India become evident. Her home is the margosa (neem) tree, and after their cattle raids[58] the Maḻavars offer her cows. She is a hunter, and she rides on a stag.[59] Murukan̲, the "young" god, becomes her "son."[60] She is the goddess of the warring tribes.[61]

58. *Akanānūr̲u,* 309.1–6.
59. *Cilappatikāram,* XII.22–39.
60. *Tirumurukār̲r̲uppaṭai,* 258: *Kor̲r̲avai cir̲uva.*
61. Kanakasabhai, *Tamils,* pp. 227f.

3

The Landscapes in the Period of the "Great Empires": The Example of Mhasvaḍ and Kharsuṇḍī

1. The Period of the "Great Empires"

References in Caṅkam literature to the basic division of South India into five landscapes would be irrelevant if there were no correspondences with or similarities to Maharashtra. In contrast to other regions of India, the plateau of Maharashtra (the Deś) is not characterized by rice cultivation. Rather, the Deś is traditionally a region of cattle raising and millet cultivation. Rice is grown primarily along the eastern side of the Ghāṭs and in the coastal region, the Koṅkaṇ. With perhaps the exception of Nāgpūr, in fertile Vidarbha, which is more subject to the northeast monsoon, and the town of Śolāpūr,[1] which developed later, the earliest plateau settlements that are still important today lie on the borderline between the rice-growing area near the Ghāṭs and the drier regions to the east. Along this line are found Nāsik,[2] Poona,[3] Sātārā,[4]

1. *Gazetteer of the Bombay Presidency,* vol. 20, Sholāpur (Bombay, 1884), p. 501: "The earliest trace of Sholāpur would seem to be about the end of the fourteenth century when its fort appears to have been built. [Note:] The Hemādpanti temple remains in the fort are older and appear to belong to the twelfth or thirteenth century." Śolāpūr seems to have been originally a settlement of Vakkaligas—essentially herdsmen-farmers.

2. In the upper valley of the Godāvarī. Mentioned by Ptolemy (VII, 1, 63): Nāsikya. See also *Mahābhāṣya* on Pāṇini 6, 1, 63. Sylvain Lévy, "Le Catalogue Géographique des Yakṣas dans la Mahāmāyūrī," *Journal Asiatique,* 5 (1915) 41, 93.

3. At the beginning of the Rāṣṭrakūṭas' rule, we hear of Pūnaka Viṣaya (King Kṛṣṇarāja I's gift of the village Koregāv-Muḷā to a group of Brahmans from Karhāḍ, A.D. 780), in *Epigraphia Indica,* vol. 13, pp. 275–92.

4. First mentioned during the reign of the fourth Bāhmanī king, Muhammad Śāh (1358–1375). The Sātārā fort is thought to have been built during this period (*Maharashtra State Gazetteer,* Satara District [Bombay, revised edition, 1963], p. 903).

Karhāḍ,[5] and Kolhāpūr.[6] Large areas in the Ghāṭs and also in the interior of the plateau still remain the preserve of tribal groups.

The first settlement of Maharashtra in historical times began in Vidarbha, east of Nāgpūr; then came the Mulaka land, with the town of Paiṭhaṇ (Pratiṣṭhāna); and Aśmaka, also in the valley of the Godāvarī River. Paiṭhaṇ was the terminus of the "southern trade route" (*dakkhiṇa-patha*). According to the *Suttanipāta,* which is probably the oldest text in the Pālī canon, Bāvari, a Brahman from Kosala, came south on the *dakkhiṇa-patha.* He settled on the bank of the Godāvarī, where it meets the valley of the Muḷā River, in the region of the "horse tribe" (Assaka). Bāvari and his disciples lived by gathering wild fruits and the like. When a large village came into existence in the neighborhood, he could use the offerings collected there to arrange for a Brahmanical fire sacrifice.[7] This is a typical example of early Brahmanical expansion in the Deccan, a development which is symbolized in the Purāṇas by the figure of Agastya.

Parts of the Godāvarī river valley early developed into a nuclear agricultural region.[8] The Sātavāhana dynasty had its beginnings in this region in approximately the second century B.C.[9] Along the Western Ghāṭs there arose the Buddhist cave monasteries of Junnar, Kārle, Bhājā, Beḍsā, and others. Near them were passes that led to trading centers on the coast, and regular agriculture also developed nearby. Still today some plows found around Junnar and in the Māvaḷ resemble those on Buddhist Kuśāṇā reliefs in the north. Although trade—even with Rome—flourished in these northern and western nuclear regions, and regular plow-based agriculture spread, yet the broad forests of the Ghāṭs remained the preserve of tribal groups, as did a bush jungle landscape stretching over much of the plateau.

It seems unlikely that during the millennia after the Sātavāhanas and the Ābhīras the part of the plateau east of Poona and Kolhāpūr and south of the

5. Karhāḍ appears in inscriptions from 200 B.C. and A.D. 100. There are sixty-three early Buddhist caves approximately three miles southwest of Karhāḍ (*Maharashtra State Gazetteer,* Satara District [Bombay, revised edition, 1963], p. 812). Lévy, "Catalogue," p. 41: the guardian spirit (*yakṣa*) of Karhāḍ was named Vīra: *vīraśca karahāṭake.*

6. The beginnings of the modern town of Kolhāpūr (Karavīra) predate the reign of the Sātavāhana king Gautamīputra Satakarṇi (A.D. 106–130) (*Maharashtra State Gazetteer,* Kolhapur District [Bombay, revised edition, 1960], p. 849).

7. *Suttanipāta,* 976–78, cited in D. D. Kosambi, *Myth and Reality* (Bombay, 1962), p. 111.

8. The term "nuclear agricultural region" (*landwirtschaftliches Kerngebiet*) is adapted from the terms "nuclear area" and "region of settled village agriculture" used by Burton Stein in his article "Integration of the Agrarian System of South India," in *Land Control and Social Structure in Indian History,* R. E. Frykenberg, ed. (Madison, Wisc., 1969).

9. The Assakas, who were still a tribe at the time of the *Suttanipāta,* have been identified with the Sātavāhanas by Kosambi, *Myth,* pp. 111f.

Godāvarī basin essentially lost its character as a region of cattle-raising and millet-cultivation. This is despite the fact that parts of the region fell, even if often only nominally, into the domain of one or the other of the great dynasties: the Traikuṭakas in the fifth century A.D., the Vākāṭakas, the Kalacuris, the Cālukyas,[10] and the Rāṣṭrakūṭas.[11]

The most loyal "feudal lords" under the Rāṣṭrakūṭas were the Śilāhāras. These presumably came from Ter (Tagara) in Usmanabad District. One family of them ruled over the northern Koṅkaṇ (in what are today the districts of Kolaba and Thana), another family over the southern Koṅkaṇ (in Goa, Iriḍige land, including Sāvantvāḍī and Ratnagiri District), and a third family over Kolhāpūr (including Satara and Belgaum districts).[12]

In the eastern part of Maharashtra the Cālukyas of Kalyāṇī ruled from the tenth century until the second half of the twelfth century, when they were superseded by the Kalacuris. An inscription from A.D. 1142 shows that a Kalacuri named Bijjala who ruled the region of Karhāṭa (Karhāḍ) was a provincial ruler (*mahāmaṇḍaleśvara*) dependent on the Cālukya king Jagadekamalla.[13] The headquarters of the Kalacuris was Maṅgaḷavāḍ (modern Maṅgaḷveḍhā, south of Paṇḍharpūr), until eventually they usurped the Cālukyas' throne and ruled from Kalyāṇī from A.D. 1162.[14]

Although the nuclear agricultural regions of the great empires, with their imprecise, fluctuating borders, were separated by forest regions and pastoral regions, and although even ecologically favored areas (those favored, that is, principally by the monsoon) like the Western Ghāṭs were still interspersed with great forests, trade nevertheless developed among the nuclear regions. Thus there were certainly trade routes that led from the north and northwest, out of the region of Broach (the Barygaza of the *Periplus*), via Nāsik and Paiṭhaṇ (Pratiṣṭhāna), to Ter (the Tagara of the *Periplus*), and from there onward toward Andhra Pradesh or south to Karnatak. Between the nuclear regions in the west and those in the east and southeast, the routes followed the river valleys—those, for example, of the Bhimā, Karhā, Nirā, Māṇ, and Kṛṣṇā rivers.

Along these east-west routes there developed bases and small trading centers. Thus Phalṭaṇ (Paḷayaṭṭhāṇa), for example, on the south bank of the Nirā

---

10. The Cālukyas of Badāmī in Karnāṭak, 6th to 8th century.

11. Between the 8th and 10th centuries. They probably came originally from Laṭṭalūra, modern Lāṭūr, in Usmanabad District. The Rāṣṭrakūṭas' nuclear area lay in northern Maharashtra and Berār (*Maharashtra State Gazetteer,* Ancient Period [Bombay, 1967], pp. 234f.).

12. Ibid., pp. 259ff.

13. Ibid., pp. 339, 347. *Annual Report of South Indian Epigraphy,* 1940–41, BK. No. 128.

14. *Maharashtra State Gazetteer,* Ancient Period, p. 347.

River, is mentioned in a copper-plate inscription from as early as A.D. 687.[15] Later the Cālukya king Vinayāditya I (of Badāmī) had his camp in the village Bhāḍalī (modern Bhāḍalī Budruk, five miles southeast of Phalṭaṇ). From the beginning Phalṭaṇ was connected with the Jainas, and it has two old but undated Jaina temples.

As is otherwise also the case in the history of northern and western India, such extra-Brahmanical sects as the Buddhists, the Jainas, and the Liṅgāyats seem to have been associated with interregional trade and supraregional trade guilds. Although during the period of the local kings Phalṭaṇ comprised a small, compact state under Rājā Naik Nimbāḷkar,[16] around 1854 it was still essentially a trading center for the exchange of goods from the interior and the coast.[17]

Just as Phalṭaṇ lies on a road running from west to east, so Mhasvaḍ is found in the dry valley of the Māṇ River, on the route that leads west to east from Sātārā through Dahīvāḍī and Mhasvaḍ to Paṇḍharpūr, and finally on to Śolāpūr and Bijāpūr.

2. Mhasvaḍ and Kharsuṇḍī as an Example of the Origin and Development of Cults in the Forest and Pastoral Area

2.1 Mhasvaḍ

Mhasvaḍ lies at a crossroads. The area was not developed until very recent times, and in the rainy season it is nearly impassable. Mhasvaḍ provides an example of how such an area became connected with the nuclear regions while its surroundings and the place itself preserved their pastoral character.

The superstructure of the temple at Mhasvaḍ dates from the Peśvā period. It was erected on the foundations of an old shrine. In front of the newer temple lie the ruins of a temple from the Yādava or Cālukya period; at the foot of these ruins is a stone on which is depicted a mounted warrior's battle with a demon. In the left-hand wall of the forecourt of the present temple is a slab bearing a Kannaḍa inscription dated Śaka 1060 (A.D. 1138); it states that an ancestor of the Kalacūri king Bijjala of Kalyāṇī, ruling from Maṅgaḷveḍhā as a dependent of the Cālukya king (Jagadekamalla of Kalyāṇī), gave a piece of

---

15. *Epigraphia Indica,* vol. 19, pp. 62f.

16. The Nimbāḷkars were appointed *sardeśmukh* under the kings of Bijāpur. Their original name was Pavār. See below, 7.2. See also *Maharashtra State Gazetteer,* Satara District, pp. 870f.

17. T. C. Loughnan and Lieutenant H. B. Sandford, "Brief Notes on the Satara Jageerdars," in *Selections from the Records of the Bombay Government,* n.s., 41 (Bombay, 1857) 23, 178.

land to a Brahman of the Kapi *gotra* so that food offerings could be presented daily to the god.[18] In the inscription the god is called Siddheśvara. This deity, who is still widely influential today even beyond the Māṇ valley, is called a living god—*jivant* or *jāgṛt dev*[19]—by Mārāṭhās, Dhangars, Māḷīs, and devotees from other castes. He is alternately called Śidobā, Mhasvaḍ-Śid, Siddhanāth, or simply Nāth. In the inscription the place is called Mahiṣavāḍā ("buffalo camp"); from this name derives the present name, Mhasvaḍ. The inscription designates Mhasvaḍ as the chief village among "twelve villages."

The oral traditions about the beginnings of Mhasvaḍ and the origin of the temple appear to the analytical observer, as always, a mixture of *purāṇic* mythology, legend, and actual events. Here I cite two versions of the traditions, as narrated by two Guravs—that is, non-Brahman temple priests. The versions were recorded on different days.

Text 1

Version 1

There used to be a forest here. They called it the Daṇḍakāraṇya. In those days, even the village (*gāv*) was not here. All that was here was a demon named Mhaśā [*mhaiśā, mhaśā* = buffalo]. Because Mhaiśāsur [Sanskrit, *Mahiṣāsura*] was killed here, the place got the name Mhasvaḍ.

In Sonārī [in modern Usmanabad District] there was a demon (*daitya*) who swelled up to an uncontrollable, arrogantly huge size. So Śaṅkar sent Kāḷbhairav to kill this Sonyādaitya. Kāḷbhairav took on the form (*avatār*) of Siddha.

The temple was completed in 1151. Before this time, there was Daṇḍakāraṇya here. There was no village here. In those days a Gavḷī named Mhasojī [also from *mhaśā, mhaisā*] lived here. While that Mhasojī Gavḷī lived here, a man named Bāḷojī Ḍubal from the family of the Cālukyas lived in the town of Karhāḍ, in Brahmapūrī.[20] He used to come to this neighborhood.

At that time there lived here a Gurav named Yamajī; by himself he used to wash the *mūrti* with water and worship it. That is, he poured water on the *piṇḍ*[21]

---

18. The inscription has not been published. A summary of its contents was published by the historian G. H. Khare in the newspaper *Samartha* (Sātārā, July 25, 1932). I am indebted to Mr. K. B. Mhaske for a copy of the summary. The temple priests and the residents of the village are unaware of the contents of the inscription.

19. On this concept, see below, Text 1, Version 2.

20. The *Maharashtra State Gazetteer,* Satara District, p. 526, refers to Bāḷojī Ḍābal (*sic*) as a Deścaugula from Karhāḍ who is supposed to have built the temple 200 years ago. The Gurav sees no difference between the Cālukyas and the builder, who lived in the time of the Peśvās.

21. Marāṭhī *piṇḍ* is a rounded lump. It means "a cake offered to the manes," but also "embryo." In many temples there is a round stone in which the god or goddess was originally manifested. It is set in the ground at the foot of the actual *mūrti*. It is often covered with a silver mask. *Piṇḍ,* then, is identical with *piṇḍī,* the *liṅgam* symbol of Mahādev.

[the narrator improves on the word *mūrti*] in the hollow [underneath the sanctuary of the present temple]. When he did that, his wife was pregnant. Later this priest (*pūjārī*) was killed by his brother-in-law. . . .

The priest's wife bore a son. This son had three sons. . . . [There follows the story of the origin of the three Gurav families. See Version 2.]

Śivājī Ḍubal, the son of the devotee (*bhakta*) from Karhāḍ, built the temple of Mhasvaḍ-Siddha. . . . Later the village developed.

Version 2

Śrīsiddhanāth is an incarnation (*avatār*) of Śaṅkar. He came south to kill the demon (*asura*) Kāḷ. And he killed the demon Kāḷāsura near Kolhāpūr. Then he went to Tuḷjāpūr. There all the gods were preoccupied with the thought, "How can Kāḷāsura be killed?" They had arranged a fire sacrifice (*hom*) in front of Ādimāyā-Śakti—that is, Bhavānī. At that time, Kāḷbhairav also arrived there, with the head of Kāḷāsura. The pots of the nine nights (*navrātra*) had also been set up before Bhavānī.[22]

At that time, Kāḷbhairav said, "I will lay the head of Kāḷāsura in front of the fire sacrifice." But all the gods cried out, "New Kāḷāsuras will come out of the drops of his blood."

"If that does not happen, what will you give me as a reward? And what will you let me have as a special privilege before all the gods?"

At that, all the gods and Māyā-Śakti said, "The pots of the nine days have been set up. Therefore from now on people will also set up the pot of Kāḷbhairav, from the first day of the bright half of the month of Kārttik until the twelfth day of the bright half of the month of Kārttik. And because you have killed Kāḷāsura, everyone will know you by the name Kāḷbhairav."

Thereupon Kāḷbhairav was deeply gratified. Thus, because he was an incarnation (*avatār*) of Śaṅkar, he came to the bank of the Māṇ Gaṅgā, saw the quiet and isolated place, and settled here.

This took place about 1,250 years ago. In those days this area was known by the name Daṇḍakāraṇya. At first there were no human settlements. In those days a Gurav named Yamajī worshiped the *piṇḍ* [= *piṇḍī*]. In those days there were some Gavḷī camps (*vasti*). At that time Mhasojī Gavḷī's *vāḍā* extended from the bank of the Māṇ Gaṅgā to the Paṇḍharpūr road, and from the Koṭeśvar temple to the carpenters' lane.

A devotee (*bhakta*) named Bāḷojī Ḍubal, from Brahmapūrī, from the family of the Cālukyas, was the first to come regularly to Mhasvaḍ-Siddha. Brahmapūrī is the present-day Karhāḍ, on the bank of the Kṛṣṇā River. He used to come here as a pilgrim, and so he developed a desire to build a temple. So he brought stone masons together, and he gave the good, well-known stone masons

22. *Ghaṭasthāpanā* = "The rite of placing a vessel (generally of earth) filled with water, having a mango-sprig, a cocoanut, or a plantain over its mouth, and the red-lead mark called Yantra on its fore part, upon *āśvinaśuddhapratipadā*, in the ceremonies of *navarātra* and upon numerous other occasions. Into this *ghaṭa* as a temple the entrance of *devī* is supplicated" (Molesworth, *Dictionary*).

three paisā a day, and the simple workers two paisā. And when the stone temple was finished, Bāḷojī went to Karhāḍ.

In those days, Yamajī's wife was pregnant. Sometime later, Yamajī's brother-in-law killed him while he was doing the *āratī* ceremony. He cut off his head. The head fell in the temple, and the body finished the *āratī* ceremony and then fell behind the elephant, where the "father temple" is.[23]

Yamajī's wife was pregnant, and now she was in a difficult situation. When Bāḷojī Ḍubal came to the temple and saw her difficulty, he brought her to his house. Later she bore a son. She named him Śidojī. He had three sons. The descendants of the oldest son live in the highest lane, those of the middle son in the middle lane, and those of the youngest son live in the lowest lane. Thus there are three lanes of priests (*pūjārīs*) here, because [the right to conduct the worship] was divided into three parts so that there would be no hindrance to the worship.

When Bāḷojī had built thirteen or fourteen layers of stones, he died. Then his son, Śivājī Ḍubal, donated the *mūrti* that one can see today. At that time the installation ceremony alone (*udyāpan*) cost about a thousand rupees. The outlay for the dome (*śikhar*) of the temple came to 75,000 rupees. Śivājī donated a *mūrti* of his father, which is on Nāth's right.

This incarnation (*avatār*) of Siddhanāth is fierce in form (*ugra svarūpācā*) and this god is truly living (*sākṣāt jāgṛt*). His devotees (*bhaktas*) call him Mhasvaḍ-Śīd, Kāḷbhairav, Bhairavnāth, Śrīsiddhanāth, or Kāśīviśvanāth. Nāth took form (*avatār*) here to help anyone who is having great difficulties and comes running to him because of them. To this day he does away with difficulties.

From both versions it is clear that Mhasvaḍ was originally a *vāḍā* of Gavḷīs. Here I cannot consider the question of whether forest tribes preceded the Gavḷīs, although such a conclusion is made feasible by microlith finds quite close to Mhasvaḍ, on a small tributary of the Māṇ River not far from the present Birobā and Nāgobā temples. The hero stone (*vīragaḷ*) installed in the small "father temple" also points to Mhasvaḍ's close connection with herds of cattle. Its lowest relief depicts a warrior protecting his cattle. The herds are not only the usual prey of marauding tribal groups; during the disintegration of the Kalacuri empire, up until the death of King Bijjala (ca. A.D. 1167), the primary interests of the feuding *daṇḍanāyakas* seem to have been cattle theft and the abduction of young women.[24]

---

23. The head and trunk of Yamajī are still pointed out today in the form of corresponding pieces of stone. The worship of the head in the temple and of the trunk at the entrance to the temple occurs in South India in the cult of Marīammā/Yeḷammā, and is associated with the legend of Reṇukā and Paraśurām. See V. Moeller, *Die Mythologie der vedischen Religion und des Hinduismus* (Stuttgart, 1966), s.v. Reṇukā.

24. *Maharashtra State Gazetteer,* Ancient Period, pp. 350ff. *Epigraphia Carnatica,* vol. 7, Sk. no. 236; vol. 8, Sb. no. 389.

Other evidence indicates that the Gavḷīs worshiped another god before the worship of Kāḷbhairav was founded. This is surely the Mahiṣāsura or Mhasobā ("father buffalo") mentioned in Version 1. As the deity of the Gavḷīs—or, historically speaking, rather a *yakṣa* or an ancestor than an already fully developed deity—he is "killed" by the invading Kāḷbhairav/Mhasvaḍ-Śīd, and he reappears as Kāḷ in Bhairav's name Kāḷbhairav.[25] Mhasobā is connected especially with the Gavḷīs, but also with the bullock caravans that traverse the forest and pasture regions. One of the roads intersecting at Mhasvaḍ leads from there to the southwest, toward Dighañcī. Not far from Dighañcī is Loṭevāḍī. The widely known god Mhasobā of Loṭevāḍī is reminiscent of the merchants who traveled through this region with caravans of pack bullocks. According to the oral tradition of the temple:

Text 2

This god came to Loṭevāḍī in a bullock's hoof. There used to be no trucks (*moṭārī*). So people took bullocks and packsaddles to the bazaar at Sāṅgolā. The god came in the hoof of a bullock, and stopped here. A merchant (Vāṇī) came here from Sātārā with his bullocks, and a stone got stuck in the hoof of one of the bullocks and fell out here. Some little boys picked up the stone and started the worship of the god. Later the god began to protect people and animals, and a temple was built for him. Then a *jatrā* [pilgrimage festival] was started. Actually, there is a *jatrā* here eleven months of the year. In the month of Śrāvaṇ [July–August] there is no *jatrā,* not even on Monday or Saturday. Otherwise they kill twenty-five sheep for the god each day, and forty or fifty in the month of Phālgun [February–March].

Today Loṭevāḍī lies somewhat off the road to Paṇḍharpūr. Hardly anyone takes the bullock track through Loṭevāḍī to go from Sātārā to Sāṅgolā; instead, people go by the roundabout way on the better road through Māhud. But still today Mhasobā is an important god who protects people and animals. The motif of the god hiding in the form of a stone stuck in the hoof of an itinerant merchant's pack animal occurs frequently in the case of Birobā and Khaṇḍobā as well.

A further characteristic of the Loṭevāḍī temple deserves to be emphasized here, because it is closely related to the Mhasobā cult and the Gavḷīs. On the roof of the temple is a sort of dome resembling the terracotta shrines of the Mhasobā cult near Khandālī (Māḷśiras Taluka), which have been noted by D. D. Kosambi.[26] The shrines are about seventy centimeters high and look like tents (yurts) with smoke holes. They are generally connected with Mhasobā

25. The reappearance of the "killed" demon's name in the name of the invading god is a frequent phenomenon in the focal area of my research.

26. D. D. Kosambi, *Myth and Reality* (Bombay, 1952), p. 131.

and the Gavḷīs. Such shrines are widely diffused in this region: they are also found, for example, near Paṇḍharpūr, near Maṅgaḷveḍhā (Sholapur District), and near Jhare (Khānapūr Taluka, Sangli District). They are almost always Mhasobā shrines. But sometimes—as, for example, near Āṭpāḍī—the shrines hold Nāgobā, an ancestor who is the guardian of the fields, *kṣetrapāl,* in the form of a snake.

The first Gurav's narrative (Version 1) also draws attention to the connection of the Mhasvaḍ cult with Sonārī in Usmanabad District. As the Gurav says, Siddha is understood to be an *avatār* of Kāḷbhairav (or Sonārsiddha) of Sonārī. Sonārī is the famous Maharashtrian cult place of Kāḷbhairav, and a center for the Gosāvīs—ascetics and magicians or yogis who travel through the wilderness alone or in groups. Like Sonārī, Mhasvaḍ also has a small monastery of Kānphaṭā Gosāvīs.

A Dhangar woman from Mhasvaḍ, about sixty years old, mentions in her narrative that Siddhanāth was an ascetic (*sannyāsī*) and a Gosāvī. She heard the account from *pūjārīs*. She also tells about Siddha's relations with the goddesses Mariāī and Yellammāī, and about his marriage to Jogāī-Jogeśvarī. The story must be reproduced here in its entirety, despite the repetitions at the beginning:

Text 3

Why did Nāth [Śaṅkar, Śiva] incarnate himself here? In order to kill Mhaśā. [Nāth] was a Gosāvī. [Śaṅkar] said to him, "This is not for you. If you do not get married, you cannot act according to the rules (*vidhi*)."

So he asked Śaṅkar, "Where should I go for a wife?"

[Śaṅkar] told him to go to the underworld. "Jogubāī, Śeś's daughter, lives there. Go there."

This is the Siddhanāth of Mhasvaḍ. He comes from Kāśī [Banaras, Vārāṇasī] and so he is called Viśvanāth [Śiva's name at his principal temple in Kāśī]. So what happened? First there was a *sannyāsī*. Then Śaṅkar challenged anyone to kill the *dait* [*daitya,* demon] Mhaiśāsūr. Then the *sannyāsī* said, "I accept the challenge."

Śaṅkar said, "You are not married, so you cannot do battle."

Then he said, "I have nothing against it: I'll get married so that I can kill the demon (*rakṣasa*). What is there against it, even though I am a *sannyāsī?* I'll stay married until I kill him."

"Good."

"You must also tell me," he said to Śaṅkar, "where I am to find a wife. How is a *sannyāsī* supposed to know that?"

Śaṅkar said, "Go to the underworld (*pātāḷ*). Jogeśvarī is there. Marry her. After you get married, kill the demon!"

Now he went to the underworld. There on the road to the underworld were the two old mothers Yalammāī (*sic*) and Marīmāī (*sic*): "Here is a young man, seventeen or eighteen years old. What is this vagabond doing here? He'll be ruined. He must be helped. If it pleases Śaṅkar, it should also please us a little to help him.'' Such was their wish.

What did Marīāī do now? She gave him a stone, a pebble. She said, ''If anyone stands in your way, throw it!''

''All right.''

''If someone says something, say yes [that is, do not contradict anyone]; if someone says yes, take it.''

He took the stone.

''Afterward you'll have hard times.''

''What kind?''

''Someone will fight with you. An enemy will try to kill you.'' What did Yalammāī give him for that? A cloth to wipe his face. ''As soon as you feel dizzy [and think,] 'Now I'm going to die; it's all over now,' when you feel this way, then wipe this handkerchief over your face. Then you'll be yourself again.''

[A question to the listeners:] Who gave it to him? Yalammāī! When he had gotten these two things, he went to Yogeśvarī in the underworld; the way was over there, in Hyderabad State, where Jogeśvarī Ambā is. When he had gone there, the whole army of Śeśnarāyan [Śeṣanārāyaṇa] was there. There were no people there!

But Siddhanāth was a man!

When the Bhagavān reveals himself in a form, on earth they call him a man. That's why Śeśnarāyan said, ''Hey! A man has come from the world of men.''

Then the whole army of Śeśnarāyan set at him. Snakes (*sarp*), Nāgas, and so on, whatever serpents (*ajgar*) there were, folk like that. Whatever poisonous folk there were attacked him. Now when a man sees this here, he gets frightened. But when he had just gotten there! How would they let him move forward? Now, he had been given a weapon.

[To the listeners:] By whom? By Marībāī (*sic*)—the stone. He threw it. When he had thrown it, that was the end. The commander (*pradhān*) ran away, terrified. ''O Mahārāj, look what has happened. There is a man there who has come from the human world. Listen to whatever he says. But get rid of this evil.'' He [the *pradhān*] had said to Śeś, ''His business should be taken care of.'' So Śeś said to the *pradhān:* ''All right.''

[And to Siddhanāth Śeś said,] ''Come, Mahārāj. We will do whatever you say.''

Now they invited him to sit down, to eat. And he said, ''I would like to marry your daughter. Śaṅkar told me to. You are my prospective in-laws (*sthal*). And I would like to marry Jogeśvarī.''

''All right, that's fine. I have no objections.''

His army was gone, so Śeś had to say yes to everything. But he did not want to give his daughter to this man. What was he to do now? So he thought up a trick. He put poison into Siddhanāth's food, in order to finish him off (*khalās karāicā*). ''We are saving our daughter from being given to a human.''

We've reached the end of the story.

The meal was ready. And what is there there? Is there a shortage of anything in Śeś's house? Do the snake folk have any shortage of poison? He ate. Then *pān*. There was poison in that too.

[To the listeners:] After a meal there's *pān,* isn't there? There was poison in that too. Within two minutes he forgot everything.

"Whatever is going on? What have I come for? What has happened? What is going on?"

Fear!

"Alas, alas, alas! Now everything I was to do is ruined. I'm finished now."

[To the listeners:] Do you understand? He was like someone who had become unconscious. Then he remembered Yalammāī. "But somebody along the way has helped me." He took the cloth. He wiped his face. He became himself again.

Śeś was frightened. "Oh, no! We went to so much trouble, and he is himself again."

"Now, let's go. I've finished eating."

Thus he went to Jogeśvarī in the underworld.

That's it, then [to the listeners]. He had overcome [the snakes], and he had overcome the girl's father. Now he had gotten everything. There was a large rock there. The one who broke it would get to hang the garland [around the girl's neck—that is, to marry her]. So there was this treacherous obstacle waiting for him there too. What was to be done now? Śaṅkar was pleased with him, wasn't he? He [Siddha] took [Śaṅkar's] trident (*trisūḷ*), threw it, and broke the rock into a hundred thousand pieces. And the door opened. A brilliance like that of the sun, the brilliance of the maiden, shone out. And he said, "How splendid! So much light!"

And he said to her, "Can't you take on a somewhat more normal form? I don't want this glitter. Otherwise I like you very much. But for the sake of the world, make your form a little less radiant."

"All right."

After he had shattered the rock, he hung the garland on her, and she had to obey all his commands. She took on a simple form. And he brought Jogeśvarī here. The marriage took place. Everyone agreed that it was a perfect wedding. And he killed the demon (*rakṣasa*). And when he had killed the demon, there were good people in those days, and they were astonished at the many wonderful deeds of Siddhanāth.

And so [Śaṅkar] said: "What do you wish for?"

"I don't want anything at all. Just remember me, and let me always stay near you. There's no reason to give me anything."

Śaṅkar said, "All right."

Today Gavḷīs have almost entirely disappeared from the region. They live on only in the mythological songs (*ovīs*) of the Dhangars and in the local traditions of Mhasvaḍ—and, as we will see, of Kharsuṇḍī. But Dhangars are represented in great numbers. West of the village of M(h)asāīcīvāḍī and about three miles southwest of Mhasvaḍ is a group of Dhangar temples. In them, Nāgobā and Birobā are the principal objects of worship, but there are also a temple of the goddess Marīāī, some ancestor temples, and a temple of Māṅgobā. Of Nāgobā it is variously claimed that he was a Dhangar, a Liṅgāyat, and a Vāṇī.

The annual pilgrimage festival that takes place near M(h)asāīcīvāḍī is primarily for the god Birobā; Nāgobā is supposed to have been a devotee (*bhakta*) of Birobā. The following account is given of Birobā's arrival:

Text 4

In the course of his travels (*phirat phirat*), Birobā came from the direction of Paṇḍharpūr to the seven water goddesses [*sāt āsarās*, or *māvalyā*] in a pool (*ḍoh*) near where the temples are today. He sat in an oleander tree [*kanherīcyā jhāḍāt; Nerium odorum*]. Then Birobā came from the seven Āsarās to the place where seven roads meet (*sātī rastyācyā mokyāvar*). Because there are seven roads, many people come here. That is why the god came to this place.

Mhasvaḍ and the Dhangars' temple complex do in fact lie at the intersection of seven roads; comparison of older and newer maps confirms this, as does on-site verification.

Still another goddess deserves to be mentioned here: the goddess Marīāī or M(h)asāī, the goddess of M(h)asāīcīvāḍī ("the herdsmen's camp of mother buffalo"). She too must have already been here when Birobā arrived. The goddess M(h)asāī/Masā is connected above all with the Gavḷīs and their herds of cattle.

Finally, Mhasvaḍ and its environs were the home of the Māṇe family. The Māṇes were *śīledārs,* "cavalrymen with their own horses," and were in the service of the Adil Śāhī dynasty of Bijāpūr (1489–1686). But even they did not change the image of the landscape: quite the opposite. The pastures served as grazing grounds for their horses and were thus the basis for their military campaigns.

2.2 Kharsuṇḍī

Kharsuṇḍī is a famous cult place about thirty miles south of Mhasvaḍ, in Khānapūr Taluka of Sangli District. The god of Kharsuṇḍī is Siddhanāth of Mhasvaḍ, who came from Sonārī and originally from Kāśī. The name "Kharsuṇḍī" has been said to be derived from Marāṭhī *kharvas,* "the first milk of the cow after the birth of a calf," and *piṇḍī,* and is supposed to be the name of the god's chief wife. But this view is the isolated statement of one Brahman, who also related the following:

Text 5

He came forth from the third eye of Śaṅkar. Because the demons were becoming powerful here in the Daṇḍakāraṇya, people were in greater and greater danger. For that reason, Śaṅkar sent the Siddhapuruṣa who had come out of his third eye. First he came to Sonārī. After he had annihilated all the demons (*rakṣasas*) there, he came to Mhasvaḍ and stayed there for many days. One mile from Kharsuṇḍī is the village of Cincāle. At that place, there was the herdsmen's camp of Nayābā Gavḷī, alias Gāikvāḍ. Every day he used to take cow's milk to Mhasvaḍ for the god, and then return. He did this for many years, and when he had gotten old, the god appeared to him and said, "Don't come any more now; I will come to you. I will be born in the belly of a barren cow."

The Gavḷī wasn't sure. But among his cows there was one that never had calves and did not move around. When the cows were grazing on the mountain, milk suddenly came spurting out of that cow, and she began to run. And [the Gavḷī] ran after her. And there where the temple is today, where you can see the [two] *liṅgas,* her milk began to flow.

The Gavḷī said, "I want to give my god the milk of the barren cow."

He took a vessel, and when it was filled with the first milk (*kharvas, kharas*), he found in it two self-formed (*svayaṃbhū*) *liṅgas*; and one of the *liṅgas,* the one made of the first milk of the barren cow, was named Kharaspiṇḍī, and is the first wife of the god.

In Kharsuṇḍī the assimilation of six local goddesses through the god is especially clear.[27] The goddesses become his wives. There is general agreement that Bāḷubāī, who has her place next to Kharsuṇḍī-Śīd in the temple, is the god's first wife. His second wife is Māḷāī; her place, too, is inside the *sabhāmaṇḍapa,* the temple hall. The third wife is Jānāī, whose place is outside the walls of the temple. The fourth is Yogeśvarī/Jogāī, the wife of Kāḷbhairav of Sonārī, with whom Kharsuṇḍī-Śīd is identified; Jogāī has an independent temple. The fifth and sixth wives are the "older" Jākhāī and the "younger" Jākhābāī (Jākhāī is derived from *yakṣī*). The temple of the "older" Jākhāī is in the village of Nelkarañje, and that of the "younger" goddess is on a nearby hill.

Three hermits are said to have been the first human beings in what was then a forest area. The first was a fakīr named Indarśākā, the second Giribuvā (the "Holy Man of the Mountain"), and the third an "outcaste" named Sārṇabā. Sārṇabā had—and still has today—the ability to cure animals. His shrine is outside the precincts of the main temple. Stone or wooden votive figures of bulls and cows are placed in front of the shrine in gratitude for the cure of animals and in fulfillment of vows (*navas*). These animal figures face away

27. See *Census of India,* 1961, vol. 10, Maharashtra, part 7-B. *Fairs and Festivals in Maharashtra* (Bombay, 1969), p. 146.

from the shrine, so that each new offering increases the herd and Sārṇabā looks like a herdsman behind his flock. He is identified with Mhasobā.

Giribuvā is a Gosāvī. A temple priest narrates the following about Giribuvā's relations with the Gavḷīs:

Text 6

Every day this Nayābā Gavḷī would hang two pots of milk from the ends of his carrying pole (*kāvaḍ*), place it across his shoulders, and go to Mhasvaḍ. At that time a Gosāvī was living in his cattle pen (*goṭ*). He was a celibate (*brahmacārya*) Gosāvī. That was the heritage that had been handed down to him. And so when [Nayābā Gavḷī] returned in the evening he would make three breads of wheat dough [*paṅga,* a bread baked in leaves] and bake them on cow dung. He would give one of the breads to the Gosāvī, and one to a guest; and the third he would eat himself. And this sufficed him for nourishment. In the morning he would milk the cows, take the milk to Mhasvaḍ, return, and make the bread—thus he was a man who practiced asceticism (*tapaścaryā*).

And when he had done his service (*śeva*) in this way [and had grown old], the god felt compassion and said, "Now don't you come any more. I myself will come to your house." And so he came.

Gosāvī-buvā's seat is over there, in the *bhaṇḍār* house.[28] By tradition his disciples do not get married. The tombs (*samādhīs*) of all the Buvās are near the temple of Gaṇpatī.

The characteristic coalescence of cults and their simultaneous coexistence at the places that have been described here make it possible for Siddhanāth (= Bhairav) to be a partial manifestation of Śaṅkar and at the same time a Gosāvī, or for Mhasobā to live on despite having been killed (as at Mhasāīcīvāḍī and Loṭevāḍī). At other places, we even find Mhasobā and Bhairav identified; Mhasobā is also identified with Kāḷbhairav of Sonārī and has Yogeśvarī/Jogāī as his wife.

This identification of the buffalo demon (as Mhasobā) with Kāḷbhairav represents a later development. The primary cults were those of the cattle deity who has the name Mhasobā, and those of such female deities and spirits as Yelammāī, Mhasāī, and Jākhāī. The goddesses, principally Bāḷubāī and Yogeśvarī; the gods, Mhasobā, Birobā, Siddhanāth, and Kāḷbhairav; and the Gavḷīs (or Dhangars), Guravs, and Gosāvīs—these are the principal features and primary elements of the origin of Mhasvaḍ and Kharsuṇḍī. Both places are in a region bounded to the southwest by Kolhāpūr, to the south by Cinclī and Saundattī, to the east by Tuḷjāpūr, and to the north by Sonārī. This is a zone still traversed every year during the monsoon season by herdsmen who spend the rest of the year near Kolhāpūr.

28. A monastery and at the same time a place where Gosāvīs are fed.

In the center of this zone lies one of the most important cattle-raising areas of Maharashtra. Here also are the cult centers whose yearly temple festivals are held in conjunction with important cattle markets. Still today large cattle and horse markets are held on the occasion of the great annual temple festivals in Mhasvaḍ on the first day (*pratipadā*) of the bright half of Mārgaśīrṣa (November/December) and the full-moon day of Pauṣ (December/January), and in Kharsuṇḍī on the twelfth day of the dark half of Caitra (March/April). Similarly, the pilgrimage festival in honor of the goddess Yallamma in Jath (Jath Taluka, Sangli District) is famous for the cattle market that takes place during the festival, from the ninth day of the dark half of Mārgaśīrṣa to the first day of the bright half of Pauṣ.

Besides the weekly cattle markets, large annual cattle markets are held in Satara District in Māyaṇī, Aundh, Pusegāv, Vadūj (Khaṭāv Taluka), Koḷe (Karhāḍ Taluka), and Vīhe (Pāṭaṇ Taluka). The district of Kolhapur, in the west, which is now fully developed agriculturally, gets the famed Khilārī cattle from the eastern districts of Sangli (for example, from Kharsuṇḍī and Dighañcī) and Sholapur (Māhud, Pilīv, Sāṅgolā), as well as from the town of Cinclī in Belgaum District. Again, it is no accident that a holy place of the Dhangars is found in Cinclī. Māyavvā is the goddess who, along with her sister Ekavvā, found the Dhangar god Birobā in a thicket and brought him up in Cinclī.

Similarly, Poona District used to get draft animals, which are so important for agriculture, from the north,[29] but also from the eastern parts of Satara District. According to the old Poona gazetteer, there was "no class of professional cattle-breeders" in Poona District.[30] Even now one can realize the importance of draft animals for regular plow-based agriculture when one sees plows that are still pulled by as many as twelve oxen. These are to be seen especially in the region around Śirvaḷ, near the principal center of the Mhaskobā cult, Vīr. The hard black soil in the river valleys can be worked only with this large a number of draft animals.

---

29. The Mhasobā pilgrimage of Mhase, Murbad Taluka (Thana District), is famous.
30. *Gazetteer of the Bombay Presidency*, vol. 18, Poona (Bombay, 1885), part 1, p. 56.

4

Forest and Pastoral Goddesses: Independence and Assimilation

1. The "Seven" Goddesses

The examples of Mhasvaḍ and Kharsuṇḍī point to the existence of such goddesses as M(h)asāī, Yeḷammā, and Marīāī. These are often called "mothers" or "ladies." In many cases they are tree goddesses—or rather, tree spirits—who have developed into goddesses with their own cults. The goddess Vaḍjāī at Kheḍbudruk in Khaṇḍāḷā Taluka of Satara District (in the Nirā valley) is an example. Her name is composed of *vaḍ* (m.), fig tree (*Ficus indica*), and *jāī* (f.), jasmin (*Jasminum auriculatum*), and thus perhaps means "the goddess Jāī of the fig tree."[1] Originally the goddess came from the heavily forested "Koṅkaṇ"—that is, more precisely, from the Māvaḷ. She was brought from there by a Dhangar who used to travel back and forth between the Māvaḷ and the Deś. At Kheḍbudruk she disappeared into the ground. One day, when a farmer's plow struck a rock, blood flowed out of it: it was the goddess, transformed. She revealed herself and has been worshiped there ever since.

Accordingly, the first right (*mān*) to worship the goddess at her pilgrimage belongs to a pastoral Dhangar family named Hakke. The Hakkes, and before them the Gavḷīs, used to stay in this area. They were followed by farmers of the Māḷī ("gardener") caste, but the Māḷīs and members of other castes secured only secondary rights of worship.

Often the witchcraft of a demoness or a goddess living in a tree or grove is so powerful that even breaking off branches brings on her curse. This is the

1. Cf. *vaḍ-jakhīṇ* = "a female goblin residing on a *vaḍ* or Ficus Indica" (Molesworth, *Dictionary*).

case, for instance, in the Paunā valley, in Māvaḷ Taluka of Poona District.[2] Elsewhere, four devotees of the gods Iṭṭhal and Birāppā of Paṭṭaṇ Kuḍolī wanted to cut down a tree for wood to build a temple. They were Nārubā Gāvḍā, a Dhangar; Jakāppā Caugule, a Liṅgāyat; Jānyā Sutār, a Liṅgāyat-carpenter; and Narayā Tarāḷe, a Koḷī. In the tree there lived a demoness (*rakṣasī*), Yeḷmakkaḷtāī ("the mother of seven children," a Kannaḍa name). Only by taking her captive could they cut down the tree:

Text 7

The tree was so thick that a rope fifteen feet long would not go around it. They looked at the tree. After they had thoroughly examined the tree, they unyoked the oxen. Narayā Tarāḷ took them to the pasture. Jānyā Sutār, Nārubā Gāvḍā, and our Jakāppā Caugulā (*sic*) decided to cut down the tree. As they set to it, what did they find in this tree? Yeḷmakkaḷtāī—the mother of seven sons. It was a colossal, gigantic goddess place (*bāīdevasthān*).

What did Narayā Tarāḷ do then? He called out the name of [the goddess] Kāḷambā and swung. He missed the tree and cut off his leg. He cried out to Nāru Gāvḍā: "Your god [Iṭṭhal/Birāppā] is no god. You have brought other people's children into the woods as sacrificial victims. You have deceived us!"

Nāru Gāvḍā could not collect his thoughts: "O God Iṭṭhal, you trickster,[3] you wonder-worker,[4] what have you done, Iṭṭhal and Birdev? Come quickly and help." He ran toward Kaduli (*sic*). As he was on the way there, the god realized everything intuitively. What did Birdev say then to Iṭṭhal? "Elder brother (Dādā) Iṭṭhal, Jānyā Sutār has called out the name of Kāḷambā, taken a swing at the tree, missed the tree, and cut off his leg. He is yelling at Nāru Gāvḍā, and Nāru Gāvḍā is in a desperate fix."

What did Iṭṭhal do? He took a coconut with three black eyes and . . . ,[5] and some turmeric powder, and he flew like a bird. Where? To the boundary of the village of Kāgal, and to Hamsvaḍ, to the boundary of three villages. Nāru Gāvḍā came running there. What did he give to Nāru Gāvḍā? The coconut with three eyes and three lines, and the turmeric powder. "Throw turmeric on the tree, break the coconut with the eyes and the three lines on it, and cut down the tree, calling out the names of Iṭṭhal and Birdev. Throw a pinch of turmeric on Jānyā Sutār's leg, and his leg will be healed. Cut down the tree."

Nāru objected: "Yeḷmakkaḷtāī, the mother of seven sons, is here. She will wake up, roaring like thunder, and devour us along with our carts and oxen. Then what will we do?"

---

2. See D. D. Kosambi, *Myth and Reality* (Bombay, 1962), p. 92.

3. *Gāruḍyā* = written *gāruḍī*—"A snake-charmer, also a juggler or conjurer" (Molesworth, *Dictionary*). *Gāruḍ* = "Juggling or leger de main. Arts, tricks, chicanery, evil devising and scheming" (ibid.).

4. *Navalyā,* from *naval,* a wonder, marvel.

5. *Tīn śīrcā nāral* [?]. Presumably, three diagonal lines.

> "Call out the names of Iṭṭhal and Birāppā, throw the turmeric powder, grab her by the hair, pull a rope through her nose,[6] tie her to the cart, and come here."
>
> Nāru Gāvḍā returned to the Bhaleghol pond, threw turmeric powder on Jānyā Sutār's leg, broke the coconut on the tree, threw a pinch of turmeric, and—calling out the names of Iṭṭhal and Birdev—made a gash in the tree. He struck at it over and over again, and after a time the tree fell down. It was the place of Yeḷmakkaḷtāī, a goddess's place, huge. She stood there, terrifying, and said, "I will devour you, along with your oxen and your cart."
>
> Following the word of Iṭṭhal, Nāru Gāvḍā threw turmeric on her and called out the names of Iṭṭhal and Birdev. He grabbed her by her braids and threw her to the ground. He bored a hole in her nose with an iron rod, and tied her to the cart, to the back of the cart. They made boards out of the tree and loaded them into the wagon and hurried home. . . .
>
> [The local Muslim ruler intervenes, and after further adventures, the four finally arrive in Paṭṭaṇ Kuḍolī.]
>
> Jakāppā, Narī Tarāḷ, Nāru Gāvḍā and Jānyā Sutār brought the cart to the "Bamboo Pasture" and then to the "Toran Pasture,"[7] and they began to lay the foundations of the temple. According to the god's command, they buried the goddess, whom they had tied to the cart, in front of the temple.

A second group of goddesses is connected with water. These are the seven water goddesses, *sātī āsarās* (Sanskrit, *apsaras*). Dhangars do special worship of them twice a year, before and after the bathing of the sheep. Before the beginning of the bathing, which is necessary for shearing the sheep, a ewe is milked in the water.[8] After the bathing, the goddesses are embodied in seven chalcedony stones on the bank of the lake or the river; these are worshiped by being sprinkled with water and turmeric powder (*bhaṇḍār*). All the Dhangars' gods and their famous devotees have encounters with *āsarās*.

The seven Bhivayyā of Kām(b)aḷeśvar, which lies between Phalṭaṇ and Bārāmatī, become the seven fictitious "sisters" (*māvācyā bahiṇī*) of the god Dhuḷobā of Phalṭaṇ.[9] They live in a deep pool in the river. Appropriately enough, Koḷīs, who have been fishermen from time immemorial, also have hereditary ritual rights (*mān*) along with Dhangars in the pilgrimage festival in honor of Dhuḷobā.

Sometimes the seven goddesses put their devotees to the test. The goddess Jānāī and the seven *āsarās* test the integrity (*sattva*) of the devotion (*bhakti*) of Khilubā, the famous devotee from Āñjangāv. They stand in his path as he is

6. As is generally done to draft oxen.
7. Particular places in Paṭṭaṇ Kuḍolī.
8. See below, Text 21.
9. See below, 5.1.1.

going on pilgrimage to Iṭṭhal and Birāppā in Paṭṭaṇ Kuḍolī. Jānāī is not otherwise mentioned in connection with the seven water goddesses, but she appears here as a goddess who lives in the water. It is also she who later helps Khilubā cross the Bhimā river at Paṇḍharpūr, on his way to Paṭṭaṇ Kuḍolī.

Text 8

. . . The four or five yellow-robed Gosāvīs[10] set off. In the first Satya Age, Khilubā the Śid [from Sanskrit/written Marāṭhī *siddha*] took the right-hand road. They went to the bank of the pond. How beautiful this place looked in the black night! [Khilubā's] disciples were happy. "The Pāṭil of Vākaḷ has lied to us. How strongly he advised us against going to this place! He said, 'Such and such [minor] deities are there.' How pleasantly cool this place is! Nāgābāī's son [Khilubā] has brought prestige to his name."

Khilubā the Śid said, "Let's see whether his prediction is true or false. If all these gods have gone to sleep in the pool, then we'll wake them up. And if they're sitting up, we will make them stand. Because if we sneak quietly away from them, then they'll say that we have run away from them in fear."

Khilubā the Śid blew his conch-shell horn at the pond. Where did the sound of the horn go? Into the underworld! The sound reached the ears of Jānābāī in the water. She sprang up full of anger, the way we do when we get stung by a horsefly. She said to the seven *āsarās:* "Wake up our gods. A man has come into our territory. We will seize him, drag him over here, and test his integrity (*satva*). Only if we rob him of his integrity can we survive."

The seven *āsarās,* with Maśāsur [Mahiṣāsura] as the eighth, Narsing [Narasiṃha][11] as the ninth, Etāl [Y ∼ Vetāḷ] as the tenth, and even the *pālkhī* of the ugly Yetāḷ, all took torches and went up from below. When the four disciples saw the gods and the torches, they said to one another, "Bābā, we've had it now. What can anyone do here now? The Pāṭil was right." They went off, terrified. "Let anyone who can save himself do so. Hide somewhere!" They ran and hid behind rocks. But Khilubā stood in the Rājāvaḷ Pond, in the first Satya Age, his chin propped on his stick, his blanket[12] on his body. He was not worried.

The seven *āsarās* surrounded him. And the ugly Yetāḷ seized Khilubā by the hips and placed him before Jānubāī in the underworld. Jānubāī spoke to the seven *āsarās* like lightning and thunder in the heavens: "Put him on a mat of scorpions. We want to test his integrity. If we don't rob him of his integrity, we won't be able to exist." The seven *āsarās* laid down a mat of scorpions.

Khilubā said lovingly to Jānūcandanī: "There are scorpions in my nails; snakes are curled in my hair.[13] What can a mat of scorpions do to me?"

---

10. Who come from the Dhangar caste.

11. On Narasiṃha as one of the fifty-two ghosts, see Rā, Ciṃ. Ḍhere, *Lokasaṃskṛtīcī Kṣitije* (Puṇeṃ, 1971), pp. 47ff., 56f.

12. *Ghoṅgaḍī,* a woolen blanket typical of the Dhangars.

13. So powerful was Khilubā, who lived in the Satya Age.

And, in the Satya Age, Khilubā, the god, sat down on the mat. Jānubāī, who lived in the water in the first Satya Age—how excited she became [in the hope of being able to rob Khilubā of his integrity]! But Jānubāī's [enthusiasm] sank the way dirt sinks in water.

[After another futile attempt to disturb Khilubā's composure, Jānubāī said to the *āsarās:*]

"Seven *āsarās,* take off your blouses, take off your saris, dance naked. If he sees you naked, his integrity will dwindle away."

Now Khilubā the Śid was in a fix. He sat down. When he had sat down, he took the blanket he was wearing and wrapped it over his head. He laid his head on his knees and closed his eyes. The seven *āsarās* took off their blouses and saris, and began to dance naked. The seven *āsarās* began dancing near Khilubā. The dance was so [lovely] that the gods who were present were completely speechless. The seven *āsarās* danced and danced, and finally they got tired. Khilubā did not once open his eyes, not once did he raise his head. He did not look at their nakedness, and he did not let go of his integrity. Now the seven *āsarās* were in a fix. What did they say to one another?

"Oh dear, how many days we have danced, and how long we have played these games of ours here—and this man does not once open his eyes, and does not once lift his head. He won't give up his integrity." So they put their clothes back on.

Jānubāī asked, "Bābā, what land are you from? What village do you come from? Through whose womb was this gem born? Why are you wandering about the countryside? All right, at least tell me your name and your village."

From inside the blanket, the crazy[14] Khilurājā said: "I am Khilubā, from Āñjangāv. The gem was born from Nāgābāī's womb."

Full of joy, Jānu said, "Oh, Khilubā, my Dādā, I beg your forgiveness. You are my brother according to dharma."[15]

"Oh, Jānūcandanī, I will be your brother, but promise me something."

"Tell me what I must promise you."

"Your gods have great magical powers. This is the Satya Age. We five are on our way [to Paṭṭaṇ Kuḍolī]. In the Kali Age thousands will come in bullock carts and on horses to the pilgrimage festival. It will be dangerous for them. Mothers with children in their wombs will come to my festival. Children will come whose hair has not yet been cut. If they should be in danger, you must do something for them. First promise that you will do this; then I will be your brother." Jānūcandanī promised this to Khilubā with pleasure. "Jānūcandanī, I am now your 'younger brother.' Now I want to go to meet my guru."

Jānūcandanī said, "Wait a little while."

To the seven *āsarās* she said, "Hurry up and give my brother a bath. We'll fix a meal with five different dishes. When we've fed him, we'll send him on

14. "Crazy" primarily because of his unshakable devotion (*bhakti*) and the equanimity he had gained through asceticism (*tapas*).

15. Dādā is an elder brother; a brother according to dharma is not a blood relative.

his way.'' The seven *āsarās* set busily to work. One of them brought the pot of water, another scrubbed him.

When had the crazy Khilubā last had a bath? He had been practicing asceticism (*tapas*) for twice twelve years, and he had no idea what a bath is. Vultures and falcons lived in his matted hair. He said, ''It's good that you're pouring water on me, but it's making my companions die. Pour less water.''

Khilubā shook his head and the birds flew away. The seven *āsarās* washed him with water from seven pots. They washed him and bathed him and cooled him, in the first Satya Age. When this was finished, the seven of them set down seven earthen pots. Thus they provided him very lovingly with food, in those days. . . .

A third category of goddesses comprises those of disease and death. The narrative from Mhasvaḍ mentions the goddess Marīāī along with Yeḷammā. There is no particular cult center for Marīāī in Maharashtra, but this cholera goddess, who is widespread elsewhere in India as well, is found in every village. A Dhangar from Jāvḷī (Phalṭaṇ Taluka, Satara District) explains:

Text 9

When cholera (*kalrā*) breaks out, people say that Marīāī has sent the cholera: ''Marīāī's cholera.'' What do people do because of it? They worship the goddess. Dressed in wet clothes, they pour water on the goddess with the words, ''You've come; but don't cause any suffering'' [*śītaḷ jā,* actually, ''become cool''].

Thus they plead with her. After that the villagers bring the goddess out. They make a small cart. They set the goddess on it. They dress her in a blouse and a sari, and sprinkle her with turmeric powder (*haḷaḍ*). Then they pull the small cart out of the village, bring the goddess to the village boundary, and place her outside the boundary of their village and inside the boundary of another village, with the words, ''Go, O Queen.''

Lakṣmīāī, also called the harsh (*kaḍak*) Lakṣmī, is a somewhat milder and kinder form of Marīāī. Among the pastoral and nomadic castes, she is usually not identical with the wife of Viṣṇu, and she is worshiped independently of him. She gives wealth in the form of cattle. As long as the sheep are in the *vāḍā*—the sheep-pen—Lakṣmī is also there, and one must remove one's sandals when one enters the pen.

The goddess who, as Marīāī and Lakṣmīāī, brings cholera—but also, if she is duly worshiped, wealth—is driven out of the village by the farmers, even though she has a permanent temple. She is basically a nomadic goddess, and is still today carried by wandering groups in shrines resembling wooden caskets, which they exhibit at weekly markets or at pilgrimage festivals. Perhaps Marīāī is most closely connected with the nomadic population and with the caravans of merchants. These groups brought prosperity, grain, cattle, and the like, but also diseases, from affluent regions to poorer areas.

Under the number "seven" the Dhangars classify not only goddesses or mothers who are known to them locally and are worshiped by them, but also goddesses or mothers whose cults lie in the region of their migration or at its end point. For example, a Dhangar from near Jejurī names as seven local goddesses Marīāī, Ekkayā, Mhākkayā, Tukāī, Nāgāī, Kāḷubāī, and Kanāī. In the view of another Dhangar, a priest (*pūjārī*) of the gods Iṭṭhal and Birāppā of Paṭṭaṇ Kuḍolī, the following are the widely influential, not merely locally important, goddesses who appear as "mothers" or "sisters" in the Dhangars' myths:

1. Sirsaṅgīcī Kāḷavā—the Kāḷubāī (Sanskrit, *Kālikā*) of Sirsaṅgī, in Belgaum District. Another Kāḷubāī center is found southwest of Śirvaḷ, at Māṇḍhardev in Wāī Taluka of Satara District.
2. Ḍoṅgarcī Yallavvā—the goddess Yallavvā (Yeḷammā) of the hill—that is, the hill of Saundattī (Saṃvadattī) in Belgaum District.
3. Cincṇ(~l)īcī Māyavvā—the goddess Māyavvā of Cinclī in Belgaum District.
4. Kolhāpūrcī Ambikā—the goddess Ambikā or Mahālakṣmī of Kolhāpūr.
5. Bādalcī Baḍdavvā—the goddess Baḍdavvā of Bādalcī(?). In the stories of a Kuruba from Eksambe (Belgaum District), Bādalcī is the famous Badāmī in Karnatak. The actual name of this famous forest- and water-goddess is Banśaṅkarī or Śākambharī.
6. Tuḷjāpūrcī Tukavvā—the goddess Tukāī of Tuḷjāpūr in Usmanabad District. Tukāī's center is actually Koṇḍanpūr in the Māvaḷ (Havelī Taluka, Poona District), but she is becoming more and more closely identified with the goddess of Tuḷjāpūr.
7. Āmbyācī Jogavā—the goddess Jogeśvarī in the story told by the Dhangar woman from Mhasvaḍ (Text 3). Ambājogāī is Mominabad in Bhir District.

Still another Dhangar gives a third list of seven goddesses. Sixty years old and blind, he comes from Tārgāv near Sātārā, where he is the priest (*pūjārī*) of the god Birobā. He is famous for his knowledge and well known in Dhangar cult centers for his skill as a performer of *ovīs*. He lists the goddesses as follows: Yalammā, Kolhāpūrcī Ambikā, Lakṣmī, Ekavvā, Māyavvā, Jānāī, and Māḷāī (the "mother" on the highland pasture).

2. The "Mothers" and "Sisters": Protection, Help, and Magical Power

The goddesses Yeḷammā and Marīāī in the story told by the old Dhangar woman from Mhasvaḍ (Text 3) are two of the many goddesses connected time and again with the divine child. In Maharashtra this relationship can be traced back to at least the third century B.C., if one interprets certain archeological finds[16] as showing the goddess accepting the male god when he appears as a child. In Nevāsā and Bahāl there are female terracotta figurines in the chalcolithic layers of the first millenium B.C.[17] Sitting mother goddesses are found in the layers of the third to second centuries B.C. in Kolhāpūr, Nāsik, Nevāsā, Ter, and Karhāḍ. Because these goddesses are usually connected with the layers of the Sātavāhana period, they might be identical with the village deities (*grāmadevatās*) mentioned by Hāla in the *Gāthāsaptaśati*.[18]

Statuettes of naked female deities from the first century A.D. are found, among other places, in Ter; and the goddesses of Ter and Nevāsā, who are generally depicted feeding, fondling, or playing with a child, date back to approximately the third to the fifth century A.D. In layers of the third century B.C. to the third century A.D. at Nevāsā and Ter, heads from figurines of boys have been found.

The god Birobā appears as a child when he first comes into contact with goddesses. Thus, when the seven great goddesses or seven sisters go hunting and find little Birobā abandoned, they argue over which of them should raise him. Only when Mhākubāī/Māyavvā begins to lactate is the dispute settled in her favor. Birobā becomes *her* "brother."[19] The goddess Mhākubāī of Cinclī helps Birobā, the Dhangar god and her younger "brother," in all difficulties:

Text 10

When Birobā went to Śolāpūr to graze his sheep there, the obstreperous Reḍeśvar [Lord of the Buffalo] was living in the forest. He ate one sheep after another. Here [i.e., in Kavlapūr, Sangli District] Mhākubāī realized intuitively (*antarāt jānleṃ*): "My 'brother's' sheep are being eaten." Mhākubāī went there and killed the demon (*daitya*) Reḍeśvar. When the demon fell to the ground and was about to die, he said to Mhākubāī: "If I die now at your hands, my last wish is for you to wear my clothes during one of the twelve months." So in the month of Māgh [February/March] Mhākubāī's temple priests (*pūjārīs*) wear the clothes of the demon Reḍeśvar.[20]

16. For the information that follows, see the *Maharashtra State Gazetteer,* Ancient Period (Bombay, 1967), pp. 48ff.

17. See also B. and R. Allchin, *The Birth of Indian Civilization* (Harmondsworth, 1968), p. 314.

18. At 2, 90; 1, 64; 2, 72. In the temple of Arya (= Candikā) is hung the string of bells from around the neck of a dead buffalo.

19. From a story told by a Kuruba from Eksambe (Belgaum District). The story of the sisters' fight is told in many versions. Perhaps the six mouths of Skanda-Kārttikeya also can be explained as the solution to an impending fight among the six Kṛttikās (*Mahābhārata,* 9, 43–46; *Rāmāyaṇa,* 1, 37).

20. This text comes from Kavlapūr (Sangli District).

Like Birobā, the young Gosāvī of Mhasvaḍ is also helped by the two goddesses Marīāī and Yeḷammā. He owes his victory to their magical powers as well as to Śaṅkar. The god who conquers demons with the help of the goddess is frequently found in temple legends. The Bhairav of Sonārī can kill the demon only with the help of the sixty-four Yoginīs, one of whom, at any rate, is Tukāī of Tuḷjāpūr.[21] Tukāī or Bhavānī of Tuḷjāpūr also gave the famous Marāṭhā King Śivājī (1627–1680) the power to conquer his enemies. She appeared to Śivājī in a dream and informed him that she was incarnated in his sword "Bhavānī."[22]

Like Khilubā, Birobā also meets the seven *āsarās* in the course of his travels and secures their assistance:

Text 11

Twelve years passed. For twelve years he played to the full in Māyavvā's *vāḍā*. Thus twelve years passed. Now the god began to have misgivings. "For twelve years she has served me, and now it is at an end." Twelve years—that is, a *tapa*[23]—had passed. He had accepted her service (*śeva*) for twelve years. "Other mothers and sisters will serve me. How can I stay here? How will I grow in the world (*mājhā jagāt vāḍhāvā kasā hoṇār*)? And how will I become known in the world? How will I become skillful and clever (*mājhī kartabagārī kaśī hoṇār*)?" Such thoughts came to him. "Twelve years have passed. To whom should I go now?" . . .

[Birobā meets a widow and her son, and is worshiped by them for twelve years.]

In that place there was the boy Vīr Velhāḷ, who guarded the chest [with Birobā in it],[24] and who stayed nearby in the *vāḍā* built for the cows. The old woman used to go to the pasture with the cows. And when she had grazed the cows, she used to return in the evening. Some days she would take them to the forest of Kātar Bilāgī.[25] Again twelve years passed. Now he wanted to leave these people. At this time the boy Vīr Malhār was sleeping. And what did Kāśīliṅg Birāppā do? He took the form of a snake and bit the boy, and the boy died. Birobā got back into the chest.

In the evening the old woman came back to the *vāḍā* with the cows. She called to the boy: "O, Bābā, untie the calves and let them drink milk. Have you been sleeping from early morning until I got back with the cows?" But he lay

21. See the end of chap. 5, and chap. 8, section 1, below.

22. *Devikoś* (Pra. Kṛ. Prabhudesai, *Ādīśaktīce viśvarūpa arthāt Devīkośa*), vol. 1 (Puṇeṃ, 1967), p. 347. See *Śrīchatrapati Śivājī Mahārāja yāṃcyā ājñe varūna lihileleṃ kavīṃdra Paramānanda kṛta Śrīśivabhārata*, Sadāśiva Mahādeva Divekara, ed., *Bhārata Itihāsa Saṃśodhaka Maṇḍaḷa puraskṛta granthamālā*, no. 3, chap. 18.19–22, and chap. 20.23.

23. A period of twelve years.

24. In the chest was the *mūrti* of Birobā, which the widow had found in a river. To this day, nomadic groups carry their deities on their heads in chests that serve as shrines.

25. That is, in Karavīr (present-day Kolhapur District).

> there dead. Did he stand up after that? He couldn't stand up. She began to cry loudly. "Get up," she said. But he wouldn't get up. Angrily she milked three potfuls of milk and placed it near his bed: "Drink, at least, and then go back to sleep." But there was no way he was going to get up; he was stiff and dead. Then she began to shout: "Twelve years I've served you [Birobā], and what have you done? How skillfully you've done this to me!"
>
> Angrily she took the chest and threw it away. The chest fell into a deep pool of water (*ḍoh*) named Kāḷā Pīparyā.[26] Even if you tied together the ropes from twelve woven rope cots (*cārpāī*), you couldn't reach the bottom of it. After the chest had fallen down into it, the god lived twelve years in the pool.
>
> We say the god is not good (*cāṅglā nāhī*). After twelve years, the devotion (*bhakti*) of the boy [that is, of Vīr Velhāḷ or Vīr Malhār] pleased him. He absorbed him into his form (*teneṃ [tye]lā āplā rupāt vilin karūn ghetleṃ*). Then the chest stayed in the water for twelve years. For twelve years the seven *āsarās* worshiped him (*pūjā kelī*). . . .

The text does not in fact state directly that Birobā wins the magical powers of the seven *āsaras*. From another text we learn that the disciple Mhāliṅgrāyā Māḷāppā and his guru Birobā withdraw into the depths of a lake, where the disciple gets his knowledge from the guru. But in a broader sense, the seven goddesses are also the personified, supernatural, feminine powers, the seven—or rather, eight—*siddhis,* who serve the one who wins them by his asceticism or in some other way.[27]

3. Mhākubāī—the Dhangar Goddess

Buchanan mentioned the goddess Mhākubāī/Māyavvā/Māyakkā (Sanskrit, Mahākālī) of Cinclī, along with Birāppā, as an important goddess of the Kurubas. She is the family goddess of many Dhangar families, especially in Satara and Sangli Districts. For example, ten out of the sixteen exogamous groups of Dhangars in the village of Limbavḍe (Āṭpāḍī Taluka, Sangli District), northeast of Kharsuṇḍī, name Māyakkā as their family goddess along with other Dhangar deities. Mhākubāī, Mhasāī, and Māyavvā are certainly identical.

In Mhasāīcīvāḍī (= the camp of the "buffalo mother"), near Mhasvaḍ, the goddess of the village is Mhākubāī. In a verse attributed to the seventeenth-century saint-poet Tukārām we read:

---

26. That is, dark blue water with pipaḷ trees on the bank (the narrator's explanation).

27. Molesworth, *Dictionary*. See David N. Lorenzen, *The Kapālikas and Kālamukhas: Two Lost Saivite Sects* (New Delhi, 1972), pp. 92–95.

navhe jākhāī jokhāī / māyārāṇī mhaisābāī
He [Viṭhobā of Paṇḍharpūr] is not [like] Jākhāī, Jokhāī,
Māyārāṇī, or Mhaisābāī.[28]

Mhaisābāī—"the buffalo woman"—is another name for Māyārāṇī. Jākhāī and Jokhāī are linked etymologically with *yakṣī* and with (Y)ekavvā, who is Māyavvā's sister in Dhangar mythology. (Y)ekavvā is certainly identical with Jākhāī and Jokhāī. In Cinclī it is primarily Dhangars and Kurubas who worship the goddess Māyavvā/Mhākubāī independently of Birobā, with whom she is otherwise very closely linked in mythology and ritual. This shows the strength and independence of the original mother-goddess cult. Village tradition confirms that in Mhasāīcīvāḍī near Mhasvaḍ, for example, the cult of Mhasāī/Māyavvā/Mhākubāī was established before the interloper Birobā arrived.

In Ārevāḍī, one of the principal cult places of Birobā, Birobā gained his present place of worship relatively late. It lies in a grove under his special protection. Birobā's original temple lies "on the border of three villages," three miles from the grove, on a hill. That Mhākubāī had her place of worship in the grove prior to Birobā is also shown by the old votive sculpture of Mhākubāī behind the present Birobā temple. It represents a woman sitting with her legs spread apart in the typical mother-goddess pose. To her left is the small figure of a herdsman (or Gosāvī?) with a staff. Today Mhākubāī still has a pilgrimage festival in Ārevāḍī. Although the festival is small in contrast with the huge *jatrā* in honor of Birobā in the month of Caitra, it nevertheless indicates her independent significance.

The mythology from Ārevāḍī expresses the reverence that Birobā feels for the older goddess. Even though she is only his "fictitious sister" (*māvācī bahīṇ*), Mhākubāī takes precedence over Kāmābāī, the wife whom Birobā won in battle:

Text 12

. . . He took Kanakāmā [~ Kāmābāī] on his horse and rode to the Hivar forest [the grove of Ārevāḍī]. Then he thought to himself, "Māyavvā and Ekavvā have come from Karnatak to the Hivar forest. This is Sunday, bazaar day at Ḍhālgāv." The brother and sister went to the bazaar at Ḍhālgāv.

Kāmābāī was angry, and thought: "He took so much trouble to win me, and now he goes off to the bazaar with his sister without a thought for me."

The god Kāśīliṅg[29] was angry at what she said and at the fact that she was grumbling about his sister. So Birobā grabbed her by the arm and threw her behind his temple, at the feet of his sister. He was angry with her, but still she said, "He takes his sister and goes to the bazaar."

---

28. *Devikoś*, vol. 2, p. 456.
29. An epithet of Birobā.

And he took her by the arm and threw her toward the rear. And when the procession of the god comes near her—that is, the *pālkhī* of the god—even if ten carts are carrying it, it doesn't move toward her—the god's anger is still that great. Thus, behind [Birobā's] temple, on the left-hand side, there is a temple of Kāmābāī. Thus, in the Satya Age, the god threw his wife at his sister's feet. In the Kali Age can we do this?

In the mythology of the Dhangars, Ekavvā and Mhākubāī are two sisters "without children." Ekavvā and Mhākubāī set out on a hunt and find Birobā abandoned—like Skanda—in a forest. An *ovī* of the nomadic Dhangars says:

Text 13

[*Ovī:*] . . . Over there was the camp (*vāḍā*) of Bāḷubāī. Her daughters were Hākāyā and Mhākāyā. These two went hunting every day. They were barren. There was no lack of wealth: nine *lākhs* of lambs, and nine *lākhs* of sheep. Innumerable barren animals. A herd of cows and water-buffalo cows.

She had servants. She had a troop of herdsmen. Her daughters were devoted to hunting.

In the Dhangars' legends and in local narratives from cult sites of Mhākubāī and Birobā, Mhākubāī is clearly regarded as having existed before Birobā was born. Only once do we hear that Ekavvā and M(h)ākāyā were fashioned out of Śaṅkar's ash and Pārvatī's *kuṅkum,* in order to bring up Birobā.

If one follows these clues, it seems that pastoral groups also worshiped goddesses like Mhākubāī. Archeological finds from even chalcolithic layers at Ināmgāv in Ahmadnagar District and Nevāsā in Aurangabad District include unfired clay figurines of female deities in a predominantly pastoral context.[30] In addition, inconographic and literary indications from Braj (the region around Mathurā, and the homeland of Kṛṣṇa), along with many vestiges in contemporary ritual and in oral traditions, point to the widespread worship of the goddess (*devī*), snake deities (*nāgas*), and spirits of the hills and forest (*yakṣas*) on the part of pastoral groups. This is still the case today as well. Even Kṛṣṇa seems to have belonged to these strata before he appeared on the scene as a child and his form gained sharper contours.[31]

4. M(h)asā—Rukmiṇī—Padubāī

It is possible that Mhākubāī/Mhasāī/M(h)asā is also the original independent goddess underlying the Viṭhobā-Rukmiṇī cult of Paṇḍharpūr. D. D. Kosambi has pointed out that Rakhumāī ("Mother Rakhu") and Viṭhobā have separate

30. H. D. Sankalia, "Mahārāṣṭrācī Ādimātā," *Kesarī,* May 16, 1971.
31. Ch. Vaudeville, "Braj, Lost and Found," *Indo-Iranian Journal,* 18 (1976) 195–213.

temples within the temple complex in Paṇḍharpūr.[32] It was at Paṇḍharpūr that Kṛṣṇa sought out Rukmiṇī (= Rakhumāī) in the Diṇḍīra forest when she was angry with him.[33] The Diṇḍīra forest is a small grove west of the Viṭhobā temple on the bank of the Bhimā (Candrabhāgā) River. There are two temples here, one belonging to M(h)asā, and the other to Rukmiṇī. Along with members of other castes, the principal adherents of M(h)asā still today are Gavḷīs, whose herds of water buffaloes are a familiar sight along the riverbank in front of the temple. In a retaining wall along the river in front of the temples there is also a small shrine of Lakṣmī, who is primarily worshiped by the Gavḷīs. And on the opposite bank of the river is found a cult of Mhasobā, who is here a god of cattle herders and not the "guardian of the fields" into which he has otherwise for the most part developed.

A Brahman who serves in the Rukmiṇī temple in the Diṇḍīra forest told the story of Viṭhobā and Rukmiṇī as follows, showing that here M(h)asā is older than Rukmiṇī:

Text 14

Viṭhobā's [Kṛṣṇa's] chief queen is Rukmiṇī. At that time, Rādhā sat on his lap. Then Rukmiṇī was angry, and she came here sulking. Here there was the Diṇḍīra forest, outside the village, on the bank of the river. She sat here and practiced asceticism (*tapaścaryā*) near Masādevī. Then Viṭhobā went to Puṇḍalik. Puṇḍalik was looking after his parents and worshiping them [and hardly took care of Viṭhobā at all]. Viṭhobā got onto the brick that Puṇḍalik tossed to him and stood there [patiently]. And Rukmiṇī sat here, in this place.

After Puṇḍalik had looked after [his parents] and worshiped them, Puṇḍalik and Viṭhobā took a cart and came to search here. Here in the Diṇḍīra forest is the place where she hid. She said to the god: "There are four pilgrimage festivals, in the months of Āṣāḍh, Māgh, Kārttik, and Caitra. At these times there should be *darśan* twenty-four hours a day." Accordingly, there is *darśan* twenty-four hours a day.

So in this way Viṭhobā and Kṛṣṇa came here.

Viṭhobā sat in that place, and Rukmiṇī in this place. Rukmiṇī sat here in order to practice asceticism. The *mūrti* of Rukmiṇī has four arms. It is a holy place that has "originated from itself" (*svayambhū devasthān*).

Other informants state that M(h)asā herself hid Rukmiṇī in a rock in front of Kṛṣṇa. M. S. Mate suggests that a local goddess has been identified with Rukmiṇī.[34] Perhaps this is the goddess M(h)asā/Mhasāī, who has preserved

32. *Myth and Reality,* p. 86.

33. See 5.1.1, below.

34. "Pandharpur: Myth and Reality," in *Studies in Indology and Medieval History* (Prof. G. H. Khare Felicitation Volume), edited by M. S. Mate and G. T. Kulkarni (Poona, 1974), p. 132ff.

her own separate cult, even though she is almost identified with Rukmiṇī. It is certainly not necessary to suppose that M(h)asā/Mhasāī *became* Rukmiṇī; the very fact that the two goddesses have separate temples shows this. The goddess who was already residing in the place helped the wife of Kṛṣṇa who came from Dvārkā. Furthermore, according to the oral traditions of the Gavḷīs, Viṭhobā/Viṭṭhal of Paṇḍharpūr is not Kṛṣṇa from Dvārkā, but a Gavḷī who came from Karnatak.[35]

In the Dhangars' stories, Viṭhobā/Viṭṭhal's wife is Padubāī (Padmiṇī), who comes from the Gavḷī caste. In the version of one Dhangar, reported by Durgā Bhāgvat, Padmiṇī, who lives in a *tīrtha* in Paṇḍharpūr, comes into being by metamorphosis when Viṭhobā and Rukmiṇī quarrel and Rukmiṇī dies as a result of Viṭhobā's curse.[36] The connection between Viṭhobā and Padmiṇī/Padubāī, as well as the contrast between them, appears again in the dispute between Viṭṭhal and Padubāī in Paṭṭaṇ Kuḍolī.[37] Like M(h)asā in the Diṇḍīra forest, Padmiṇī/Padubāī is connected with the Gavḷīs, but she is above all a goddess of the forest. The Padubāī of Paṭṭaṇ Kuḍolī comes "from the forest region" (*vanācyā bhāgyātūn*). She dies—cursed by Viṭhobā—in the forest. A snake drives away from her corpse the relatives and members of her village who are searching for her. Also affected by Viṭhobā's curse, Padubāī's parents, "Nandāī Pāṭlīn and Maṅgrāvaḷ Pāṭīl," become "gods in the forest."

The independent goddess of the forest, Padubāī, is still to be found primarily in forest regions. There are relatively independent Padmāvatī cults in the forested areas of the Māvaḷ favored by Gavḷīs and Dhangars, as well as in Muḷśī, Māvaḷ, Khed, and Junnar Talukas of Poona District. Bhūgāv in Muḷśī Taluka has an old, almost forgotten, Khaṇḍobā temple two miles away, on a hill. Padubāī is found in front of the temple—a *śendūr*-painted stone in the underbrush. Inside the temple are old votive sculptures of Khaṇḍobā, Mhāḷsā, and Bāṇāī. To the left and right of these are two female figures (Gavḷṇīs) with milk pots. Today Padubāī's principal temple is in the village. She came to the village from a hill in the forest. "The villagers brought her from there."

This accords with a slow development that took place everywhere in this region for centuries: the settlement of people from the hills in the valleys, and

35. See also Durgā Bhāgvat, "Paṇḍharīcā Viṭhobā," in *Paisa* (Bombay, 1970), p. 38: ". . . *Viṭhṭhala Kānaḍā āhe. to Gavaḷī āhe. . . .*" A. P. Karmarkar et al., *Mystic Teachings of the Haridāsas of Karṇāṭak* (Bombay, 1939), p. 25: "God Viṭhobā is called as a Kannaḍa God belonging to Karnāṭak in one of the Abhaṅgas ascribed to the authorship of Jñāneśvara." See T. H. Avate, ed., *Jñānadeva Gāthā* (Poona, 1923), no. 7, p. 30.

36. Bhāgvat, ibid.

37. G. D. Sontheimer, "Eine Tempellengende der Dhangars von Mahārāṣṭra," in H. Berger, *Mündliche Überlieferungen in Südasien. Fünf Beiträge* (Weisbaden, 1975), pp. 83–110.

the concomitant transition from a predominantly pastoral economy to agriculture, especially to rice cultivation in the valleys.[38] Also, the Gavḷīs are no longer Gavḷīs by caste, but "Marāṭhās," and "Gavḷīs by profession." The villagers today are Marāṭhās, and their knowledge of the history of the cults is in the process of dying out. Their knowledge is focused rather on the *bhakti* cult of Viṭhobā in Paṇḍharpūr. The local deities are indeed worshiped, but with little interest in their mythology or their recent history.

The mythology has a tendency to become standardized and assimilated to the Purāṇas. People do know that Padubāī came from the forest, but they see in her solely a manifestation of Pārvatī:

Text 15

[Pārvatī saw Rām in the Daṇḍakāraṇya, wandering in search of Sītā. Astonished, Pārvatī asked Śiva why he persisted in meditating on Śrī Rām, who behaved like an ordinary mortal. Śiva answered that she had not understood Śrī Rām.][39]

Śaṅkar said, "Pārbatī [Pārvatī], don't go there. Rām won't be deceived by you in this form. You must act according to the curse Rām gives you."

She went to Rām, and, in order to deceive him, she took on the form (*avatār*) of Sitā (*sic*). [But] Rām recognized her: "*tu kā gā āī ithe[ṃ] ubhī*?" ["Why are you standing here, Mother?"].

From that originated Tu-kā-āī, Tukāī. Padubāī, Tuḷjābāī, and Kāḷubāī originated in a similar way.[40] All goddesses originated through Rām because of Pārbatī's curse [*sarāp*, written *śāp*]. Pārbatī had to take the form of all these goddesses. The goddess is Pārbatī. Whose daughter is she? The daughter of King Bṛhaspatī. She practiced asceticism (*tapas*). As a result of her asceticism, she attained the rank of a goddess. She was cursed, and because of the curse she attained the divine status [of Tukāī and the others].

[How did the name Padubāī come into being?][41]

First there came to be the name Tukāī. All [goddesses] Tukāī in the world are the same. As she [Pārbatī] wandered around after Rām, she became Kāḷubāī. Wherever [the goddess] Kāḷubāī is found in the world, she is always the same. She became Kāḷubāī of Maṇḍhardev,[42] didn't she? So wherever [the goddess] Kāḷubāī is found, she is always the same. And then he said "Padmāvatī" and

38. Thus it is said, for example, of the small village Bhājā, for which the Buddhist Bhājā caves are named, that with the coming of agriculture the village moved from the heights above the Bhājā caves into the valley.

39. The text has been supplemented with the help of a legend referred to in D. R. Amladi, *Tuḷajāpūr Bhavānī*, Government of Maharashtra, State Board of Historical Records and Ancient Monuments, Monograph Series, no. 2 (Bombay, 1961), p. 8.

40. The informant could give no folk-etymological explanation of these names.

41. This question is asked by the interviewer.

42. In Wāī Taluka, Satara District.

changed [Pārbatī] by a curse into Padmāvatī. Rām was like a madman, as he searched for Sitā. Sitā had been carried off by Rāvaṇ. Pārbatī said, "I am going to cure Rām of his madness."

She took Sitā's form and stood behind Rām. Rām looked back, and said: "*tu kā gā māī ubhī?*" ["Why are you standing there, Mother?"]. As she [Pārbatī] wandered around again, she became Kāḷubāī, then Phirkāy,[43] then Jāvkāī, then Padmāvatī. When she had become Padmāvatī, she said, "I will live alone in a forest." With her is Aṣṭabhairav.[44] He is the doorkeeper. From whom [did he derive]? From Śaṅkar.

In Padubāī's temple in the village of Bhūgāv, old votive sculptures of Bhairav and Jogeśvarī are found on the right side, and thus not in front of or close to the aniconic representation of the goddess Padubāī. In front of them stands a female figure in a worshipful attitude who holds a pot full of oil in her hands. She is called simply Devī ("Goddess"), but presumably she is Padubāī. Bhairav is called the guardian (*rakṣak*) of Padubāī or the doorkeeper (*dvārapāl*).

In Kāsārambol̤ī, ten miles farther west than Bhūgāv and even deeper in the forest area of the Māvaḷ, Padubāī shares a temple with Vāghjāī—the Tiger Goddess. Here too the goddess's close connection with the forest and with cattle herds is historically indisputable. And once again the Gosāvī appears in the picture:

Text 16

There used to be a vast jungle here. Then the king (Rājā) of Bhor asked a Gosāvī, intending to defraud him: "Do you want the city of Amaravantī or do you want Supe and Sāsvaḍ?"[45]

He answered: "I want the city of Amaravantī."

Then he came here, and there was only jungle. Supe and Sāsvaḍ were naturally better [than the putative Amaravantī]. And so he took his life [*samādhi ghitli,* written *ghetlī*] here.

He had been given the Rājā's promise, and he could not go back to him.

When he took his life, then, [and buried himself alive], he left a tube leading into his grave. They poured milk into it, and he drank through the tube as long as he was alive. But when he died, the tube stayed full of milk. And they built a shrine over him.

In Kāsārambol̤ī, Padubāī protects not only people but especially cattle:

43. The goddess Phiraṅgāī of Kurkhumb, Indāpūr Taluka, Poona District. Here too are found legends of Pārvatī being disseminated by assimilating local mother goddesses. The somewhat primitive folk etymology is: *kā phirtis āī?*—Why are you wandering around, Mother?

44. See below, after Text 17, and chap. 9, section 3.

45. East-southeast of Poona, in the Karhā valley.

Text 17

A buffalo cow was bitten by a snake. They brought the animal to the goddess. Halfway through the night the animal got better again.

Bhairav is also present in Kāsāramboḷī. Between the two large, *śendūr*-painted lumps of rock representing the goddesses Padubāī and Vāghjāī is a much smaller one of Bhairav. The tiger goddess Vāghjāī is particularly dangerous to cattle.[46] In Padubāī and Vāghjāī there are combined in one place, in two different goddesses, elements of protection and danger to animals.

In Vaḷunj one might question the thesis that Padubāī was a goddess of the forest. Vaḷunj is near Sāsvaḍ, on the bank of the Karhā River. Since the high Karhā valley was by no means as thickly wooded as the Māvaḷ, this is not really the region for Padubāī; and people in Vaḷunj know little about her except that "she came from the Māvaḷ." Bhairav as the guard or doorkeeper (*dvārapāl*) of Padubāī is represented here by a *mūrti* to the left of the entrance of Padubāī's shrine. Frequent applications of red lead have made it almost aniconic.

Bhairav is the doorkeeper or guardian of Pārvatī/Padmiṇī in the forest. His restless character as the leader of Śiva's troops (*gaṇas*) and his life outside villages and permanent settlements made him—like Mhasobā—a celibate (*brahmacārī*) despite his propinquity to the *śakti*.[47] By contrast, in the traditions of the Gosāvīs and Gavḷīs (see Text 3 from Mhasvaḍ), Bhairav became the husband of Yogeśvarī/Jogāī or Bāṇāī/Bāḷāī, who came from the underworld.

5. The Quarrel Between Kāḷbhairav and Yeḷammā

The god's assimilation of the goddess does not always take place easily. Instead of the invading god becoming the goddess's "brother," "son," or

46. There is a god Vāghobā who is worshiped among other places in a pass that leads from the Paunā valley into the valley of the Indrāyaṇī. In earlier times, before the railway and modern roads, tigers were a threat not only to cattle in general but especially to the pack animals of caravans traveling through the pass. Votive sculptures representing cattle are still today placed before the tiger god by worshipers intending to placate the god or to fulfill their vows to him.

47. Like Bhairav and Mhasobā, Bharmappa or Bharma, a god found in Karnatak, represented as a horseman with a sword, is a guardian spirit who protects village and temple, but who also circles the village dangerously at night on his horse. Just as Bhairav is associated with Padmāvatī (Jogeśvarī), so the Jainas and others in Karnatak associate Bharmappa/Bharma/Brahmā with Padmāvatī. See S. Settar, "The Brahmadeva Pillars," *Artibus Asiae,* 33 (1971) 17ff., 34ff. Bharmappa/Brahmappa/etc. is also found among the Kurubas—as, for example, on the wall of the Birappa temple in Eksambe (Cikoḍī Taluka, Belgaum District), where he clearly plays the role of a guardian.

"husband," a struggle can develop between the two of them. Pastoralist groups often see the goddess as a demoness dangerous to cattle. Thus Syed ul Hassan reports of the Gollas:

> Another tradition, purely of a local character, comes from Kurvinal in the Atrafi Balda district, and represents the Gollas as having sprung from one Irānnā, the son of king Pidiraj of Donakunda in Telingana and his wife Padmā. Irānna and his brave brother Kathanna saved the bovine race from a female goblin and have been, in consequence, elevated to the rank of gods.[48]

In the following legend the powerful Kāḷbhairav invades the territory of the goddess Yeḷammā. This legend was narrated by a sixty-year-old Dhangar who died shortly afterward during the migration to the Koṅkaṇ. The reference to Baṅgāl in the legend can be traced to the folk belief that special magical powers are to be obtained in Bengal. Thus, Yeḷammā is also referred to as the goddess who rules over the fifty-two magical sciences. On the other hand, it is possible that the Dhangar, who knew the cult place of Yeḷammā only from hearsay, connected *Baṅgāl* with the district of *Belgaum,* where Yeḷammā's principal cult place is found on a mountain at Saundattī.

The other places in the story—Vīr, the principal cult place of Mhaskobā, in Purandar Taluka of Poona District, and the Nirā River—were more familiar to the narrator. The god Mhaskobā of Vīr, and especially Mhasvaḍ-Sīd, who is identical with him but older, were the narrator's family gods. Although the god is described as Kāḷbhairav and is found in a garden at Vīr near the Nirā River, the name "Mhaṅkāḷ" is also mentioned. Here the narrator brings together Mhaskobā of Vīr and Dhuḷobā of Phalṭaṇ, gods who exhibit a great number of similarities. Before the latter god became Dhuḷobā, he was Mahākāl of Ujjain.

Text 18

In those days, the three hundred fifty gods got together and made plans. After they had made their plans, they said, "Let's see how large the earth[49] is." They traveled through the nine continents and came to the tenth, that is, to Kāśī. Then they made more plans and said, "We want to go to Baṅgāl land, on the eleventh continent." So they went to Baṅgāl land; and what did the powerful Yeḷammā do, she who commands the fifty-two magical sciences (*bāvan [v]idyā*)? She did not let any of the gods into the continent. She sprinkled [magical] ashes (*vibhūt*), and the gods' horses fell down. Again and again the gods returned; she sprinkled ashes, and the horses fell down. Thus she drove away the horses of the three hundred fifty gods. Then the gods were fed up with it, and said, "We

48. *The Castes and Tribes of H. E. H. The Nizam's Dominions* (Bombay, 1920), s.v. Gollas.
49. *Pirthivī,* written *pṛthvī.*

haven't managed to see the eleventh continent. We have traveled through all the continents; we have traveled through the tenth; only the eleventh is left.'' Yeḷammā stood there at the door. She said, ''If you want to see Baṅgāl land, you must pass through my legs. If you don't want to see it, you must go back.''

''No,'' they said. ''We want to see Baṅgāl land.''

''If you want to see Baṅgāl land, the eleventh continent, you must pass under my legs.''

They reflected, ''We ought not to pass under her legs. We could become [ritually] impure.''

Then the three hundred fifty gods passed through under her outspread legs. Then she urinated. When she had urinated, there arose a flood like one in a river, and the gods nearly drowned. ''Where is all the water coming from? The water tastes salty. Yeḷammā has urinated!'' In this way, having fallen into the water, they reached an island, and they sat there trapped. There was no way forward or back. Now, the gods were trapped for six months, and they said, ''What should we do now? We have to endure great deprivations.[50] Our nails are as long as from the thumb to the little finger of a stretched-out hand. Our beards are as long as a forearm.[51] Our hair is as long as a whole arm. There is no razor and no barber. We have to spend the days with only the leaves of the paḷas tree for clothing, and only the fruits of the umbar tree for food.''

And when they went to sleep in the evening, crab apples[52] would fall on their chests. ''Don't hit me. Don't hit me,'' they would say to one another, and a quarrel would break out. Six months passed, and no one came to set them free. Then came the Divāḷī festival, and the seven sisters, Ekāyā, Mhākāyā, Ṭakayā [Tukāī], Nāgāyā, and so on, said, ''Where are the gods? They have been trapped. For whom should we prepare the bath?'' So they went to Bhoḷā [Śiva] and said: ''Bhoḷādev, whom should we bathe now?'' Bhoḷā looked in his lists: ''One of the three hundred fifty gods is missing. Who is missing? Ujanī Mhaṅkāḷ [Mahākāḷ of Ujjain in North India] is missing.''

What was Ujanī Mhaṅkāḷ doing? In Vīr there is a garden with pān plants and flowers. He was sitting there. After he had bathed in the Nirā, he was smoking a pipe of *gāñjā* [hashish]. ''He is sitting by the Nirā River,'' and ''How can he be brought here?'' Pārvatī and Īsvar [Īśvar] occupied themselves with these thoughts. ''How should we get him to come? He is smoking *gāñjā*—what will make him come here?''

''I'll get ready all the *gāñjā* that he needs. We must say to him, 'All the *gāñjā* you need is waiting for you, so come.' '' So what did Pārvatī do? She got dressed in leaves from the paḷas tree[53] and went. Where? To heaven, to see the god. He had let down his hair and was sitting there as a Gosāvī, devoting

50. *Vanvās,* living in the forest. This term is generally used to express deprivation.

51. *Hāt,* from the elbow to the fingertips.

52. *Kavāṭ,* written *kavāṃṭ: Feronia Elephantum* (Molesworth, *Dictionary*).

53. *Paraṅgyā,* leaves of the paḷas tree.

himself to his vice. He was crushing tobacco in his hands, smoking it, and sitting there. She went a little closer and called out, "Hello, Kāḷbhairī."

Kāḷbhairī thought, "Who's calling me, damn it?"

She went still closer and called again, "Hello, Kāḷbhairī!"

He looked around. "Damn it, somebody's calling me again!"

A third time she called, "Hello, Kāḷbhairī. I'm calling you."

"Why have you come, Mother? You haven't been here in so long. Why have you come here today?"

"Bābā, I've been searching very hard for you. And why," she said, "are you sitting on the river bank?"

"No, no," he said. "I won't leave here."

"Why, Bābā?"

"I have to have *gāñjā*. If I don't smoke *gāñjā* with tobacco, I don't feel happy."

"Oh, Bābā, I've filled the whole house with it for you. I've gotten sackfuls and sackfuls—and who else will smoke this *gāñjā?*"

"All right, Mother," he said. "I'll come."

Then what happened? The god left and came with his mother to Bhoḷā. [Bhoḷā] opened the doors of the house and showed him the rooms filled over and over again with *gāñjā*. *Gāñjā* means, you press the dudhāni plant[54] and sprinkle the extract with . . . ,[55] and fill the sacks with it.

"Look, Bābā," she said. "Smoke as much *gāñjā* as you want."

Now what happened? He dedicated himself to his vice, crushed the *gāñjā*, and smoked it until he fell into a state of intoxication. Then he looked around. And he saw the trident above him, and said, "Mother, what is that?"

She said, "That is Bhoḷā's trident."

"Give it to me!"

"Take it."

Again he looked around, and then he saw the begging bag.[56] "What is that for?"

"That is Bhoḷā's begging bag."

"Give it to me."

"Take it, Bābā."

When he looked around again, he saw an eating dish.

"What is that?"

"That is Bhoḷā's eating dish."

"Give it to me."

---

54. A flowering and milky shrub. *Ipomoea turpethum* (Molesworth, *Dictionary*).

55. The narrator either could not or would not express this. The Dhangars who were listening said, "*kāyhtarī sāṅgtoy*" (written *kāhītarī sāṅgto āhe*): "He's just talking nonsense [on this point]."

56. *Jhoḷī*, a small bag in which is kept the magical turmeric powder (*bhaṇḍār*) or ashes (*vibhūt*).

''If you want it, just take it.''

''What is it for?''

She said, ''When we're traveling around, if we become hungry somewhere, then we do *pūjā,* and we get five kinds of cooked food.''

''Is that so? Give it to me!''

''Fine. Take it.''

What happened then? As he was traveling around there, he came to an underground hole where wind was blowing. The wind blew, and he asked, ''What is blowing there?''

She said, ''That is Bhoḷā's wind.''

''Give it to me!''

''If you want it, take it.''

He took it. It was [a horse,] dark black, white on the forehead, with a white tail and a reddish–brown back. He saddled the horse, fastened the silver saddle straps and the golden stirrups, and mounted it. He mounted the horse, and the Divāḷī festival was approaching. Bhoḷā said, ''Kāḷbhairī should be sent to the land where the three hundred fifty gods are to be found.''

So Kāḷbhairī set off to search. When he had traversed the nine continents, and Kāśī, the tenth, he came to the eleventh—that is, to the land of Baṅgāl. There Yeḷammā stood in his path, she who commands the fifty-two sciences. When he saw her from far off, he leaped down from heaven on the horse. Yeḷammā let him come. She sprinkled ashes and his horse fell down. He lifted the horse high, and again she threw it to the ground. A third time he forcibly lifted up the horse. Again she threw it down. ''Damn it!'' He was addicted to *gāñjā,* so what did the god do? When the horse had fallen to the ground, he dismounted. There was a pond there. And he crushed *gāñjā* and took water to help him, and he smoked the *gāñjā.* And then he went to set the horse upright. He grabbed it by the tail, and the tail broke off. ''Bhoḷā's horse,'' he said, ''is no good.'' He grabbed it by the ear, and the ear broke off. ''Bhoḷā's horse,'' he said, ''is no good.'' He grabbed it by the neck—and the neck broke off. ''Bhoḷā's horse,'' he said, ''is no good.'' Then he grabbed the horse by the leg, and the leg broke off. ''The god's horse,'' he said, ''is worthless.''

What happened then? Only the body was left. ''How can I ride back now?'' What did he do? He reached into the bag and, calling out the name of Bhoḷā, he sprinkled ashes; and the horse stood there again, saddled and bridled. It neighed. It danced. He cracked the whip. The horse was very impetuous; it flew up to heaven. Then Yeḷammā said, ''The horse may not pass through.'' Then he guided it toward her a fourth time. When he tried to pass her on the left side, she stood on the left side; and when he tried to pass her on the right side, she stood on the right side. Then he speared her with the trident. He placed the trident on her breast. Then she said, ''God, spare my life. I am a woman! Don't kill me. Spare my life.''

What happened then? He put her in the bag, and went into the land of Baṅgāl. When he arrived there, he found the gods in a bedraggled state and in great misery. How their beards and hair had grown! They were living on the fruits of the umbar tree.

"Now what's to be done?" he said.

"Why have you come? We have been in captivity for six months now, and there is no way out."

When he had cleared a path for them, the skeletons of three hundred fifty horses lay there. Then he said, "Gather the skeletons together!" So they gathered the skeletons and joined them piece by piece. He sprinkled nectar (*amṛt*) on the horses and, calling out the name of Bhoḷā, brought the horses to life. Then he brought the procession of gods to Bhoḷā.

Then the seven sisters said, "How can we bathe them? Mustaches like shrubs, eyes like limes, swollen lips as thick as your wrist." The sisters trembled with fear. Thus they bathed the gods. The Divāḷī festival passed.

The end of my story . . .

The warlike Kāḷbhairav, who appears as a Gosāvī, takes it upon himself to subdue obstructive goddesses, to fight demons, or to cut off the fifth head of Brahmā. Śiva does not do these things himself, but he finds in Kāḷbhairav someone who will do the dangerous deeds for him. For that purpose. Kāḷbhairav is given the characteristic possessions of Śiva that in Maharashtra are time and again connected with Kāḷbhairav: the trident and the horse. He also receives Śiva's magical bag (*jhoḷī*). He puts Yeḷammā into it and thereby wins still further magical powers, for Yeḷammā is the goddess who commands the fifty-two magical sciences. *Gāñjā* serves as an indispensable means for the Gosāvī-yogī and for Kāḷbhairav to acquire magical powers; it is also used liberally by the famous god Mhaskobā in Vīr.

The principal cult center of the goddess Yallammāī or Ellāmmā/Yeḷammā is in Saundattī (Saṃvadattī) in Belgaum District. Saundattī also lies in the north-south cattle-herding tract. Of the various explanations of her name, the most plausible seems to be the one that derives it from Kannaḍa *ēḷu* + *ammā*, "the seven mothers"—who also appear, when conditions demand, as a single entity. Of course, the name could also mean "the mother of the seven" (see Text 7, on Yeḷmakkaltāī).

Yeḷammā is one of the great mother goddesses who have retained their own independent cult. The association with a male god or with a sage (*ṛṣi*) of Brahmanical literature has not essentially touched the original cult, even though Yeḷammā is treated as equivalent to Reṇukā, the wife of the *ṛṣi* Jamadagni.[57] The story of her son Paraśurāma killing her at his father's

57. *Mahābhārata*, 3.116.6ff. *Viṣṇu Purāṇa*, 4.7.35f. The legend is found in N. Ramesan, *Temples and Legends of Andhra Pradesh* (Bombay, 1962), pp. 35f., and in H. Whitehead, *The Village Gods of South India* (Calcutta, 1921), p. 116. The *Devīkoś*, vol. 2 (Puṇeṃ, 1967), p. 458, questions the association between Reṇukā and Yeḷammāī in Saundattī.

command reflects on the mythological plane the conflict between different sets of ideas. According to the Gavḷīs, Paraśurām was born without a father from a tumor on the palm of Yeḷubāī's (Yeḷammā's) hand.

In Gavḷī and Dhangar myths, Yeḷammā also appears as Yalu (~ Yeḷu) Gavḷan, the mother of a youthful cowherd (Gavḷī) named Bābū Ballāḷ.[58] He was born of Yalu miraculously, without conception, on account of her devotion to Śiva.

6. Tukāī/Durgāmahiṣāsuramardinī

Dhangars and Gavḷīs do not worship the goddess as Durgāmahiṣāsuramardinī. The motif of her victory over the buffalo demon (Mahiṣāsura) does not accord primarily with the notions of pastoralist groups, but with the ideas of a population living in permanent settlements, particularly in the rice area.

In the focal area of my research, the goddess Tukāī is represented as Durgā who kills the buffalo demon. She has one of her principal cult places in Koṇḍanpūr, in the rice-growing area of the Māvaḷ. Farther east, in Vīr (Purandar Taluka, Poona District), one can observe particularly well the synthesis of Mahiṣāsura/Mhasobā with the cult of Tukāī. Mhasobā/Mhaskobā is killed by Tukāī on the highland pasture of Vīr: this can be clearly seen in the Durgāmahiṣāsuramardinī relief in the small Tukāī temple. Undoubtedly Tukāī was the goddess already established in the place before immigrant Dhangars brought Mhasobā/Mhaskobā with them. During the annual pilgrimage festival in Māgh (February/March), Mhaskobā's procession goes first of all to the goddess Tukāī, to whom Mhaskobā thereby shows respect as the elder deity.

Having developed from a "demon" into the dominant deity of the village, Mhasobā/Mhaskobā, the simple god of cattle and of herdsmen, is equated by the Gosāvīs with Kāḷbhairav. Although Mhasobā came to Vīr without a wife, on this level, as Kāḷbhairav, he can now marry Jogubāī/Jogāī/Yogeśvarī—that is, Durgā. Thus, Mhasobā/Mhaskobā of Vīr is married to the goddess Durgā, who kills the buffalo demon. Mhasobā, who as such is popularly said to be "without a wife,"[59] becomes fused with the cult of Kāḷbhairav in many places in the area of my study. As in the case of Kharsuṇḍī, the cult has assimilated the prevailing local goddess, making her into the wife of the god. This happens, it must be added, not only with the Purāṇic, celibate Kāḷ-

58. See Text 22, below.

59. *Saṭavāīlā nāhīṃ navarā āṇi mhasobālā nāhīṃ bāyako* [Saṭvāī has no husband, and Mhasobā has no wife.] Ya. Rā. Dāte and Ciṃ. Ga. Karve, editors, *Mahārāṣṭra Vāksaṃpradāya Kośa* (Puṇeṃ, 1942), vol. 2, p. 557.

bhairav, but also with a manifestation of the god that resembles Murukan̲ with his two wives.

As Durgā or Kālī the goddess of the Purāṇic-Sanskritic pantheon regains her explanation and her proper place in the villages of Maharashtra and South India ruled by independent mother goddesses. No one but she is supposed to be able to kill Mahiṣāsura: this is Mahiṣāsura's wish when he is condemned to die, and Śiva grants it to him. Durgā carries out the deed, and wins in this way her place among the village deities.[60]

In Telaṅgaṇa and other parts of South India the buffalo demon is not worshiped as an independent deity, as at Loṭevāḍī (Text 2), nor as a dominant god of the village to whom the goddess is subordinated, as at Vīr. In Telaṅgaṇa and Tamilnāḍu the *poṭṭu-rāju* ("the King of the Buffalo")[61] is sometimes the brother and sometimes the consort of the village goddess,[62] but he never has the dominant position of Mhaskobā of Vīr. Whitehead cites a case in which Ellammā/Yeḷammā is the sister of the "Pot-Razu." He describes "Pot-Razu" as a wooden figure three feet high, painted red, depicting a warrior with a sword. "Pot-Razu" holds a small lime and wears nine glass bangles, which belong to his sister Ellammā. At each of his feet there is a cock. Here *poṭṭu-rāju* most closely resembles Kāḷbhairav/Vīrabhadra, who has a sword, whereas the cocks suggest a relationship with Murukan̲/Skanda. But Whitehead also reports that such representations of *poṭṭu–rāju* are rare.[63]

In Maharashtra, besides the independent Mhasobā cult (as at Loṭevāḍī), and Mhaskobā of Vīr, to whom the goddess is subordinated, there is also the *potrāj*, who is found among the Māṅgs and Mahārs. The *potrāj* is a servant of the goddess; he dresses himself in women's clothes and cracks a braided, ropelike whip.[64] A woman carries the goddess (Marīāī or Kaḍak Lakṣmī) in a box on her head. If the goddess is well disposed, she possesses the woman, who begins to dance. In a high voice, accompanied by the boom of drums and the clang of a handbell, the *potrāj* importunes the goddess to appear:

> Oh, Woman! Open the door, Woman!
> Marīāī, O woman!
> Open the door.
> Lakṣmīāī—O woman! Open the door![65]

---

60. Whitehead, *Village Gods,* p. 18.

61. *Madras District Gazetteer*. Salem (Madras, 1913), vol. 1, part 1, p. 99. *Dravidian Etymological Dictionary,* 3747: Tamil, *pōttu;* Telugu, *pōtu.*

62. Whitehead, *Village Gods,* p. 18.

63. Ibid.

64. The following observations were made in Maravḍe, Mangaḷveḍhā Taluka, Sholapur District.

65. See also Rā. Ciṃ. Ḍhere, *Marāṭhī Lokasaṃskṛtīce Upāsaka* (Puṇeṃ, 1964), p. 72.

By cracking his whip, the *potrāj* forces the goddess to possess him, and it appears as if she symbolically kills him. The stricken *potrāj* rolls around on the ground. Occasionally the lashes of the whip draw blood, and he gives a few drops of it to the woman who for a short time has become the goddess. The goal, above all, is to force the goddess to manifest herself, and for the *potrāj* to become identified with her. The ''demon's'' desire to assimilate himself to the goddess is also expressed in his women's clothing. As we have seen, the dying demon asks the goddess to wear his clothes for one month each year.[66]

There is an echo of this in the Purāṇas, in Mahiṣa's wish to die at the hands of a beautiful woman. Śiva grants him this wish. Mahiṣa wants to marry the beautiful Tripurasundarī, who is provided with all the weapons of the gods. She agrees, on condition that Mahiṣa vanquish her. Instead, Tripurasundarī kills Mahiṣa.[67]

7. The Marriage to the Goddess of the Forest and the Tribe: Bhairav/Mhaskobā/Khaṇḍobā and Bāḷāī ~ Bāṇāī ~ Bāḷubāī

Frequently the local, autochthonous goddess has preserved her position along with Yogeśvarī. Sometimes she even takes priority. At Kharsuṇḍī, for example, Bāḷāī ~ Bāḷubāī is the first and favorite wife of Kharsuṇḍī-Śīd; his fourth wife is (Y~)Jogeśvarī. Kharsuṇḍī is an exception in that here the god is married to seven goddesses. Mostly—and this applies to many temples of the Deccan all the way down to Tamilnadu and Kerala—the god corresponding to Kharsuṇḍī-Śīd is married to two wives. The first comes from a ''higher'' caste, and she is Sanskritized—that is, she is more in accord with the Brahmanical pantheon or with the regionally dominant group and its religious ideas. The second wife is from a ''lower'' caste, or often from a tribe.

The differentiation between the autochthonous, local goddess and the Sanskritic, often supraregional, goddess is clearly illustrated at Biḷūr. Biḷūr, a small village near Jath in Sangli District, lies in the forest and pasture region. Jogeśvarī/Jogubāī is supposed to have come here with Kāḷbhairav from Kāśī, whereas Bāḷubāī—Bhairav's favorite wife—came with her brother from Sūrdī in Jath Taluka in Sangli District.

For Bāḷāī to be the first wife, as at Kharsuṇḍī, is unusual. It appears that in the case of this cult, the Jogeśvarī cult from the north did not manage to assert

66. Text 10.

67. *Śivapurāṇa, Umāmaheśvara Parvan,* chap. 46. *Devībhāgavatapurāṇa,* 5.20. *Matsyapurāṇa,* 152. *Mārkaṇḍeyapurāṇa,* 79–80.

itself fully in a cattle-herding region. Here Bāḷubāī, who is closely connected with the pastoralist groups, maintains her importance; her position as first wife expresses this. By contrast, in Vīr only Jogeśvarī has found a place next to Mhaskobā/Kāḷbhairav. Although the god of the place, Mhaskobā, was brought by Dhangars, the place itself has long been settled by farmers and Brahmans. It is famous for its garden land (*bāgāīt*), and it lies near the path of the southwest monsoon.[68] For this reason, there was no place here for the herdsmen's goddess; here Jogeśvarī, who is closer to the "Brahmanical" pantheon, won out. This was surely due in large part to the help of the Gosāvīs, who contributed greatly to the dissemination of the cult of Kāḷbhairav. But here too the dichotomy between Bāḷāī and Jogeśvarī can still be discerned. In the stories of the Gosāvīs of Vīr, the autochthonous Bāḷāī transforms herself into Jogeśvarī.

When he rides into the underworld to marry the daughter of Śeṣnārāyaṇ, Mhaskobā/Bhairavnāth meets many obstacles. Finally he suceeds in winning Bāḷurāṇī, Śeṣnārāyaṇ's daughter. But as Mhaskobā/Nāth departs, Śeṣnārāyaṇ makes one last attempt to prevent his union with Bāḷurāṇī:

Text 19

As they were leaving, the girl fell at everyone's feet. Nāth started out. He sat on his horse. He set Bāḷurāṇī next to him. Her name was still Bāḷurāṇī. At that time, Śeś [Śeṣ] said to Mhaskobā, "Wait a minute, son-in-law." He brought two small drinking vessels, one filled with nectar (*amṛt*), the other with poison—the one with poison for Bhairavnāth, the one with nectar for Bāḷurāṇī. He gave them to them. Bāḷurāṇī saw what he was up to. She said to Śeś, "I won't talk about what you've done for so many days. But now Bhairavāth is my husband."

When Nāth had taken the vessel in his hand, Bāḷurāṇī knocked it out of his hand, and the poison spilled out. Śeś saw this, and he said to Bāḷurāṇī, "You have taken the side of this Jogaḍā. So now your name is Jogubāī. Nāth is a Jogī [yogī], and you have taken him as your husband, so you are Jogubāī." From then on, Bāḷurāṇī was named Jogubāī.

After that they rode away immediately.

Bāḷurāṇī ~ Bāḷāī is Bhairav's wife who comes from the underworld. The underworld is in many respects identical with the pasture and forest areas beyond humanized, established settlements. Thus the god's second wife derives either from the forest tribes or from the pastoralist tribes of the herding region. Not only is the world of the Nāgas and of Bāḷubāī a reality in the Gosāvīs' imagination; it also finds tangible expression in their cult. Behind

68. See *Mhaskobā Devācem̩ Caritra,* part 2 (Appendix). See also Text 18: Bhairav is sitting in a garden with pān and flowers.

the snakes lies the reality of the forest and the pastures and their inhabitants. About a mile southwest of Biḷūr, the place in Jath Taluka of Sangli District that has been referred to above, we come across a grove called Vanśrī ("the Lord of the Forest," Kāḷbhairav). In the grove are mango trees and clear water, as well as *ketakī* trees, the scent of whose flowers is pleasing to cobras. On many days Nāgrāj ("the King of the Cobras," and also often a collective name for cobras) dances there, it is said. In the small temple there is a large, round stone that lies between two icons of Bhairavnāth, dominating them; it represents Bāḷubāī. Jogeśvarī/Jogāī is not found in this "forest" temple. But in the village temple, the shrine of Bhairavnāth and Bāḷubāī is on the right side, and the shrine of Jogeśvarī is opposite it, on the left side, also inside the temple.

Bhairav's marriage with Bāḷurāṇī, who is from the underworld and derives from the Nāgas, corresponds to the union of Khaṇḍobā (who is likewise a form of Bhairav: Mārtaṇḍa Bhairava) with Bāṇāī/Bāḷāī, his second wife. She is a Dhangar—or even, according to some, a Gavḷī. In Karnatak, the second wife, Kurbattyavva, comes not from the Dhangar "tribe," but from the Kurubas. Her temple is outside the village, and Khaṇḍobā/Mailār visits her each year during the nights from the first day to the tenth day of the bright half of the month of Āśvin. He travels in a palanquin, except on the seventh day of the bright half of Āśvin, when he comes on a horse.[69]

In Maharashtra, by contrast, Bāṇāī's temple is inside the village, although outside the main temple. It is said that Mhāḷsā did not take kindly to the arrival of Khaṇḍobā's second "wife." Dhangars in Maharashtra regard Bāṇāī as a "legal" wife, but Kurubas in Karnatak consider her a kind of concubine. The Dhangars are also aware that Khaṇḍobā's marriage with Bāṇāī was not completely proper. People strongly influenced by "Sanskrit culture" describe the marriage as a *gandharva* marriage. The Dhangars relate:

Text 20

There was no Brahman present at Khaṇḍobā and Bāṇāī's wedding. No wedding band played. Sheep dung was tossed instead of rice. They decided that their wedding music would be the bleating of the sheep coming home in the evening, and of the lambs left behind in the *vāḍā*. That evening, all the herdsmen (*gāvḍe*) came together, pronounced the *maṅgalāṣṭaka* verses, and married them. It was more a marriage by abduction[70] than a marriage [according to the proper rules] (*lagna*). They gave all the sheep to the herdsmen. Then they [Khaṇḍobā and Bāṇāī] came to Jejurī. . . .

69. Ga. Ha. Khare, *Mahārāṣṭrācīṃ cār daivateṃ* (Puṇeṃ, 1958), p. 120.

70. *Paḷvūn neṇyāpekṣā aseṃ tyānī[ṃ] lagna keleṃ*. Cf. the *rakṣasa* marriage of the *smṛtis*. This is also still found among the Bhils and others, where the abduction is often in fact only pretense.

Dhangars believe that Khaṇḍobā spent three years in Bāṇāī's/Bāḷāī's *vāḍā*. They say that she was the overseer[71] of twelve Dhangar *vāḍās*. Many Dhangars relate that Khaṇḍobā was out hunting when he met a Dhangar who brought him to Bāṇāī's *vāḍā*.[72]

The following version of the story comes from Citaḷenagar, (Māḷśiras Taluka, Sholapur District):

Text 21

[*Ovī:*] *sumbarāṇeṃ maṇḍileṃ.*

We are ready to remember the god. Which god? Bhoḷā,[73] my god. He had difficulties [because he wanted Bāṇubāī for his wife]. Bhoḷā set off. He went into the forest, into a second forest, into a fifth forest. Then Bhoḷā went to the *vāḍā* of Bāṇubāī. The Dhangar women Umyā and Dhumyā were there. They woke up.

[Prose:] What happened then? God Bhoḷā went there. What did he do there? He changed his form. [Now he was an old man.] He was bleeding [because of his long journey through the five forests]. In this form he went there. Nine *lākhs* of lambs; nine *lākhs* of sheep; innumerable barren animals. When he arrived there [the two Dhangar women] gave him a pot full of water, they gave him a pot full of buttermilk. He drank them to the bottom, and his fatigue went away. When his fatigue had gone away, he said, "Up your mother's. . . .[74] Now who will take me on as a servant? I must stay here."

Then he went to Bāṇubāī. He said, "Will you take me on as a servant?"

"Yes," she said. "You'll get *bhākrī* for the work you do."

"Fine," he said. "I'll do whatever work you give me."

The Dhangars thought it over and said, "That's good. During the rainy season we can't get the sheep pen clean. The old man will sweep it and clean it. That will save us some work."

What happened then? In the early morning the old man got up. "My work has begun."

[*Ovī:*] In the early morning. He put on his shirt with twelve tie strings. Wrapped his turban on his head. Put on his shoes and tied his bag at his side. He set off, went to the *vāḍā*,[75] and entered it; into the sheep pen he went, took a pinch of turmeric (*bhaṇḍār*), and tossed it into the sheep pen.

[Prose:] What happened then? It used to take a hundred or five hundred Dhangars to do the work. But in five minutes he swept [the dung] in the *vāḍā*

71. *Mirdhin,* from *mirdhā,* "a village overseer, a captain of a company of spearmen, etc." (Molesworth, *Dictionary*). In the neighborhood of Jejurī the leaders of Dhangar settlements are often called *mirdhā.*

72. For instance, in Koḷvihire (Purandar Taluka, Poona District).

73. See chap. 6, note 67, below.

74. *Ailā.* A curse alluding to sexual intercourse with one's mother, used frequently in rural areas without awareness of its actual meaning.

75. Here, the sheep pen.

into a mountain. Everywhere it was sparkling clean. After he had made everything spick and span, he ate. Then he went to sleep.

What happened then, when the light was in the Māvaḷ [the west]? The shepherds returned from all over, and everything had been washed sparkling clean. "Ei, ei!" they said. "Wherever can this old man have come from, to ruin us? What should we do now? There were many of us, and now our livelihood is threatened. We will give him especially difficult work. Then at night he will go away of his own accord."

What did they think up then? They said, "We have nine *lākhs* of sheep and nine *lākhs* of lambs. He should lead the [lambs, who have stayed in the *vāḍā* all day] to the sheep [when they return home in the evening] to be suckled. A hundred or five hundred of us Dhangars do this job. But even so we find it difficult to manage for all of them to nurse. And what can an old man do all by himself? He will run away without more ado."

Evening came. They ate. Bāṇubāī thought, "What is the old man to do?" She said, "Tomorrow you must look after nine *lākhs* of sheep and nine *lākhs* of lambs."

He said, "But how can an old man manage this?"

She said, "Can you do it? If you work, you get *bhākrī*—that was our agreement."

"Fine," he said. "It has to be fine—what can I do?" What did he do? In the early morning he took his bath.

[*Ovī:*] He put on his shirt with the twelve tie strings. Wrapped his turban on his head. Put on his shoes, and tied his bag at his side. He went to the sheep [pen], pulled the dried thorn bushes away from the entrance, and put [the sheep] in a row one behind the other; he went into the terrifying forest; into the terrifying forest went the sheep then. There was a bad drought. He dragged his blanket along on the ground.

[Prose:] What happened then? There was a bad drought. He dragged his blanket along on the ground; no dried blades of grass clung to it. The sheep began to roam around. What did the old man do then? He reached into his bag and took out a pinch of turmeric. He took it out and threw it into the scrub jungle. When he had thrown it, grass and water appeared there. The sheep were exhausted from the hot summer day. Now they began to graze. What did he do? He took the blanket from his shoulder, laid it on the ground; their tiredness disappeared.

What had happened every day [before this]? [On the days when the Dhangars had watched the sheep,] even at eight o'clock in the evening none of the sheep was ready to begin bleating, because none of them had had enough to eat. On the day when the old man watched the sheep, they were already full at two o'clock. From the third watch of the day on, they began to bleat. And when they began to bleat, the old man woke up. Then he put on his clothes. He put on his shirt with the twelve tie strings, wound his turban on his head, put on his shoes, tied his bag to his side. He took his staff in his hand, and returned to the sheep. Slowly he set off.

[*Ovī:*] He went to the *vāḍā*. The light was in the Māvaḷ [the west]. He was close to the *vāḍā*.

[Prose:] What happened now? The old man's sheep came close to the *vāḍā*. The Dhangar women Umyā and Dhumyā let the lambs out of the pen. Then the nine *lākhs* of sheep peacefully nursed the nine *lākhs* of lambs. But the Dhangar herdsmen, who had held their heads so high, now let their heads hang. "Even though we worked out such a good plan, this old man has made it come to nothing. What should we do now? Yesterday's work was too easy for him. Even though he has hard work to do today, he is going to accomplish it. Be on the lookout for someone who has a good idea." So they arrived at the idea that there were five hundred women, and they had five hundred children. "So of course the old man should take care of the five hundred children. If even one of them cries, he will be sent home."

What did he do? He ate his dinner. Then the old man said to Bāṇubāī: "I have no work for tomorrow."

She said, "Tomorrow you must take care of the five hundred children. If even one of the children cries, you must leave."

"How can an old man keep five hundred children quiet?"

"You will get *bhākrī* according to how well you do your assigned work. If you don't do this work, there's no help for you."

"Fine," he said. "What can be done then? A person has to work somehow or other to fill his stomach." And what did he do? In the early morning he took his bath.

[*Ovi:*] He put on his shirt with the twelve tie strings. Wound his turban on his head. Put on his shoes, and tied his bag at his side.

[Prose:] What happened then? He said, "My aunts, look out for a mango tree in this scorching heat, and put [your children] under it. Somehow or other I will look after them."

"No, not just somehow or other. If even one of the children cries, you must go away."

The women took the five hundred children and put them under the mango tree. Then what did the children do? They raised a fuss. They began crying in various ways. And what did the women do?

They had nothing to do, and they went away. But they hid somewhere, so that they could go home and tell Bāṇubāī as soon as they heard a sound. The old man took his bag and sprinkled a pinch of turmeric over the swarm of children. All the children died. The aunts strained to hear: "Is my child crying?" They kept [hoping] to hear something. He killed the children who had been alive in the morning.

When the light was in the Māvaḷ, the children were quiet. From all sides came the aunts. They said, "Bābā, why haven't our children woken up yet? What has happened? It's time for them to get up."

Then what did he do? He took out his bag and sprinkled a pinch of turmeric over the herd of children. The children began to cry.

"What should we do now?" [the women] said, and they scratched their heads and thought it over. "This old man has done work we couldn't get done: our work in the *vāḍā,* the nursing of the lambs, and now even our work with the children. Our husbands beat us every day and say, 'These sheep and these lambs are left over [that is, the lambs have not found sheep whose milk to drink], our children are starting to cry.' From now on we will take good care of this old man." Then some of the aunts took care of the old man. There was something godlike about him.

The shepherds said, "He goes into my house, but if I see him there, I'll beat him with my stick." But how could anyone beat him? He would go into the house and eat *capātīs* and rice. As soon as they came, he would transform himself in a wondrous way. When he had done this for eight days, he began to jump around [like a lamb, so strong and boisterous had he become because of the food]. And finally his behavior became very annoying to the Dhangars. They said, "Now we must really try to do something about that old man." Though he is weak and old, he jumps as high as a doe. We're tired out from thinking about it. Here is our last resort: tomorrow is Monday, and we will be doing the washing of the sheep [*prugram,* from English *program*]. And we'll give the old man the nine *lākhs* of sheep to wash all by himself—and the lambs besides. He won't be able to keep the sheep together. How can he keep them in line all by himself? And we hundred or five hundred Dhangars will go away."

And they said to the old man: "Tomorrow you must wash the nine *lākhs* of sheep and the lambs all by yourself."

"Now, that's just fine," he said. "What am I to do?"

"If the work isn't done, you won't get any *bhākrī.*"

He said to Bāṇāī: "Come at noon tomorrow with offerings of food (*naivedya*) and water. I will go on ahead."

And what did he do?

[*Ovī:*] In the early morning, he formed a line of sheep, a line of sheep, in those times, in those times. To the river he went, to the river, he left them in the river.

[Prose:] On the way to the river he let the sheep spread out. So the sheep had slowly dispersed themselves over four or five *kos* [eight to ten miles]. What did the hundred or five hundred Dhangars do? They came to have a look: "How is he managing our animals, how is he keeping them in the river, how is he giving them water to drink, how is he keeping them together? Has anyone come to such and such a place to wash them, is anyone helping him?"

What did the old man do? He let the sheep, who were spread out over four *kos,* drink water peacefully. He stood there calmly, with his beard propped up on his shepherd's staff as if he were tired. And they laughed: "Who is guiding the sheep, who is washing them?"

When the sheep had dispersed themselves over three or four *kos* across the rocky ground, he took out his bag and made a gentle breeze blow. And [thus] he kept together the sheep who were spread out over four *kos.* He found some rocky ground and drove them all together in one place [on the rocky ground]. And he sprinkled a pinch of turmeric over the herd.

They were packed closely together. They couldn't move this way or that. He took off his shirt with the twelve tie strings, set aside his turban, and took off all his clothes. He pulled a young sheep into the river and milked it and began the washing. He pulled each sheep into the water and washed it sparkling white. He led it out of the water and killed it. He skinned it, and heaped the skins on one side, and the meat on the other side. In this way, he killed the nine *lākhs* of sheep.

The Dhangars were delighted.[76] "Up your mother's. . . . To no avail did [Bāṇubāī] hire him. Many *lākhs* have been lost. Now the old man will get nothing to eat in the evening."

So now he had finished "washing" the sheep. He washed himself and left. At noontime what did Bāṇubāī do? She took the food offering (*naivedya*) and went there. When she arrived, the old man said, "Bāṇubāī, give me something to eat. I am very hungry." Then Bāṇubāī saw the disaster. She quickly set down the basket, and writhed on the ground, screaming.

What did he do while she was writhing on the ground? He said, "I am hungry now." He took two pancakes. He threw them into the river [as a food offering] and said, "O river goddess, take this and be satisfied with it. I'm starting to eat now."

And what happened then? He ate until he was full. Meanwhile, Bāṇubāī kept writhing on the ground, screaming. "Bāṇubāī, you aren't used to heat or wind [that is, you do not leave the *vāḍā,* you do not subject yourself to any trouble]. Don't go rolling around in your [dead] herd."

"Bābā," she said, "my loss is simply immense. You have done me harm. Now bring my sheep back to life."

"Am I a god, that I can bring them back to life?"

"No, no. You must bring them back to life."

"All right," he said, "I'll bring them back to life for you, but you must become my wife."

She was sad and alarmed. She thought to herself, "I'll wait until he has brought my sheep back to life, and then I'll say no. After all, have we tossed the rice?"

"All right," she said. "Yes."

"No, no," said he. "We can't do it that way. We'll do it this way: we'll have our wedding, and once the rice is tossed, then it will be complete and proper. If not, then it won't be."

"Is there a Brahman or anyone else? There's no one."

"We have everything: Brahmans, rice."

"Where is the Brahman and where is the rice?"

"There is sheep dung; we'll collect that. And I'll take half of what we've collected and throw it at you, and you'll take the other half and throw it at me."

"Fine," she said.

76. *Cikḷūn gilī,* written *cekaḷūn gele*. This could also mean "became angry."

Now they had firmly agreed on it. There was nothing more to keep him from bringing the sheep back to life. He got dressed. Everything was in order. He took a pinch of turmeric and threw it over the sheep. What happened when he had thrown it? Dripping and snorting, the sheep shook themselves and lined themselves up in a row.

What happened then?

[*Ovī:*] In those times, he formed a line of sheep; they shook themselves and started moving.

[Prose:] Bleating, they started moving. What did the old man say to Bāṇubāī? "Bāṇubāī, hold them back. I'm just going to take a drink of water."

Bāṇubāī ran around and around, but she could not keep the sheep together. What did the old man do? From behind he spoke magical words [*matīr,* written *mantra*], and the sheep stayed where they were. "Ah," she said, "is he an old man, or is he a god?"

What happened from then on?

[*Ovī:*] They set off, traveled back. They set off and traveled, went farther along the track through the woods, stopped along the way. The dogs began to bark. The barking of the dogs. He took Bāṇu with him, Bhoḷā, the god. They set off and went to his land. They went to his land then, to Bhoḷā's village, they went to his village.

[Prose:] And what happened? When the old man had gone to the village, he changed his form. When he had changed it, what else happened? They said to the sun, "Don't rise," and to the moon, "Don't set," so [bright] did his form become.

[*Ovī:*] The *ovī* is finished. The god sat in his place.

In this version, Bāḷāī/Bāṇāī/Bāḷubāī becomes the *wife* or concubine (*rākh*) of *Khaṇḍobā,* but there are also stories in which Bāḷubāī becomes the "fictitious" *mother* [*māvācī āī*] of *Birobā.*[77] Birobā's two "fictitious" sisters, Māyavvā and Ekavvā, find Birobā in the forest:

Text 22

[*Ovī:*] Mhākavvā, his sister, Mhākavvā, his sister, set out and started toward Bāḷubāī's *vāḍā,* toward Bāḷubāī's *vāḍā.*

[Prose:] And what did she do then? [The audience and the other singers repeat the question:] What did she do?

She took the small boy with her, Mhākavvā, his sister. Where did she go? To Bāḷubāī's *vāḍā.* When she arrived there, what did Bāḷubāī say?

[Response:] Well, what did she say?

"Oh Mhākavvā, my daughter, what have you brought with you from the forest?"

"I've brought a small child to show you."

"A boy or a girl?"

77. A story from Limbavḍe (Ātpāḍī Taluka, Sangli District), for example.

"It's a boy."

Then what did Bāḷuśākkā [*ākkā* means "sister" in Kannaḍa] say to Mhākavvā?

[*Ovī:*] "I have no son. You have no brother. So it has been well ordained. A good thing has happened."

In a similar *ovī* from Mhasāīcīvāḍī, near Mhasvaḍ, Bāḷubāī is called the "mother" of Birobā. She appears as the owner of cows, and as a Gavḷī. Birobā is responsible for the creation of sheep.

Today Bāḷubāī is only rarely worshiped independently of Khaṇḍobā. Apart from the *ovīs* of the Dhangars, little is known about Bāṇāī/Bāḷāī and Khaṇḍobā. All the same, in Jejurī, the principal cult center of Khaṇḍobā, many prayers for plentiful cattle are directed to Bāṇāī. Stone votive images representing animals are offered in front of her temple, which lies at a distance from that of Khaṇḍobā.

D. D. Kosambi suspects that in Bāṇāī there has been preserved a recollection of the fourth-century tribe and dynasty of the Bāṇas.[78] This becomes all the more plausible when one recalls that the dynasty of the Bāṇas ruled in Rāyalasīma, a traditionally pastoral region with little water.

Whereas nowadays Khaṇḍobā is offered no animal sacrifices but principally only a food offering (*naivedya*) of *poḷī* (*capātīs* sweetened with molasses), Dhangars kill rams for Bāṇāī and "show" her a *naivedya* consisting of pieces of liver, meat, and rice. This happens on Dasarā, which is the traditional day for setting out for battle or on a journey, and on the full-moon day of the months of Māgh and Caitra.

From the examples provided here we can gather that the tribal or local goddess, as the second wife of the god, has preserved her autonomy just like the first wife, who comes from the "higher" strata. Mhāḷsā, Khaṇḍobā's first wife, who comes from the Liṅgāyat caste, keeps her position along with Bāṇāī, who comes from the pastoralist tribes; in Kharsuṇḍī, Bāḷubāī has priority independently of Yogeśvarī. In Vīr, Bāḷubāī becomes Yogeśvarī (Text 19): the Gosāvīs see the two originally separate goddesses as growing into a unity. An even further step is taken when Pārvatī is identified with the local goddesses (Text 15).

To be sure, Mhāḷsā is also equated with Pārvatī, but no one has yet supposed that Pārvatī and Bāṇāī are identical. The closer we get to the classical Purāṇas, the more frequently is Pārvatī equated with the goddess of the tribe. For example, on Cauragaḍh mountain, near Pañcmāḍhi (Madhya Pradesh),

78. *Myth and Reality,* p. 121.

the faithful, who come primarily from Maharashtra, have set up thousands of tridents for Śiva. According to the legends of the Korkūs, the second wife of Śiva here comes from their tribe. Her name is Girjā, and the place from which she came, near Cauragaḍh, is precisely identified. But Śiva's priests at Cauragaḍh—*sādhūs*—equate Girjā with Pārvatī. This assimilation of the local tribal goddess is reminiscent of the legends of Pārvatī wearing the clothing of a woman of the Bhil tribe and searching in the jungle for Śiva, when he is angry with her. Before she reveals herself, Śiva falls in love with her.[79]

79. *Kāśīkhaṇḍa,* chap. 49. Abridged version of Śrīdhara's text, *Sacitra Śrīkāśīkhaṃḍa Kathāsāra,* printed and published by Dattātreya Viśvanātha Pāṭhaka (Bombay, 22nd edition, 1964), pp. 215ff.

5

Forest and Pastoral Peoples: Hunters, Robbers, Traders, Ascetics

1. The Koḷīs

1.1 Traditional Occupations and Gods

By tradition, Koḷīs are hunters, warriors, fishermen, and boatsmen, but also cattle-breeders and farmers. In 1921 Enthoven wrote that a Koḷī who takes up settled agriculture usually becomes a Kuṇbī, thus contributing to the recruitment of Marāṭhās.[1] *Koḷī* is the Marāṭhī word for spider, and a connection can be seen between spiders and the Koḷīs' fishing nets. In Sanskrit the word *kolla* can have the sense of "petty warrior of mountains and jungles."[2] The ocean fishermen of the coastal Koṅkaṇ region, the Son Koḷīs, are to be distinguished from the Koḷīs of the Ghāṭs and the plateau, Mahādev Koḷīs and Malhār Koḷīs.[3] Today the Mahādev Koḷīs live primarily in the region from Junnar up to the vicinity of Trimbak in Nasik District. Captain Mackintosh places their original home in Bālāghāṭ, south of the Godāvarī River (or in the Mahādev mountains).[4]

In the Mahādev Koḷīs' area of the Western Ghāṭs there are two Śiva shrines with which they are closely connected: Bhimāśaṅkar, at the source of the Bhimā River, and Tryambakeśvar, at the source of the Godāvarī River. There seems to be no essential difference between the Mahādev Koḷīs and the

1. *The Castes and Tribes of the Bombay Presidency* (Bombay, 1921), vol. 2, p. 243.

2. I. Karve, *Maharashtra State Gazetteer, Maharashtra—Land and Its People* (Bombay, 1968), p. 28.

3. G. S. Ghurye, *The Mahadev Kolis* (Bombay, 2nd edition, 1963), p. 2.

4. Captain A. Mackintosh, "An Account of the Tribe of Mhadeo Kolies," *Transactions of the Bombay Geographical Society*, 1 (1836–38), 236.

Malhār Koḷīs, except that the Malhār Koḷīs live in the area south of Poona and generally serve as water-carriers in villages. Perhaps the division is based only on the two groups' respective worship of the gods Mahādev (the original Śiva) and Malhār-Khaṇḍoba (an *avatār* of Śiva). The Malhār Koḷīs are also called Cumḷīs, after the ring of cloth (*cumḷī*) they place on their heads, or they are called Pānbharīs—that is, water-carriers. They are one of the twelve service castes (*bārā balutedārs*) of village society in Maharashtra. According to Enthoven, Malhār Koḷīs are supposed to be *yeśkars,* or guardians of the village gates, in the vicinity of Paṇḍharpūr.[5]

The 1884 Sholapur gazetteer provides an interesting bit of information from a work entitled *Mālū Tāraṇa Graṃtha*. This work states that King Śālivāhana[6] and his minister, Rāmacandra Udavanta Sonār, sent four Koḷī headmen south from Paiṭhaṇ to put down a rebellion in the Diṇḍīra forest. After the revolt had been quelled, the forest was ceded to the Koḷī headmen, and the Koḷīs were told to earn their living as boatsmen and as priests in Mahādev temples. Later two more Koḷī headmen and their relatives followed them.[7] Although the details of such accounts are not authenticated, in the absence of reliable historical data they at least offer clues about the history of the region and traditional Koḷī duties.

Paṇḍharpūr was originally a center of Śiva- and *devī*-worship, before the Vaiṣṇava *bhakti* cult won out.[8] The town is referred to in the seventh century (A.D. 616) as Pāṇḍaraṅgapallī.[9] The original meaning of *palli* is "a small village, (esp.) a settlement of wild tribes" (Monier-Williams, *Dictionary*). Koḷīs and pastoralist groups first determined the character of the town. G. A. Deleury claims to see as an element of the history of Viṭhobā a hero killed in Paṇḍharpūr while defending his herd.[10] According to the Marāṭhī poet Śrīdhar

5. Enthoven, *Castes,* vol. 2, p. 256. *Yeśkar* is derived from *ves* (village gate) + *kar*.

6. Śālivāhana is used as a synonym for the Sātavāhana dynasty. Only since the 13th century has the word been used in connection with the Śaka era, which King Śālivāhana is supposed to have founded in A.D. 78 (*Maharashtra State Gazetteer,* Ancient Period [Bombay, 1967], p. 71).

7. *Gazetteer of the Bombay Presidency,* vol. 20, Sholāpur (1884), pp. 152f. Although inquiries in Paṇḍharpūr did not bring to light the manuscript of this work, I did discover a printed summary, or table of contents, based on it. I have used this document to supplement the information given in the gazetteer. *Mālū Tāraṇa Graṃthācā adhyāya 32vā sāraṃśa arthāta Koḷyāṃci vaṃśāvḷi* (2nd edition, Śake 1890 [A.D. 1968/69]).

8. See especially Māṇika Dhanapalavāra, "Vaiṣṇavāṃcyā Paṃḍharīcī Śaivaparamparā," in *Jīvana-Vikāsa,* vol. 7 (September 1972), pp. 360ff.

9. G. A. Deleury, *The Cult of Viṭhobā* (Poona, 1960), pp. 181–84, 192–98, etc. Contrast V. V. Mirashi, "Note on Pāṇḍaraṅgapallī Grant of Āvidheya," in *Studies in Indian Culture,* Ghulam Yazdani Commemoration Volume (Hyderabad, 1966).

10. Deleury, *Cult,* pp. 197f. Cakradhara, the founder of the Mahānubhāv sect, which polemicized against the Viṭhobā cult and its followers, describes the origin of Viṭhobā in a story disparaging to the cult:

(late 17th–early 18th century), the site from which the later Paṇḍharpūr developed was in the Diṇḍīra forest; and there Kṛṣṇa, accompanied by cowherds, came searching for Rukmiṇī.[11] Koḷīs are priests, or at least have rights to the offerings, in many of the temples of Paṇḍharpūr—for example, in the

---

Mahadaṃbā asked Cakradhara, "How is it that Vīra Viṭhṭhala Cakravarti is called an *avatār* of Śrīkṛṣṇa?"

And Cakradhara answered, "Viṭhṭhala, the son of an old Brahman; and Nemdev, a Koḷī; and a Gurav named Mhāyā always used to steal cattle and rob people. One day they stole some cows in Maṅgalveḍhā. Mhāyā got away with the cows. Nemdev and Viṭhṭhala fell in battle fighting off their pursuers. At the place where Viṭhṭhala fell, his sons erected a hero stone (*bhaḍakhaṃba* = *vīragaḷa*). They also installed a *liṅgam* at the same place. These deities were 'alive' (*jāgṛt*) then; they began to fufill wishes [addressed to them]. Vīra Viṭhṭhala's wife was named Lakhāī. His sons composed verses and arranged them in *abhaṅgas*. That is Viṭhṭhala. He enjoys women, eats betel, and does all sorts of other things as well."

See Gaṇeśa Harī Khare, *Mahārāṣṭrācīṃ cāra daivateṃ,* Bhārata Itihāsa Saṃśodhaka Maṃḍaḷa puraskṛta graṃthamālā, no. 54 (Puṇeṃ, 1958), pp. 186f. *Līḷācaritra,* S. G. Tulpule, ed. (Puṇeṃ, 1964–1967), "Uttarārdha," Līḷā 411. [The genuine version of the *līḷā* has since appeared in the new edition by Vi. Bhi. Kolate (Muṃbaī, 1978). In it we are told that Vīṭhalu, the hero, died defending cows, but there is nothing about his being a cattle thief.]

Even when one takes into consideration the prejudiced attitude of the Mahānubhāvs, there remains the fact that cattle thefts were frequent at that time—even the *daṇḍanāyakas* seem to have taken part in them (see above, 3.2.1)—as well as the fact that hero stones were erected for heroes who had died in battle defending their herds. Indeed, a hero stone depicting a battle over cattle is built into a wall in front of Viṭhobā's temple in Paṇḍharpūr. It is located next to the *samādhī* of Cokhāmeḷā at the main entrance to the temple. Hitherto this fact has been overlooked. The stone, which derives from the Yādava period, has in its middle relief the usual depiction of the hero being carried to heaven by *apsaras*. The upper relief is missing, but by comparing this hero stone with others in Sholapur District one can conclude quite definitely that the upper relief depicted the hero worshipping a *liṅgam*.

Presumably Viṭhobā developed out of a Śaiva hero cult connected with cattle raids. Because the erection of a hero stone depends on the attitude of the dead hero's relatives, it is not impossible that the members of his family would erect a memorial stone for him even if we would consider him a "robber." Moreover, cattle robbing has always been a way of declaring war, and it often carried no social stigma. In the Ṛgveda, "searching for cattle" is synonymous with war (Grassmann, *Wörterbuch zum Ṛgveda,* s. v. *gaviṣṭi. Mahābhārata,* 4, *Goharaṇaparvan*). Oral traditions about the identity of "stealing cattle" and "starting a war" are still found in Gujarat. See also Dinkar Desai, *The Mahāmaṇḍaleśvaras under the Cālukyas of Kalyāṇi* (Bombay, 1951), pp. 53f., 381.

This is not to claim that the god Viṭhobā is a cattle robber. With the arrival of a new trend in belief, the cult changed its nature and transformed itself into the cult of the Vaiṣṇava Viṭhobā, or a new cult established itself next to the old. On the origins of Vaiṣṇava *bhakti* in Paṇḍharpūr, see M. S. Mate, "Pandharpur: Myth and Reality," in M. S. Mate and G. T. Kulkarni, eds., *Studies in Indology and Medieval History,* Prof. G. H. Khare Felicitation Volume (Poona, 1974), pp. 132ff.

11. *Pāṃḍuraṅga-māhātmya,* chap. 1. See I. M. P. Raeside, "The Pāṇḍuranga-māhātmya of Śrīdhar," *Bulletin of the School of Oriental and African Studies, University of London,* 27 (1965) 81–100.

temple of Puṇḍalik and in the Śaiva Mallikārjuna temple. Today Brahman priests (Baḍvās) make the offerings in the temple of the goddess Ambābāī, but it is certain that they have taken the place of Koḷīs. The Koḷīs' monopoly as boatsmen was especially important because of the pilgrimages and trade routes that pass through Paṇḍharpūr; the monopoly was finally broken in 1926, when a railway bridge was built over the river.

The following extract from the legends about the devotee (*bhakta*) Khilubā is one of several dealing with the origins of the symbiosis among traders, pilgrims, and Koḷīs. Khilubā was a Dhangar from Āñjangāv (Māḍhā Taluka, Sholapur District), who was a devotee of Viṭṭhal and Birobā. Every year he still comes with about a hundred of his followers to the great pilgrimage festival in Paṭṭaṇ Kuḍolī (Hātakanaṅgale Taluka, Kolhapur District). The journey, which most of the participants make on foot, is about one hundred eighty miles long. It begins two days before Dasarā and lasts for twenty-one days. The pilgrimage crosses the Bhimā River at Paṇḍharpūr. Here too it is possible to see, with D. D. Kosambi, the close connection between pilgrimage routes and the—often prehistoric—migratory routes of pastoralist groups. During the monsoon, to avoid the heavy rainfall in Kolhāpūr, Dhangars take their herds of sheep from there to the dry areas around Paṇḍharpūr, along the route that Khilubā travels every year. At the time of the Dasarā festival, they return to Kolhāpūr.

Text 23

Birdev[12] and Viṭṭhal[13] came to bind the devotee Khilubā to themselves: "O Yeḍyā[14] Khilu Rājā! O Bābā! Devote yourself to your worldly life for eleven months of the year, and in the twelfth month take the road to us."

Khilubā said, "O god, I can't manage that. To me, Khilubā, my sheep are everything."

Then Iṭṭhal and Birdev said, "We have wandered around for six months because of you. If you don't honor Bhāgubāī, Bhāgubāī will kill herself. And, Yeḍyā Khilubā, the sin will fall on your head."[15]

---

12. Birobā.

13. Viṭhobā ~ Iṭṭhal.

14. Written *veḍā,* "crazy." This refers to the steadfastness brought on by his intense quietude in the practice of asceticism (*tapa*), and to his equally imperturbable devotion (*bhakti*).

15. Khilubā is the *māvacī bhāū,* the "brother," of Bhāgubāī. Bhāgubāī is the daughter of Viṭṭhal and Padubāī. Padubāī dies because of Viṭṭhal's curse, and Bhāgubāī does not forgive her father for this, even though Viṭṭhal grants her the first right in the pilgrimage festival (*jatrā*) at Paṭṭaṇ Kuḍolī. Khilubā is understood to appease her, and to worship her at the *jatrā.* On the legend of Viṭṭhal, Padubāī, and Bhāgubāī, see G. D. Sontheimer, "Eine Tempellegende der Dhangars von Maharashtra," in *Mündliche Überlieferungen in Südasien. Fünf Beiträge,* H. Berger, ed. (Wiesbaden, 1975), pp. 83ff.

Khilubā said, "I have practiced asceticism (*tapa*) for twenty-four years, and it's done me no good. All right, I'll practice devotion (*bhakti*), but you must make whatever I say come true." Thus spoke Khilubā.

Then the gods said, "If you wish, we will sit on the tip of your tongue. Whatever you say, wherever, we will make it come true." The gods bound the devotee to themselves, went on their way, and settled down in their place [in Paṭṭaṇ Kuḍolī].

Yeḍyā Khilubā dedicated himself to worldly life for eleven months. And in the twelfth month he set out. Following the old custom,[16] he left Āñjangāv in Pharaṇḍe land[17] and set out for Kolvadī [= Paṭṭaṇ Kuḍolī]. Where did he go? To the Candrabhāgā,[18] to the town. When he arrived there, the river was flooded. In the Satya Age there was no bridge. Now how could he cross the river? He said to his disciples, "How are we supposed to get across?"

What did the four of them say? "Over there are tied the boats of Āmbyā and Limbyā Koḷī. We'll go to where their boats are tied, put turmeric powder (*bhaṇḍār*) on their [foreheads], and ask them to take us across."

The five "Gosāvīs"[19] from Pharaṇḍe land went to where Āmbyā and Limbyā's boats were tied, and put *bhaṇḍār* on their foreheads. When they had done this, they said to Āmbyā and Limbyā: "O Āmbyā and Limbyā! Take us across to the other shore. We are on our way to see our guru."

What did the Koḷīs say? "Our boats are loaded with pearls and corals belonging to the merchant (*sāvkār*) Lāṭyā from Miraj. First we must take these across, and only then can we take you across in the boat of dharma."[20]

What did Khilubā say now to Āmbyā and Limbyā? "We Gosāvīs won't sit in a boat of dharma."

The Koḷīs said, "If you want a boat of *hukam*,[21] then you must pay."

What did Khilubā say? "I paid you when I arrived. What did I give you? I gave you as payment the *bhaṇḍār* that I put on your foreheads."

What did Āmbyā and Limbyā say? "In your land, *bhaṇḍār* may stand for gold. But we don't recognize it. You got the turmeric for free, smashed it to pieces on a rock, then ground it and put it into your bag. And you hang around like swindlers, putting a pinch of it on people's foreheads?"

---

16. *Nemādharamān,* written *nemādharmaneṃ*.

17. The village of Pareṇḍā is in Usmanabad District. Āñjangāv is actually in Māḍhā Taluka (Sholapur District), which borders on Usmanabad District. Pharaṇḍe land (*p[h]areṇḍā-deś*) is a more comprehensive, older term.

18. At Paṇḍharpūr the Bhimā River is called Candrabhāgā, on the model of the Ganges at Kāśī (Banaras).

19. They looked like Gosāvīs or *sādhūs*.

20. That is, take the boat across for free. Through dharmạ they are only religiously or morally bound to take the boat across. According to Manu 8.407, ascetics are to be given toll-free passage on ferries.

21. Written *hukūm*. By paying, one gets an imperative right to the boat and the passage. Compare Text 33, below.

> "O Bābā, we aren't swindlers. We're showing you the strength of our trustworthiness.[22] With Parameśvara's help, we are on our way to Paṭṭaṇ Kaḍulī. *Bhaṇḍār* is our gold. You ought to know that."
>
> Then Khilubā, filled with the power of his god, said the following: "Āmbyā and Limbyā, you Koḷī children, it may be true that you have loaded your boats with goods belonging to the merchant Lāṭyā from Miraj. If you won't take me across, then listen to my *piṅgḷyā* prophecy."[23] And Khilubā cursed them as follows: "You'll push the loaded boats into the river, you'll row to the middle of the river. Through the power of the existence of Viṭṭhal and Birobā, your boats will be caught in a whirlpool, and they will sink. As you swim, you'll be carried down the river, and finally you'll be thrown up on the bank. You'll climb up at a steep place and reach land. And the money and goods will be sunk, and the two of you will moan and wail. In Paṇḍharpūr, Lāṭyā the merchant will hear about it, and he will take proceedings against you at the Divān. He will say, 'Āmbyā and Limbyā haven't let my wealth sink; they've stolen it. They've been working on the river for twenty-four years. No matter how high the water is, have Āmbyā and Limbyā ever let their boats sink?' ". . . .

The impatient Khilubā, inspired by god, got across without the Koḷīs' help:

> . . . He folded his blanket[24] into a rectangle and laid it on the water of the Candrabhāgā. He reached into his bag, took out *bhaṇḍār,* and sprinkled it on the blanket. What did he say? "I call on the thirty-three hundred thousand *lings,* I call on my guru, I call on Iṭṭhal and Birdev." He called to mind the water goddess Jānāī, his sister according to dharma.[25] Jānābāī was on her guard. She hurried into the water and held up the blanket with her hand. The four disciples sat on the four corners, and Yeḍyā Khilubā sat in the middle. His staff served as a rudder. . . .

Āmbyā and Limbyā suffered the disaster Khilubā had foretold. But Khilubā helped them, and thus established his right to be taken across on his yearly pilgrimage to Paṭṭaṇ Kuḍolī—a right that continues to this day.

As security the Koḷīs offered him the rocks in their village, Kāsegāv, near Paṇḍharpūr. But Khilubā declined this:

> "This is the Satya Age, and you're giving me the rocks. In the Kali Age the turbaned Mughals will come. They will break the rock and make stone slabs of it. They will build many-storeyed houses. . . .[26]

---

22. *Sattvācā jor.*

23. *Piṅgḷyā,* written *piṅgaḷā,* "little spotted owl, *Noctua Indica*" (Molesworth, *Dictionary*). It is believed that humans can understand this bird's language, and that what it says comes true.

24. *Jāḍ* ~ *ghoṅgaḍī* ~ *kāmblī.* This is indispensable for a Dhangar. It serves as a shelter against the rain, as protection against the cold and the sun, as a seat for guests, and so on.

25. That is, a sister to whom he is not related by blood.

26. Paṇḍharpūr was occasionally also called Sultānpūr. It belonged to Bijāpūr. Aurangzeb came into the Deccan in 1636. There is a series of legends about Aurangzeb's encounter with Viṭhobā in Paṇḍharpūr.

"But there is one security I will accept: my right (*mān*) will last as long as the sun and the moon rise in the east and set in the west. My right should last as long as the Narbadā and the other rivers take their normal course and flow from above to below. My right should last as long as the Rāvaḷ mountain stays in its place. When the moon and the sun rise in the west and set in the east, then my right should come to an end. When the Narbadā and the other rivers flow backward, then my right should come to an end. When the Rāvaḷ mountain starts moving, then my right should come to an end."

[The Koḷīs said,] "But still, O god, ask for something."

"O Bābās, today, in the Satya Age, five or six people go on the pilgrimage (*jatrā*), but in the Kali Age thousands will come by bullock cart to the pilgrimage festival (*jatrā*) at Paṭṭaṇ Kuḍolī. They must cross the river, and you should not ask them for any money. . . ."

At many other places along the Bhimā River also, as well as along the Nirā River, Koḷīs are boatsmen and have long-standing fishing rights. Here too, according to tradition, they were the first priests of Mahādev (Śiva), as of the famous god Mahādev of Śiṅgṇāpūr in Māṇ Taluka, Satara District. Here as well there are still today Baḍvā priests in addition to Koḷīs. A Koḷī from Kāmbaḷeśvar, about twenty miles from Śiṅgṇāpūr on the bank of the Nirā in Phalṭaṇ Taluka, gave the following answer to the question of the derivation of the name Mahādev Koḷī:

Text 24

We do the worship (*pūjā*) of Mahādev of Śiṅgṇāpūr. But the Brahmans [Baḍvās] demanded that we give the god's *pūjā* to them. We gave them the *pūjā*. They gave us the cloth ring and said, "You are Koḷīs. Take this cloth ring and provide people with water."

The Koḷī said this without regret, in a matter-of-fact tone. For him *pūjā* is an occupation for which the ritually higher Brahmans are better qualified, although for the Brahmans this temple service is more likely to be ritually demeaning. This example also shows how Brahmans, having penetrated the forest and pasture region, assigned to other castes their natural rights and duties within the caste system.

At Kāmbaḷeśvar on the Nirā River the Koḷīs' close connection with water and with the Bhimā, Karhā, and Nirā rivers, as well as with water goddesses, is particularly clear. The goddess Bhivāī (or the seven Bhivāyā) is identical with the seven river goddesses. She lives in a great water hole (*ḍoh*) in the Nirā River. This is supposed to be immeasurably deep, even in the hot season, when the rest of the river bed threatens to dry up—especially since the construction of the Vīr dam. Bhivāī is one of two wives (or, more frequently, the sister) of the Dhangar god Dhuḷobā near Phalṭaṇ. During the pilgrimage festival (*jatrā*) in honor of Bhivāī in the month of Caitra, worshipers throw sheep from the rocky bank into the water for the goddess, in the hope of increasing their herds. Koḷīs swimming in the water hole below take the sheep and bring them back to land. Children who have been born in answer to a prayer or because of a vow (*navas*) to Bhivāī must be shown to the goddess during the *jatrā* in fulfillment of the promise. They are placed on rafts and immersed by the Koḷīs, and then received back by their parents. Near the goddess's shrine is another shrine with an aniconic, *śendūr*[27]-painted stone. In the story told about this shrine, worshipers see a reflection of the dangerousness of the goddess:

Text 25

A woman prayed to the goddess for a son. A boy baby was born to her. She brought the boy to the goddess. The boy was placed on the raft. He was supposed to be immersed. She was afraid. The boy really sank. Through the Koḷīs' intercession she had another son. This time she was not afraid. She came to set him in the basket. . . .

The first boy surfaced again, alive, after a year. His skull was coated with *śendūr*. The woman was happy. The boy said, "I want to take on the state of lifelessness while I'm alive here (*jīvant samādhī ghyāycī*)." He did this. A shrine was built near Bhivāī.

Another legend tells of utensils[28] like water jugs (*haṇḍī*), bowls (*carvī*), and rolling pins (*lāṭṇeṃ*) that used to emerge from the water during the pilgrimage festival (*jatrā*):

Text 26

People used to take them, use them during the *jatrā,* wash them, and sink them back in the water. One Dhangar took a *lāṭṇeṃ* to use at Dhuḷobā's pilgrimage. When he had gotten halfway to Phalṭaṇ, he died. In this way people come from Bhivāī's *jatrā* and go to Dhuḷobā's. Halfway there they offer coconuts, and the like, to Dhangar Bābā and then go on to Dhuḷobā's *jatrā.*

Bhivāī is said to have come to Kāmbaḷeśvar before Dhuḷobā. Then Dhuḷobā came to Ghoḍe Uḍḍāṇ[29] and settled in Phalṭaṇ. Bhivāī is supposed to have come from Vāḷaṇḍ. This is the Veḷvand that lies upstream in the Bhātgar reservoir, near the Western Ghāṭs. There Bhivāī is called "the seven Veḷvand-women." There too Koḷīs act as ferrymen. It is said there that when rice grown in the Ghāṭs is thrown into the water as an offering, the fish eating the

27. Sanskrit, *sindura,* red lead paint (minium).

28. Pots that come up from a river are also referred to by D. D. Kosambi, in connection with the goddess Mhātyrāī at Theūr, among others. Kosambi suspects that these are prehistoric finds that believers take to be holy (*Myth and Reality,* p. 120).

29. The modern temple lies between Kāmbaḷeśvar and Phalṭaṇ: literally, "the place where the god's horse took off from the ground." The term is also found in the case of Khaṇḍobā in Jejurī and Mhaskobā in Vīr. See *Mhaskobā Devāceṃ Caritra,* part 1 (Appendix.)

rice make seven concentric circles. Anyone who sees the seventh ring dies. Prehistoric reproductions of these circles are found on rocks, especially in the valley of the Bhimā River.[30]

1.2 The Encounter with Birobā

According to the old gazetteer of Sātārā,[31] Khaṇḍobā (Malhār) and Birobā are the favorite gods of the Koḷīs. Otherwise Birobā is almost exclusively a god of the Dhangars. How did the connection between Birobā and the Koḷīs come about? The following excerpt from what was actually an all-night *ovī* performance suggests how the relationship began. We also see how Birobā taught the Koḷīs the correct behavior toward the river goddesses.

The *ovī* comes from nomadic Hāṭkar Dhangars from Ṭhombrevāḍī (Bārāmatī Taluka, Poona District). Without the usual interruptions for spoken passages,[32] it consists entirely of a series of lines (*caraṇas*) without verse divisions and without rhyme. In the second half of a *caraṇa,* the first half is repeated by the two singers, one of whom is usually learning from the other. The two "repeaters"—as the Dhangars themselves call them[33]—repeat the whole *caraṇa.*

Here I present the first halves of the *caraṇas* in a translation that resembles the original as closely as possible even in its sentence structure, and from which punctuation has been omitted as far as possible, to correspond to the sung text:

Text 27

[On his way to Iṭhū/Viṭhobā's pilgrimage festival, Birjī/Birobā comes to the edge of the village of Limbgāv:]

Ovī: He set out
Toward the west
Came to the edge of Limbgāv
On the Kisnā River.
Birjī, my Bhagavān

30. Kosambi, *Myth and Reality,* p. 136, refers to concentric "mother goddess circles" on rocks in the middle of the Bhimā River at Kanoṭā (Dhoṇḍ Taluka, Poona District). These circles are worshiped by fishermen (in this case, Bhoīs rather than Koḷīs). According to Kosambi, they are megaliths.

31. *Gazetteer of the Bombay Presidency,* vol. 19 (1885), p. 106.

32. *Sampādnī,* written *saṃpādaṇī* ~ *saṃpādaṇūk,* "the dressing up (. . . of any legend-exposition) with rhetorical embellishment. . . . [To] act out the part according to its requirement" (Molesworth, *Dictionary*). Generally in these spoken portions the contents of the *ovī* are elaborated or continued.

33. *Māge[ṃ] mhaṇāre.*

Said
The Dhupārtī ceremony of my sister
Is taking place.
It is the month of Caitra
On the side of the mountain
In the foothills of the mountain
Rain fell.[34]
The river is flooded.
Kisnā, my sister!
He joined his hands
Touched her feet.
The brother's sister!
Let me go across.
The river was high on both banks
The god's pilgrims
Could not cross the river.
Birjī, my Bhagavān
How clever was Birobā
He called
Māyā and Hiryā, the policemen[35]
He said:
Go to Limbgāv
Bring Limbā Koḷī.
He will untie a boat
It should take us across
The god's policemen
Ran
Along the path through the forest
They hurried.
The god found
Limbā, the Koḷī.
The policemen said:
Birjī, my god—
The god's pilgrims
Are going to Viṭṭhal, my god
To play.[36]

---

34. Extremely rare in Caitra (March-April). When it does happen, people say, "*Mahādevāce[ṃ] taḷeṃ bharāyla ālā āhe*—It has come in order to fill Mahādev's lake." The month of Caitra has the greatest number of pilgrimages, one of the largest of them in Śiṅgṇāpūr, the famous seat of Mahādev.

35. *Pulīs,* from English *police.*

36. *Kheḷ,* literally, "play," is dancing, playing music, and beating drums in front of the temple during the pilgrimage, or before the start of the migration after the Dasarā festival. The god takes possession of one of the dancers (*aṅgāt yeṇe[ṃ],* to come into the body) and speaks through him. Compare the *sīds* in *Mhaskobā Devāceṃ Caritra,* part 3 (Appendix).

The river is flooded
The flood has come.
Birjī, my god
Has called to you
Take
Your wages.
You must untie the boat.
The Koḷī said:
The Dhangar caste—
This caste is stupid.
They are afraid
Of the summer rain.
The flood will run off
You will get across
The god's policemen
Joined their hands
Touched his feet
But the Koḷī would not have pity.
Now the policemen were disappointed.
They went back
To Birjī, my god
They went before him
They said
Limbā Koḷī
Refused.
Birjī, my Bhagavān
Was upset
He sat there hanging his head
On the bank of the Kisnā.
He made his staff into a pillow[37]
Laid his chin on his knees
Sudrasain [Sudarśan] Bhagavān
Birjī Nārāyaṇ
Slept.
After he had fallen asleep
The brother's sister
Came to him in a dream
She said
O brother
[Give me] a blouse, a sari
Fill my lap[38]

37. By propping his chin on his staff, a stance typical of a Dhangar grazing sheep.

38. With, for example, grains of wheat (*gahū*); unripe, dry dates (*khārīk*); pieces of dry coconut; a betel nut (*supāri*); a whole coconut.

Give me bangles
Give me lemons and coconuts
A bag of [red] *kuṅkum* [powder].
Birjī, my god
This mischievous rogue[39]
Woke up
Rinsed his mouth.
He joined his hands
Before Kisnā Bāī
He called
Māyā and Hiryā, the policemen . . .

[In what follows, Birjī tells Māyā and Hiryā to bring the gifts for Kisnā Bāī. Birjī and his followers throw the gifts into the river. Then the Dhangars cross the river and resume their journey to the *jatrā*. The *ovī* continues:]

Limbā Koḷī
Took his mother, father, brother
Sister-in-law, brother-in-law
Into his boat
He cast off.
Limbā Koḷī
Began to row
Got to the middle of the river
Lost the oars
The boat was carried away
Began to sink.
The mischievous god
Caused a disaster
Iṭhū [and] my Birū
The lords on the throne[40]
The Sambhā [Śambhu] of Kailās
Circled
In the sky
The boat sank
Limbā the Koḷī
Nearly drowned
He couldn't find the boat.
On the bank of Kisnā Bāī
He began to shout
He began to cry[41]

39. *Kaḷiyācā nārand,* written *kaḷicā nārad,* "an incendiary, a mischiefmaker, a make-bate or embroiler" (Molesworth, *Dictionary*).

40. They sit in the temple like kings, on the cushion that serves as a throne (*gādī*).

41. Because everybody else had drowned.

He called the god to mind
Iṭhū [and] my Birū.
He was in despair
He went to the god,
Iṭhū [and] my Birū,
To Ḍhagevāḍī
He heard
The boom of *ḍhol* and *ḍapha* drums
He ran
His lips were cracked
His eyes were red
Limbā, the Koḷī
In those days—
He joined his hands
Touched them to his forehead
What happened?
Limbā Koḷī
Called to mind the god
Came imploring the god
Touched his feet. . . .[42]
He stood there
On one leg.
Birjī, my god
The king would not have pity
Would not show love
What happened?
Limbā Koḷī
Spoke
To Iṭhū [and] my Birū
Strode away backward[43]
Beat his head on the tree.
I will shed my blood
I will take my life
I am the guilty one.
He forgave him
Go now!
Why should I live?
What is the use of living?
The god had pity.
Birjī, my Bhavānā

42. *Daṇḍvat gheū lāgalā.* The devotee lies down on the ground and makes a line with his staff in the dust in front of him. The next time he lies down, his feet must touch that line. A devotee often covers several miles this way.

43. Without turning his back to the temple.

Iṭhū, my Bābā
Said
In those days,
Before you get into the boat
Take off your sandals
Make a salutation
Then step into the boat
Then sit down in the boat
Do not let a menstruating woman
Sit in the boat
Unless you are not told about it.
Do not make fun of anyone
On the Nāraḷya-Puṇav[44]
Give what you can,
Or only a coconut
This custom is to be preserved in the family
Blouse, sari
Her lap must be filled
Limbā Bābā! A coconut
The gifts for my sister
Kisnā, my sister
Koynā, my sister
Nirā, my sister
Karhā, my sister
Bhivrā [Bhimā], my sister
Candra, my Candrabhāgā
Bhāgirthī, my sister
Yamunā, my sister
Kāśī [= Gaṅgā?], my sister
Make for her, O Bābā
A house of a mother
You must come worshiping
Kisnā, my sister
Joining your hands
And touching them to your forehead.
You must reveal
Your inmost heart to my sister
My sister will have pity
Kisnā, my mother!
Limbā the Koḷī
Took ashes,

44. Nāraḷī Paurṇimā, "The day of full moon of Śrāvaṇ on which a coconut is thrown into the sea, and the monsoon is declared to be broken up" (Molesworth, *Dictionary*).

A pinch of ashes
He threw them
On the bank of sister Kisnā
He came pleading. . . .

1.3 The Assimilation of the Koḷīs

The Koḷīs as a tribe were also dreaded warriors and robbers, from whom even in the British period the government still ran into organized resistance. Because they could not be completely conquered anyway, the traditional Indian policy toward them had as its basic idea to subdue them and install them as military commanders with police authority over territories that were still only minimally developed. Thus, during the period of the Bāhmanī kings, for example, the Koḷīs were practically independent under their Nāīks,[45] ruling over the Bāvan Māvaḷs, the "fifty-two" valleys on the eastern side of the Ghāṭs. The Koḷīs retained their important positions at court during the rule of the Ahmednagar kings as well.

The Emperor Śāh Jahān came up against the Koḷīs' opposition when he tried to introduce Ṭodar Mal's land-taxation system in the regions he had conquered. The Koḷīs still held to the tribal notion that their land was their sovereign territory: they refused to let their estates be measured or to pay a regular tax. After this revolt was quelled, Aurangzeb treated them favorably.

The Koḷīs were held in great awe during the Peśvā period as well, especially because of their skill at robbing forts. In 1760 the Koḷīs revolted under Nāīk Jivājī Bomlā. After a twenty-year stand-off, they surrendered to Tukojī Hoḷkar, the Peśvās' general. At his instigation, Nāīk Jivājī Bomlā was installed as the ruler of an area that included sixty villages. He had power over life and death for Koḷī robbers and for outlaws. In 1798 a new revolt broke out under Rāmjī Nāīk Bhaṅgriā. When there finally appeared to be no hope of suppressing the revolt by force, the government pardoned the Nāīk and gave him an important police post, "in which he did excellent service."[46]

The British government also followed this traditional Indian method. It took twenty years to put down the Koḷīs' revolts, but in return the British made use of the Koḷīs' warlike abilities in 1857.

Much in this traditional policy of Indian kings toward the tribes is reminiscent of the adjustments made by a god more closely related to the Sanskritic pantheon who forces his way into the forest and pasture land: thus the con-

45. Syed Siraj ul Hassan, *The Castes and Tribes of H. E. H. The Nizam's Dominions* (Bombay, 1920), s.v. Koḷī.

46. Ibid.

quered demon reemerges in the name of the god, for example; and often, although the demon is killed, he lives on in an independent cult or becomes identified with the invading god.

2. The Rāmośīs: Professional Robbers and Devotees of Khaṇḍobā

Except where the Koḷīs have become incorporated into village society, like the Malhār Koḷīs or Cumlīs, they are even still today a tribelike group. The Rāmośīs, by contrast, were a motley company of robbers reinforced by members of various castes, such as Kuṇbīs, Māḷīs, Mahārs, and Māṅgs.[47] Originally, the Rāmośīs are supposed to have immigrated as a tribe from the Hyderabad-Karnatak region or from Telaṅgaṇa, and to have spread northward from Māṇdeś, the valley of the Māṇ River.[48]

Dhangars, Gavḷīs, Kuṇbīs, and others also call the Rāmośīs Byārāḍ ~ Berāḍ. This name is probably derived by metathesis from Beḍar. The Beḍars or Beḍas were predatory forest tribes who lived in Karnatak, Arcot, and other parts of south India and who gave Hindu kings considerable trouble, principally by stealing cattle. There are numerous Kannaḍa inscriptions about them. These are found on hero stones (*vīragaḷs*) installed in honor of *gāvuṇḍas* (village headmen) who had been killed defending their herds of cattle against the Beḍars.[49] Eventually the Beḍars became *jagīrdārs* or formed small kingdoms of their own. The kings of Śorāpūr in Gulbargā District became especially famous: they revolted against Aurangzeb, and in 1857 against the English.[50]

The attempts to give an etymological explanation of the caste name "Rāmośī" reflect the Rāmośīs' original place of residence and their claim to be integrated into the caste system of other groups living in nuclear agricultural areas. Mackintosh derives "Rāmośī" from Marāṭhī *rānvāsī:* residents of uncultivable deserts or of forests (*rān*).[51] His second etymology

47. A gripping depiction of the Rāmośīs is found in Captain Alexander Mackintosh's book, *An Account of the Origin and Present Condition of the Tribe of Ramoossies, Including the Life of the Chief Oomiah Naik* (Bombay, 1833).

48. Ibid., p. 7; *Mysore State Gazetteer,* Gulbargā District (Bangalore, 1966), p. 74.

49. See the inscriptions cited by B. A. Saletore in *The Wild Tribes in Indian History* (Lahore, 1935), pp. 60ff.

50. *Mysore State Gazetteer,* Gulbargā District, p. 470.

51. Mackintosh, *Account,* p. 3. See also *Gazetteer of the Bombay Presidency,* vol. 18, Poona (Bombay, 1885), part 1, p. 409. Today *rān* is also used for dry but still cultivable land. The meaning "forest" is less accurate today, except in the sense of "scrub jungle."

derives the name from *Rāma* and *vaṃśī:* descendants of Rāma, supposed to have been created by him when he went to Laṅkā.[52] Finally Mackintosh gives "Rāmabhaktas" ("devotees of Rāma") as a synonym for "Rāmośīs"—for those Rāmośīs, that is, who do not eat meat.

Mackintosh accurately describes the historical career of the Rāmośīs:

> There can be little doubt that the Ramoosies in their primitive state, led a roving unsettled life, like many of the nomadic tribes, keeping at some distance from the inhabitants of the more civilized orders of society, and occasionally, when opportunities offered, plundering travellers; they also attacked at night the houses of the inhabitants of towns and villages near which they halted; as a measure of precaution, with the view of protecting their property from such troublesome and dexterous robbers, the inhabitants of various places deemed it most advisable, to employ some of these people in the capacity of preventive police; and it may be observed, that it has frequently become necessary in many parts of the country, to continue a system perfectly analogous in modern times.
>
> This led to the institution of the village Rickwalldar[53] and Juglahs[54] (the guardian or watchman), which in the course of time, became hereditary.[55]

Rāmośīs also served as night watchmen guarding the pack oxen of merchants' caravans in their special resting places or outside a village. In the area of Sātārā, Poona, and Ahmadnagar, they were primarily one of the twelve service castes of village society.[56] But again and again the Rāmośīs took up their traditional occupation, robbery. Finally the British broke their resistance to an ordered way of life. The famous leader Umājī Nāīk was captured after a long pursuit, and hanged in 1832.

In addition to Mhasobā and Mhaskobā, Vetāḷ, Vāghobā ("Tiger Father"), Bhavānī of Tuḷjāpūr (the Koṟṟavai of Maharashtra), and various other goddesses, the Rāmośīs' principal deity is and has long been the god Khaṇḍobā of Jejurī. Jejurī lies in an area that can turn into "desert" (Tamil, *pālai*) during the hot season, and where the monsoon is unreliable (see above, chap. 1). Consistent with this picture is the fact that Khaṇḍobā also shares certain features with Skanda, the north Indian guardian deity of robbers and thieves. When Khaṇḍobā's palanquin is brought down to the Karhā River in the great procession of the Somvatī festival at Jejurī, Rāmośīs have the right (*mān*) to carry it from behind. This fact is attributed to the god's close connection with Umājī Nāīk.

---

52. Mackintosh, *Account,* p. 3.
53. *Rākhvaḷ* or *rākhaṇāvaḷ,* wages for the night's watch.
54. *Jāgal,* to keep watch, and the watchman's wages.
55. Mackintosh, *Account,* p. 3.
56. Ibid., pp. 10f., 3.

To this day, whether rightly or wrongly, Dhangars still feel that the Rāmośīs (as well as the tribal Kātkarīs in the Western Ghāṭs) are a threat to them during their migration to the Koṅkaṇ. But also in their monsoon camps, if they are remote, the Dhangars fear for their sheep and horses:

Text 28

Rāmośīs from Dharmapurī [Māḷśiras Taluka, Sholapur District] came and settled on the mountain near our *vāḍā* [near J., Phalṭaṇ Taluka, Satara District]. Dhangars were grazing their horses on this mountain. The Dhangars saw the Rāmośīs there. Immediately the Dhangars returned to the *vāḍā*. They all gathered together and finally went toward the Rāmośīs. They said, "If we hadn't seen them, our *vāḍā* would have been robbed. We will attack them from the side and catch them. If they see us, they will run away."

When the Rāmośīs saw the Dhangars, they began to run away. The Dhangars surrounded the Rāmośīs, and they could not escape. The Dhangars came from all sides and caught the thieves. Then they brought the Rāmośīs to the *vāḍā*. Then they went into the village and informed the Pāṭīl. And in order to convince others that these Rāmośīs were indeed thieves [because they had not yet stolen anything], the Dhangars gathered together stones [which the Rāmośīs were allegedly planning to use in their assault on the *vāḍā*] in a spot at the side of the *vāḍā*. Then the Dhangars informed [the Pāṭīl] in B. Then the police came, put handcuffs on them, and took them away.

But Rāmośīs also appear in the legends of the Gavḷīs and Dhangars. I will present here a brief summary and the conclusion of an *ovī* about Yelu Gavḷaṇ and her son Bābū Ballāḷ. Bābū Ballāḷ was killed by Rāmośīs and became "Bābīr," a herdsmen's god. Bābīr's is not a simple ancestor cult or the cult of the ghost of a young herdsman who was violently killed—as is the case, for example, with Ceḍā, the ghost of a Māṅg boy who cannot be pacified until a cult is established for him and he is exorcised by being sent into a stone. Bābīr becomes connected with Śiva because of his mother's worship of Bhoḷā (Śiva/Śaṅkar).[57] In this way he himself becomes a god and also one of the manifestations of Śiva. A huge pilgrimage during Divāḷī brings together devotees from as far away as Khāndeś:

57. For Gavḷīs and Dhangars this is above all the Mahādev of Śiṅgṇāpūr in Phalṭaṇ Taluka. This god is himself something of a deity of pastures and herdsmen, and so he is not satisfied with just *one* Nandī. Five gigantic Nandīs stand facing him in the temple hall (*sabhāmaṇḍapa*). Hunting scenes are depicted on the pillars, which are in the late Hemāḍ-Pant style. The place is associated not only with the Yādavas of Devgiri—the name Śiṅgṇāpūr is supposed to be derived from Siṅghaṇa, the name of the Yādava king who ruled from 1210 to 1247—but also with Śivājī, who used to go hunting in this area. Motifs similar to those in the legend of Bābīr pointing to the antagonism between Dhangars and Berāḍs occur in an *ovī* from the village of Khāṇḍerājurī (Miraj Taluka, Sangli District). See Sarojinī Bābara, editor, *Eka hotā rājā* (Bombay, 1964), pp. 136ff.

Text 29

Ya(∼e)lu Gavḷaṇ and her husband, Malu Gavḷaṇ, used to graze their cattle in the forest (*rān*) of Nhāī Rūī [Indāpūr Taluka, near Kaḷas]. She had no children. One day a black cow named Kapilī appeared to her in a dream and said, "Worship Bhoḷā (Śiva) and you will have a child."

Yalu Gavḷaṇ took all the things needed for worshiping the god, and went to worship the god. She did this regularly every day, and finally Bhoḷā was pleased with her worship. He asked her, "Do you want a son who is wise but who lives only twelve years, or do you want one who is born stupid?"

She asked for nine months' time to think. After six months the god came to her. Yalu Gavḷaṇ recognized him. When he came back after nine months, he first tried to take a child from a Gavḷī woman who had many children and give it to Yalu Gavḷaṇ. But this failed, and he himself took form in her womb. Yalu Gavḷaṇ bore a son. He was named Bābū Ballāḷ. When he had grown up, he used to take the cows to pasture. He also let them graze in fields of standing grain, which were guarded by Rāmośīs. The Rāmośīs of Mhaiman Gaḍ were out to rob the cows. But they couldn't manage to do so.

Bābū had a flute. When he played a joyful melody on it, the cows would spread out over a wide area to graze. When he played a sad tune, the cows would hurry over to him. After twelve years his life as a man was over. . . .

One hundred fifty Byārāḍs (Rāmośīs) killed Bābū.

[*Ovī:*] He went to his *vāḍā*. He went with his cows. He said to his mother, "I'm going to the pasture."

His mother said to him, "Don't go, O Bābū. You must let me know what good things and bad things happen."

"If something bad happens to me, your left breast will hurt.
The tuḷśi birdāvan [*vṛndāvan*] bush will dry up.
The palmyra tree will fall down.
Some such omen will occur."
Bābū set out
for the forest of Nhāī Rūī.
He began to graze the cows.
One day
the colossally strong Byārāḍs came looking for Bābū
and they drove away the cows.
They seized Bābū,
they killed Bābū.
They stuffed him into a porcupine's den.
Branches of the līmb tree
began to grow upward
through the vāghāṭī bush.[58]

58. *Vāghāṭī,* written *vāghāṃṭī,* "a scandent shrub, Capparis Zeylanica or Corymbosa" (Molesworth, *Dictionary*).

Bābū appeared to his mother in a dream.
"I have lost my life in the forest of Nhāī Rūī,
I've been stuffed into a porcupine's den."
His mother woke up and looked around.
Her left breast hurt.
The tuḷśi birdāvan bush had dried up.
the palmyra tree had fallen down.
His name, Bābū, had died out.
Bābū was killed in the month of Kārttik, at Divāḷī.
A great radiance descended.
He acquired the quality of a god (*devpaṇālā lāglā*).
Now he could help the poor
He was given the ability
to fulfill people's wishes.

Today Rāmośīs are farmers and watchmen, and sometimes also shepherds who, like the Dhangars, pen their sheep in farmers' fields. They are hardly distinguishable any longer from the rest of the rural population.

According to the Bombay gazetteer of 1885,[59] some Rāmośīs believed that Khaṇḍobā was the apotheosis of a Liṅgāyat Vāṇī. The Rāmośīs are supposed to have been Liṅgāyats themselves once, and to have worshiped the *liṅga* in the form of Khaṇḍobā. At that time their priests were not Brahmans, but Jaṅgamas (Liṅgāyat priests). Even today it is generally undisputed that Khaṇḍobā's first wife in Jejurī is from the Liṅgāyat caste, and his second wife a Dhangar.

The cult of Khaṇḍoba brings together sections of the population who were especially important outside the nuclear regions in southern Maharashtra: the Liṅgāyats, who were very influential in this area in the pre-Marāṭhā period; the Rāmośīs, who often had the job of protecting merchants and their caravans, or who took on police functions in the forts; and finally pastoralist groups such as the Gavḷīs, Dhangars, and Kurubas, who formed a significant tribal element in the population and whose economy was founded on cattle-raising as well as on plow-based agriculture.

3. The Liṅgāyats: Ascetics, Priests, and Merchants

3.1 The Liṅgāyats as a Link Between Nuclear Agricultural Regions

Today the Liṅgāyats live primarily in the pastoral areas of the western Deccan, which I have sketched above. They are found in Karnatak—in Dharwar,

59. *Gazetteer of the Bombay Presidency,* vol. 18, Poona (Bombay, 1885), part 1, p. 413.

Belgaum, Gulbarga, and Raicur districts—and in southern Maharashtra. Once the Liṅgāyats were even more widely disseminated in Maharashtra, especially when the districts of Ahmadnagar, Satara, Sangli, and Sholapur still belonged to Kanarese kings.[60]

According to Enthoven,[61] Liṅgāyats can be divided into three groups:

1. The highest group consists chiefly of priests called Jaṅgamas—that is, the walking abodes of *liṅgas.* Still higher than the regular (*sāmānya*) Jaṅgamas are the Viraktas, Liṅgāyats who do not marry and who live a life of wandering, supporting themselves by begging. The highest merchant castes, the Bañjiga (Sanskrit, *vāṇija, vāṇijaka*), also belong to this highest group.[62]
2. The middle group includes about seventy professional endogamous "castes." Like the first group, they are strict vegetarians, at least in theory, and they wear a *liṅga* on their body in a small silver container.
3. The lowest group corresponds to the Untouchable castes of the Hindus.

The Liṅgāyat sect is founded primarily on the premise of the *equality* of all people, on the rejection of the concept of pollution (pollution of the individual and of the family by birth and death, as well as pollution through contact with lower castes), on the worship of Śiva (but not of Viṣṇu or Brahmā), and on an esteem for the Vedas that is, however, subordinated to a rejection of Brahmanical superiority. In addition, the Liṅgāyats reject child marriage and allow widow remarriage. In contrast to Hindus, they bury rather than burn their dead.

Louis Dumont points out that many of the characteristics of this sect are reminiscent of the institution of world renunciation: their "monasteries" (*maṭhas*), for example; the importance of gurus; and the position of the Viraktas—whose task, theoretically, is to practice devotion (*bhakti*) not only for themselves but also for the laity.[63] The goal of devotion is unity with the god, not a nebulous fusion with the divine.[64] Dumont describes the Liṅgāyat sect as an "incomplete caste system" founded not on the oppositions of caste vs. world renunciation, pure vs. impure, and Brahman vs. Caṇḍāla, but on world renunciation, either direct or through the medium of the sect's priests,

60. See A. P. Karmarkar, "Boundaries of Ancient Mahārāṣṭra and Karṇāṭaka," *Indian Historical Quarterly,* 14 (1938) 776–86.

61. Enthoven, *Castes,* vol. 2, p. 343. Syed Siraj ul Hassan, p. 383.

62. Today there is hypergamy between Jaṅgamas and Bañjigas—that is, Jaṅgama men can marry Bañjiga women, but Bañjiga men cannot marry Jaṅgama women.

63. *Homo Hierarchicus. The Caste System and Its Implications,* translated by Mark Sainsbury (London, 1970), pp. 189f.

64. Ibid., p. 190. Cf. the Śiva *bhakti* of Siddhanāth of Mhasvaḍ.

and on the tendency of sects to become divided into castes. On this tendency also rests, in part, the definition of the Jaṅgama priests.

We can also consider the characteristic traits of the Liṅgāyat sect from another point of view. Next to the Liṅgāyat priests, the merchants were historically the most important group in this sect. The sphere of the Liṅgāyats lay outside the nuclear agricultural regions, where the caste system had become firmly established. In the nuclear region there lived the settled Brahman, who followed strict marriage rules. By contrast, the renouncer (*sannyāsī*) lived outside the established settlements and often followed the rule of celibacy. The *sannyāsī* in the forest and the pastoral region had more contact with Śiva and his manifestations. For the Brahman, Rudra and Śiva were more likely to be connected with impurity. For the strict Brahmans of an *agrahāra* in southern Karnatak, the Brahman priests of Śiva are impure, and members of the two groups usually do not enter into marital alliances even if they belong to the same subcaste.[65]

Merchants, and the Buddhist, Jaina, and Liṅgāyat sects connected with them, were among the first to traverse the forest areas. They opened up these areas, primarily along the trade routes, and formed a link between the nuclear regions of the great kingdoms. The merchants of the Liṅgāyat sect are closer to the Viraktas than to the Brahmans. Their trade between kingdoms brought with it contact with people of all classes and of unknown origin. This presupposed a relatively high degree of equality. Their cult sites lay at the intersections of trade and migration routes, and at places where rivers had to be crossed. Their cults were often connected with a pilgrimage and a market, as, for example, at Paṇḍharpūr and Mhasvaḍ.

According to Fleet, the Liṅgāyat sect was a development of the 500 Svāmīs of Aihole (in Bijapur District), who were the protectors of the Vīra-Banañju-dharaṇa, the dharma of the master merchants. They carried the image of a bull on their banner, and, according to inscriptions, were known for their daring "all over the world." They dealt in elephants, horses, jewels, spices, and perfumes. They filled the king's treasury and received special trade privileges from rulers.[66] One of the groups of these merchants and soldiers were the Gāvuṇḍas and Gāvuṇḍasvāmīs. Hereditary "village mayors" in Mysore were also called Gāvuṇḍas or *gāvḍās* ~ *gauḍās*. Their wealth consisted of cattle, and "Gauḍā" is generally connected with Sanskrit *go*, cow.[67] The Gāvḍās

65. Pandit K. P. Aithal on conditions in Kota.

66. K. A. Nilakanta Sastri, *A History of South India* (Oxford, 3rd edition, 1966), p. 331.

67. For example, E. Thurston, *The Castes and Tribes of Southern India* (Madras, 1909), vol. 2, s.v. Gauda. *Mahārāṣṭra Śabdakośa: gāvaḍā—dhanagarāṃtīla eka mukhya adhikārī* (Sanskrit, *gau? gāṃva?* Kannaḍa, *gauḍā*).

are also called *hāl-vakkalu-makkalu,* "children of the lineage of milk." This is reminiscent of the Kurubas, who call themselves the descendants of (Pārvatī's) milk.[68]

3.2 The Liṅgāyat Merchants and Khaṇḍobā and Mhāḷsā

Although in its strict interpretation the Liṅgāyats' religion forbids image (*mūrti*) worship and allows the worship of Śiva only in the form of the personal *liṅga* (*iṣṭaliṅga*) received from one's guru, since early times the laity has worshiped various manifestations of Śiva, such as Vīrabhadra.

The Vīra-Baṇañjas were also represented by their merchant guilds in southern Maharashtra, which at that time belonged to Karnatak. In inscriptions from Kolhāpūr and Miraj from the years Śaka 1058 (A.D. 1136) and Śaka 1066 (A.D. 1144), we read of a guild organization (*śreṇī*) of Vīra-Baṇañjas, which extended over four districts.[69] This group had a mountain (*guḍḍa-dhvaja*) as the coat of arms on its banner. This brings us to Khaṇḍobā, who is himself understood as the apotheosis of a Liṅgāyat merchant (Vāṇī), and whose first wife, Mhāḷsā, is understood to come from the Liṅgāyat merchant caste. Another name of Khaṇḍobā is Mallārī (or Malhārī), "the enemy of the demon Malla." According to the *Mallārī Māhātmya,* Khaṇḍobā killed the demons Maṇi and Malla when the *ṛṣis* called on him for help.[70]

Still another name of Khaṇḍobā, which occurs primarily in Karnatak but also in Kolhāpūr, is Mallayya. The most common names for Liṅgāyat and Kuruba men are Mallayya, Mallāppā, Malleś, and Mallināth. As an "*avatār*" of Śiva, Khaṇḍobā/Mallayya has a close connection with mountains;[71] this points to the possibility that Kannaḍa *male* ("mountain") + *ayya* ("father")[72] is the derivation of the name "Mallayya."[73] Like Khaṇḍobā/Mallayya, Murukan̲ is the "lord of mountains" (Tamil, *malaikil̲avōn̲*).[74] A mountain is also often like a *liṅga,* and so it is not surprising that Kuruba mythology tells of the congenitally mute son of a Gauḍa couple, Siddarāmayya, who, while grazing cattle

68. See below, chap. 6, section 2, Version 5.

69. *Epigraphia Indica,* vol. 19, p. 33.

70. *Malhārī Māhātmya* (Sanskrit version), ascribed to the *Brahmāṇḍa Purāṇa,* but not included in the Veṃkateśvara Press edition.

71. Compare Sanskrit *girīśa, girika,* as a name of Śiva. Besides Mallayya the names Guḍḍāppā and Parvatāppā also occur in Kannaḍa.

72. *Dravidian Etymological Dictionary,* 3883: Kannaḍa, *male* = mountain, forest. Ibid., 163: Kannaḍa, *ayya, aya* = father, grandfather, master, lord, teacher.

73. According to Śan. Bā. Jośī, *Marhāṭī Saṃskṛti* (Muṃbaī, 1952), p. 132.

74. See above, 2.2.

in the woods, worships Śiva in the form of a *liṅga* and calls him Mallayya.[75]

Khaṇḍobā/Mallaya's connection with mountains does not mean that Malla, who threatened the *ṛṣis* and was conquered by Khaṇḍobā, cannot also be a mountain spirit. The fact that Śiva/Khaṇḍobā forgives the demons Malla and Maṇi, and spares their lives, expresses an ever-recurring process: the older cult is absorbed, is tolerated, lives on. Malla becomes a devotee (*Śivabhakta*) and asks Khaṇḍobā to allow his name to be a part of Khaṇḍobā's: Mallārī.[76]

Because a mountain was depicted on their banner, we can assume that the Vīra-Baṇañjas of Miraj and Kolhāpūr worshiped the mountain, an early form of Khaṇḍobā.[77] Khaṇḍobā's connection with the Vīra-Baṇañjas/Liṅgāyats is still expressed today in the conviction that his first wife, Mhāḷsā, came from the Liṅgāyat merchant caste, and that one of his two ministers is a Liṅgāyat. This conviction is shared not just by Liṅgāyats, but by all of Khaṇḍobā's followers.

3.3. The Liṅgāyat Gurus

The founder or reviver of the sect was Basava, who, according to legend, was an incarnation of Nandī, Śiva's mount. Basava was a Brahman who had refused to be invested with the Brahmanical thread. Along with his sister Nāgambā, he took refuge with the Cālukya king Bijjala Rājā of Kalyāṇī. He married the daughter of the minister Baḷadeva and succeeded him in office. King Bijjala is supposed to have given him his younger sister, Nīlalocanā, as a second wife. The birth of Basava's nephew is described as follows:

> Basava was busy praying, and he saw an ant emerge from the ground with a

---

75. Yallanagauḍa Ph. Attikoḷḷa, *Hālumatada Caritra* (Dharvāḍ, 1949), chap. 5. On the similarity between the *liṅga* and the mountain, see, for example, Merutuṅga Ācārya, *The Prabandhacintāmaṇi or Wishingstone of Narratives,* translated by C. H. Tawney (Bibliotheca Indica, n.s., nos. 931, 950, 951), p. 96.

76. *Malhārī Māhātmya* (Marāṭhī version), 17.36. In Naḷdurg (Usmanabad District) Dhangars worship Maṇi-Malla separately, in addition to Khaṇḍobā. Compare the explanation given by the Gurav from Mhasvaḍ (Text 1): the god is called Mhasvaḍ Siddha because he killed Mahiṣāsura. Śiva is called Mahābaḷeśvar at Mahābaḷeśvar (Mahābaḷeśvar Mahāl, Satara District) because he killed the demon Mahābaḷi there. "Kandārī" means "enemy of Kandāsura"; see section 4.2, below.

77. According to P. B. Desai, *guḍḍa* in this context is a Jaina term meaning "a lay follower or disciple of the Jaina faith" (P. B. Desai, *Jainism in South India,* pp. 122–23, cited by S. Gururajachar, "The Vira-Bananjus of Karnataka," in *Studies in Indian History and Culture,* Professor P. B. Desai Felicitation Volume [Dharwar, 1971], p. 311). "Mountain" could nevertheless be the original or popular meaning in this context. See also *Epigraphia Carnatica,* vol. 12 (Kolar), p. 170: ". . . *Bīra-Banañja-dharmma-pratipālaṇa viśuddha-guḍḍa-dhvaja-virājamāna. . . .*—Protectors of the Bīra-Banañja dharma, distinguished by the flag of the white mountain. . . ."

seed in its mouth. He took this seed home with him. There his sister swallowed it and became pregnant. From this conception was born a son named Cannabasava, who then together with his uncle spread the Liṅgāyat faith.[78]

In addition to these legends, which must be supplemented by inscriptions to discern their historical kernel, the five *pūrva-ācāryas,* the "first Ācāryas," are also very important. These are understood to have come out of the five mouths (*pañcamukha*) of Śiva; they are named Revaṇa, Maruḷa, Ekorāma, Paṇḍita, and Viśva.[79] It is principally Revaṇa and Maruḷa who play a role in the myths of the Dhangars in southern Maharashtra and the Kurubas in Karnatak. Liṅgāyats, Kurubas, and Gosāvīs all claim Revaṇasiddha as their *ācārya,* the Gosāvīs naming him as one of the "Nine Nāths." But there have been different historically authenticated Revaṇasiddhas.[80] According to Kuruba mythology, Maruḷa is none other than the congenital mute, Siddarāmayya,[81] who has been mentioned above. According to the *Hālumatada Caritra,* Siddarāmayya's birth took place as follows:[82]

> There was a Gauḍa named Muddugoṇḍa[83] in a village called Hirēvūru. His wife was named Suggaladēvē. Both of them were faithful devotees of Śiva. For a long time they had no children. Sadāśiva (Śiva) wanted to bless them. He came to them in the form of Revaṇa and granted them a boon. A son was born to them, and they named him Siddarāmayya. But he was born dumb.
>
> Even when the child was five years old, he couldn't talk. His parents were sorrowful. They sent him with two other shepherd boys, Ekkayya and Jogayya, to graze the cattle in the forest. There the boy did nothing but worship the *liṅga,* which he called Mallayya. Once Śiva came to him in the forest and asked him for something to eat. But the boy had already eaten everything, and could not give him anything. Śiva told him to go home and get some food. Śiva gave him the power of speech; the boy hurried home and asked for something to eat. Nobody could believe that the boy could speak. He ran back into the forest, but Śiva had already disappeared. The boy was determined to search for Śiva, even though his friends laughed at him. He ran toward Śrīśaila. . . .[84]

---

78. These legends are found in Enthoven, *Castes,* vol. 3, and in Thurston, *Castes,* vol. 4, s.v. Liṅgāyat.

79. S. C. Nandimath, *A Handbook of Viraśaivism* (Dharwar, 1942), p. 13.

80. Ibid., p. 15.

81. *Siddha* is not aspirated in Kannaḍa: *Sidda.*

82. Synopsis of chapters 4–6 of Yallanugauḍa Ph. Attikoḷḷa, *Hālumatada Caritra.*

83. Kannaḍa, *goṇḍa* ~ *gauḍa.*

84. In Nandīkoṭkūr Taluka, Kurnool District (Andhra Pradesh)—a famous Śiva shrine (Mallikārjuna), and one of the religious centers of the Liṅgāyats. The tribal group connected with this holy place is neither the Dhangars nor the Kurubas but the Ceñcūs. On a hunting expedition, Śiva meets a beautiful Ceñcū maiden and marries her. See N. Ramesan, *Temples and Legends of Andhra Pradesh* (Bombay, 1962), pp. 11ff. Many Gollas come to worship Mallikārjuna, and the ubiquitous legend of a cow and a cowherd discovering the god in a termite mound is found here as well.

> After searching for a long time and encountering many obstacles, he entered a forest and fell down exhausted on a stone. When he woke up, Śiva (Mallikārjuna) appeared to him. The boy threw himself down before him and prayed to him. They ate together. Sadāśiva said to him: "You will be known as Maruḷasidda, and you will be the guru of the lineage of milk." He commanded Kālabhairava (*sic*)—who was created out of a hair of Śiva's head—always to be at Maruḷasidda's service.

This legend of Siddarāmayya is closely connected with the story of Siddheśvar of Śolāpūr:[85]

> In a hamlet there lived a Pāṭīl named Muddaya and his wife Suggalādevī. They had been born in the Kuḍuvakkaliga caste of the Liṅgāyats. At that time, Revaṇasiddheśvar was traveling around to spread the Liṅgāyat sect. He visited the hamlet of Sonnaligī and blessed the old couple with the promise that they would have a son. And so, after five months—without any sign of the imminent birth—a son was born to them, and they named him Dhuḷi Mahāṅkāḷ.[86] Pārvatī herself named him Siddha.
>
> Siddharām's youth was full of strange occurrences. His parents were sad that he was mute. But he understood his name when he was addressed as Siddharām. Because he could never speak, people took him for an idiot. He was given the task of taking care of his father's cattle. One day it happened that Mahādev appeared to him in the form of a Jaṅgama and asked him for some *hurḍā*.[87] Siddharām gave it to him. Then the Jaṅgama, whose name was Mallaya (that is, Śrīśaila in person), asked for some rice mixed with yoghurt. Siddharām ran to his mother and asked for the food the Jaṅgama wanted. His mother was astonished that her son could speak.
>
> Siddharām ran back to the place in the field which is still known today as *gurubheṭ*,[88] but the Jaṅgama had disappeared. . . .

---

85. *Census of India,* 1961, vol. 10. Maharashtra, part 7–B, *Fairs and Festivals in Maharashtra* (Bombay, 1969), pp. 166ff. The *Caritra* is also narrated in *Śrī Sonnalāpūra [Śolāpūr] yethīla grāma daivata Śrīsiddheśvara Caritrābābata Tarkatīrtha Ṣa. Bra. Pra. Nīḷkaṃṭha Śivācārya Siṃhāsana Bṛhamaṭha Hulī yā pūjya svāmīṃce saṃdeśa kṛta Satyadarśana* (Śolāpūra, 1964). On p. 2 is the statement, "*Śrī Siddharāmeśvarācā itihāsaca yā śaharācā itihāsa* . . .—The history of Śrī Siddharāmeśvar is the history of this town. . . ."

86. Dhuḷi Mahākāḷ is now especially the Bhairav of Ujjayanī. But "Ujjayanī" can also refer to one of the five Vīraśaiva/Liṅgāyat centers (*pīṭhas*) in Karnatak. On the connection of the Liṅgāyats with Ujjayanī in Mālvā, see *Gazetteer of the Bombay Presidency,* vol. 10, Sholāpur (Bombay, 1884), p. 75. For further information about Dhuḷobā = Ujjanī Mahākāḷ ~ Mahāṅkāḷ, see 8.2, below. Marāṭhī *kaṅkāl* means "skeleton." Sanskrit *kaṅkālamāla-bharin* means "wearing a necklace of bones, a name of Śiva" (Monier-Williams, *Dictionary*).

87. Immature kernels of *bājrī* or *jondhaḷā,* lightly roasted. A delicacy typical of the Maharashtra plateau, available shortly before the second harvest (*rabi*). In Andhra Pradesh rice is more plentiful; this is shown by the subsequent request for rice.

88. "The place where he met his guru."

[The events that follow are essentially the same as those outlined in the *Hālumatada Caritra.*]

Afterward Siddheśvar turned Śolāpūr into a holy place, a *kṣetra*. In A.D. 1136 Siddheśvar is supposed to have built the great water reservoir in Śolāpūr. By doing *tapas* he attained many supernatural powers (*siddhis*). He built sixteen temples in the town. He is supposed to have buried himself alive in A.D. 1167.[89] In the case of Śolāpūr, then, we find another of the Siddhas of the Liṅgāyat caste standing at the beginning of the development of a region. Sixteen separate hamlets in this area grew together into what was not only a holy *kṣetra* but also an important trading center. From the twelfth to the sixteenth of January each year there is a great pilgrimage festival in honor of Śrī Siddheśvara. Typically, an important part of this festival is its great cattle market, to which cattle from far away are brought and offered for sale.

4. The Gosāvīs and the Cult of Bhairav

4.1 The Groups of Gosāvīs

Another group whose members penetrated the forest and pasture region of Maharashtra were the Gosāvīs, who primarily spread the cult of Bhairav. In addition to Śiva (Ādināth), the Gosāvīs principally worship the nine Nāths. These are the Gosāvīs' nine great, deified, immortal teachers or religious leaders.[90] Russell and Hiralal[91] note correctly that the Gosāvīs have contributed much to the "Hinduization" of the tribes. In Verrier Elwin's anthology *Folk Tales of Mahakoshal*[92] there appears the figure of the Gosāvī or *sādhu* who, as a hermit and ascetic, becomes connected with Śiva and the termite mound. In the myths of the Dhangars, Śiva again and again takes the form of a Gosāvī. The Kānphaṭā Gosāvīs were also the religious preceptors of Koḷīs,[93] Gavḷīs, Kuṇbīs, and other groups outside the sphere of Brahmanical influence.

89. *Fairs and Festivals in Maharashtra,* p. 171.

90. George W. Briggs, *Gorakhnāth and the Kānphaṭā Yogis* (Calcutta, 1938; reprint, Delhi, 1973), p. 137. This work contains a wealth of details about the Gosāvīs and their gurus. In Vīr and Vālhā (near Vīr, Purandar Taluka, Poona District) the names of the nine Nāths were listed as follows: Gorakhnāth, Macchindarnāth, Jālandharnāth, Sarpaṭīnāth, Cauraṅgīnāth, Āḍbaṅgīnāth, Mīnīnāth, Gahinīnāth, and Kanīphnāth.

91. *Tribes and Castes of the Central Provinces of India* (London, 1916), vol. 3, p. 159.

92. London, 1944, p. 330.

93. *Gazetteer of the Bombay Presidency,* vol. 20, Sholāpur, p. 16.

In the region of my research, the principal contribution to the spread of the Bhairav cult has been made by the Ḍavryā Gosāvīs. Their name derives from Marāṭhī *ḍaur* (Sanskrit, *ḍamaru*), the hourglass drum of Śiva or Bhairav, which they carry with them along with a small trident (*triśūl*). Gosāvīs can still be found at pilgrimage festivals of Bhairav, where they present the *bharāḍ,* a performance of religious songs glorifying the god Bhairav or Mhaskobā. They use their hourglass drum as accompaniment. The Śinde Gosāvīs, an exogamous subgroup of the Ḍavryā Gosāvīs, also still travel from one pilgrimage festival to another as well as to the holy places of northern India—to the shrine of Kāḷbhairav in Banaras, for instance. They wear ocher garments and bring cows with them. For the most part, their destination is Nāsik and Trimbakeśvar in Nāsik Taluka, the site of the first of the twelve famous *jyotirliṅg* temples. Legend holds that Jñāneśvar's elder brother, Nivṛttināth, who is connected with the Nāth sect, had himself buried alive at Trimbakeśvar in 1294; Gorakhnāth and Macchindranāth are supposed to have devoted themselves to asceticism there. There too Gahinīnāth became the guru of Nivṛttināth, who in turn became the guru of Jñāneśvar.[94]

Aside from the strictly monastic Gosāvīs, who—in Sonārī, for example—are dedicated as young children to Kāḷbhairav in fulfillment of vows made by their parents, a majority of groups of Gosāvīs have long recognized the institution of marriage. This has led to the formation of exogamous groups. Some of the "laity" are sedentary, but others still tend to lead a nomadic life. Thus, for six months of the year, the twelve to fourteen families who form one group of Marāṭhā Gosāvīs work their poor land in Māhud, near Āṭpāḍī (Sāṅgolā Taluka, Sholapur District), but they also travel every year from Māhud, via Veḷāpūr, Aklūj, Nātepute, Bārāmatī, Jejurī, Sāsvaḍ, Poona, Āḷaṇḍī, and Bhimāśaṅkar, to Nāsik and Trimbak. The group returns home via Dhoṇḍ, Bhigvān, Indāpūr, Bavḍe, Aklūj, and Veḷāpūr. Besides their meager income from farming, these Gosāvīs' "profession" (Marāṭhī, *dhandā*) is to take care of cows and to beg in the villages they visit in the course of their travels. Their work also includes exhibiting deformed bulls or a four-horned ram. Other Gosāvīs trade in buffaloes; for example, they buy buffalo oxen on the plateau, where they are not very popular as plow animals, and sell them for a profit in the rice region of the Koṅkaṇ.[95]

Gosāvīs, who often traversed unsafe regions in armed groups, seem to have been important as merchants and bankers in the eighteenth and nineteenth centuries. Their monasteries (*maṭhs*) also functioned as banks or business

94. M. S. Mate, *Temples and Legends of Maharashtra* (Bombay, 2nd edition, 1970), pp. 140, 145f.; see also *Fairs and Festivals in Maharashtra,* pp. 98ff.

95. See also *Gazetteer of the Bombay Presidency,* vol. 20, Sholāpur, p. 16.

houses, and the pilgrim routes were at the same time their trade routes. Like Kāḷbhairav, they traveled from *tīrtha* to *tīrtha*, from market town to market town. The spread of modern means of transport in the British period deprived the Gosāvīs of their position as merchants and bankers.[96]

4.2 The Gosāvīs and Kāḷbhairav of Sonārī

The Ḍauryā Gosāvīs and the Kānphaṭā Gosāvīs are closely connected with Sonārī, one of the most important Kāḷbhairav cult places in Maharashtra. Sonārī is in Pareṇḍā Taluka (Usmanabad District). From here, according to tradition, the Bhairav cult spread to Mhasvaḍ, Sāṅgoḷā, Kharsuṇḍī, Kārande, and Jāvḷī. More common than the cult of Kāḷbhairav is that of Aṣṭabhairav, who is to be found as the guardian deity of almost every village in the northern districts of Maharashtra, but who is marked by a certain uniform anonymity. The cult places of Kāḷbhairav, by contrast, display a multilayered background.

Many cults in the region of my research reveal the influence of the cult of Kāḷbhairav: for example, Mhasvaḍ, Kharsuṇḍī, Biḷūr, Jāvḷī, and Vīr. The deities in these places are for the most part identified with Kāḷbhairav, and Kāḷbhairav is then called an *avatār* of Kāḷbhairav or Sonārsiddha of Sonārī.

As for the history of Sonārī, first we read in the old *Gazetteer of the Bombay Presidency* that the *garbhārā* (sanctum) is old and of unknown date—that is, that it must have been built at least before A.D. 1680. In that year the temple hall (*sabhāmaṇḍapa*) was built by the Pāṭīl of Devgāv, a village about ten miles from Sonārī.[97] This was corroborated at the site by the testimony of the temple priests. The outer walls with rooms on their inner side were built by a member of the family of the Nimbāḷkars, the Rājās of Phalṭaṇ, who held the region around Karmāḷā as a *jāgīr*.[98]

Whereas the temple at Sonārī thus dates back to before the year 1680, the Bhairavnāth of Kandārī must surely be even older. Kandārī is about six miles north of Sonārī in a region that until now has been nearly inaccessible. This Bhairavnāth is popularly called the elder brother (*vaḍīl bhāū*) of Sonārī, an expression used frequently in Maharashtra for the earlier of two otherwise similar cults. The seniority of the god of Kandārī is expressed in ritual by the

---

96. See Bernard S. Cohn, "The Role of the Gosains in the Economy of Eighteenth and Nineteenth Century Upper India," *Indian Economic and Social History Review*, 1 (1964) 1ff.; Sir Jadunath Sarkar, *A History of Dasnami Naga Sanyasis* (Allahabad, n.d.), pp. 274–84; and Gosvāmī Pṛthvīgīr Harigīr, *Gosāvī va tyāṃcā saṃpradāya* (Yavatamāla, 1926).

97. *Gazetteer of the Bombay Presidency*, vol. 20, Sholāpur, pp. 502f.

98. Ibid.

fact that the great cart festival at Sonārī in Caitra cannot start until the *kāṭhīs* (the flagpoles of the god) of Kandārī appear.

With the village traditions of Kandārī we enter the sphere of legend. But inasmuch as legend also adapts itself to local realities, we get after all a little insight into the history of Kandārī. Śaṅkar is supposed to have come to the region of present-day Kandārī when he had taken the form of Kāḷbhairav and was wandering from *tīrtha* to *tīrtha* in expiation for having fought with Brahmā and killed him.[99]

At that time, at the place where the temple is now, there were Daṇḍakāraṇya, jungle, and wasteland inhabited by four demons (*asuras*) named Bhaumāsur, Kandāsur, Suvarṇāsur, and Pracaṇḍāsur. After Bhairav had killed Kandāsur, he first settled in Kandārī. Whereas in the case of Khaṇḍobā the name of the demon became an epithet of the god, Mallārī,[100] the name of the demon Kanda, as an epithet of Bhairav (*Kanda* + *arī* = "the enemy of Kanda"), became the name of the place, Kandārī. The god let his horse dance and rear up in Kandārī, and then crossed over to the present-day Sonārī to kill the demon Suvarṇa. In the region of my research, the place where the god first set off on his horse or prepared to leap to a new place (Marāṭhī, *ghoḍe uḍḍāṇ*) often indicates an earlier stage of a cult.[101]

Kandārī developed from a small hamlet (*vastī*) into a village through amalgamation with the residents of four other hamlets. One of these hamlets was inhabited by Gavḷīs, the others by Gosāvīs. The original residents of Kandārī were thieves—*bhāṃtyās*. *Bhāṃtyās* were professional robbers and thieves. In many local traditions of the forest and pasture region, robbers and thieves stand at the beginning of the history of a village; this fact is often even expressed in the village's name—Corācī Āḷaṇḍī, for example, "Thieves' Āḷaṇḍī" (Havelī Taluka, Poona District), or Corācī Uṇḍavḍī, "Thieves' Uṇḍavḍī" (Bārāmatī Taluka, Poona District). The thieves disappeared from Kandārī, and the new inhabitants stayed on: "Here the god is near us. That is why we stay."

Guravs related the following account of the origin of the village of Sonārī:

Text 30

The goddess Bhadrakālī practiced asceticism (*tapaścāryā*) in Sonārī. And Suvarṇāsur [= the golden demon, or the demon with a good background] tested her constancy and prevented her from completing her religious exercises in the

99. *Compare Mhaskobā Devāceṃ Caritra,* part 1 (Appendix).

100. See above, section 3.2.

101. Compare *Mhaskobā Devāceṃ Caritra,* part 2 (Appendix A). Similar earlier layers of cults—that is, places called *ghoḍe uḍḍāṇ*—are found in Jejurī (Khaṇḍobā) and at Phalṭaṇ (Dhuḷobā).

proper way. And she told Suvarṇa that she would marry whoever killed him. Bhairavnāth came to kill him. And he married Bhadrakālī, whose name was Jogeśvarī. Indeed, he had taken form in Kāśī in order to kill demons. He established Vetāḷ on the boundary of the village. There he struck the stone with his trident, and water gushed out;[102] there he let his horse rear up, so that one can still today see the impression of its hoofs. And the battle began again. After the wedding, the killing (*saṃhār*)[103] of the demon took place, and Kāḷbhairav said to Yogeśvarī, "If I succeed, I will come back; if I don't succeed, I will not come back." Then he called for the sixty-four Yoginīs—Tukāī of Tuḷjāpūr, for example—and they drank the demon's blood. Because if a drop of it had fallen to the ground, a thousand new demons would have sprung up.[104] He killed the demon with his bow and arrows, and he washed the weapons in Lohatīrtha. Suvarṇa said to Kāḷbhairav that there should be some way for people to remember him. Thus there came to be the name Sonārī—that is, Suvarṇapurī.

102. Compare *Mhaskobā Devācem Caritra*, part 2 (Appendix).

103. According to Dowson, *Saṃhāra* is one of the eight forms or manifestations of Bhairava, or Śiva (*A Classical Dictionary of Hindu Mythology and Religion, Geography, History and Literature* [London, 10th edition, 1961], s.v. Bhairava).

104. This story is found in the *Matsya Purāṇa* (179.2–40; 252.5–19), among other places; the names of the Mātṛkās with whose help Śiva killed the demon (*asura*) Andhaka ("Blind") are listed in verses 179.10–34.

6

Forest and Pastoral Peoples: Pastoralist Groups

1. Gollas/Gavḷīs

After the disintegration of the Sātavāhana kingdom around the middle of the third century A.D., the Ābhīras founded a kingdom in Khāndeś. The Ābhīras were the classical cattle breeders of Sanskrit literature; they are supposed to be identical with the Ahīrs of today. According to the Purāṇas, a line of ten Ābhīra kings ruled for sixty-seven years after the Sātavāhanas.[1] Whatever the truth of that claim, an Ābhīra king named Mādharīputra Īśvarasena left an inscription dated A.D. 250 in one of the Nāsik caves.[2] During the centuries after the Sātavāhanas, we hear again and again of feuds between the Ābhīras—who are equated with "Gaulas" in Sanskrit literature[3]—and the great dynasties of the Cālukyas, the Hoysaḷas, and the Yādavas of Devgiri. An inscription from A.D. 1341 speaks of the Hoysaḷa king Viṣṇuvardhana Vīra Ballāladeva as the "terror of the Gaulas."[4]

Still today forts and temples in the region serve as reminders of pastoralist Gavḷīs (Ābhīras) or their kings: two examples are the fort of Songīr at Dhuḷe (Dhulia District) and the Hemāḍ Pant temple (Gondeśvara) at Sinnar, near Nāsik, which is supposed to have been built by a Gavḷī king (Rāv Govinda). There are stubbornly persistent traditions that Devgiri, near Auraṅgabād, was

1. *Matsya Purāṇa,* 271.18. Cf. *Viṣṇu Purāṇa,* II.37 (*Bibliographia Indica* edition, p. 453). See Bh. Suryavanshi, *The Abhiras, Their History and Culture* (Baroda, 1962), pp. 34f.

2. *Epigraphia Indica,* VIII, 88–89.

3. Suryavanshi, *Abhiras,* p. 22.

4. This seems to be one of the last inscriptions in which the Gaulas appear as an independent political group.

also founded by a Gavḷī (Dhangar) king.[5] These traditions cannot be completely dismissed as inventions, and it should be remembered that some of the greatest dynasties had their origin in a pastoral environment. Defending and rescuing cattle was a successful way to begin a dynasty. Such a feat would make the defender a hero and secure him prosperity—or, if he was killed in battle, bring renown to him and his descendants. Thus, according to a Jaina tradition, the first of the Yādavas of Devgiri, Dṛdhaprahāra, entered history by recapturing stolen cattle. The Brahmans and other residents of his city made him a guardian (*daṇḍanāyaka?*) of the city and recognized him as their ruler by paying a tax as tribute.[6]

According to Syed ul Hassan, the two principal groups of Gavḷīs are "Nagarkar" and "Vajarkar"; these accept cooked food from each other but do not intermarry.[7] Enthoven, who also lists "Nagarkar" and "Vajarkar" among the seventeen endogamous groups of Gavḷīs, conjectures that the designation "Nagarkar" derives from this group's former residence in *Ahmadnagar* (for which is sometimes used the short form, Nagar).[8] What is more likely is that both of the designations refer to the two groups' habitats and modes of life. Nagarkar Gavḷīs are those Gavḷīs who have settled as a pastoralist caste on the edges of villages or towns (*nagar*). Vajarkar Gavḷīs are pastoralist Gavḷīs who lived in forested areas with better grazing, and who still live in such areas today—in the Western Ghāṭs, for instance (see below under Mhaske Dhangars). *Vajar* is derived from Sanskrit *vraja,* a word that has been attested since the Ṛgveda.[9] It means a cattle-shed, a corral or paddock for cattle, or a "pasture"—like the one on the wooded bank of the Yamunā River, which eventually gave the name *Braj* to the region around Mathurā. *Vraja* is also a "settlement" of cowherds and cattle-breeders, who move out from it when there is a shortage of good pastures or of rain after the end of the monsoon. The word already appears in this sense in the Pāli canon: the monks spend the rainy season in the *vaja.* When the *vaja* is moved, the monks go to another *vaja.*[10] In contrast to *vaja,* the term *goṇisādiniviṭṭho gāmo* is used for an established village of cattle herders.[11]

---

5. See *Cārayugācī Bakhara,* Ms. 1799–1802, Madras Government Oriental Library, Madras.

6. See O. P. Verma, *The Yādavas and Their Times* (Nagpur, 1970), pp. 14f.

7. *The Castes and Tribes of H. E. H. The Nizam's Dominions* (Bombay, 1920), p. 196.

8. *The Castes and Tribes of the Bombay Presidency* (Bombay, 1921), vol. 1, p. 368.

9. Grassmann, *Wörterbuch zum Ṛgveda:* "a) Hürde, Stall (der Rinder, Pferde); b) Viehstand, Stall."

10. *Vinaya Pitaka,* I, p. 152. Cited by N. Wagle, *Society at the Time of the Buddha* (Bombay, 1966), p. 14.

11. *Vinaya Pitaka,* III, p. 46; *goṇisadika* ~ *goṇisadi* = *go* + *nisadi* + *nivittho. ni* + *sad* = to set down, settled, well organized. Cited by Wagle, *Society,* p. 14.

Like the distinction between "Nagarkar" and "Vajarkar," there is one in Karnatak and Telaṅgaṇa between Ūru Gollas (village Gollas) and Kāḍu Gollas (forest Gollas). The Ūru Gollas have become a pastoralist caste in the villages of Andhra Pradesh or on their borders, and have also taken up other occupations. They generally live in a specific part of the village.[12] They have legends about their glorious past and about a dynasty of Golla kings, and to this day they still claim a high rank in the caste hierarchy. Many Gollas have become shepherds, presumably because the expansion of agriculture and the reduction of pasture lands have made it impossible for big cattle-breeders, relatively independent of agriculture, to continue to support themselves. According to Iyer, the Kāḍu Gollas are scattered over the districts of Bangalore, Tumkur, and Chitaldurg.[13]

Buchanan visited the Gollas during his journey through Mysore at the beginning of the nineteenth century. His description of them and of their cattle-raising is of the greatest interest, and so I quote some of his observations:

> Their families live in small villages near the skirts of the woods, where they cultivate a little ground, and keep some of their cattle, selling in the towns the produce of the dairy. Their families are very numerous, seven to eight young men in each being common. Two or three of these attend the flocks in the woods, while the remainder cultivate their fields, and supply the towns with firewood, and with straw for thatch.[14]

Then Buchanan describes the two types of cattle in Karnatak. One type is brown or black and is kept in fixed settlements, primarily for milk; the other type, which is less tame, the Gollas keep in the woods, exclusively for breeding. The majority of the breeding herds belonged to rich residents of the villages, who employed the Gollas and who would send all their spare cows to the Golla forest settlements for breeding better oxen.

Some Gollas also, to be sure, were themselves wealthy, possessing something on the order of two hundred cows, thirty buffalo cows, fifty sheep, a hundred goats, and enough plow oxen to pull three plows. The Gollas lived in huts near small villages in areas where there was a good deal of undeveloped land. The huts were encircled by fences made of thorny branches. In them the Gollas kept as many animals as the pasture land of the village would permit. But when the rain failed and made grazing near the settlements difficult, some of the men would take the herds to other areas where there had been more

12. Cf. *Dravidian Etymological Dictionary,* 3347. Tamil, *pāṭam,* street of herdsmen.

13. Anantakrishna Iyer, *The Mysore Castes and Tribes,* vol. 3 (Mysore, 1930), p. 219.

14. Francis Hamilton Buchanan, *A Journey from Madras through the Countries of Mysore, Canara and Malabar* (London, 1807), vol. 2, p. 5.

rain. These men would live, then, near the huts of other Gollas, and let them have dung for their fields as recompense for the trouble to which they had been put. Alternatively, they would live in the woods at places where there were small reservoirs for watering their animals. On this migration all the breeding cattle and calves would be taken along, as well as all the sheep and goats. Only a few plow oxen and buffaloes would be left at home in the care of the women and of those men who were not needed to accompany the herds. During the whole period of their absence, the Gollas would never sleep in a hut; rather, they would lie among the herd inside the enclosure, wrapped in their blankets and accompanied by their dogs. All night long they would keep a fire going inside the corral to ward off tigers. But this was not always enough, and tigers would still break in on the herd. The Gollas had no firearms, but relied only on their shouts and on the barking of the dogs. They were also harassed by robbers, who would kill or carry off sheep or goats. The breeding bulls were dangerous, so enemies could not carry them off.[15]

A "settlement" or "camp" of Kāḍu Gollas was called a *haṭṭi*. According to Iyer,[16] the leader of a *haṭṭi,* called the *yajamān,*[17] settles disputes and serves as the priest (*pūjārī*) of the temple; and the deity manifests himself through him. He heals snake bites with medicines and by magic. If an epidemic breaks out or some other misfortune occurs, he arranges for the *haṭṭi* to be moved. He is assisted by a member of his own caste, called the *kōlkar,* and by a member of the Beda caste, called the *halemaga.* Meetings of the tribal council are held in the *pattemane,*[18] where such matters as violations of caste customs are investigated and penances are prescribed.

The details given by Iyer are important for us, because the remains of a similar tribal system are found among the Dhangars, as well as among the Nandīvālās and other pastoral castes of Maharashtra. Buchanan mentions "Jinjuppa" (*sic*) and "Ramuppa" (*sic*) as the Kāḍu Gollas' special gods, worshiped in small temples in the form of aniconic stones. Whereas Brahmans equated "Jinjuppa" with Lakṣmaṇ, the Gollas were not aware of this association. Buchanan mentions that the Kāḍu Gollas had as their guru a Śrī Vaiṣṇava, a Brahman, whose name and place of residence the Gollas did not know. This Brahman came every two or three years, and admonished them to wear the sign of Viṣṇu on their foreheads, and so on.

---

15. Ibid., pp. 10f.

16. Iyer, *Mysore,* vol. 3, p. 219.

17. Literally, in Sanskrit, a person who initiates a sacrifice and has it carried out, and who also bears the expense of the sacrifice; or generally a patron, host, guardian, or lord. In South Karnatak the *yejamāna* is the manager of the family group.

18. A house open on all four sides and used for assemblies.

According to Buchanan, the Gollas sacrificed animals in the forest to a god named Mutrāya. If an ascetic happened to be present, he would receive the head of the sacrificed animal, along with some bread. According to Iyer, the Junjappa mentioned by Buchanan is the chief god of the Kāḍu Gollas. He is a glorified cowherd, who is supposed to be a later incarnation of Kṛṣṇa.[19] Junjappa is supposed to have broken through his mother's back when he was born. This is reminiscent of the birth of Birobā, who was born from the side of his mother, Sūravantī.

The many endogamous groups into which the Gollas and Gavḷīs of Andhra Pradesh, Karnatak, and Maharashtra are divided have nothing more in common than the occupations that they still practice today or that they traditionally practiced in the past: breeding cattle and small livestock, trading in cattle, and selling milk and butter.[20]

Besides these occupations, the landscape has also made its mark on the Gollas/Gavḷīs and their religion. Thus when people who are traditionally farmers (Kuṇbī/Marāṭhās) migrate into areas characterized by pastures and still today only superficially affected by regular plow-based agriculture, they work primarily as cattle breeders. The fact that such immigrants can start as outsiders and come to be called Gavḷīs on the basis of the occupation they practice can lead to an endogamous subcaste of Gavḷīs being formed from an immigrant group of Kuṇbīs. The village of Mhasobāvāḍī, near Bārāmatī (Bārāmatī Taluka, Poona District), is still today a typical example of a village based on cattle-raising. Broad expanses of pasturage (approximately twenty-five hundred acres), far better than those in the true "famine tract" farther west, provide fodder for approximately fifteen hundred head of cattle and four thousand sheep. The god of the village is Mhasobā. His mount is considered to be a male buffalo (*reḍā,* not *mhaśā*). But in front of the *mukhavṭā,* the mask of the god, there is actually not a buffalo, but a small brass bull whose horns swing out toward the rear and then curve broadly forward like those of a Khilārī bull. The Khilārī breed is typical of this area.

Long ago the god is supposed to have come from "the Koṅkaṇ." This need not necessarily mean the coastal region beyond the Ghāṭs: given people's imprecise notions of geography, it could equally well be the region close to the Ghāṭs, on their near side, which is intended. Thus, for example, for unlettered residents of the area around Sāṅglī, the region of the Ghāṭs is "the Koṅkaṇ."

If one comes to the vicinity of these pastures, which stretch north from Bārāmatī and reach as far as Indāpūr and the Bhimā River (and thus belong to

19. Iyer, *Mysore,* vol. 3, p. 231.

20. See, for example, Enthoven, *Castes,* vol. 1, p. 368.

our north-south pastoral region), one is struck by the fact that not only cattle herders but also farmers live in huts fenced in by thorn hedges. At the same time, the size of the cattle herds increases the farther southeast one goes toward Paṇḍharpūr, Mhasvaḍ, Sāṅgoḷā, or Maṅgaḷveḍhā.

The village of Gavḷyāncī Undavḍī, near Bārāmatī, is another place where immigrants began to practice the same occupation as their predecessors. Here the immigrants were ready to take over their predecessors' caste designation. Initially the name of the village would lead one to suppose that it was a settlement of Gavḷīs. But village tradition holds otherwise:

Text 31

There used to be Kāsar Gavḷīs [Gavḷīs with brass pots] here. They all died of cholera. After that came the Bhosles [Bhosle is a typical Kuṇbī/Marāṭhā name]. They brought yoghurt (*dahī*) and milk to Śiṅgṇāpūr [the famous seat of Mahādev; see above, chap. 5, n. 57], and so they came to have the name Gavḷī. Before this time, the Gavḷīs had kept cows and buffalo cows, and had sold milk and yoghurt. After that came people with the name Bhosle. They carried on the same trade, and in this way they came to have the name Gavḷī. . . . The first Gavḷīs brought the god.

The adoption of not only the occupation but also the caste name of the predecessors can be ascribed to the relatively high caste rank of pastoralist groups, economically independent and not fully integrated into village society. Thus, on the plateau Dhangars are considered almost equal to Kuṇbīs/Marāṭhās—for example, Kuṇbīs accept cooked food from Dhangars. According to Syed ul Hassan, Gavḷīs in the districts of Marāṭhvāḍā had (or came to have) a higher rank than Kuṇbīs/Marāṭhās.[21] In the rice region (the Koṅkaṇ), Dhangars are considered to rank beneath Kuṇbīs—and, indeed, Dhangars accept cooked food from Kuṇbīs, but not vice versa. The Dhangars come to the Koṅkaṇ with the change of the seasons, and pen their sheep in the farmers' fields; although their relationships with the farmers are good and enduring, the Dhangars represent only a valuable supplement to agriculture. They are not of essential economic importance.

2. Kurubas

The Kurubas are an important element in the history of South India, and they also have considerable influence in southern Maharashtra. By tradition they

21. Syed Siraj ul Hassan, *Castes*, p. 199. The Gollas' high status is widespread in the Deccan. For example, see also *Madras District Gazetteer, Salem* (Madras, 1913), vol. 1, part 1, p. 171.

are shepherds—their name is popularly derived from *kuri,*[22] which means "sheep"—and thus they correspond to the Dhangars of Maharashtra. Today they are still shepherds as well as farmers and weavers of woolen blankets, but they are also engaged in other occupations. According to Buchanan, the Kurubas were shepherds, militiamen from the hills, armed vassals, or postmen.[23]

The Kurubas' religious ideas and practices correspond in important ways with those of the Dhangars, who will be discussed in detail below. Birobā/Birāppā is identified as having come from Karnatak and as speaking Kannaḍa. Viṭhobā/Iṭṭhal is also described as a Gavḷī from Karnatak. Birobā is found throughout Karnatak and Andhra Pradesh as an exclusively Kuruba god.[24] But Yeḷammā and Khaṇḍobā (Mailār, Mallanna) are also deities of the Kurubas and Dhangars. Khaṇḍobā/Mailār/Mallanna is supposed to have come originally from Ādimailār near Bīdar in Karnatak to Naḷdurg in Usmanabad District. Many of the Kannaḍa-speaking so-called Dhangars in Sholapur District could as easily be called Kurubas. The great festival in honor of Iṭṭhal/Birāppā in Paṭṭaṇ Kuḍolī brings together not only Bande Dhangars from Usmanabad District and Dhangars from villages near Kolhāpūr, but many Kurubas as well. "Heggaḍe," the name of Khaṇḍobā's minister, is the Kannaḍa designation of a caste or village leader, or (for example) of a priest to whom is entrusted the service of the god Birāppā.

The most striking division among the Kurubas, who are also divided into many subcastes, is that between Kāḍu Kurubas (jungle Kurubas) and Ūru Kurubas (Kurubas who live in villages or towns). The fact that the Kuṟavars of Caṅkam literature worship Murukaṉ and his Kuṟavar wife, Vaḷḷi, and that the Kurubas worship Mailār/Mallanna and his Kuruba wife, Kurubattyavva, lends some support to the supposition that the Kurubas are ethnically related to the Kuṟavars. Moreover, it is difficult to think of the name "Kuruba" as being ultimately a collective term lumping together as a caste with a number of endogamous subcastes different ethnic groups practicing the same occupation. To be sure, there are great social and religious differences between the Kurubas of the jungle—those in the Nilgiris, for instance—and the Kurubas of the Malnāḍ and Karnatak. But whereas the Kurubas or Kuṟumbas of the forest preserved their original condition or reverted to it, and are probably also to be associated racially with the original inhabitants, the Kurubas of the pastoral regions were exposed to many more new religious, social, and economic influences and have probably also mixed with other groups. In this way

22. *Dravidian Etymological Dictionary,* 1799. Kannaḍa, *kuṟi, koṟe;* Telugu, *goṟe, goṟṟe.*
23. Buchanan, *Journey,* vol. 1, p. 396.
24. Syed Siraj ul Hassan, *Castes,* p. 363, s.v. Kuruma. Iyer, *Mysore,* vol. 4, p. 54.

new groups of Kurubas have been formed. In addition, among Kurubas who live in the pastoral region—in Karnatak and Rāyalasīma, for instance—the division into Uṇṇikaṅkaṇ and Hattikaṅkaṇ Kurubas indicates rather a later cleavage of a group which was originally homogeneous. The two groups still accept food from each other, but they no longer intermarry.

In addition to the Uṇṇikaṅkaṇ and Hattikaṅkaṇ Kuruba castes, there is a third group, which calls itself (Hā-)Āṇḍe Kurubas. Together these make up the Ūru Kurubas. In Salem District, the (Hā-)Āṇḍe Kurubas claim a position higher than that of the other two castes; here the (Hā-)Āṇḍe Kurubas constituted an important component of the armies of Haidar Ali and the Ankusagari Poligārs, and the preferred title of their caste is Nāyaka. Nāyakas were military leaders who often became *ināmdārs*.[25]

The Uṇṇikaṅkaṇ and Hattikaṅkaṇ Dhangars in the vicinity of Paṭṭaṇ Kuḍolī in southern Maharashtra explain the origin of the two castes by the legend of a Dhangar who had extramarital relations with a demoness (*rakṣasī*) during his migration. The offspring of this union are the Uṇṇikaṅkaṇ Dhangars, whose position in the caste system is lower than that of the Hattikaṅkaṇ Dhangars. It is also believed that a younger brother, a shepherd, was cast out by his older brother, a farmer, because of the stench and dirt spread by the sheep. These notions suggest that a split took place wherein the contrast between farmers and herdsmen, agriculture and grazing, fixed settlements and nomadism (or transhumance), *kṣetra* and *vana,* played a role in the formation of the castes.

This contrast is already expressed in the names *uṇṇikaṅkaṇ* ("woolen bracelet") and *hattikaṅkaṇ* ("cotton bracelet"). Cotton is the symbol of the Kurubas who practice agriculture or even simply live in a fixed village, and wool is the symbol of the Kurubas and Dhangars who roam through the forest and dedicate themselves to the impure occupation of keeping sheep. Here I quote six versions of the legend of the origin of the Kurubas and of the division between Uṇṇikaṅkaṇ and Hattikaṅkaṇ Kurubas, showing how widespread this legend is.

Version 1

In Kolhāpūr, Revaṇa Siddheśvar killed the goddess Māyī, who held captive by her valor nine hundred thousand Siddhas or Liṅgāyat saints. And he freed them.[26] He commissioned one half of the saints to wander around begging for alms in his name. He could not think of anything to do with the other half, so he changed them into sheep, drove them into a hole in a field, and closed up the opening with a stone. The field belonged to a certain Padmaṇṇa and his brother. As Padmaṇṇa was plowing the field, his plow struck a rock, and when he

25. *Madras District Gazetteer,* vol. 1, part 1, p. 169.

26. Compare Text 18, above.

moved it away the sheep came out and surrounded him. He drove them into a nearby forest, and while he was grazing them he saw a beautiful girl who had been kept hidden there by an ogre. The girl wanted to marry him; she ran up and placed a garland around his neck. At that moment Śiva came and conducted the wedding ceremony. Because there was no cotton in the forest, wool was used for the bracelet.

And so there came into being the group of Uṇṇikaṅkaṇ Kurubas, who are considered descendants of Padmaṇṇa. The other group, that of the Hattikaṅkaṇ Kurubas, claims Padmaṇṇa's brother as their progenitor. At his wedding cotton bracelets were used.[27]

Version 2

Padma or Padmākhya was the ne'er-do-well son of a chief (*heggaḍe*) of the Vakkaliga caste.[28] His father kicked him out of the house so that he would earn his own living by farming. He was especially warned not to dig up anthills or to cut down a certain palāśa tree. But in his uselessness he did just that. When he dug up the anthill on which this tree stood, six kinds of sheep came out, bleating, and sought his protection. But he did not know what to do; and the prayer he directed to Śiva brought Bīre Devaru (Vīreśa), who became his guardian deity. He gave up cultivating the land and took up sheep-breeding as his occupation. They say that the Kāḍu Kurubas are the descendants of this man and his wife, a demoness (*rakṣasī*) who was the daughter of Hiḍimbā, and that the other group of Kurubas derive from his union with Sumālinī, the daughter of Sunandā.[29]

Version 3

Originally the Kurubas were Kāpus. Their ancestors were Masi Reddi and Nilamma, who lived on the eastern ghats by selling firewood, and had six sons. Taking pity on their poverty, Śiva came begging to their house in the disguise of a Jangam, and gave Nilamma some sacred ashes, while promising prosperity through the birth of another son, who was called Undala Padmanna. The family became prosperous through agriculture. But, unlike his six brothers, Undala Padmanna never went out to work in the fields. They accordingly contrived to get rid of him by asking him to set fire to some brushwood concealing a white-ant hill, in the hope that the snake within it would kill him. But, instead of a snake, an innumerable host of sheep appeared. Frightened at the sight of these strange black beasts, Undala Padmanna took to his heels. But Śiva appeared, and told him that they were created for his livelihood, and that he should rear them, and live by their milk. He taught him how to milk the sheep and boil the milk, and then sent him to a distant town which was occupied by Rākshasas (demons) to fetch fire. There the giants were keeping in bondage a Brahman

27. Summarized from Enthoven, *Castes,* vol. 2, p. 318.
28. A caste of farmers many of whom raise cattle.
29. Adapted from Iyer, *Mysore,* vol. 4 (1931), p. 28, s.v. Kuruba.

> girl, who fell in love with Undala Padmanna. They managed to escape from the clutches of the Rākshasas. . . . To save her lover, the girl transformed him into a lizard. She then went with him to the place where his flock was, and Undala Padmanna married a girl of his own caste, and had male offspring by her as well as the Brāhman. At the marriage of these sons, a thread *kankaṇam* (bracelet) was tied to the wrist of the caste woman's offspring, and a woolen *kankaṇam* to that of the Brahman girl's sons. . . . The latter are considered inferior, as they are of hybrid origin.[30]

The fourth version is reported by Syed ul Hassan.[31] The legend comes from Telaṅgaṇa, from the Kurumas, the caste of shepherds and woolen blanket weavers of this region.

Version 4

> Mallanna [identical with Khaṇḍobā of Maharashtra and Mailār of Karnatak] had two wives. One was Padmākṣī, a Kāpu girl, who was married in the usual way by having cotton bracelets tied to the wrists of the bridal couple. His other wife was Ratnāṅgī, the daughter of a Brahman woman who had been devoured by a demoness (*rakṣasī*). The demoness had raised the newborn child. One day as Mallanna was grazing his sheep in the jungle, he came close to the girl. He was so overwhelmed by the girl's beauty that he fell in love with her. He killed the demoness and married the girl, but the wedding bracelets were made of wool instead of cotton, which was not available in the forest. That is why wearing woolen bracelets distinguishes the descendants of Ratnāṅgī from those of Padmākṣī, who wear cotton bracelets.

The descendants of Padmākṣī presumably claim a higher rank in the caste hierarchy. But Syed ul Hassan[32] writes:

> He killed the demon and married the girl, but the wedding bracelets on this occasion were made of wool instead of cotton, which could not be procured in the jungle. Hence Mallanna's descendants by Ratnangi have been distinguished from those by Padmaksi by the name *unni* (wool) Kuruma and are said to hold a position superior to that of the latter.

This last statement is intriguing, for a hypogamous (*pratiloma*) marriage—in this case the marriage of a Kuruba man with a Brahman girl—can hardly lead to recognition of the union as fully legitimate, with the marriage with a woman of the same caste being given a lower rank. This is opposed to the prevailing testimony of the legend, as well as to reality. Even the wording, "Hence," seems to suggest that the author has erred. The basis on which the Uṇṇikaṅkaṇ caste is here given priority is not evident.

---

30. From the *Mysore Census Report,* 1901, cited by Iyer, *Mysore,* vol. 4, pp. 29f.
31. *Castes,* p. 363.
32. Ibid.

Version 5 comes from the *Hālumatada Caritra* cited above.[33] This *caritra,* which shows many parallels to the myths of the Dhangars and Liṅgāyats, is something between a precisely fixed historical tradition and a Purāṇa detached from time and place.

Version 5

Pārvatī formed a male figure out of earth mixed with milk from her right breast, and she formed a female figure out of earth mixed with milk from her left breast. Śiva gave life to the figures, and named them Muḍḍāppā and Muḍḍavvā; he married them to each other and told them to propagate themselves. Because they were born from milk, their descendants were called "those of the lineage of milk" (*hālumatada*). They had a son, Ādigoṇḍa ["the first Goṇḍa ~ Gauḍa"]. Ādigoṇḍa had six sons, of whom the youngest was called Padmagoṇḍa. From him derive the two groups of the lineage of milk: Hattikaṅkaṇ and Uṇṇikaṅkaṇ [chap. 2].

[Chap. 3 describes Pārvatī's creation of sheep and goats.] . . . Sadāśiva [Śiva] and Pārvatī thought it would be better to keep the sheep in a *haṭṭi,*[34] and for this purpose they went to see Ādigoṇḍa in Tammāpura, to ask him for a piece of land. Śiva went to the Gauḍa in the form of Revaṇasiddha, asked him for a piece of land measuring five *molas,* dug a hole in it, and shut the sheep up in the hole. He closed it up with Pārvatī's nose ring, which grew into a muttala plant [chap. 3].

Padmagoṇḍa frittered away his time, while his five elder brothers devoted themselves to household tasks. His idleness annoyed his brothers' wives, and he was forced to work. When he weeded the field, he removed the muttala plant as well. The sheep came out. Padmagoṇḍa was full of anxiety; he drove the sheep back into the hole, covered the opening with dry bushes, and set it on fire. Some of the sheep jumped out; they were black from the smoke. The ones that remained in the hole were reddish-brown. When the fire died out, all the sheep emerged and scattered all over. Padmagoṇḍa was very frightened. A Jaṅgama came and encouraged Padmagoṇḍa to follow the sheep and earn his living with them. . . .

One day Padmagoṇḍa could not find fire to heat the milk. As he was searching, he came upon the house of a demoness (*rakṣasī*). But only her daughter Cannavvā was at home. . . .

[There follows the story of the killing of the demoness, who before she died created wolves out of vengeance, then the account of Padmagoṇḍa's marriage to Cannavvā in the forest and the return home to Tammāpura. Chap. 7].

After returning to Tammāpura, Padmagoṇḍa let his sheep graze on the ancestral land. His brothers objected, and they refused him a portion of their father's land.

[His mother recognized him. . . .]

---

33. Ya. Ph. Attikoḷḷa, *Hālumatada Caritra* (Dharvāḍ, 1949). A versified version of this *caritra,* which certainly exists, could not be found.

34. An enclosure for cattle, corresponding to the *vāḍī* or *vāḍā* of the Dhangars.

Padmagoṇḍa brought Cannavvā and lived happily with her and his first wife, Siddavvā. When the father's land was divided, Padmagoṇḍa got only a house and some land for grazing his sheep. After a certain period of time, he divided his fortune into two equal parts and gave them to his two wives, each of whom had twenty sons and twenty daughters. When the daughters married, Siddavvā's daughters received cotton bracelets and Cannavvā's daughters received woolen ones.

[The names of the forty sons follow; chap. 8.] Chapter 9 describes the journey of the forty Kurubas with their herds of sheep to Kalyāṇa, where they had been invited by Basaveśvara, the minister of King Bijjala of the Kalacuri dynasty. After some time they returned, because the people there looked down on them on account of their sheep. Chapter 10 describes the Kurubas' return once again to Kalyāṇa at the request of Maruḷāsidda. By bringing back to life a dead Nandī bull—the bull is especially worshiped by Liṅgāyats—Maruḷāsidda won over the residents of Kalyāṇa, got the Kurubas admitted and settled there, and made it possible for them to sell milk and milk products.

The last version comes from Balapālapalle, south of Kurnool, in Kurnool District, Andhra Pradesh. The existence of this version shows how widespread among the Kurubas is the story of the youngest, shepherd son.[35]

Version 6

Ādireḍḍi and his wife Ādemmā were Kāpūs. They had seven sons. Their last son, Elenāgireḍḍi, was a son blessed with signs promising good fortune. As a village leader, he watched over seven villages [*reḍḍipani*]. His six elder brothers were jealous, and, in order to get rid of him, they asked him to get himself some oxen and to migrate to a region where they supposedly had a hundred acres of land. They said that he should cultivate this land. The site was north of Balapālapalle, near Śrīśailam in Kurnool District. The land was called Munnimodakamānu *puṭṭa* [termite mound], because there was a tree on it that was named Munnimodakamānu. It is said that Śiva had put a Brahma Rakṣasī in this tree. Because the land belonged to this ogre and she kept watch over her land, Elanāgireḍḍi's brothers believed that if the tree were cut down the ogre would fly into a passion and devour him. Elanāgireḍḍi suspected nothing of this scheme of his brothers', and he set out to cut down the tree with an axe weighing three *maunḍs*.[36] When the six demon children of the Brahma Rakṣasī rushed at him, Elanāgireḍḍi killed them.[37] The demoness went to Śiva and complained about the intruder and about the killing of her demon children. Śiva said to the demoness that the intruder was his chosen son (*varaputra*), and that from now on the place should belong to him.

Some time earlier, on Kailāsa, Pārvatī had asked Śiva for a sheep. Śiva

35. I am extremely grateful to Dr. M. L. K. Murty of the Department of Archaeology, Deccan College, Poona, who recorded this version in Balapālapalle at my request.

36. A weight of varying size: one *maunḍ* equals approximately 37 kilograms.

37. Cf. Text 7: the killing of Yeḷmakkaḷtāī.

created a sheep for Pārvatī. It reproduced itself quickly, and the sheep inundated Kailāsa and dirtied the gardens. Thereupon Śiva brought the sheep to Munimodakamānuchenu [the area characterized by the Munimodakamānu tree], dug a passage [to the *nāgalok*—that is, strictly speaking, the underworld, the world of snakes], drove all the sheep into it, and blocked the entrance with a stone slab.

Elanāgireḍḍi began to plow in this area, and as he was doing so he struck the slab of rock. Curious, Elanāgireḍḍi lifted the slab, and, to his astonishment, he heard the sheep. At that moment, Śiva appeared there and said that he should take care of the sheep and take them along with him. With the sheep following him, he should go to Kalyāṇapaṭṇam, somewhere in the west, but he should not look back, because if he did so the sheep would stop coming out of the passage. Last of all there appeared a golden sheep (*goṟṟe*) and a golden ram (*poṭṭelu*). Unfortunately, Elanāgireḍḍi looked back exactly at the instant when the golden sheep and the golden ram appeared. They fell back into the passage. Śiva ordered him to go to Kalyāṇapaṭṇam with the rest of the sheep. When Elanāgireḍḍi reached the edge of the town, the king refused to let him into the town. He and his sheep were seen as dirty. For twelve years, Elanāgireḍḍi had to lead a nomadic life with his sheep in the forest.

In Kalyāṇapaṭṇam everyone wore a *liṅgam,* and every object had a *liṅgam* tied to it. Even the cattle wore *liṅgams* on their horns. Every day Nandī (Basavaṇṇa) would come from Kailāsa to Kalyāṇapaṭṇam, and when he had been worshiped by the people, he would return to Kailāsa.

The legend goes on to narrate such subjects as the evolution of relations between the Kurubas and the Liṅgāyats, and the development of the name (or title) Bīradeva, which would be given to Elanāgireḍḍi (see below).

It is not yet known whether the Kurubas in this region cite a legend explaining the difference between Uṇṇikaṅkaṇ and Hattikaṅkaṇ Kurubas. It is certain that they make this distinction, and that the two groups do not intermarry. The Kurubas are spread over several villages and are frequently the numerically dominant group. In the village of Balapālapalle, for example, where Version 6 was recorded, 90 percent of the residents are Kurubas.

Almost all versions of the legend are based on the assumption that agriculture is the original and basic occupation of the ancestors, or of the parents or elder brothers of one of the ancestors. The Kurubas assume that their ancestors, or the parents or brothers of one of their ancestors, were really farmers (Version 1) or Vakkaligas (Version 2) or Kāpūs (Version 3), or that the members of one branch of the descendants were Kāpūs (Version 4), or at least that the members of one branch of the descendants are, although Kurubas, nevertheless farmers (Version 5). This places the Kurubas close to the Vakkaligas of Karnatak and the Reḍḍis of Telaṅgaṇa. Vakkaligas and Reḍḍis are the dominant farmers of the pastoral region; they hold the same rank in the caste system as Kurubas—that is, the two groups accept food from each other, and so on. At the end of the fifteenth century, during the time of the Vijayanagara empire and under its protection, the Vakkaligas seem to have settled, under the leadership of their Gauḍas, in areas that were still uninhabited.[38] Vakkaligas even call themselves the first settlers of Śolāpūr.[39] As with all agriculturalist castes in the pastoral region, cattle-raising is also important for the Vakkaligas and Reḍḍis.

The majority of Hattikaṅkaṇ Kurubas now dedicate themselves to farming and cattle-breeding, and many Uṇṇikaṅkaṇ Kurubas are also farmers; but both groups also own herds of sheep. It is usually the youngest son of the family who must take care of the sheep. This is probably the origin of the cleavage represented in the legends. In addition, it is primarily the younger male members of Kuruba groups living in fixed settlements who must drive their own family's or others' sheep over great distances and bring them back again. For the Dhangars from villages around Kolhāpūr, who differ from Kurubas only in name and language, transhumance begins with the start of the monsoon.[40] On all the roads leading east and northeast, herds of sheep are driven away from the moisture of the monsoon, which is harmful to the animals' hoofs and wool, into the drier part of Maharashtra. Thus, for example, Dhangars named Wāghmoḍe travel from the village of Vāśī (about ten miles from Kolhāpūr) to the neighborhood of Dhoṇḍ (Dhoṇḍ Taluka, Poona District), and return to Vāśī after three or four months. This group consists of about sixty Dhangars, with horses and about fifteen hundred sheep. On the way they pen the sheep in farmers' fields for the night, and they are paid for this fertilizer service in money or grain. At Sāsvaḍ, near Dive Ghāṭ (Purandar Taluka, Poona District), it is said that as recently as the British period the Mahārājā of Kolhāpūr allowed the armed Dhangars entrusted with herding his sheep to use rifles, when necessary, in order to intimidate farmers into letting the sheep graze on standing crops.

In the narratives, thc youngest brother—heroic, foolish, or "bad"—is generally connected with sheep, and travels around with them in the wilderness. Khilubā, the devotee (*bhakta*) of Iṭṭhal/Birāppā of Paṭṭaṇ Kuḍolī (see above, Text 8), who lives at the end of the migration route of the Dhangars from Kolhāpūr—in Āñjangāv (Māḍhā Taluka, Sholapur District)—is also the youngest of five brothers in a Dhangar Pāṭīl family. It is said of him, "Breed-

38. See Iyer, *Mysore,* vol. 4, pp. 22ff., s.v. Morasu Okkalu.

39. The work *Satyadarśan* (see above, chap. 5, n. 85), pp. 8f., refers to Kuḍuvakkaligas and calls them *śetkarī*—that is, farmers.

40. Here "transhumance" means the periodic driving of cattle to another region by some male members of the family group.

ing sheep is sweet to Khilubā.'' He is an imperturbable, even crazy (*veḍā*) adherent of Iṭṭhal and Birāppā.

The rejection of Elanāgireḍḍi according to the version from Balapālapalle and that of the forty Kurubas according to the *Hālumatada Caritra* suggest what it was that moved the Liṅgāyats not to accept the Kurubas: the Kurubas and their herds of sheep were impure. Moreover, the Liṅgāyats are strict vegetarians, and sheep sacrifices and meat-eating are opposed to their customs. The legend from Balapālapalle continues:

> From Kailāsa, Śiva observed that Elanāgireḍḍi, his *varaputra,* spent twelve years leading a life of privation, wandering in the forest with his sheep. Śiva felt compassion for him and decided that Elanāgireḍḍi should be accepted in Kalyāṇapaṭṇam so that he could live a comfortable life there. Śiva hit upon an idea: he let one of the sheep die. At the same time, the Nandī in Kalyāṇapaṭṇam, who was fervently worshiped, died. The king and the Liṅgāyats were deeply dismayed and distressed, and they began to sing prayers to bring him back to life again.
>
> As soon as the sheep died, Śiva appeared and commissioned Elanāgireḍḍi to go to Kalyāṇapaṭṇam and sell the sheep's wool and meat. Elanāgireḍḍi and his seven sons carried the dead sheep to Kalyāṇapaṭṇam. The residents again refused to admit them, and so much the less would they buy the meat and wool from them. To do this would have been opposed to their traditional practice.
>
> Then Elanāgireḍḍi took the dead sheep to a pond at the edge of the town of Kalyāṇapaṭṇam and laid the dead animal on a funeral pyre. The stench and smoke from the funeral pyre spread through the town, while the citizens were devoting themselves to singing and dancing in order to please Śiva, trying to persuade him to bring the Nandī back to life. They were angry that Elanāgireḍḍi had chosen such an inauspicious moment, and they wanted him to tell them the reason. Elanāgireḍḍi did not allow himself to get upset, and he asserted—because they were trying in vain to bring the bull back to life—that he could revive his sheep. The condition was that they must accept whatever meat and wool he would offer them. The residents of Kalyāṇapaṭṇam attempted in vain to revive the Nandī with their urgent prayers and their most beautiful songs and dances. When they finally tired of their efforts, they asked Elanāgireḍḍi to try his luck with the sheep.
>
> Elanāgireḍḍi took what was left of the sheep from the funeral pyre and was about to cut it into pieces. To do that, he needed a board as a support. But the people of Kalyāṇapaṭṇam pointed out to him that each object in the town had a *liṅgam* attached to it, and that therefore he could not have anything, for whatever they gave him would become impure. He asked them to open the main gate of the town and to take away the *liṅgam* mounted on it, so that he could use the door as a plank. Finally they agreed. Elanāgireḍḍi cut the sheep into pieces, put the pieces into a large pot, and began to cook them. Śiva, who was watching this from Kailāsa, sent Revaṇa Siddheśvar down to Kalyāṇapaṭṇam to help

Elanāgireḍḍi with his undertaking. At the crossroads leading toward Kalyāṇapaṭṇam, he asked for turmeric powder and *kuṅkum* [turmeric powder colored red]. But it turned out that only diamonds (*vajra*) and lapis lazuli stones (*vaidūrya*) were to be found in the shops there. Even so, he asked the merchants for turmeric and *kuṅkum,* and when they said no, he asked them to look into their pouches. When they finally, reluctantly, did this, they found, to their surprise and dismay, that the pouches they had filled with diamonds and lapis lazuli stones now held turmeric powder and *kuṅkum.* They asked Revaṇa Siddha to excuse them for their mistake. He had them give him a little turmeric powder and *kuṅkum,* and in return he gave them back the diamonds and lapis lazuli stones.

When Elanāgireḍḍi saw Revaṇa Siddheśvar coming, he fell down as stiff as a stick and then raised himself from the ground high into the air. He asked Revaṇa Siddheśvar to sit down on his breast [?]. Revaṇa did so. The seven sons of Elanāgireḍḍi began to beat drums, dance, and pray. Revaṇa sprinkled turmeric powder and *kuṅkum* into the pot. Because of the prayers, and because of the sound of the musical instruments, and because Revaṇa threw turmeric powder and *kuṅkum* into the pot, the pieces of the ram fitted themselves together again, and it came to life. The ram jumped out of the pot and ran amuck in Kalyāṇapaṭṇam. The residents of the town could not bring it under control, because it was endowed with divine power. Even the king took refuge on a conical rock (*suḍiguṇḍu ray*). The ram ran at the rock, making it totter. Then the king asked Elanāgireḍḍi to bring the ram under control; the king promised that he and his subjects would accept the meat and woolen blankets that Elanāgireḍḍi offered them, and that they would follow Elanāgireḍḍi's traditions. But Elanāgireḍḍi was not able to control the ram; only Revaṇa could do that. Revaṇa took his golden staff and bent the ram's horns toward the back; the ram died. (Since then, rams' horns have been curved toward the back.)

Most of the residents of Kalyāṇapaṭṇam were now convinced of Elanāgireḍḍi's greatness; they threw the *liṅgas* into the water and adopted Elanāgireḍḍi's way of life—for example, they now eat meat. Some residents, who were not inclined to go along with the new way of life, emigrated to Śrīśailam, the pilgrimage place dedicated to Mallikārjuna. People believe that the present-day Liṅgāyats are the descendants of these emigrés.

The story of Elanāgireḍḍi gives expression to the contrast between the religious conceptions of the Liṅgāyats and the magical power of Elanāgireḍḍi, who comes from the pasture and forest region. The Liṅgāyats worship Śiva with prayer and dance. This simple method of worship does not allow for the iconographic representation of Śiva, and—according to the strict version of the teachings—does not even allow for the worship of a *liṅgam* in a temple. The religion of Elanāgireḍḍi and his guru Revaṇa is entirely devoted to magic. Revaṇa cannot get along without turmeric powder and *kuṅkum.* Dance plays an important role, and the full significance of the magical power of the drums beaten by Elanāgireḍḍi's seven sons can be fully measured only when one experiences them as an essential component in the Dhangars' and Kurubas' worship of deities. The god takes possession of his devotee (*bhakta*) in the rhythm of the drums. With the help of drums and the use of huge quantities of turmeric powder, the god speaks through those he has possessed. People even go so far as to equate the magically powerful *bhaṇḍār* (turmeric powder) with Birobā and Khaṇḍobā.

In Paṭṭaṇ Kuḍolī and in Vīr, a *śīd* (*siddha*) hits himself with a sword—in a good many other places (for instance, Gāykvāḍvāḍī, in Havelī Taluka, Poona District), with a stick—in order to compel the god to possess him. Of Sūryabā, Birobā's devotee (*bhakta*) in Ārevāḍī, it is said:

Text 32

. . . He took the sword and "played" with it, and they intentionally played the drums out of tune. When they played out of tune, he hurt himself. When he hurt himself, he fell to the ground and his life (*prāṇ*) escaped him. . . .

So it is not surprising that many Liṅgāyats, who often came from Kuruba families, and among whom there were many groups not completely assimilated to the strict version of the teachings, allowed themselves to be convinced by the deified spirits of the forest and the pasture region. Kalyāṇapaṭṇam becomes almost the prototype of a town in which Kurubas, Dhangars, or other pastoralist and nomadic groups who want to settle there must come to terms with a resident Liṅgāyat population.

The case of Paṭṭaṇ Kuḍolī is similar to that of Kalyāṇapaṭṇam. In the course of their wanderings, Iṭṭhal and Birāppā came from the east to Paṭṭaṇ Kuḍolī. Previously the two Dhangar gods had met at the Varṇā River; this is the event with which the following narrative starts:

Text 33

. . . There they became brothers. And they traveled all around the world on horseback, and where did they end up? Near Kolhāpūr. They came to the village Kaḍulī (= Kuḍolī), Kaḍulī Paṭṭaṇ, the "resting place[41] of deer and cows." They rode to the high Toraṇ pasture (*māḷ*). And when they got there, they liked the place. And the gods sat down there in the tamarind[42] grove. In the neighborhood there lived a god named Kalīśā.[43] The god was a Liṅgāyat. His temple was also there. In the early morning they got up quickly. "Good," they said, "we'll stay here, that's right. But won't we want to have someone as a servant?" [The narrator addresses himself to his two listeners:] Suppose, if you

41. *Goṭhān,* "a shady spot near a village whither the pasturing herds resort at noon and rest" (Molesworth, *Dictionary*).

42. *Cinc; Tamarindus Indica.*

43. Kalīśā/Kalleśvar, identical with Śiva.

two are *puḍhārīs,*[44] then you need someone like me to see to your affairs, don't you?

For this reason they took some dirt from their neck and formed a figure out of it; they dripped nectar (*amṛt*) onto the figure and brought it to life. And they gave it the name Somā Mahāldār and the epithet "Ocean of Wisdom."[45] They said to him: "Go in the early morning to Kalīśā's temple. Greet Kalīśā with the words "Rām, Rām." As soon as you arrive, he will offer you a seat. Then say, 'I won't sit on a seat (*gādī*) of dharma; I want a seat of *hukm* (*sic*).'[46] Speak to him this way." So he went. He went, the servant they had created to do the work assigned to him. As soon as he arrived there, Kalīśā told him to sit down in front of him. But Somā Mahāldār said, "I won't sit there."

"Why not?"

"I want a seat of *hukm* on the highland pasture of Kaḍulī. I don't want this seat of dharma."

"Crazy sir,"[47] said he, "that god belongs to the Dhangars. He will have a hundred or five hundred drums resound before you. Sheep will be sacrificed before you. And I, your god, am a Liṅgāyat. I cannot tolerate this wild uproar, and the drums will burst my eardrums. That won't do."

So he returned and told this to Iṭṭhal and Birāppā. They said, "What's to be done now? Go and say that even if five hundred drums are played in front of my door you won't hear it. If they sacrifice sheep before me I won't allow even a single drop of blood to be seen."

Somā Mahāldār returned and said this. Kalīśā answered: "Well, I will give you a place, but in the village I am Kalīśā, the god of the Liṅgāyats. Go, in the village are the *puḍhārīs* Narubā Gāvḍā, Liṅguśā Pāṭīl, and Jakāppā Caughule. Go and ask them for a place in the village."

When Kalīśā had said this, Somā Mahāldar left. Still to this day he goes to Kaḍulī [and asks the *puḍhārīs*]. In the middle is a wall.[48] And on this side a

---

44. A *puḍhārī* is a leader, one who assumes leadership or provides an example; also, a leader of a caste, a village, or a Dhangar *vāḍī*, etc.

45. One of Somā M(ah)āldār's descendants had no sons. His daughter was married into the family of the Khaṭāvkars in Candūr (five miles from Paṭṭaṇ Kuḍolī). Nowadays one of the descendants has the right of worship (*mān*) there. His tasks include assembling the articles needed for the procession (*pālkhī*), helping at the conclusion of the procession, sending invitations to everyone connected with the cult and the pilgrimage festival, aiding the *pūjārīs,* and so on. By caste the descendants are Śimpīs (tailors).

According to Molesworth, *Dictionary,* a M(ah)āldār is a "revenue officer in charge of a Mahāl" and the term is sometimes confused with Bhāldār, "an attendant on great men who waits with a wand in his hand, an usher."

46. One offers a guest a seat of dharma out of politeness and courtesy, but he is not invited to stay for a long time; by contrast, the seat of *hukūm* guarantees a long-lasting right. See Text 23.

47. *Girastā,* from *gṛhastha* in Sanskrit and written Marāṭhī.

48. That is, directly to the right, between the present-day temple of Iṭṭhal/Birāppā and the temple of Kalīśā. The wall is a part of the compound wall around the present-day temple of Iṭṭhal/Birāppā. The two temples are about 200 meters apart.

hundred or five hundred drums resound. I [the narrator] myself have sat in [Kalīśā's] temple, and not even the slightest sound has reached my ear. And when you come out, you see a big cloud of dust [or rather: clouds of *bhaṇḍār*] and you hear a stupendous noise [that of the drums]. . . . That happens on the Bhūmi Pūrṇimā day, between Divāḷī and Dasarā. There is a big pilgrimage then.[49]

They sacrifice sheep and carry them away, and not once does a drop of blood remain on the ground. Still today, too. Not a trace of a drop of blood remains.[50]

Now Iṭṭhal and Birāppā said again to Somā Mahāldār, "Go and ask the *puḍhārīs* in the village." He went to the village. The leaders of the village, Jakāppā Caughule and Liṅguśā Pāṭīl, were sitting on a platform (*pār*) at the foot of the village tree. When Somā arrived, they asked, "Who are you? Where do you come from?"

"We[51] come from Khān-Māṇ Deś.[52] We are gods from Māṇ Deś, Iṭṭhal and Birāppā. And we should be given a place on the highland pasture of Kaḍulī."

[The *puḍhārīs* speak to the gods through Somā Mahāldār:] "The Dhangar god is someone great, and he says, 'Give me a place.' You are a god, aren't you? Good. This pipaḷ tree in front of the village hall has been dried up for twelve years now. When leaves break out on it, I will know that he's a god. And I will give him as much space as he wants."

Somā Mahāldār went back immediately to convey the message: "The *puḍhārīs* said so-and-so." And what did the gods do, Iṭṭhal and Birāppā? They threw turmeric powder with fourteen magical powers [*caudā idyācā bhaṇḍārā*].[53] He threw at the tree the *bhaṇḍār* that has fourteen magical powers. Out of the dried-up pipaḷ tree there grew a fresh green pipaḷ tree. In the early morning—the *puḍhārīs* had slept in the village hall—they got up and chewed tobacco, and as they got up the pipaḷ tree began to crack: *phāḍ, phāḍ, phāḍ, phāḍ*. What's cracking outside there today?" they said, and they bent over and looked out at an angle from the hall. Green leaves had sprouted from the pipaḷ tree.

"Why, yesterday someone came and said to us that leaves would sprout on this pipaḷ tree. What he said is true." Because it was now daylight, he [Somā

---

49. In his enthusiasm, the narrator, a Dhangar and a *convinced* devotee of Iṭṭhal and Birāppā, repeats three more times his experience in Kalīśā's temple.

50. When I visited the pilgrimage in 1970, I learned that the sheep sacrifices had been brought to a complete halt several years earlier.

51. Somā, who is speaking for the gods, even uses the plural form, "we."

52. The region around Mhasvaḍ and Āṭpāḍī, the valley of the Māṇ River.

53. For Brahmans, the fourteen *vidyās—the bhaṇḍār*'s "magical powers"—are the fourteen fields of the sciences—namely, the four Vedas, the six Vedāṅgas (1. *śikṣā*—the science of correct pronunciation, 2. *candas*—prosody, 3. *vyākaraṇa*—grammar, 4. *nirukta*—explanation of difficult Vedic words, 5. *jyotiṣa*—astronomy, 6. *kalpa*—"ritual"), the eighteen Purāṇas, Mīmāṃsā, Nyāya, and Dharma. For this Dhangar, *bhaṇḍār* is almost personified, and contains fourteen magical powers. (Monier-Williams, *Dictionary,* s.v. *vidyā,* also "a spell, incantation, magical skill, a kind of magical pill.")

Mahāldār, who had said this] came now too. "All right, then, leaves have now appeared on the tree, as you asked. So at least now give us a place."

"Go away," they said. "You do some magic and then you want something. Do you think that if we gave space to everyone who does some trick, the people of the village would have made us *puḍhārīs?*"

So they got angry with him and drove him away. He went immediately to Iṭṭhal/Birāppā and made his report. The god said, "They won't listen. What are they saying then? That I will come, use a magic trick, and get myself a place in the village. That won't do!" So then Iṭṭhal/Birāppā, the gods from Karnatak, threw the fourteenfold powerful *bhaṇḍār* and made all the residents blind. Big and little, good and bad—all became blind. Only Liṅguśā Pāṭīl had one eye left. When Liṅguśā Pāṭīl got up in the early morning, he could not see out of one eye, and he could see out of the other eye. Everyone else was wandering around lost in the village. They were standing up and falling down. No one could see. "What's to be done now?" [said Liṅguśā Pāṭīl]. "Someone hit on the idea that now suddenly I am the *puḍhārī* of the village; the responsibility for the whole village rests on me."

Then in the early morning, Iṭṭhal/Birāppā said to Somā Mahāldār: "Go and declare yourself to be a nose-and-eye doctor [*sic! nākā-doḷyācem vaid*]. Then Somā went into the village and said, "I am a nose-and-eye doctor." Liṅguśā Pāṭīl said, "It's lucky that you've come. The whole village has gone blind. Give us back our sight."

"All right, I'll give you your sight, but what will you give me?"

"I'll give you whatever you ask for."

"If I give your village back its sight, then give me a place in the village three and a half times the size of the stick in my hand."

"All right, why not?"

"But it won't be as simple as that. All the residents must come to the highland pasture of Kaḍulī with a coconut as an offering (*nivad,* written naivedya). I am really just the compounder.[54] The doctors are there."

"All right, but how can we get there?"

"I'll give [everyone] one eye until we reach there."

That's what the god's play (*līlā*) was like. He did something, and they could see out of one eye. So all the people of the village took coconuts and went singing and dancing to the highland pasture of Kaḍulī. When they had arrived there, Liṅguśā Pāṭīl said, placing his hands together in greeting, "All my people in the village have gone blind. Take whatever you want, O god, but give my people their sight."

At that time, the gods said, "Give me a place on the highland pasture of Kaḍulī. The place should be three and a half times the size of this stick. I want nothing else."

---

54. Marāṭhī, *kampaunḍar,* from English "compounder," a clerk in a doctor's anteroom who mixes the medicines and sells them. The narrator is recalling here his own trips to an ear, nose, and throat doctor, whom he had to visit many times because his hearing deteriorated after a bout of typhus.

"Why should this not be? It's given to you." Then the Pāṭīl of the village said, "Measure out the place with this staff." He gave Jakāppā Caughule the stick the god had in his hand, to have him measure off the land. The play of the god—he gave the rule for measuring! When a piece three times that size had been measured off, it extended over half the area of the village. What did Jakāppā do then? He wanted to keep back the half measure, and he counted: ". . . three-and-a-half!" But the god realized this and said, "You have not done right," and he cursed him: "Wherever there is a family of Caughules, they are to be looked down upon. You have acted like a swindler and done harm to my interests. So from this day on, people will have a low opinion of your descendants." In this way the gods cursed him at that time.

Now the gods were staying on the highland pasture of Kaḍulī. Jakāppā, what happened to him? He had seven cows that had been barren for the past twelve years. They couldn't get pregnant, nor could they bear calves—nothing! They were just seven barren cows. "Good," he said, "if the seven cows bear calves, I will set the seventh cow's calf free for you. And I will yoke the seven calves to the cart, bring wood, build your temple, and drive around your temple in the cart." He made this vow (*navas*). The play of the god—the seven cows became pregnant. They gave birth to seven calves. Three days passed. Then Jakāppā yoked them to the cart. He offered coconuts as *naivedya*. In the Satya Age, Jakāppā Caughule yoked three-day-old calves to the cart. "Why shouldn't three-year-old oxen be yoked to the cart?" they thought.[55] But he yoked three-day-old calves to it. And the seventh he let go. And now he wanted to build the temple. . . . [See Text 7.]

The narrator of this legend does not himself come from Paṭṭaṇ Kuḍolī. He is a priest (*pūjārī*) of a Birobā temple in Kuṇḍal (Tāsgāv Taluka, Sangli District), and he comes to the Paṭṭaṇ Kuḍolī pilgrimage almost every year. But this legend of the arrival of the Dhangars and their gods in Paṭṭaṇ Kuḍolī is in its essentials the common property of all the groups in this village.

An interesting variant comes from the Muslims. They say that the present temple of Iṭṭhal and Birāppā arose from the shrine (*dargā*) of a Muslim saint. Iṭṭhal and Birāppā asked him for permission to settle in his place of residence. The Muslim "god" (*sic*) was afraid that the drums would disturb his peace. So he allowed Iṭṭhal/Birāppā to settle there, and he himself moved out to Rūī (approximately one mile outside of Paṭṭaṇ Kuḍolī). When he left, the great vaḍ tree (*Ficus Indica*) in front of the temple—near which the gods' procession (*pālkhī*) stops—caught fire. The typical Muslim gravestone (*madār*) which is found today in the temple of Iṭṭhal/Birāppā and which is described as the seat (*gādī*) of Bhāgulek, the daughter of Iṭṭhal and Padubāī, appears to

55. Perhaps because in the Satya Age three days were like three years, or because the god changed three-day-old calves into three-year-old oxen.

confirm the Muslim origin of the temple. Furthermore, the actual shrine of Birāppā and Iṭṭhal, onto which a modern structure has been added (as a temple hall), looks like a small mosque. Many signs point to an earlier correspondence between Birobā (from *vīr,* hero) and *pīr* (Muslim saint). For example, in the year 1610 the gravestone of a Muslim *pīr* in Masur (Karhāḍ Taluka, Satara District) was worshiped by Hindus as Vīr.[56]

In Paṭṭaṇ Kuḍolī there live Jainas, Brahmans, Marāṭhās, Muslims, Kaikāḍīs (basket-weavers), Mahārs, and Māṅgs, but especially Dhangars and Liṅgāyats. Dhangars and Liṅgāyats are the dominant groups of the village. The group of Liṅgāyats is composed of actual Liṅgāyats, of Tirāḷes, and of members of Liṅgāyat artisan castes such as Śimpīs (tailors) and Sutārs (carpenters). All are connected with the cycle of legends of the Dhangar gods of Paṭṭaṇ Kuḍolī, and have a fixed function (that is, are *mānkarīs*) in the ritual of the annual pilgrimage festival.

The Brahmans are an exception, but nevertheless a Brahman has composed a work in Marāṭhī in praise of the Dhangar gods. The style and contents of this unpublished manuscript (*pothī*) are detached from the concrete background of the place. For example, "Kuḍolī" is connected with the *ṛṣi* "Kauṇḍiṇya" on the basis of a superficial phonological similarity.

The residents of the village accepted the new gods. To be sure, they continued to worship their own gods and to follow their own religious customs. But the annual pilgrimage festival unites all the groups, including the Liṅgāyat Pāṭīl Rāygoṇḍa, whose forefathers built parts of the Dhangar temple. The older Kalleśvar [Kalīśā], the god of the Liṅgāyats, occupies an old, venerable temple in the Hemāḍ-Pant style, but this temple seems deserted in comparison with the bustle in the Dhangar temple.

The fact that sheep are not sacrificed to Iṭṭhal and Birāppā today is to be ascribed to the influence of the Liṅgāyats—or, according to the legend, to the influence of the Liṅgāyat god Kalleśvar. The Liṅgāyat influence is so great, especially in Karnatak and in the parts of southern Maharashtra influenced by Karnatak, that many Dhangars or Kurubas call Birobā a Liṅgāyat—as, for example, in Hunnūr in Maṅgaḷveḍhā Taluka (Sholapur District). Here the almost aniconic *mūrti* of Birobā wears the Liṅgāyats' amulet, which contains a *liṅgam.* The Hāṇḍe Kurubas mentioned above are an example of a group who gave up eating meat and even changed their occupation. From sheepbreeders, they became weavers of woolen blankets (*kāmbḷīs*).[57]

---

56. Viśvanātha Kāśīnātha Rājavāḍe, *Marāṭhyāṃcyā itihāsācīṃ sādhaneṃ* (Bombay, 1912), vol. 15, p. 6. *Bombay Law Reporter,* vol. 15 (1913), *Journal,* pp. 97–108. See also Molesworth, *Dictionary: vīr-pīr,* "a term . . . for a man of daring and energy."

57. Enthoven, *Castes,* vol. 2, p. 319.

Another group of Kurubas are the Oḍeru, who are priests of Birobā and, in the neighborhood of Bijāpūr, gurus of the Kurubas. They avoid eating meat and they wear the *liṅgam,* and to that extent they resemble the Liṅgāyats' Jaṅgamas. The influence of the Liṅgāyats led one informant to make the following comment:

Text 34

The dharma of the Dhangars is Liṅgāyat—but what happened! Keeping sheep is our dharma, and eating sheep became our fate. We still have some Liṅgāyats. They are called *vaḍaḍ*.[58] They do not allow us to touch them. "You eat," they say, "sheep." They wear the *liṅgam* around their neck. "By eating sheep you have drowned the dharma." Our dharma is Liṅgāyat.[59]

3. Dhangars

3.1 The Groups of Dhangars

The number of endogamous groups of Dhangars listed by Enthoven is certainly not exhaustive, nor, surely, is the number of exogamous groups identified by their last names. In the focal area of my research, the principal endogamous groups are the Saṇgars, who weave large woolen blankets (*ghoṅgaḍīs*); the Mhaskars (or Mhaskes), who own buffaloes and cows; and the Khuṭekars, who also make woolen blankets. I encountered Saṇgars principally in Māṇ Taluka (Satara District) and in Khānapūr and Jath talukas (Sangli District). The Mhaskars or Mhaskes are found in the western part of Satara District—in the forests of the Koynā valley, for example.

Gavḷīs are often also called Dhangars. Gavḷī Dhangars are for the most part identical with the groups that primarily keep buffalo cows. According to several concurring accounts from the Nirā and Māṇ valleys, the Gavḷī Dhangars and the Meṇḍhe (shepherd) Dhangars are understood to have formerly constituted a single endogamous group. The division into two endogamous groups is explained as follows by a Hāṭkar Meṇḍhe Dhangar from Jāvḷī, Phalṭaṇ Taluka:

Text 35

In the past there was no difference between Meṇḍhe Dhangars and Gavḷī Dhangars. They were the same. In the past, a Meṇḍhe Dhangar once went to the Gavḷī Dhangars in order to enter into a marriage alliance with them. He sat down in their house. A buffalo calf of theirs had died. They had removed the hide and hung it up to dry, and they were planning to sell it after it had dried.

58. Probably Kannaḍa, *(v)oḍeru.*

59. From Kuṇḍal (Tāsgāv Taluka, Sangli District).

A Vāghyā (a mendicant dedicated to the god Khaṇḍobā) from the Dhangar caste. Over his shoulder are a blanket and a chain, at his side a pouch for turmeric powder, and in his hands a "spear" and a begging bowl.

A Dhangar as a medium (*devṛṣī*) of the god Khaṇḍobā (or Bāvanvīr) making predictions during a pilgrimage festival (Muḷśī, Muḷśī Taluka, Poona District).

Dhangar women.

A Dhangar from *vāḍī* B.

A young Dhangar bridegroom.

An ancestor relief in front of the temple of the god Dhuḷobā near Phalṭaṇ (Phalṭaṇ Taluka, Poona District).

Ancestor stones in front of a Birobā temple near Wāī (Satara District). The reliefs resemble images of Khaṇḍobā and Mhāḷsā with a horse and a dog.

Khaṇḍobā of Jejurī. In the rear, Mārtaṇḍa Bhairava. In the middle row, standing images of Khaṇḍobā and Mhāḷsā donated by Marāṭhā princes. In front, a dark semicircular stone (*svayaṃbhū liṅga*); behind it, to the left, the silver mask (*mukhavṭā*) that serves as a cover for the *svayaṃbhū liṅga*.

An ancestor stone at Dhuḷobā's temple. The ancestor has been fed a *capātī* and rice during a pilgrimage festival.

Khaṇḍobā and Bāṇāī. In front of Bāṇāī's temple in Jejurī (about 80 centimeters high).

Khaṇḍobā and Mhāḷsā. A form for stamping (hence reversed) small silver plaques, which are mainly used for the worship of gods and ancestors in household shrines. Notice the dog and, below right, a woman (Bāṇāī?).

An ancestor stone, modeled after representations of Khaṇḍobā and Mhāḷsā. The dead couple are absorbed into Khaṇḍobā and Mhāḷsā.

Mhaskobā. A form for making small silver plaques, which are used for worshiping the god. Original, 4.2 by 3.6 centimeters.

Palanquins (*pālkhyā*), parasols (*chatryā*), and yak-tail fans (*cavryā*) during the pilgrimage festival for Mhaskobā in Vīr.

Khaṇḍobā and his devotees (*bhaktas*), probably the Peśvā, Hoḷkar (standing), Śinde (standing), and a Gosāvī with a cap that covers his ears. From *Śrī-Māṇika-prabhu-kṛta sacitra Malhārī Māhātmya* (Beḷagāṃva, 1917).

The Khaṇḍobā temple at Jejurī.

Birobā of Kātecīvāḍī (Bārāmatī Taluka, Poona District). In the foreground, masks of Dhangar ancestors.

Bhairav and Jogeśvarī/Jogāī in the temple at Nāygāv in the Karhā valley (Purandar Taluka, Poona District). The stone is covered with red lead, and the shape of the original *mūrti* is no longer recognizable. The bulges of the original *mūrti* are covered with silver masks.

Bhairav (Vandev) and Yogeśvarī/Jogāī hunting (Mūrti Moḍhve, Purandar Taluka, Poona District).

Kāḷbhairav in the attire of a Marāṭhā *sardār* (Biḷūr, Jath Taluka, Sangli District).

A *ṭāk* (a form for stamping small silver plaques) of Viṭhobā and Rukmiṇī of Paṇḍharpūr (reversed). Original, 3.2 by 4.5 centimeters.

A representation of Māyavvā and Birobā in Ārevāḍī (Miraj Taluka, Sangli District).

A Mhasobā shrine of fired clay resembling a yurt. The "smoke hole" is covered with a stone. Notice the raised seams, the sun and the moon, and the trident (*triśūl*).

A modified shrine at the entrance to a house in Mhasvaḍ (Khaṭāv Taluka, Sātārā District), with a basil (*tulśī*) plant and Mārutī (Hanumān) over the shrine.

Here a Mhasobā shrine (yurt) serves as the pinnacle (*śikhar*) of a temple of Mhasobā in Loṭevāḍī.

From the "smoke hole" appears the anthropomorphic head of Mhasobā as the guardian of the field.

Potrāj ("The King of the Buffalo").

The mask (*mukhavṭā*) of the god Birobā of Hunnūr (Maṅgaḷveḍhā Taluka, Sholapur District) during the pilgrimage festival at Huḷjantī.

A *mūrti* of Durgāmahiṣāsuramardinī, here the goddess Yamāī in Śivare (Purandar Taluka, Poona District).

A typical Aṣṭabhairav temple (Sonārī, Purandar Taluka, Poona District).

Mhasvaḍ-Śīd (Mhasvaḍ, Khaṭāv Taluka, Sāt-ārā District).

The five *vāhanas* of the god Mahādev of Śiṅgṇāpūr. The temple lies in an old cattle herding region.

The lowest relief of a hero stone, showing the hero defending cows (Yādava period).

Hero stones at Nāygāv-Peṭh (Havelī Taluka, Poona District): most of the stones commemorate the defense of cattle (Yādava period).

Detail of a hero stone: the cattle stand over the fallen hero (Mūrti Moḍhve, Purandar Taluka, Poona District).

Temple of Satobā-Birobā (who comes from Paṅgrī, Dahīvāḍī Taluka, Sātārā District) near Śiṅgṇāpūr.

A Dhangar shrine and the Dhangars' huts during the monsoon stay in the Deś (Algujdarā, "The Valley of the Flute," near Rākh, Purandar Taluka, Poona District).

Gavḷīcā Bābā, a divinized cowherd near Navlākh Umbare (Māvaḷ Taluka, Poona District). To the original, aniconic stone has been added a hero stone (covered with *śendūr*).

Statuettes of Bhairav, 20 and 15 centimeters high. On the left, Bhairav with a trident (*triśūl*), a sword (*khaḍga*), a skull (*kapāla*), and a discus (*cakra*). At the bottom is the dog, which licks at Dakṣa's severed head. On the right, Bhairav and Jogeśvarī/Jogāī.

The Dhangar saw this, and when he had seen it, he said, "Now I will not enter into a marriage alliance with you. Your behavior (*vāgṇūk*) is filthy." So he left again, and from then on there have been no marriage alliances between Meṇḍhe Dhangars and Gavḷī Dhangars.

Many informants divide Dhangars into three endogamous groups: Khuṭekar, Hāṭkar, and Gavḷī Dhangars. Because the number three-and-a-half is also of great importance among the Dhangars, the number of groups is sometimes reckoned as three and a half. In the Nirā valley, for example, the following groups are counted: Hāṭkars, Khuṭekars, Mhaskars, and, as the "half," the caste that is somewhat less highly regarded and is given less social and religious recognition, the Khāṭīks. According to Enthoven, the Khāṭīks are also called Kāsāīs, and they seem to derive from Marāṭhās and Dhangars who as meat-sellers eventually came also to butcher the animals themselves, like Muslims of the Khāṭīk caste.[60]

Another group is that of the Bande Dhangars, who live in Sholapur District: in Āñjangāv (Māḍhā Taluka) and in Huljantī (Maṅgaḷveḍhā Taluka), for example. Huljantī is the place where the famous "disciple" of Birobā settled. The population of this village consists almost exclusively of Bande Dhangars. The number of cattle in this village far surpasses that normal in other areas. To this day the village is protected by a stone wall. Mhāliṅgrāyā Māḷāppā himself is supposed to have come "with the cows" from Bārāmatī. His temple is on the *māḷ,* the pasture, on the opposite side of the river. Microliths found in the pasture suggest that this was a prehistoric tribal area. "Māḷāppā" means "the father on the highland pasture." In front of the impressive temple stand stone votive figures representing cattle.

Āñjangāv, in Māḍhā Taluka, is the home of Khilubā *bhakta,* the devotee of Iṭṭhal and Birāppā of Paṭṭaṇ Kuḍolī. He is a Bande Dhangar.

3.2 Hāṭkar Dhangars

To describe the numerous groups of Dhangars in detail would lead us too far afield. Here I will confine myself to a more detailed description of the Hāṭkar Dhangars.

1. *Bargi Dhangars.* Little is known about the origin of the Hāṭkars. They are supposed to have immigrated from the north. Syed ul Hassan lists them as a "cultivating and hunting caste" and also calls them Bargi Dhangars. Hāṭkar or Bargi Dhangars are numerous in the districts of Parbhani and Nanded. In the focal area of my research, the designation "Bargi" is not found for

---

60. Enthoven, *Castes,* vol. 1, pp. 313, 315f.

Dhangars. Syed ul Hassan cites the observations of Captain FitzGerald, an "Assistant Commissioner in Berar":

> They declare that they emigrated from the north to this part of India many years ago, supposed to be some time prior to the Nizam becoming Subedar of the Deccan on behalf of the kings of Delhi. But the "Ain-i-Akbari" seems to suppose that the Hatkars were driven westward across Wardha by the Gonds.[61] The Hatkars are all Bargi Dhangars, or the shepherds with the spear. . . . The Hatkars say that they formerly, when going on any expedition, took only a blanket seven hand long and a bear-spear, and that on this account they were called "Bārgir" or Bargā Dhangars. They would appear to have been all footmen. To this day the temper of the Hatkar is said to be obstinate and quarrelsome. They will eat with a Kunbi.[62]

The name Bargi would thus seem to be connected with "spear." However, Enthoven conjectures: "Barges (*sic*) claim to be Marāthās, and were perhaps Bārgirs or mounted troopers during the time of the Marāthās."[63]

In my opinion, "Bargi," with its various spellings, seems to be derived from Marāṭhī *barcī* ~ *-chī* ~ *-śī*.[64] *Barcā* and *barsā*[65] also occur. All mean a kind of spear. Hunting and warfare are important components of the Hāṭkar past still evident in the present-day Hāṭkar Dhangars' worship of Khaṇḍobā. This is especially clear in the case of the Dhangar Vāghyās ("Tigers"), who have pledged themselves to the service of Khaṇḍobā, or whose ancestors were consecrated to Khaṇḍobā by their parents in fulfillment of a vow. A Vāghyā in particular, but often also the eldest man in an exogamous group, carries a spear that—perhaps originally at the initiative of the British government[66]—has a knob on its point to make it less dangerous. Just as Śivājī's sword was identified with the goddess Bhavānī, the Vāghyās identify their spear with

61. According to R. Russell, *Tribes and Castes of the Central Provinces of India* (London, 1916), vol. 3, p. 507, a Gaoli (Gavḷī) dynasty of Devgaḍh was overthrown by the Gonds. There was probably no great difference between Gavḷīs and Dhangars originally, because both followed pastoral occupations. At first they gradually differentiated themselves into two groups that finally no longer made marriage alliances with each other. Cf. Text 35. The northern origin of the nomadic Hāṭkar Dhangars and Gavḷīs is also to be surmised from their characteristic dark-red turban, which is not to be seen farther south than the southern part of Satara District, but is very similar to the turban of the Jāts and Rabārīs in Rajasthan.

62. Syed ul Hassan, *Castes,* pp. 248f.

63. Enthoven, *Castes,* vol. 1, p. 313. *Bārgīr* (Molesworth, *Dictionary*): "a trooper that is mounted and equipped by the chief or state that employs him." The opposite is said to be *śiledār,* "a horse-soldier who provides his own horse." Compare the Māṇe family of Mhasvaḍ, above, chap. 3, end of section 2.1.

64. *Mahārāṣṭra Śabdakośa.*

65. Noted in the field.

66. Compare *Mhaskobā Devācem̧ Caritra,* part 3 (Appendix).

Khaṇḍobā. They worship it each morning, even during their travels or in the ancestor shrine of their monsoon camp. Vāghyās are thus the "warriors" of Khaṇḍobā, who is a god of war and the territorial guardian of Maharashtra.

In the Dhangar worship of Khaṇḍobā at Jejurī (Purandar Taluka, Poona District), the element of the hunt appears especially clearly once or several times a year, at the Somvatī Amāvāsyā festival. This festival, which occurs whenever the no-moon day falls on a Monday, is the day of the conjunction of the moon and the sun. The greatest number of Dhangars celebrate the festival when it occurs during the month of Śrāvaṇ (August/September). The monsoon season does not seem especially suitable for hunting expeditions, but right in this period there comes the so-called "break of the monsoon;" moreover, during the monsoon game animals—which were more plentiful in the past—used to return from the moister areas in the Ghāṭs to the drier plateau. In the hunting expedition on Somvatī Amāvāsyā, the god is carried in a palanquin (*pālkhī*) from his temple on the mountain to the Karhā River, about three miles away, where he takes a "bath" in the river. Most present-day participants in the festival understand that the god is simply taking a purifying bath, or that the sun (Khaṇḍobā, who is Mārtaṇḍa) and the moon (in the form of the river) are meeting one another,[67] but the Dhangars understand the procession as a hunting expedition of the god. In the past, they say, they used to go as far as the temple of the god Bhuleśvar, on the *māḷ* on the opposite side of the valley. If on the way to the river a game animal is killed, the god (that is, his *mūrti*) gets a drop of blood put onto his forehead by the successful hunter. A veritable horde of red-turbaned, spear-carrying Dhangars runs at the double ahead of the palanquin, in order to be at the river on time to bathe along with the god.

2. *Hāṭkar Dhangars.* An investigation of the origin of the caste name "Hāṭkar" also throws light on the origin of the Hāṭkar Dhangars themselves. The folk-etymological interpretation of their name, which derives Hāṭkar from Marāṭhī *haṭ* (Sanskrit, *haṭha*), "stubbornness" or "obstinacy," expresses the instinctive attitude toward pastoralist groups on the part of people who live in fixed settlements. Nomadic Dhangars are chiefly viewed by villagers and townsfolk as above all self-willed and obstinate, but also as limited in intelligence, and yet as models of simplicity and sincerity.[68] The

---

67. John M. Stanley, "Special Time, Special Power: The Fluidity of Power in a Popular Hindu Festival," *Journal of Asian Studies,* 37 (1977) 27–43.

68. For an example see *Mhaskobā Devācem̱ Caritra,* part 4 (Appendix). Molesworth, *Dictionary: devabhoḷā* = "simple, credulous, confiding;" *bhoḷā* = "simple, honest, artless, silly." Bhoḷānāth appears as an epithet of Mahādev and of his anthropomorphic manifestations: the Lord of simple men or of true devotees (*bhaktas*).

Gollas of Andhra Pradesh were proverbially trustworthy guardians of store-houses and of valuable freight.

Although the folk-etymology gives other important information, it says nothing about the origin of the Hāṭkars. Here the same Captain FitzGerald who has been cited above gives some further help, as he writes the following about the Hāṭkars:

> The general idea is that, originally, there were twelve tribes of Bargi Dhangars, who came from Hindustan, and that the country about Hingoli (the Parbhani District) was called Bār Hatti, which, the Hatkars say, is a corruption of the words "Bārā Hatkar," or the country of twelve Hatkar. At present there are only three families. To one or other of these families all the Hatkar about Berar, Hingoli, etc. belong. The names of these families or clans are: (1) Poli, (2) Gurdi, (3) Muski.

Rather than being a bowdlerization of the name Hāṭkar, "Bār Hatti" seems to be derived from *haṭṭi;* and thus *bārā haṭṭikar* means "the Dhangars of twelve *haṭṭis.*" According to the *Dravidian Etymological Dictionary* (3199), *h(~p)aṭṭi* has the following meanings: in Kannaḍa, "pen or fold," "hamlet;" in Malayalam, "fold for cattle or sheep;" and in Tamil, "cowstall, sheep-fold," or "hamlet, village." I have already mentioned *haṭṭi* as a sheep pen, or as the camp or settlement of pastoralist groups. S. B. Joshi derives "Hāṭkar" from *hāṭa/haṭṭi, vāḍā/vāḍī* (in the sense of "sheepfold, cow pen, stable"), and *pāḍā/pāḍi* (*Dravidian Etymological Dictionary:* Tamil, *pāṭi,* "town, city, hamlet, pastoral village"). He indicates that the term *haṭṭikara* occurs in old Kannaḍa lexicons as a synonym for *govāḷī,* cowherd.[69]

The *District Gazetteer* of Khāndeś refers to the "Kānadās." This was a group of cattle drovers and dealers whose special breed of black and white cattle, called *hāṭakara,* was the favorite type of draft animal of farmers in the Koṅkaṇ.[70] The same gazetteer also mentions that the Hāṭkars had formerly been Dhangars—that is, "shepherds." They had migrated into this district from around the Godāvarī River—that is, from Parbhani District.[71] Similarly, it is clear from the *District Gazetteer* of Sholapur that the Hāṭkars were settled in that district in 1884. According to them, they had migrated there from Bijāpūr about one hundred twenty-five years earlier. Still today they work as "landholders, potters. . . . house servants, shepherds," and so forth.[72]

69. S. B. Joshi, "Etymology of place-names *'paṭṭi-haṭṭi,'*" *Annals of the Bhandarkar Oriental Research Institute,* 13 (1952) 50ff. Śan. Bā. Jośī, *Marhāṭi Saṃskṛti* (Muṃbai, 1952), pp. 37ff.

70. *Gazetteer of the Bombay Presidency,* volume 12, Khandesh (Bombay, 1880), p. 106. Cited by F. R. Allchin in *Neolithic Cattle-Keepers of South India* (Cambridge, 1963), p. 110.

71. P. 69.

72. *Gazetteer of the Bombay Presidency,* vol. 20, Sholapur (Bombay, 1884), p. 87.

It can also be conjectured that folk etymology would connect the Hāṭkars/Haṭṭikaras secondarily with Marāṭhī *haṭ* (Sanskrit, *haṭṭa*)/*haṭṭī*. *Haṭ*/*hāṭ* means "a market, bazar; esp. a moveable market or a fair" (Molesworth); *haṭṭī*, as the diminutive of *hāṭ*, means "a petty or small market or fair," or "a knot or cluster of houses of people of one calling or caste . . . a cluster or row of huts (of agriculturists, shepherds, goatherds, graziers) at a little distance from the village to which they belong" (Molesworth). "Market" or "moveable market" clearly appears as a secondary meaning—especially from a historical point of view—because the groups traded in oxen, transported goods by oxen between the agricultural centers, and supplied the markets that were held on the occasion of pilgrimage festivals. Still today Hāṭkar Dhangars sell their Khilārī oxen during pilgrimage festivals, and thus supply farmers with draft animals. By contrast, the nomadic Khilārī Hāṭkar Dhangars often sell sheep belonging to farmers in the Deś for a profitable commission in the Koṅkaṇ. For these Dhangars, *vāḍī* still means not only the relatively fixed monsoon camp, but the "camp during the migration," which also carries on trade in sheep. This seems to correspond to the meaning of *hāṭ*/*haṭṭī*.

Although in colloquial speech Hāṭkar Dhangars, including nomadic Hāṭkars, no longer use the term *hāṭ*/*haṭṭī*, but rather *vāḍā* or *vāḍī*, for the Dhangar camp or the sheep pen, "*haṭṭī*" still occurs in their oral traditions. The term occurs, for example, in an *ovī* from Jhirāpvāḍī (Purandar Taluka, Poona District), in which Bhoḷā (that is, Śiva) sets out in search of Yelu Gavḷaṇ:

Text 36

Ovī: . . . Bhoḷā got up from his sleep.
Bhoḷā spoke to Pārvatī.
"Things have not gone well. I must go to Yelu's *vāḍā*.
I must go to Yelu's *vāḍā*."
Bhoḷā set out from there.
He bridled Nandī. He mounted Nandī.
The god went to Yelu's *vāḍā*, he followed the road through the forest.
He came to the second forest. He traversed two forests.
He came to the third forest. There he came upon a *vāḍā* of Gāvḍās.
He approached the *vāḍā*, called to the Gāvḍās.
A *vāḍā* of twelve *haṭṭīs*.[73] Three hundred Saṇgar Dhangars [and]
A crowd of three hundred Gāvḍās. The god called out.
He reached Yelu's *vāḍā*. The Gāvḍās said to him:
"Ei, ei, old man. Why are you calling her?" . . .

Here *haṭṭī* can equally well be interpreted as "sheep pen" or "cow corral." But it can also have been a *vāḍā* of "twelve" family groups, each of which had a *haṭṭī*, a pen.

73. *Bārā hāṭicā kāī* [written *kāhī*] *vāḍā*.

The following text can be given a similar interpretation. It comes from Hunnūr in Maṅgaḷveḍhā Taluka of Sholapur District. The narrator himself thinks it necessary to explain the term *haṭṭī*.

Birobā is going to go to the continent of men, and he asks Śiva:

Text 37

"What am I to do [there]?"

[Śiva answers,] "There is a *bārāhaṭṭī* village (*gāv*)." [The narrator explains:] *Bārāhaṭṭī* means a village (*gāv*) that consists of twelve *vāḍīs*. [The narrator again quotes Śiva:] "There is a mountain there. Go and sit on the mountain. There also is the *bārāhaṭṭī* Dhangar-*vāḍā*, and there in the *vāḍā* is a girl [the goddess of Cinclī] named Māyāvvā. . . ."

From the next text, it seems to follow that the members of a single *haṭṭī* were exogamous and that the *bārā haṭṭī* formed an endogamous group; but the narrator no longer uses the word *haṭṭī*. The text comes from Nimbāvḍe (Khānapūr Taluka, Sangli District):

Text 38

The Dhangars traveled to the bank of the Varṇā River, toward Bijāpūr, to graze their sheep. Among them were Dhangars from twelve villages (*tyāt bārā gāvce dhangar hote*). They intermarried with one another. Their leader (*pramukh*) was named Kamaḷā Śinde. He had three *lākhs* of sheep, and three *lākhs* of lambs, and innumerable barren animals. That was the world of Kamaḷā Śinde. All the shepherds now moved their world into the farmers' fields, and they filled their own and their families' stomachs with the grain they always received [from the farmers]. And they spent their days happily. . . .

The text goes on to describe the birth of the god Dhuḷobā from the ashes of the Hoḷī fire on the full-moon day (*śiṃgā*) of the month of Phālgun (February–March). Kamaḷā Śinde becomes the first devotee (*bhakta*) of the god Dhuḷobā of Phalṭaṇ. The twelve Dhangar groups reappear here as the famous twelve honorary devotees (*mānkarīs*) of Dhuḷobā, from the twelve exogamous families of Hāṭkars who still today live in the Nirā and Māṇ valleys. Behind this idea of the twelve groups of Hāṭkars there is perhaps still to be seen an earlier tribal alliance consisting of twelve exogamous clans. The number twelve also points to the number of marriage groups in a given region. Twelve *haṭṭīs* were, and are still today, an economic unit, of which one member of the group searches for partners to cooperate in penning sheep on farmers' fields. When several herds of sheep are combined in a common herd of two to three thousand head, and the herd is penned on the large fields of the plateau (in contrast to the small rice fields of the Koṅkaṇ), the farmers pay more highly for the fertilizer service.

3. *Khilārī Hāṭkars.* As we have seen, the 1884 *District Gazetteer* of Sholapur describes the Hāṭkar Dhangars as "landholders, potters, mes-

sengers, house servants, shepherds, and a few moneychangers."[74] The gazetteer also refers to the so-called Khilārī breed of cattle, which it says are raised by Dhangars with the same name.[75] Still today the home of the Khilārī cattle is the area comprised of Sangli District, the eastern part of Satara District, and the western part of Sholapur District. The breeders of these cattle were, and still are, primarily Dhangars. According to Molesworth (in 1857), a Khilārī Dhangar was a herdsman with cows, buffaloes, and sheep. But today, in the more restricted area of my research, the Khilārī Hāṭkar Dhangars are simply nomadic Dhangars who keep sheep. In the nineteenth century the nomadic Khilārī Dhangars still kept herds of cattle and smaller animals. It thus seems that there were Hāṭkar Dhangars who were farmers and cattle breeders, and that in addition there were Khilārī Hāṭkar Dhangars, who lived a nomadic life and had herds of cattle and smaller animals. In another context, I will discuss below the question of why nomadic Khilārī Hāṭkar Dhangars today have only sheep herds (along with a few goats for each herd of sheep).

74. *P. 87.*
75. *Ibid., p. 14.*

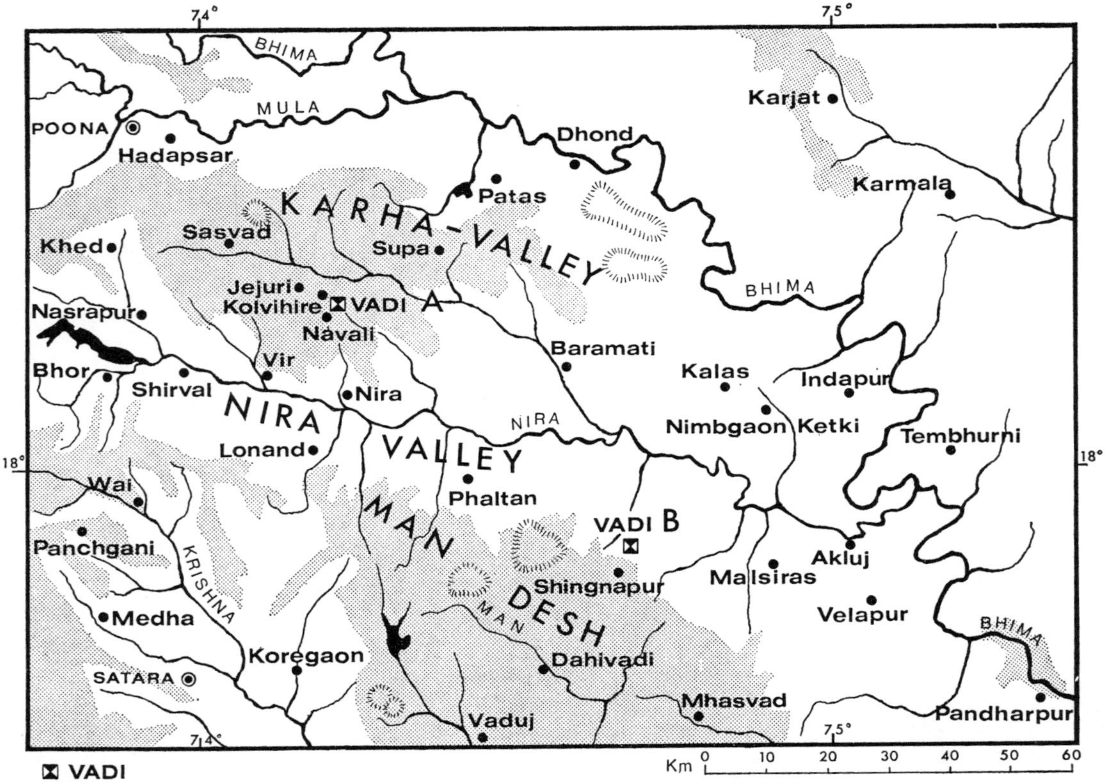

The main area of the monsoon camps of the nomadic Hāṭkar Dhangars, including *vāḍīs* A and B.

7

The Religious Milieu of Two Camps of Nomadic Dhangars

1. Description of the Camps

Vāḍī (camp) A is located about four miles east of Jejurī, in the rocky hills that separate the higher Karhā valley from the lower Nirā valley to the south. On these hills between the two valleys, as well as generally on all the west-east spurs of the Sahyādrī mountains (the Western Ghāṭs), there are many *vāḍīs* of nomadic Hāṭkar Dhangars. *Vāḍī* B is located at Javḷī, near Śiṅgṇāpūr, on the other side of the Nirā valley; it lies on the chain of hillocks of the Phalṭaṇ range, a spur of the Ghāṭs that divides the Nirā valley from the valley of the Māṇ River.

There are three types of Dhangar *vāḍīs* in the region of the Bhimā, Karhā, and Nirā valleys:

1. Some *vāḍīs* are part of a village—that is, they are located at the edge of a village inhabited by other groups. In this case it often happens that some of the Dhangar families practice regular agriculture, and others are nomadic.
2. Some *vāḍīs* are completely inhabited by Dhangars, some families of whom switch over to regular cultivation of the land.
3. Other *vāḍīs* are inhabited only by nomadic Dhangars, and the men wear the red turbans characteristic of nomadic Dhangars.

Both *vāḍīs* A and B fall into the third group, although in *vāḍī* A three of the families have plow-oxen and attempt to farm their land and that of other families in years when the monsoon is good. The other families of the camp are nomadic. The camp's economic base is sheep-raising. Each family has an average of fifty to sixty sheep. *Vāḍī* B is inhabited exclusively by nomadic Hāṭkar Khilārī Dhangars. In this *vāḍī* there are three brothers, the eldest of whom remarried after the death of his first wife. Three sons of his first marriage live separately from him; they too have children. The other two brothers also have many children, some of whom are married. The eldest member of camp B is the three brothers' mother. Her husband moved the *vāḍī* to these hills from the Nirā valley, where it had been driven out by expanding agriculture.[1] This camp also has some arable land, which Māḷīs cultivate for half the harvest in years when the monsoon is good.

In camp A the house walls consist of loose rocks, which are piled up and covered with roofs of corrugated iron. The roofs are removed and stored with farmers before the beginning of the migration. Camp A also has tents constructed of modern tarpaulins. The entrances of the houses and tents are all oriented toward the east, as are the entrances of many temples of such Dhangar deities as Birobā, Mhaskobā, and Khaṇḍobā. In camp B, which in addition to tents also has one stationary building, the entrances are oriented toward the south. To the south, visible from the camp, is the famous Mahādev temple of Śiṅgṇāpūr.

Sheep are the Dhangars' capital. Although nowadays they have come to appreciate the value of owning land, they prefer to raise sheep, because even in years when the monsoon is good, their land provides only meager harvests. Thus, when a Dhangar has lost his sheep herd and so must seek employment on the land of a rich farmer, he strives to save enough money to rejoin his *vāḍī* as quickly as possible.

Nowadays the Dhangars live in close symbiosis with the farmers of the villages surrounding their *vāḍī,* as well as with the farmers in whose fields they pen their sheep, in exchange for payment in grain or money, during their migration to the Koṅkaṇ. They live a nomadic life in the Koṅkaṇ for about seven months, and in exchange for the dung, which is extremely valuable to the farmers, the Dhangars principally receive rice. Rice is in great demand in the Deś, and so the Dhangars can sell it there in exchange for other things.

The migrations of these Dhangars to the Koṅkaṇ began not too long ago. Worsening ecological conditions and the dwindling area of pasture lands forced them to begin migrating.[2] Still today many Dhangars travel only as far as the Ghāṭs, where people and animals have migrated with the beginning of the dry season since prehistoric times, and where these Dhangar migrants still find their subsistence at the sources of the rivers and in the thick forests of the mountains.[3]

1. See 8.3.2, below.
2. See 8.3.1, below.
3. D. D. Kosambi, "Living Pre-history in India," *Scientific American,* 213/12, p. 112.

2. The Religious Year

Many of the religious festivals and rituals of camps A and B are also celebrated by castes living in the surrounding villages and towns. The following
are some of the most important:

1. The religious year begins with Guḍhī Pāḍvā. A *guḍhī* is a pole wrapped
in colorful pieces of cloth and decorated with mango boughs. It is set up in
front of the door of the house on the first day of the year in the month of Caitra
(March/April). The Dhangars' principal celebration of this festival is by a
puraṇpoḷī meal. *Puraṇpoḷīs* are flat wheat breads (*capātīs*) filled with a paste
made of unrefined sugar (*guḷ*) and boiled chickpeas (*caṇā*). A food offering
(*nived*, written *naivedya*) of *puraṇpoḷī* is shown to the family gods.

2. Caitra Pūrṇimā. This is the full-moon day of the month of Caitra
(March/April). The Dhangars celebrate it by sacrificing rams or sheep. First
Khaṇḍobā is shown a vegetarian *nived*, and then Baṇāī a *nived* of bits of meat
and liver.

3. Āṣāḍhī Ekādaśī. This is the eleventh day of the month of Āṣāḍh
(June/July). It is a festival celebrated primarily with a *puraṇpoḷī* meal and the
corresponding *nived* for the gods.

4. Nāgpañcamī. The fifth day of the month of Śrāvaṇ (July/August). This
festival is generally devoted to women's worship of termite mounds and of the
cobras that live in them. In Dhangar mythology, the termite mound plays a
major role as the seat of the god Birobā and as the place of the origin of sheep,
which are often compared to ants. As a typical symbol of the forest, the
termite mound stands outside the sphere of the established settlements, and is
an enemy of farmers. Thus this festival is much less holy in the eyes of
Brahmans who live in established settlements than it is for the Dhangars.[4]

The Dhangar women's dance around the termite mound is a fertility ritual.
In one text[5] we learn about Sūravantī, later to become the mother of Birobā,
who wanted a "child without a man":

---

4. See M. M. Underhill, *The Hindu Religious Year* (Calcutta, 1921), p. 30: *sāḍetīn muhūrttā*,
"three auspicious seasons or periods and a half-season, viz. Dasarā, Dipāvaḷī, Varṣapratipadā
and Nāgpanchamī. The latter has only a qualified auspiciousness for the performance of any
works." Similarly, the Khāṭīks, who are often Muslims, are only a "half" caste, in addition to
the three "full" castes of Hāṭkars, Mhaskars, and Khuṭekars, primarily because as butchers the
Khāṭīks become impure. See above, 6.3.1.
5. From Jeūr (Purandar Taluka, Poona District).

Text 39

It was the Nāgpañcamī festival. The women had gone to the termite mound. And Sūravantī Bāī too had started dancing hand in hand with the other girls at the termite mound. They carried pots on their heads and had *bhaṇḍār* marks on their foreheads.

When they arrived at the termite mound, they saw a pair of cobras. Sūravantī cried out, "The termite mound is a man; we should steer clear of it."[6]

Then the women and the girl Sūravantī went dancing, foot to foot, back home. . . .

5. Somvatī Amāvāsyā. A Monday on which there occurs a conjunction of the sun and the moon—that is, a no-moon day that falls on a Monday. The Dhangars celebrate this festival, if it falls during the time of their stay on the Deś, especially in honor of Khaṇḍobā. They see it primarily as a hunting expedition made by Khaṇḍobā.[7] They also break iron chains (*laṅgar*) on this day; the chains are kept in the household shrine for the rest of the year.

6. Dasarā. The tenth day of the bright half of the month of Āśvin (September/October). The pots in which the goddess has stayed for the preceding nine nights (*navrātra*) on account of the *ghaṭasthāpanā* ceremony are now thrown into the river. Around this time, but at the latest soon after Divāḷī, all the *vāḍīs* begin their migration west toward the Koṅkaṇ. At Dasarā, Bāṇāī is worshiped with a nonvegetarian *nived.*

7. Divāḷī. Āśvin Amāvāsyā, the no-moon day of the month of Āśvin (September/October). On this day no special festivities take place. The celebration essentially consists of a *puraṇpoḷī* meal preceded by *nived* for the ancestors.

8. Makar Saṅkrānt: the passage of the sun from Sagittarius into Capricorn. This festival is celebrated primarily by Dhangar women and in towns. *Puraṇpoḷī* is eaten and shown to the gods and ancestors. In towns, and among groups that are in contact with towns, it is the custom to distribute sweets on this day and to ask recipients to speak only good of one.

9. Māgh Pūrṇimā, the full-moon day of the month of Māgh (January/February). As at Caitra Pūrṇimā and Dasarā, Bāṇāī is shown a nonvegetarian *nived,* and Khaṇḍobā a vegetarian one.

10. Śiṃgā or Hoḷī. On this day in the month of Phālgun (February/March) pyres are built. In the past, among Dhangars who had cows, the pyres consist-

---

6. *vāruḷ hā purus [ā]he; hyālā dharāvā durus.*

7. See 6.3.2, above. Cf. P. V. Kane, *History of Dharmaśāstra* (Poona: Bhandarkar Oriental Research Institute, 1968–1975), vol. 5, part 1, p. 454, where the festival is referred to as being celebrated especially by women.

ed principally of heaps of dried cow dung. On the next day, Dhuḷvaḍī, the god Dhuḷobā was born in the ashes of the Hoḷī fire.[8]

3. The Dhangars' *Jatrās:* the Change to Vegetarianism

In addition to these festivals, there are also pilgrimages (*jatrās*) to the family gods, the *kulsvāmīs* of the exogamous groups. Because the exogamous groups of camp A are connected to one another by marriage, they also have more distant obligations to worship one another's family gods. Likewise, near *vāḍī* B there are other *vāḍīs* with which the members of *vāḍī* B have connections through marriage, friendship, or the common penning of sheep on fields in the Deś during the return journey from the Koṅkaṇ. Thus each family has three to five *kulsvāmīs.* Besides Khaṇḍobā, these can be Birobās of different places, or Mhasvaḍśid in addition to Mhaskobā, even though the two latter gods are essentially identical. Mhaskobā of Vīr comes originally from Mhasvaḍ, but the geographical distance obliterates this identity.

To neglect the gods to whom one is related by marriage—who are also called "guest gods" (*pāhuṇā dev*)—can bring about considerable harm. A Dhangar from camp B relates:

Text 40

Our mother is descended from the Paḍaḷkars of Muḍhal. [Their] god followed our mother. When she had come, the god protected us,[9] and he was our guest. Then we began to go on the pilgrimage (*jatrā*) of that god. Our mother died. We married our brother to the daughter of our mother's brother. When our mother died we stopped going on the pilgrimage. But when our sister-in-law (*bhāvjāī*) came, the god followed her. Sheep were dying, so our grandmother said, "Go on the pilgrimage of Iṭhubā and Birubā."[10] [We did so and] from then on the god has protected us [again].

At the *jatrās* for the family gods, each family sacrifices, if possible, a sheep or a ram, which is slaughtered by Muslims or by the Dhangars themselves. At the pilgrimage for the god Bābīr during the Divāḷī festival, the Muslims often slaughter dozens of sheep. In front of the aniconic image of the god is a *madār,* a small gravestone of a Muslim of whom it is said that he was the god's best friend. More common is the institution of the *dāvaṇ,* "a string [of rams]." Each year for five years in a row, a ram is kept for Birobā,

8. See chap. 8, Text 51, below.

9. *Dev pāvlā:* actually, "the god heard our prayers" or " . . . was pleased."

10. In Siddheśvar Kuroḷī (Dahīvāḍī Taluka, Satara District).

Mhaskobā, or Khaṇḍobā, for example. In the fifth year the rams are let loose, and the first one to reach the herd gets a reprieve. The other four are brought to the *kulsvāmī*. The Gurav priest of the temple gets one of them (in the case of Khaṇḍobā of Jejurī, the Gurav, who is a vegetarian, sells the ram), and the other three are sacrificed in the name of the *kulsvāmī*. He is shown the *nived,* and blood relatives and in-laws—at least one member of each of the eight exogamous groups of camp A—as well as friends and acquaintances are invited to eat. After a few days, the fifth ram is also slaughtered, in the name of Birobā, in the camp. After five years the practice is repeated.

This custom of the Dhangars is reminiscent of the five descendants of the five sons of the Dhangar named Kamaḷājī who brought Mhaskobā to Vīr.[11] The five sons are supposed to be sacrificed to Mhaskobā. One manages to escape by running away and hiding. The other sons are sacrificed, but the god brings them back to life—or rather, he replaces the sacrificed children with sheep.[12] It may be that this story hints at earlier human sacrifice, or it could have been made up in order to emphasize the unconditional devotion (*bhakti*) of the cult's five founding families.[13]

The Birobā of Katecīvāḍī is one of the *kulsvāmīs* of the Mhānvars and the Lakḍes (who are represented in camps A and B). In the temple of this Birobā the sheep are slaughtered inside the temple precincts in front of the ancestor shrine, and then the god is shown a *nived* of liver, heart, and *capātīs*. In other places the Dhangar gods—especially when they have been adopted by other castes—are increasingly becoming deities worshiped only with vegetarian offerings. A few examples will serve to clarify this point. In Vīr, sheep are slaughtered for Mhaskobā to the left of the eastern entrance to the temple precinct. The *nived* is shown to the god only from this entrance.[14] The famous Birobā of Ārevāḍī (Tāsgāv Taluka, Sangli District) is one of the most important *kulsvāmīs* of one of the exogamous families of camp A. Here the *nived* is received by the army of ghosts (*bhutāvaḷ*), and by a *bhakta* of Birobā's, Sūryabā, who died at Ārevāḍī after the ghosts had followed him there from the Koṅkaṇ. The army of ghosts is usually represented by a number of round stones painted with red lead (*śendūr*). Hundreds of sheep and goats are sacri-

11. See *Mhaskobā Devācem̩ Caritra,* part 2 (Appendix).

12. Ibid.

13. The oral traditions of Vīr also relate that Śivājī's government intervened when the sacrifices were made known. In northern India, the practice of substituting buffaloes for human sacrifice is supposed to have been introduced by Bhīmsen and Gorakhnāth. W. Crooke, *The Popular Religion and Folklore of Northern India* (Delhi, 2nd edition, 1968), vol. 1, p. 91. This alliance between king and Gosāvī was also in effect in the forest and pasture area in Maharashtra.

14. Cf. *Mhaskobā Devācem̩ Caritra,* part 3 (Appendix), where the author expresses his antipathy toward slaughtering and offering sheep.

ficed here. Birobā himself is a Liṅgāyat and hence a vegetarian.[15] But that does not necessarily mean that he is also a vegetarian in other places, even when he has come from Ārevāḍī. In Bhāde (Khaṇḍāḷa Mahāl, Satara District), for example, Birobā is not a vegetarian. In this place there can thus be detected an aspect of an earlier stage of the Ārevāḍī cult. The devotees (*bhaktas*) in Ārevāḍī today are mostly Dhangar *farmers,* and thereby accessible to new influences. The devotees at Bhāde are, by contrast, principally *nomadic* Dhangars.

The Birobā of Siddheśvar Kurolī also came from Ārevāḍī. A Marāṭhā relates the following about this god's conversion to vegetarian *nived:*

Text 41

The Birobā of Ārevāḍī was brought here by a devotee (*bhakta*). This devotee worshiped Birobā and so he came here. After some time Iṭubā [Viṭhobā] went from Paṇḍharpūr to the Koṅkaṇ. As he was on his way back, night fell, and he stopped here. He set up camp near the god. He thought, "I want to meet the god." And they understood each other.[16]

Birobā said, "It is very nice that you're staying overnight, but I will be eating *vaśat;*[17] I like sheep, lambs, cocks. How will you stand it?—I will do without this food in your company." Then Birobā accepted a garland of flowers and *bukkā*[18] from Viṭhobā.

After that this custom continued. . . .

Here the Vaiṣṇava Viṭhobā of the Vārkarī sect, whose followers avoid eating meat, makes himself felt. More often Viṭhobā, Birobā's elder brother, is for the Dhangars a somewhat unpredictable, even cruel, Śaiva god.

4. *Kheḷ:* The Festival for the Gods and Ancestors Before the Beginning of the Migration; the Importance of the Ancestors

One of the most important festivals celebrated by the Dhangars of camps A and B, as well as by other, sedentary groups, is the *kheḷ.*

Kheḷ, literally "play," is celebrated before the departure on the migration. On the fourth day after the full-moon day of the month of Āśvin (September/October), Dhangars from the smaller, surrounding *vāḍīs* gather together in camp A. A great dance takes place in front of the ancestors and

15. Cf. Text 34.
16. *Tyā dyāvācā* [written *devācā*] *manālā man miḷāle*[*ṃ*].
17. A typical rural word meaning "meat."
18. *Bukkā* is a black mixture of *kuṅkum* and *cunā* (lime).

gods. The gods are represented by small, stamped silver plaques. These are usually kept in the corner of the tents or houses—the corner that serves as a shrine. But on this day the plaques are displayed on a blanket (*ghoṅgaḍī*). Ignorance of the names of the gods depicted on them often blends with the belief that they represent ancestors.

During the dance on the occasion of the festival, the god—usually Birobā—takes possession of a Dhangar who is especially qualified as a *devṛṣī;*[19] this man then sets the exact time of the migration, predicts the heaviness of the next monsoon, or explains some theft. On this day, sheep are killed, particularly to feed the ancestors and for Birobā. A *nived* consisting of liver, heart, and *bhākrī* is shown. The departure on the migration is celebrated in a similar way in camp B.

The oldest man in camp B (the father of the three brothers) died during the migration to the Koṅkan. There is a small shrine for this ancestor at one of the stops on the migration route. A ram is slaughtered for him here during the migration to and from the Koṅkan, and a *nived* consisting of rice, liver, heart, and *bhākrī* is offered.

The ancestors remain behind in the camp—that is, they are not especially worshiped in the Koṅkaṇ—but the *kulsvāmī,* who is represented on a silver plaque, and the "guest gods" go along on the migration. They are wrapped up in a white cloth and the women transport them on horses to the Koṅkaṇ, along with the household goods. Devotees (*bhaktas*) of Khaṇḍobā and Dhuḷobā, like the oldest man in camp B, often have a kind of spear that embodies Khaṇḍobā; it is worshiped with turmeric powder every morning during the migration.[20]

There is one ancestor shrine in camp B, and several in camp A. The ancestor is represented on a stone slab about fifty centimeters high. Often he is a horseman with one or two wives, who sit behind him on the horse. The ancestors are thus similar to the representations of Khaṇḍobā. Often only simple stones are devoted to the ancestors, a small shrine to the somewhat more famous *bhaktas*. In Paṭṭaṇ Kuḍolī there is a whole collection of ancestor stones.

In Huljantī (Maṅgaḷveḍhā Taluka, Sholapur District), numerous ancestor shrines showing Muslim influence from Bijāpūr are grouped around the temple of the divinized Mhāliṅgrāyā Māḷāppā. Even more numerous here are shrines about thirty centimeters high, open in front, with a flat stone as a roof. These are the "memorial stones" of poorer *bhaktas*. These shrines, each of

---

19. Pronounced *devruṣi* or *devruśi,* from Sanskrit *devarṣi*. Molesworth, *Dictionary:* "a dealer with gods and devils, one that summons or exorcises them, etc."

20. See above, 6.3.1.

which contains a simple stone, resemble miniature megalithic graves. In Bhāde, Purandar Taluka, there are found to the left, in front of the Birobā temple, many rows of boulderlike stones, on each of which is carved the representation of a dead Dhangar man with one or two wives at his side. This collection of memorial stones around a Birobā temple reflects the dead person's wish to be "near the god." In popular belief it is said that Nāmdev, a famous devotee of Viṭhobā of Paṇḍharpūr, asked his god, "*tujyājavaḷ jāgā de*"—"Give me a place near you."

In addition there is the idea of merging into Śiva, which is the Liṅgāyats' conception. When Basava died he is supposed to have merged into Śiva's *liṅgam.*[21] The nomadic Dhangars have few ideas about where the dead live. Many believe that they are in the Indrasabhā, the court of the god Indra; others, again, that they reappear as ghosts—if their wishes remain unfulfilled. The following text indicates ideas about the ancestors, and shows what happens when a monsoon camp splits, and one section breaks off to found a new camp. The two camps mentioned are not far from camp A, on the hills that separate the Karhā valley from the Nirā valley:

Text 42

All the Mhānvars came from the Hākes' camp to Algujdarā ["the valley of the flute"]. First Dādū Dhoṇḍibā Mhānvar came from Hākevāḍī. His father had acquired Algujdarā. After Dādū came his brothers, Śiva, Lakśmaṇ and Bhagvān. After that, Cāṅgu Mhaskū and Bābū Mhaskū Mhānvar also came. In the beginning, they still lived in Hākevāḍī. They took their sheep over there [to Algujdarā, to graze]. There was no more room for the sheep in Hākevāḍī. Finally they couldn't live there any more. So we came to Algujdarā. Since then we have lived here. We have land, which we pay the Marāṭhās to plow. We ourselves do the other work, like weeding and harvesting.

While we were still in Hākevāḍī and Sādū Khaṇḍu [Mhānvar] was still alive, he said, "Build my temple[22] in Algujdarā. Then my spirit [*man*] will be peaceful." And with that, he died.

After four or six years we built the foundation walls there and began to build

21. This also explains the unusually large number (about 110) of small Śiva temples with *liṅgams* in Aihole; according to M. S. Mate, these are all "memorial monuments" (M. S. Mate and Shobhana Gokhale, "Aihole: an Interpretation," in *Studies in Indian History and Culture,* Professor P. B. Desai Felicitation Volume [Dharwar, 1971], pp. 501ff.).

Ancestor shrines with one or two *liṅgams* (depending on the number of dead people) on a raised platform are found in many places in India—in Kolāras near Śivpurī (Madhya Pradesh), for example. Proximity to Śiva or absorption into him or Pārvatī is depicted even more clearly on a beautiful, old *satī* stone in the museum of the fort of Gwalior (Gujarī-Mahāl). The couple is shown in the Umāmaheśvara pose. This representation is frequently found on *satī* stones in Madhya Pradesh, but seldom is the rendering as convincing as on this stone.

22. *Dyāvāḷ,* written *deuḷ.*

the temple; it was finished in two years. In the month of Ākhāḍ [Āṣāḍh] we came from the Koṅkaṇ. Then we went to Nirā and got a *mūrti*[23] made in a week. We brought it here. We made a *nived* of *puraṇpoḷī*.

We also took out in-laws with us to get the *mūrti*. [Sādhu Khaṇḍu] possessed Bābū. He and the Hākes installed the *mūrti* at five o'clock in the afternoon. While the *mūrti* was being installed, the Brahman from Rākh studied (*abhyās karto*) for half an hour.

They killed two sheep for the two *mūrtis*. They cooked a *nived*. They showed a *nived* of *puraṇpoḷī* and then a *nived* of mutton. After that he took possession of Bābū's body. Then Dādū asked the god,[24] "We have installed our father and our grandfather. Is your spirit satisfied now?"

And the god said, "I am satisfied."

And Dādū said, "If your spirit is satisfied, then satisfy us too."

Later their father came into Lakśmaṇ's body. We celebrate the play (*kheḷ*) for the gods in the evenings for nine days after the Dasarā full-moon day.[25] We invite Holārs.[26] They come from Rākh. At twelve o'clock at night we have a procession, which lasts until four o'clock. After four o'clock we kill the sheep. We prepare them and cook them. At daybreak, at six o'clock, we start the procession [again]. It generally lasts until ten o'clock. Then we bring the procession to an end and show the *nived*. Then we give a meal to "guests from four villages," and after that we eat too. At twelve o'clock we begin the "play,"[27] which lasts until two o'clock in the afternoon. During it, the god comes into someone's body. When he has come into his body, we ask him, "Did you like the *kaṇyaghugryā?*"[28]

The god says, "Yes, I liked it."

The god leaves. The dance ends.

If we have forgotten to show the *nived* for the ancestors, then he causes some problems. We ask the *devṛṣī*, and he says, "Show *nived*," or, "Free a cock [in the field]."

Thereupon the trouble decreases. And if it doesn't get better, we go to the doctor.

Later the Dhangar supplemented his remarks, also showing how a man who died young lives on in his male descendants:

Text 43

Dādū Mhānvar's father, grandfather, and uncle on his father's side are installed there. First we show the *nived* to the grandfather, then to the father, and then to the uncle, then to the brother. [The brother's] name is Bhāgū [= Bhagvān]. He

23. The "*mūrtis*," stone images, are manufactured by local stonemasons.
24. *Devālā*. That is, the ancestor.
25. The full-moon day is five days after the Dasarā festival.
26. A caste of musicians.
27. The narrator mistakenly says the word *chabinā* ("procession") instead of *kheḷ*.
28. A sort of porridge made of *bājrī*, *jvārī*, or some other kind of grain.

died at the age of eight. This Bhāgū was Dādū's brother. When Bhāgū had been dead for five years, he began to come into Mahādū's body. Mahādū is Dādū's son. When he had come into his body, we asked him, "Who are you?"

Then Mahādū said, "I, Bhāgū, have come. My desire[29] is wandering around."

Then we asked the *devṛṣī:* "Is it true that Bhāgū has come into Mahādū's body?"

The *devṛṣī* said, "It's true."

From then on we began to call Mahādū "Bhāgū." Four years later, we celebrated Bhāgū's wedding, and on the *haḷdī* day,[30] we gave him the name. We invited four relatives on our mother's side and put sugar into their mouths. Then they said, "Bhāgū." The relatives on our father's side did so too. Then they distributed pān. After that we fed them, and we ourselves ate. From then on he has had the name Bhāgū instead of Mahādū.

5. Birobā Comes to the Camp

Camp A has on its outskirts a simple place of worship for Mhasobā, and it has a small shrine for Marīāī/Lakṣmī as well. Camp B also has a Marīāī/Lakṣmī shrine. Generally Birobā and other *kulsvāmīs* have their temples, which serve as centers for pilgrimage festivals (*jatrās*), outside the camp. Many exogamous groups come together here during the *jatrās*. But sometimes Birobā also comes in person to a camp and demands a temple for himself. The following text from Algujdarā shows how this happens:

Text 44

Rāmā's father, Khaṇḍu Mhānvar, was a devotee (*bhakta*) of the god Birobā of Kāṭecīvāḍī [who had come from Hākevāḍī]. The god thought: "We have many *bhaktas* in Hākevāḍī. Among them, Khaṇḍu Mhānvar is a true *bhakta*. So we should come here [to Algujdarā] from Hākevāḍī."

After that the god came here from Hākevāḍī. A stone painted with red lead (*śendūr*) turned up on the wall of the field. At this place, there was a hivar tree.[31] After that there began to be troubles in the house. Then Khaṇḍu went to the *devṛṣī,* who said, "The difficulties (*cācanuk*) are because of Birobā."

Then Khaṇḍu asked, "Why is the god making difficulties? Have I failed to keep a vow?[32] Have I neglected my *bhakti,* or what mistake have I made? Tell me. Give us your favor (*guṇ*); whatever it is, we will accept it."

---

29. *Sardā,* from Sanskrit/written Marāṭhī *śraddhā.*

30. The day before the actual wedding. The feet and hands of the bride and bridegroom are smeared with turmeric (*haḷdī*).

31. *Mimosa tomentosa.*

32. *Navas.* On account of such "vows," in Jejurī there is an entire forest of lamp pillars (*dīpmāḷ*). A simple god like Birobā is satisfied with, for example, a votive image in the form of a cow or a sheep.

Thereupon he gave us his favor. We found out [what we had forgotten].

We went to Kāṭecīvāḍī. There we asked the god, "What have we done wrong?"

Then the god said, "I have appeared in the wall of your field. Go on, I'll show you the place." Just then there was "play" (*kheḷ*) in the village. The god had appeared under the hivar tree, at the place where the god came into Rāmā Mhānvar's body. The god [in the form of Rāmā Mhānvar] went to this place. He came into his body and said to the people: "I have come here; worship me." Rāmā Mhānvar began to worship him. His relatives said, "How are we to recognize that he is the god? If he does what we say, then we will say that he is real. If Somā Malū Mhānvar's wife has a child, then we will say that the god is real."

The god fulfilled their request. Somā's wife bore a child. The relatives had made a vow that if this happened, "we will offer a drum worth forty rupees, and an umbrella worth fifty rupees."

The god fulfilled their request, and after that they were sure that he was real. Then all the Mhānvars became devotees (*bhaktas*) of this god. [What follows tells among other things of the construction of a temple for Birobā.]

Usually the god appears to his *bhaktas* in a dream, and makes his demands of them. The oldest man in camp A had a dream in which Birobā appeared and pointed out the place in the camp where he and Māyabā, his "brother," would appear. The next day the man found two *liṅgam*like stones protruding from the ground. Stones for a shrine were brought to the place, but before the construction of the shrine was begun, the eldest member of the camp died during the migration to the Koṅkaṇ.

6. The *Devṛṣī*

Any Dhangar can become possessed by a god on the occasion of the "play" (*kheḷ*) or during a procession (*chabinā*), and for the observer it is time and again impressive how completely ordinary Dhangars who are looking on with seeming indifference at the hustle and bustle during the "play" or during a procession suddenly fall trembling into ecstasy. However, not all Dhangars who have become possessed are qualified to be *devṛṣīs*. The *devṛṣī* is not a shaman in the strict sense. There is no land of the dead into which the *devṛṣī* accompanies the dead, and no mystical shamanic flight. The god "comes" in order to take possession of the medium's body and to speak to the Dhangars.

The following text details the test that one must pass in order to be recognized as a *devṛṣī:*

Text 45

When someone comes into a man's body, then this must be brought out into the open (*tyācī phuṭ karāicī*). If a god [for example] comes into the body of our son, then we ask, "Who are you?" Then the one who has come into his body says, "I am an ancestor," or "I am a god," or "I am a goddess," or "I am a ghost (*bhūt*)." Then we ask the one who has come into his body, "Tell us exactly which god has come."

If he doesn't say, we go to the *devṛṣī* and ask him, "Is it true or false that a god has come into our son? If you say that it is true, we will send for you: come there."

If the *devṛṣī* has answered yes to the question, he says, "Get ready five small limes, four coconuts, two pieces of clothing, wood from seven trees, and *tūp* [that is, ghee, clarified butter]. I will come on the day you determine."

After that, the relatives of the one into whose body [he] comes decide on a day and get the things ready. On this day, they call together their in-laws: "Today is our son's test [*thāpaṇuk,* written *sthāpaṇuk*]. Come."

Then at five o'clock in the evening we carry out the test. We send for the Holārs with their drums, we bring water from the river. We place five small limes in a row. Then the two of them stand off far away. Then the man's relatives on his mother's side give the limes names. We send for the *devṛṣīs* and say to them, "Pick up the lime that is named after you!"

If he picks up the lime that is named after him the first time, then the god is real. If he picks up another one, then the *devṛṣī* beats him with a whip. Then we decide on new names. If he recognizes [the lime with his name] this time, then the god is real. If he doesn't recognize it, then we decide the names a third time. If he recognizes the right lime, then the god is real. If he doesn't recognize it, then he is a fraud, and the *devṛṣī* says, "It is a ghost (*bhūt*) or something like that."

If it is a *bhūt,* then he doesn't come into his body any more. If it is a true god, then we make a fire (*hom*) out of seven pieces of wood. Then we pour ghee (*tūp*) and the urine of a cow into the fire and have him dance on it.

When the god has gone out of his body, we put the [new] clothes on him. We kill sheep and give everyone a meal. After that he is a *devṛṣī* or guru. Then he is also capable of putting others to the test. Then he is also a guru for others.

If we have here, so to speak, the objective events in the investiture (*thāpaṇuk*) of a *devṛṣī,* so the following report describes the inner, subjective side of a *devṛṣī*'s experience. The narrator is the eldest member of camp A; his *kulsvāmī* is Siddhobā (Śīdobā) of Mhasvaḍ, who is essentially identical with Mhaskobā of Vīr:

Text 46

The *devṛṣī* carried out my test during the play. How did I become a *devṛṣī?* When I was young, I was seized by a ghost (*bhūt*)—it was a huge Khais.[33] At that time, what happened was that the Khais came one night while I was sleeping near the sheep. He pulled at my leg, and when he had pulled at it, I was

---

33. Molesworth, *Dictionary:* "A spirit or goblin viewed as the spirit of a deceased Musalmān."

afraid. "Up your mother's . . . ,"[34] I thought. "Who is pulling at me?" I woke up and could not see anything. "Up your mother's . . . , but somebody *has* pulled at my leg."

The next morning I went and took a bath. I went to the river, took off my clothes, and put them aside. Then I went into the water to take my bath. When I sprinkled myself with water, what did the Khais do then? He pushed me into the water. I said to myself, "Up your mother's. . . . Why is he pushing me?"

Somehow or other I finished my bath and came out. I held onto the sheep while the lambs drank the sheep's milk. Then I milked the sheep, washed my hands, and ate some *bhākrī*. Then I took my staff and drove the sheep to the pasture. Then my body began to ache. "Up your mother's. . . . My body has begun to ache." At that time I had many sheep. I had hired two herdsmen. There were two or three hundred sheep. When my body began to ache, I called to the two herdsmen. "Look after the sheep," I said. "I can't go on. I'm going to go to sleep now."

There was a platform there on which rice had been laid out to dry.[35] I went under it, laid down my dhoti, and went to sleep under the platform. I slept from twelve to four o'clock in the afternoon. Then I got up. The herdsmen had led the sheep to the pasture. I went to our tent.[36] I went there very slowly. When I got there, darkness was closing in.

What happened the next day? I got up in the morning, rinsed my mouth, and went out to defecate. When I had gone to defecate, the *bhūt* held on to me and wouldn't let me go. As soon as I squatted down, the *bhūt* came and sat on my neck. When he had sat on my neck, I did not know what to do.[37] Then he went away. I looked around and could see him—but not clearly. It was a man who was missing one arm. A number of people see him now and then, when they go to collect cow dung. His name was Mahādyā [Mahādū].

"How can he come to me," I thought, "when I have just defecated?" He made me feel ashamed.

There was a place there with a rock face on both sides. I went into this gorge, but when I got there the *bhūt* grabbed me and pushed me to the ground. A long time passed, during which the *bhūt* pushed me to the ground again and again. From four o'clock in the morning until twelve o'clock noon he did not let me stand up. He would not let me climb up the rock face.

"What am I to do now? Is it a *bhūt* or not?"

The *bhūt* came and sat next to me. I simply lay there. When it was twelve o'clock, I stood up somehow and went to the tent. I drank some water. Our father returned from the village. "What are you doing?"

---

34. See chap. 4, n. 74.

35. *Mā(ṃ)c:* a wooden scaffold about the height of a man. Rice straw is stored there to keep it away from the moist ground.

36. *Birhāḍ,* actually a Dhangar household during the migration.

37. Someone who is alone and impure (from menstruation, childbirth, sexual intercourse, or urination) is especially exposed to the danger of attack by a *bhūt.*

"Dādā, I am sick. I'm not well today!"

"Sleep somewhere in the shade. Don't go away," he said. He went to Rohā to the bazaar. There was no shade, but we had built a makeshift roof of hay over the mouth of the well.[38] I slept under that. I slept like a rock. I slept so deeply that I didn't know where my *laṅgoṭī*[39] was or where my shirt was. When the day was in the Māvaḷ, my father returned from Rohā. "Why hasn't that boy gotten up yet? Hey, Limbyā! The day is in the Māvaḷ, and you haven't gotten up yet?"

Dādā woke me up, and I said, "I don't feel well."

He got me up, he held me by the hand, got me to stand there, and said, "Get up! Come home." And he led me home by the hand. When I got home, I was even sicker. It had reached the point where a person gets ready to die. For two weeks [my father] called on the *devṛṣī*. He looked at everything, but it was no help. What happened then?

The *bhūt* had attacked me for a whole month. Then one day a Holār came. The pot ceremony for Śidobā had been arranged, and he [the Holār] had come to play music for the play (*khyoḷ,* written *kheḷ*) of Śidobā. When he came I got up. And I walked as far as from our *vāḍā* to the well [on the road to Jejurī].[40]

On this day I ate half a *bhākrī*. The next day he [the Holār] came to beat the drum. When he beat the drum, the god came into my body. When the god had come into my body, the *bhūt* ran away from it. From that day on, the god [Śidobā] has come into my body. Since then I have been a *devṛṣī*. Another *devṛṣī* carried out the test (*thāpaṇuk*).

Here there took place in an individual Dhangar, in a microcosm,[41] so to speak, the same event that appears on another plane in the struggle of the god against demons, *asuras, daityas, bhūts,* and so on. Śidobā of Mhasvaḍ defeats the *asura*. The defeat of the *asura* brings peace and makes an area into a holy *kṣetra*. And it is also Śidobā who drives out the *bhūt* in an individual. By entering into the body of the *devṛṣī,* he makes him into a "temple" and enables him to diagnose others' diseases, adversities, and so on, in the form of *bhūts,* and to recommend methods for remedying them.

The situation is somewhat different in the case of the "possession" of the descendants of the founder of the Mhaskobā cult of Vīr.[42] Through the great *bhakti* of their ancestor, it is possible for them to become possessed by the god—especially during the great pilgrimage in the month of Māgh (January/February). They hit themselves with a sword and hold the point of the

38. Where oxen or buffaloes are harnessed with ropes, go back and forth, and in this way lift water from the well for irrigation.

39. A loincloth, which is nowadays ever more frequently being replaced by the dhoti.

40. About a mile.

41. The body as temple. See Mircea Eliade, *The Sacred and the Profane* (New York, 1961), p. 172.

42. *Mhaskobā Devācem̄ Caritra,* part 3 (Appendix).

sword in their mouths as they dance, in order thus to compel the god to take possession of them. Then the god speaks through them. The Dhangars who perform this dance of possession are not priests of the temple but mediums of the god. Perhaps it is the Dhangars' special talent at getting possessed by gods, together with the fact that their ancestor brought the cult, that gives them a fixed, hereditary right as *śids*. The designation *śid* (from *siddha*) comes principally from the world of the Gosāvīs and the Liṅgāyats. Theoretically a *siddha* is a person who has perfected his magical-spiritual capacities by mastering the eight *siddhis*. But nothing is known about this any more in Vīr, and essentially the difference between the simple *devṛṣīs* and the *siddhas* of Vīr consists in the fact that the *siddhas* enjoy an established, hereditary, honorary right (*mān*) in Mhaskobā's temple to become possessed by this god.

7. The Roles of the Jaṅgama and the Brahman

In the area of my research, the Jaṅgama, the priest of the Liṅgāyat sect, was in the past often called upon to solemnize marriages for other groups as well. Gradually the Liṅgāyats seem to have lost this function to the Brahmans. Even the marriage between Mhaskobā and Jogeśvarī, the annual festival of Mhaskobā on the full-moon day of the month of Māgh (January/February), is now celebrated by a Brahman. The Dhangars of camps A and B likewise call upon a Brahman for their weddings, primarily to recite the marriage verse (*maṅgaḷāṣṭaka*).

At a Dhangar wedding, traditional, non-Brahmanical rites are thus often combined with Brahmanical ones. For example, in the case of one exogamous group it is the custom to ensure the fertility of the bride and groom by killing a pregnant sheep and burying the unborn animal under the wedding seat. But for naming a child on the twelfth day after its birth, the Brahman is consulted. Thus a Brahman even decided the name of the young god Birobā, who had been found in the forest. Bāḷubāī asked the Brahman:

Text 47

"Bāman [Brāhmaṇ]-dādā, if you are my brother, tell me the boy's *nakṣatra* name (*nāvras*)."[43]

43. *Nāvras* is the name determined according to the horoscope with the help of a person's everyday name. The word "*nāvras*" comes from written *nāṃv* + *rāśi*.

He got out the old book [*jotak*].
"Take the new book and find out the *nakṣatra* name."
The Bāman began to read the book, and said, "According to the *nakṣatra,* his name is Birojī. And he will get revenge on the king [who had him abandoned]. And he will bring the king in chains to the *vāḍā*. His everyday name is Tayājī and his *nakṣatra* name is Birojī."

Actually the name Tayājī is—today, at least—much more rare in the area of my research, whereas the name Birojī/Birobā, etc., is prevalent as far as Karnatak and Andhra Pradesh. But in this version, which comes from Jeūr (Purandar Taluka, Poona District), it is not the case, as one might suppose, that the narrator has confused the "everyday" name, Tayājī, with Birobā, the name that is usual today, but rather that this text preserves an earlier phase of the cult.

For example, in the traditions of the village of Corācī Āḷandī in Havelī Taluka, Poona District, T(∼S)āyājī and Māyājī, or Sāyābā and Māyābā, were two Gavḷī brothers who brought the god Mhaskobā to Corācī Āḷandī along with their cattle herd. Māyājī is generally a shepherd who was created to help Birobā keep the sheep under control. It seems clear that Tāyājī was a cattle herder, and that his name was "everyday" until the time when the Gavḷīs with their herds of cattle gave way to regular agriculture and became farmers or shepherds. It appears that when the divinized Gavḷī Tāyājī, who was historically earlier, became equated with Birobā, whose cult was spreading from Karnatak and Andhra Pradesh, Tāyājī acquired the *nakṣatra* name Birojī/Birobā. Perhaps too it is this that is being referred to in the request to determine the *nakṣatra* name in the *new* book.

The Brahman's task is therefore to recognize the god and to identify him. He does not impose any new system, but interprets the same phenomenon in a loftier and more prestigious way. Dumont has described this as the essence of the so-called Sanskritization process.[44]

The following text has central importance in many respects, because it shows how the Brahman is necessary for the identification of the god, an event typical of the introduction of "Hindu" deities among the tribes. The god who is identified here is Viṣṇu. It could not be a Śaiva deity, because that would be a task for a Gosāvī or Liṅgāyat. Thus the text does not come from either camp A or camp B, because the nomadic Dhangars are more inclined toward Śaiva deities; even Viṭhobā of Paṇḍharpūr is not (yet) Viṣṇu for them.

---

44. See Dumont in *Contributions to Indian Sociology,* no. 3, (1959), p. 45: " 'Sanskritization' does not consist in the imposition of a different system upon an old one, but in the acceptance of a more distinguished or prestigious way of saying the same things."

The text comes from Kuṇḍal (Tāsgāv Taluka, Sangli District). Here, despite the fact that there are still many sheep breeders among the Dhangars, the settled life, with its greater exposure to Brahmans and to their preference for Viṣṇu, is nevertheless predominant:

Text 48

Now I'll tell you a little story about how the god revealed himself to us, the Dhangars.

How was it, then? There was a Brahman who always used to go to the river to do his religious rites [*sandhyā*]. He would take a bath, do his religious rites, and so—it was in the Golden Age—he did this for many days. There was also a simple, honest Dhangar. And now what would happen every day? The Brahman would do his religious rites, hold his nose, submerge himself in the water, come up again, hold his nose, and go back under water. The Dhangar saw this, and one day he said, "Today I'll ask him." And he went to him and asked, "Uncle, why do you do this?"

"Now, my boy, I worship the god and—when I have worshiped him, what happens then!? The god shows himself to me!"

"Really?"

"Absolutely certain!" Then the Brahman left.

The Dhangar was simple. "So," he thought to himself, "to worship means to hold your mouth and nose and then to go under water. Then the god shows himself to you."

This was what he took the Brahman's words to mean.

He let the Brahman go, took off his clothes, and jumped into the water—he jumped in, held his nose and mouth tightly closed, and sank in the water. The Brahman, who had in fact done this himself, had no idea what he had thereby started. So the Dhangar sank in the water, and he was in great trouble down below; he began to die. He couldn't breathe in the depths, and he sank in the water.

The god was in an embarrassing position. He said, "This Dhangar is killing himself from simplicity. If I don't show myself, he'll die. Just because the Brahman said, 'The god shows himself to me.'" Thus the god was in difficulties.

And when under the water the Dhangar was about to lose his life, the god revealed himself as an *avatār* with four hands and arms—as a proper, four-armed *avatār* of a god. He came forward and stood there.

"You fool!" he said. "Let go of your nose and mouth," he said. "I am the god," he said. "Let go, let go," he said. "Come up, come up."

And the man came up: "*You* are the god? How can that be? I am not sure," he said.

"Now I've shown myself to you, and you're still not sure?"

"No," he said. "If this Brahman comes in person and says, 'This is the god,' then I will let go of my nose and mouth,'' he said. ''Then I'll begin to die right now. If I die,'' he said, ''the shame is on the god. So I will get the Brahman, and if he says, 'This is the god,' then I'll let go of my nose and mouth.''

''I've come to show myself to *you,*'' he said, ''I have not come to reveal myself to the *Brahman.*''

''All right, I won't let go.'' And he got a firmer grip on his nose and mouth.

''It's not nice of you,'' said the god. ''You will die,'' he said. ''Go and get the Brahman.''

''You're sending me for the Brahman, and by the time I get back you'll be gone.''

It was the simple way of *bhakti*. With his turban he tied the god tight to a tree, and he ran to the Brahman. ''Uncle,'' he said, ''get up! The god has come, and you must decide whether it's the god or someone else.''

The Brahman thought, ''For the past twelve years, I have held my nose and mouth and gone under water, and nowhere have I met the god. And you have not once put your hand into the water, but it's to *you* that the god has come and shown himself?''

''Yes, that's right,'' he answered. ''I've tied him to a tree.''

''Oh, come on, what are you saying?'' said the other.

''It's absolutely certain. Get up! Come on,'' he said, and he took him along with him.

He took him along with him, and there stood the four-armed manifestation of the Mahārāj, the four-armed divine image of Viśṇu [Viṣṇu] Mahārāj! The Brahman touched his feet worshipfully: ''The god is showing me himself because of the Dhangar's *bhakti.*''

And then he held the Dhangar's feet and said, ''Because of your *bhakti* the god is showing himself to me.''

The Dhangar said, ''The god is showing himself to me?''

Then the god said, ''Because of your *bhakti* I have shown myself to the Brahman and to you, and I am feeling kindly toward you. Ask for whatever you want.''

The Dhangar was of a simple nature. He said to the god, ''What can you give me, and what do I lack? I have plenty: I have four brothers, a mother, a father, a wife, children, a hundred sheep. What can you possibly give me? But there is one thing I ask for: you must come to my sheep pen every evening and drink milk.''

''Good,'' he said. ''Why not?'' The god promised: ''Every evening I will come to your sheep pen and drink milk.''

Thus in those days the Dhangar had bound the god to come to drink milk in his sheep pen. Now, these days it is the Iron Age. This happened in the Golden Age. In the Iron Age this is our offering. The god comes to the Dhangar settlement, and on the ground there stands a pot of milk for him. To this day,

> they heat the milk, stand it on the ground, and by evening it is cold and sour. To this day the god comes in person to the Dhangar camp. Thus the god came in the Golden Age because of the simple *bhakti* of the Dhangar. But is there really any basis for it today?

It is not the complicated, incomprehensible ritual of the Brahman, but the simple, devoted *bhakti* of the Dhangar that compels the god to appear.

8

Integration of the Landscapes of Maharashtra: The Spread of Agriculture

1. The Period of the Yādavas of Devgiri

All over Maharashtra there are temples built in the so-called Hemāḍ-Pant style. They date from the period of the dynasty of the Yādavas of Devgiri (twelfth–thirteenth centuries), and are mostly dedicated to Śiva or the goddess (*devī*). In the focal area of my research, they are found primarily at the intersections of trade routes. For example, at Veḷāpūr, in Māḷśiras Taluka (Sholapur District), there are several Hemāḍ-Pant temples at the intersection of two roads, one running north-south and the other east-west; and at Māhulī, a bit north of Māyaṇī in Khaṭāv Taluka (Satara District), there is also a temple at the crossing of a north-south and an east-west road. In Paṇḍharpūr, one of the most important intersections of trade routes, donations were made to the god Viṭṭhala (Viṭhobā) by "Hemāḍī Paṇḍita" in 1276, and by king "Rāmacandradeva Yādava" in 1277.[1] In addition, remains at the temple at Mhasvaḍ suggest that there was an earlier temple there in the Hemāḍ-Pant style.

It was during the Yādava period that Marāṭhī developed as the vernacular language of Maharashtra. Popular belief ascribes the introduction of *bājrī* millet to Hemāḍ-Pant or Hemādri, the prime minister (*mahā-karaṇādhipa*) of the last Yādava; but this can only mean that *bājrī* was now cultivated more intensively and regularly.

Although these Hemāḍ-Pant temples could point to a spread of regular agriculture in new nuclear regions in the valleys of the Bhimā and Karhā rivers, they also bear signs of the importance of cattle herds and the high value

---

1. See the inscription cited in S. G. Tulpule, *An Old Marathi Reader* (Poona, 1960), pp. 90–91.

placed on cattle. Were their sites thus the settlements and camps of *daṇḍanāyakas, nāyakas, gāvuṇḍas,* and other such local rulers with a primarily pastoral base? At many of the Hemāḍ-Pant temples that have been preserved or have had new superstructures added to them later, there are hero stones[2] whose lowest relief shows the hero who has been killed and the cattle he has protected or won back. Examples are found in Māhulī (Khānapūr Taluka, Sangli District), Koregāv Mūḷ (Haveli Taluka, Poona District), Mhāluṅg (Māḷśiras Taluka, Sholapur District), Vaḍapurī (Indāpūr Taluka, Poona District—where the migratory pastoralist caste of the Nandīvālās holds its caste assembly every three years in the month of Āṣāḍh—July/August), Bavḍe (Māḷśiras Taluka, Sholapur District), Guḷuñce (Purandar Taluka, Poona District), Mūrti Moḍhve (Purandar Taluka, Poona District), Kiklī (Wāī Taluka, Satara District—the home of the Marāṭhā family Bābar), and Corācī Āḷandī (Havelī Taluka, Poona District).

These hero stones are not always found in front of the Hemāḍ-Pant temple; sometimes they are at the entrance to the village, around the village square, or at the edge of the road. The list of places with stones that depict heroes protecting cattle can be considerably expanded. The stones are typical of the drier, pastoral region east of Poona. Kiklī, north of Satara, is the westernmost site where there are hero stones (*vīragaḷs*) depicting a struggle over cattle. The Kolhāpūr museum and Bīḍ in Karavīr Taluka (southwest of Kolhāpūr), with its more than a hundred hero stones, exhibit only one or two depicting a cattle raid (see above, 3.2.1). In the pastoral region, Veḷāpūr (Māḷśiras Taluka, Sholapur District) is an exception: it has dozens of stones representing battle scenes, but not one with a cattle raid. It seems that at this important crossroads battles between larger armies took place, and hence protection of herds was not the primary reason for erecting hero stones. Hero stones are also found where there is no temple in the Hemāḍ-Pant style, and no remains of such a temple, as for example in Cikhalavḍī, near Indāpūr on the bank of the Bhimā River, in a landscape still characterized by the villages of pastoralist groups.

Many of the Hemāḍ-Pant temples, to the extent that they are still *jāgṛt*—that is, that the god "lives" in the temple and is worshiped there by the faithful—point to settlements with pastoral traditions. An example is found at Paḷasdev, fifteen miles northwest of Indāpūr on the Bhimā river, with its famous Śiva temple. The foundation walls are from the Hemāḍ-Pant epoch, while the superstructure was built of bricks in the Peśvā style. Local tradition traces the temple, which dates from about 1680, to a donation made by cowherds.[3] The village of Ḍhālgāv in Miraj Taluka (Sangli District) also has

2. Kannaḍa, *vīragaḷa*. Unlike those in Karnatak, a *vīragaḷa* in Maharashtra generally does not bear an inscription.

3. *Gazetteer of Bombay State,* Poona District (Bombay, revised edition, 1954), p. 626.

an old temple ascribed to Hemādri. Although no hero stones have been found here depicting men protecting cattle herds, the great cattle market held here every week allows for at least the supposition that the place is an old cattle trading center. Moreover, about a mile from Ḍhālgāv is Ārevāḍī, a center of Birobā worship. As many as twenty thousand Dhangars gather here at the annual pilgrimage in the month of Caitra (March/April).

Between the nuclear agricultural regions—those in the Godāvarī basin in the north, Andhra Pradesh and the area around Sholapur in the east, Karnatak in the south, and the rice region of the Māvaḷ and the Koṅkaṇ in the west—there lay broad stretches of land still characterized by pastoral life. The connection between the nuclear agricultural regions was maintained by the successors of the Vīra-Baṇañjas: Liṅgāyat merchants and groups like the Lamāṇīs ~ Lambāḍīs ~ Briñjārīs ~ Bañjāras, and so on. The last-named, in part endogamous groups that came from the north, were salt and grain merchants, but also cattle breeders and cattle traders, who later took over the task of provisioning the armies of the Muslims and the Marāṭhās. Although it is thought that they first came south with the Muslims at the beginning of the seventeenth century, these groups are nevertheless a classic example of an element of the population that always existed and whose task was to maintain the connection between the separate nuclear agricultural regions. Even the groups' names and their interpretations point to the functions they served. "Lamāṇī" is said to be derived from *lavaṇ* (Sanskrit, *lavaṇa*), "salt." F. R. Allchin suggests that Lambāḍīs were also cattle breeders, and that "Lambāḍī" is derived from "Ālambādī," the famous cattle breed from North Salem District.[4] "Bañjārī" is said to be derived from Sanskrit *vana* + *cara,* and thus to mean "roaming in woods, living in a forest" (Monier-Williams). On the other hand, "Bañjārī" is also derived from Sanskrit *v(~b)aṇij,* "merchant, tradesman." Molesworth explains *vaṇaj* as "a mercantile excursion or sojourning abroad; the traveling on business of a trader," whereas he derives "Briñjārī" from the Persian *biriñj,* "rice."

The Bañjārīs also have a tradition that the great Durgā Devī famine, which lasted from 1396 to 1407 and devastated wide areas of the Deccan, was named for a Bañjārī woman from the exogamous group of the Lāds. She is supposed to have accumulated great wealth and to have owned a million pack oxen, which she used to bring grain from Nepal, Burma, and China. She is supposed to have saved many lives in this way, so that she was given the name Jagdambā, "the mother of the world."[5] This legend at least shows the

---

4. *Neolithic Cattle-Keepers of South India. A Study of the Deccan Ashmounds* (Cambridge, 1963), p. 108. It could be added that in Tamil *ā* (or *ān*) means "female of ox, sambur, and buffalo." *Dravidian Etymological Dictionary,* 283.

5. *Gazetteer of the Bombay Presidency,* vol. 16, Nasik (Bombay, 1883), p. 62, n. 2.

importance of the Bañjārīs as transporters of grain during the worst famines, and before the days of road connections and railroads. But at the same time Jagdambā is also the famous goddess Bhavānī of Tuḷjāpūr (Usmanabad District). Tuḷjāpūr lay on one of the important routes leading south to north between Karnatak and the nuclear agricultural regions of the Godāvarī valley. Even today, Jagdambā of Tuḷjāpūr is still an important goddess of the Bañjārīs. Especially at the Dasarā festival, many of them come to "see" Bhavānī Jagdambā and to worship her.

In the centuries during and after the Yādava period, the god Khaṇḍobā begins to become stronger. Khaṇḍobā, one of the most important gods of Maharashtra, corresponds to an earlier Kannaḍa form, Mallayya/Mailāra. As has been mentioned above, Khaṇḍobā was the god of merchants and of groups belonging to forest and pasture regions. It has been suggested that he is the apotheosis of a Yādava king, and a Jaina work assigned to the twelfth century describes Khaṇḍobā as having originally been a historical hero.[6]

Around that time, temples of Khaṇḍobā arose along the great north-south route. The traditions of these temples are associated with pastoralist groups and merchants' caravans. According to the oral traditions, it was these groups who "brought" the god. The village of Māḷegāv can be cited as an example of this.[7] Māḷegāv—derived from Kannaḍa *maḷe* or Marāṭhī *māḷ* and Marāṭhī *gāv*—means "the village on the hill" or "the village on the plateau," thus in general the abode of pastoralist groups. Māḷegāv lies on the main road from Nāndeḍ (on the Godāvarī River, in the nuclear agricultural region) to Lāṭur, and has a Khaṇḍobā temple in the Hemāḍ-Pant style, presumably from the twelfth or thirteenth century. On the twelfth day of the dark half of the month of Mārgaśīrṣa (November/December), a pilgrimage takes place here. The pilgrimage is named *ghoḍyācī jatrā* because of the horse market connected with it, at which there are traded horses from various parts of India, as well as camels, mules, and oxen. Cattle merchants from Marāṭhvāḍā, Gujarat, Mysore, Rajasthan, and Andhra Pradesh gather here. From the legends of the temple we learn:

> Many years ago, when modern means of transport had not yet facilitated communications, merchants used to carry their wares on horses and oxen. Once a caravan of merchants from Nāndeḍ was transporting sacks of rice to Bīdar in Mysore. The merchants camped overnight in Māḷegāv. The next day, when they wanted to set out, they could not lift one of their bags, which they were convinced contained only rice. When they opened it, they found, to their

6. Mentioned in R. C. Dhere, *Khaṃḍobā* (Puṇeṃ, 1961), p. 18; cf. p. 14.

7. What follows is based on *Census of India,* 1961, vol. 10, Maharashtra, part VII-B, *Fairs and Festivals in Maharashtra* (Bombay, 1969), pp. 190f., and on my own observations.

astonishment, two *śāligrāmas*,[8] which were then installed in Māḷegāv. The day on which this happened was the sixth day of the bright half of the month of Mārgaśīrṣa.

This day, Campāṣaṣṭhī, is also especially consecrated to the god Skanda, and it is partly on this basis that some scholars have identified Khaṇḍobā with Skanda. In Māḷegāv, Bāṇāī is a devotee of Khaṇḍobā, as she is in Pāl (Satara District), where Khaṇḍobā is supposed to have appeared to his favorite devotee, a Gavḷī girl named Pālāī.[9]

As a further example I can cite the village of Mailārpūr/Khānapūr (its older name is Prempūr/Peṃber). Mailārpūr lies on the road from Bīdar to Udgīr, and has, besides remains from the pre-Islamic period, a temple of Khaṇḍobā, who is here called Mailāra. It is perhaps not a coincidence that in the Islamic period the town of Bīdar, with its extensive fort, came into being farther south on this road, and later developed into the capital of the Muslim kingdom of Bīdar. In Mailārpūr too there is a great pilgrimage festival from the sixth day of the bright half of Mārgaśīrṣa (Campāṣaṣṭhī) until the tenth day of the month. There is also a cattle market at this time. Again we see the connection with Skanda, the tutelary deity of thieves; there may be an old tradition involved, for not long ago this north-south route was still seen—whether rightly or wrongly—as threatened by highway robbers.

2. The Period of the Local Rājās, Nāīks, and Marāṭhās

From the fall of the Yādava dynasty (1317/18) until the period of British rule, the Deccan was first under the influence of the Bāhmanī dynasty, and then under that of the five sultanates of the Deccan: Berar (founded in 1484, merged into Ahmadnagar in 1574), Ahmadnagar (founded in 1489–90, annexed by the Mughals in 1633), Bijāpūr (founded in 1489–90), Golkondā (founded in 1512 or 1518, annexed by Aurangzeb in 1687), and Bīdar (founded in 1526 or 1547, merged into Bijāpūr in 1618–19). The Bāhmanīs and their successors were in conflict with one another as well as with the kingdom of Vijayanagar (1336–1565). In 1648, Śivājī founded the independent kingdom of the Marāṭhās, which expanded and survived until 1818. It is uncertain whether or how the area between the agricultural centers lost its pastoral character in the centuries up to the time of the Mughals and Marāṭhās. But it

8. Strictly speaking, a *śāligrāma* is a black stone found in the river Gaṇḍakī; it is usually worshiped as Viṣṇu.

9. *Maharashtra State Gazetteer*, Satara District (Bombay, revised edition, 1963), pp. 856f. The goddess Bāṇāī also has her place in the temple at Pāl, independently of Pālāī.

can be assumed that during this period broad stretches of land in the Deccan, particularly in Maharashtra, were not yet entirely transformed into nuclear agricultural regions with intensive use of the land.

I have already mentioned the relative independence of the Koḷīs under their Nāīks during the time of the Bāhmanīs and Śāh Jahān, and the futile effort made to survey their land (see above, 5.1.3). After the downfall of the Yādavas, and still during the period of the five Sultanates, there were no attempts—or at least no successful attempts—to survey the land east of Poona and institute fixed property taxes. It was pasture land, and the population raised cattle.[10]

During the period of the Vijayanagar empire, according to Burton Stein,[11] regular agriculture expanded, at least in Mysore, primarily in what had until then been forest areas. In the process the forest population was integrated into the empire. This expansion was promoted by warriors and minor princes, the *nāīks* or *nāyakas,* who founded small kingdoms with fortresses as their headquarters. The *daṇḍanāyakas,* originally officials of the great kingdoms, increasingly became autonomous local rulers who made themselves independent, or who strove to become independent, on the basis of local power. The *nāyakas* (*nāīks*) of pastoralist groups or forest tribes likewise often developed into local rulers.

At that time it was possible to emigrate as a unified group from the domain of a tyrannical king and to resettle in new, as yet undeveloped, areas. This is typified by the legends about the Morasu Vakkaligas. The Morasu Vakkaligas were one of the endogamous groups of the Vakkaligas, whose principal occupations were agriculture and cattle-breeding. They are said to have migrated from Kāñcīpuram in the dead of night, because they were involved in a quarrel with the local ruler there. They first came in seven clans to Kolār, settled there, and then gradually spread out further in the region.

Under the leadership of Malla Bhaire Gauda, one of these clans settled in Avatī at the end of the fifteenth century. Near this village there was a small hamlet named Devana-doḍḍī, "Deva's cattle camp." Here Malla Bhaire Gauḍa built a fort to immortalize his name. The fort of Devanahalli, along with the land around it, remained in the possession of the family until 1749, when both fell to the Nañjarājas of Mysore.

The ambitious Malla Bhaire Gauḍa left the fort in the care of his younger brother Sanna Bhaire Gauḍa. Malla made further conquests to the north of Devanahalli and founded the fort of Chikbalapūr. One day when he was

---

10. See V. T. Gune, *The Judicial System of the Marathas* (Poona, 1953), pp. 8f.

11. "Integration of the Agrarian System of South India," in *Land Control and Social Structure in Indian History,* R. E. Frykenberg, ed. (Madison, Wisc., 1969), pp. 188ff.

hunting in the jungle of Koḍi-Mañcenahalli he saw how a hare resisted a dog that was chasing it. From this he realized that the place must have good soil. To two of his brothers, who were the "*pāṭīls*" of the village, he proposed building a fort and a *peṭh* (a trading center) there with the permission of the king of Vijayanagar.

An auspicious moment was set for beginning construction; the moment was to be announced by the sound of a shell horn. A Gosāvī (Dāsari) who happened to be passing by blew on his horn, and Malla Bhaire Gauḍa began construction a half-hour too early. As a result it was predicted that the dynasty would last only three hundred years—and this proved true, because in 1799 the fort fell into the hands of Sultān Tipū.[12]

There is a whole series of similar legends in Mysore about the origin of minor dynasties and local princedoms in the forest and pasture regions. Often there is a cow whose milk pours out over a termite mound in the forest and who thereby indicates the god's presence and the most favorable site for a settlement. The residents of the surrounding forest and pasture region become integrated into the small princedom. Often the ruler even comes from their ranks, or has them as his power base—as Śivājī did with the residents of the forests of the Māvaḷ. This development is illustrated by a *kafīyat* (local chronicle) of the rulers of Candī ("Ginjee") in Andhra Pradesh, which reports on the origin of Candī at the time of the Vijayanagar empire, its fate under the Marāṭhās and Mughals, and finally its conquest by Tipū Sultān:[13]

> During the rule of [Kṛṣṇadevarāyā of Vijayanagar (1509–29)], a certain Vijayaranga Nāīk came with [the king's] permission to Chandī and secured a *jāgīr*. There he cleared the forest, amassed riches, and established Chandī. In [the year] *Faslī* 852[14] a Dhangar named Ānandakoṇ[ṉ]a,[15] who was seeking some strayed flocks, met a *mahā-purusha* [generally this means a Gosāvī], who told him that through his labors Chandī would become a great place, and bade him go to Vijayaranga Nāīk. Accordingly, with Ānandakoṇ[ṉ]a's assistance, the kingdom of Chandī was established, and Ānandakoṇ[ṉ]a's son, Tristapitha, became Prime Minister.
>
> The Nāīk dynasty reigned for eleven generations. . . . The families of Vijayaranga Nāīk and Ānandakoṇ[ṉ]a remained in undisturbed possession of

12. Ananthakrishna Iyer, *The Mysore Castes and Tribes* (Mysore, 1930), vol. 4, pp. 227ff.

13. James Fuller Blumhardt and Sadashiv Kanhere, *Catalogue of the Marathi Manuscripts in the India Office Library* (Oxford, 1950), p. 83, ms. 163.

14. That is, 1442. But the dates in this *kafīyat* do not always agree with the accepted dating.

15. According to the *Tamil Lexicon,* Tamil *kōṉ, kōṉāṉ,* Telugu, *kōnāri,* is a title customary in the Iṭaiyar shepherd caste (p. 1204). *Kōṉ* also means "king," and a local tradition in Candī states that a dynasty of shepherd kings preceded the Nāīks. See E. Thurston, *Castes and Tribes of Southern India* (Madras, 1909), s.v. Idaiyan, p. 357: "Konar (cowherds)"; p. 365: "The usual title of Idaiyans is Kōnān or Kōn meaning King."

> Chandī for 225 years, that is, to *Faslī* 1077. In *Faslī* 1077 Chandī was conquered by [Sardārs sent by Aurangzeb]. Then the Marathas came to the rescue under Śivājī. . . . In *Faslī* 1082 [1672, but more likely 1675], under Śivājī's orders, his son, Rājārāma, became ruler of Chandī. Śivājī then returned to Poona. . . .

This chronicle is legendlike, especially at the beginning, but it essentially reflects the process of change in Maharashtra.[16] Sometimes an old trading center—like Phalṭaṇ, for example—became the base of a local ruler. Phalṭaṇ was an old town, known from inscriptions as early as A.D. 687,[17] which still served in 1854, as we have seen, as a trading center for goods between the interior and the coast. Goods were brought there on pack oxen.[18] Before the middle of the sixteenth century, one of the kings of Bijāpūr made Rāv Nāīk Nimbāḷkar the *sardeśmukh* of Phalṭaṇ. The Nāīks of Phalṭaṇ eventually became independent. They undertook many military expeditions and retained the old title of Nāīk. Their original name was Pavār; the name Nimbāḷkar is derived from that of the village Nimbāḷik or Nimḷāk, where the first Nimbāḷkar lived after migrating to the Nirā valley from the northeast, from Dhārāśiv in Usmanabad District. Another branch of the Nimbāḷkars, the famous Rājās of Vaḍgāv Nimbāḷkar, came from Nimḷāk and settled on the chain of hills north of the Nirā valley, an area where Meṇḍhe Hāṭkar Dhangars still live today and where Gavḷī Dhangars lived before them. There the Nimbāḷkars, one of the five highest Marāṭhā families, founded the village of Vaḍgāv:

Text 49

> In those days it was Daṇḍakāraṇya there. There was jungle. As they left it, they found a *piṇḍ* [see above, chap. 3, n. 21] named Vaṭeśvar under a vaḍ tree (*Ficus Indica*). The village that came into being near this Vaṭeśvar was called Vaṭagrāma, and from that came the Apabhraṃśa name Vaḍgāv. And because we came there, the village was called Vaḍgāv Nimbāḷkar. . . .
>
> Today if you want to buy an acre of garden land (*bāgāīt*) in our village, you have to pay ten thousand rupees. In those days they let you come, and they said, "Bābā, take fifty acres of land, and take money for oxen besides. And then sow. . . ."

Māḷavḍī is an especially typical example of the founding of a famous local Marāṭhā kingdom in the forest and pasture region. Māḷavḍī, which is surrounded by an imposing wall, is located near the source of the Māṇ River,

---

16. See also D. Rothermund, "Feudalism in India," in *The Phases of Indian Nationalism* (Bombay, 1970), pp. 165, 175ff.

17. *Epigraphia Indica,* vol. 19, pp. 62f.

18. See above, chap. 3, n. 17.

seven miles northwest of Dahīvāḍī. Even its name (Māḷavḍī, Māḷvāḍī, "the *vāḍī* on the rocky plateau") shows that the village does not have good agricultural land. And indeed, although there is some good land near the present-day village and on the bank of the nearby Māṇ River, Māḷavḍī otherwise lies in a wild and rocky landscape. Māḷavḍī was the home of the Ghāṭges, one of the most influential Marāṭhā families. One of the heads of the Ghāṭges held a *mansab*[19] or a position of similar rank under the Bāhmanī dynasty. They were awarded the title *sardeśmukh*[20] by the sixth king of Bijāpūr, Ibrahim Adil Śāh (1580–1626). Śivājī conquered Māḷavḍī shortly after his coronation, but the Ghāṭges won it back from him for the king of Bijāpūr. Under the Mughals, the *deśmukhī* rights went to the Brahman Deśmukhs of Khaṭāv. The Ghāṭges were apparently given back these rights by King Śāhū of Sātārā (1707–1749). An order of Śāhū's from the year 1726–27 states that Māḷavḍī was to be settled by Mahādjī Ghāṭge, and that the Khilārī [Dhangars?] and herdsmen (*cāraṇīvāle*) were to receive another Mahāl[21] as pasture land.[22]

According to the oral traditions of Māḷavḍī, Khaṇḍobā is supposed to have come from Ādimailār, near Bīdar, to Naḷdurg in Usmanabad District, and to have been taken to Māḷavḍī by a Dhangar before the Ghāṭges settled there. The following local legend alludes to the changing history of Māḷavḍī:

Text 50

A Dhangar named Rām Corāmble had his farmstead (*vastī*) here. Every day he used to drive his sheep to the pasture. In the early morning he would let his sheep free in the pasture and run straight to Naḷdurg, where he would serve the god Khaṇḍobā. He served in Naḷdurg for twelve whole years. When twelve years had passed, the god was in a good mood one day. And the god said, "Bābū, don't you serve me now. I'll come to your house. Don't you come tomorrow."

"Are these words true or false?" it occurred to him. "The god said to me, 'Don't come tomorrow to serve me.' " So he returned. In the evening he drove the sheep into the pen and locked them in. He ate as usual in the evening, and lay down to sleep. In the morning he got up, let the sheep free, and got his water pot. He took a bath and set out to serve the god. When he arrived, he went to the temple of Mother Bhavānī. When he had gotten there, he suddenly remembered.

---

19. Molesworth, *Dictionary:* "A rank or command formerly in the (Muhammadan) cavalry."

20. As the governor of a *subhā* ("province"), the *sardeśmukh* had the right to one-tenth of the tax revenue.

21. Mahāl used to be a common designation for a part of a district; cf., still today, Khaṇḍāḷā Mahāl, for example, in Satara District.

22. Ma. Gam. Dīkṣita [and] Vi. Go. Khobrekar, *Śāhū Daptarātīla Kāgadapatrāṃcī Varṇanātmaka Sūcī* (Nāgpūr, 1969), *Peśve Daptara Abhilekhamālā, Varṇanātmaka Sūcī,* vol. 1, p. 39 (*daptara aṃka* 2, *puḍke kr.* 4, *patra kr.* 1844).

What had the god said? "I'll come to your house. And the sign of it is that here is a churning stick for churning buttermilk. Young, fresh leaves will break out on it. And you will find a pouch of turmeric powder (*bhaṇḍār*) with two flowers on it—something, anyway, that will show you that the god has come—and a dried-out stick. So don't come to serve me any more."

He remembered that. He came back and went to his house in the enclosure. And there he saw that leaves had broken out on the churning stick. The leaves looked very fresh. Then he saw a pouch of turmeric powder and some pieces of coconut lying on the ground. And he saw two flowers. So from then on he did his service of the god there. And thus it continued for some time.

Later there came bad times (*ucitkal* = *uccedh-kāḷ?*). Some people died, some went away because they had nothing to eat. When they had left, there was only the fallen-down farmstead here. There was no way to earn a living here (*ādhār*), no people, nothing. In this way some days passed. Then Ghāṭge was given a kingdom here. He came into the jungle to hunt for hares. As he was wandering around, he came here and startled a golden hare. "It looks very beautiful. I want to catch it."

So he chased around after the hare in the jungle. And the hare hid itself under some leaves. It hid under the fallen leaves and branches of a ṭaraṭī tree.[23] Now it could no longer be seen. He saw the leaves. He was afraid. "If I dig it out and somehow I'm suddenly bitten, then what will become of me?"

So he broke off a piece of wood from a tarvaḍ tree[24] and he pushed the leaves here and there. When he had removed them, he saw a *śāḷuṅkhā* stone[25] in a hole. And he saw some turmeric powder. "This is a place sacred to Khaṇḍobā," he thought. Then he carefully took out the stone. The day was in the Māval. And it didn't occur to him [to ask], "Where am I?" or [to answer], "I am out hunting." He swept the place and cleaned it. And he sat down right there.

Then he took a bath. He returned. There were flowers growing on the bank of the stream; he laid them at the place. He brought wild fruits, showed them to the god, and stayed there performing service. He had no recollection of his kingdom or of anything else. Then his people, who had remained at home, said, "To whom has the king gone? Why is he away? He is out hunting all alone!"

So they got worried, and they went to search for him in the jungle. "He'll be hunting in this jungle." Wandering around in the jungle, they came to that place, and found him sitting there performing service. "Oh dear, King, we've been waiting for you for two or four days, [wondering] where you are."

"Oh, nothing has happened to me. I am not going anywhere. I have set up

---

23. *Capparis Erythrocarpus* (Molesworth).

24. *Cassia auriculata* (Molesworth).

25. A stone in the center of which is found a *bāṇa* (Sanskrit), the emblem of Śiva. The *śāḷuṅkhā* is the *yonī,* and the *bāṇa* Śiva's *liṅgam.*

my camp (*vāḍā*) right here, and now I'll stay here.'' So he founded a village here. He brought people from somewhere and settled them here. And they began to serve him. They built a *vāḍā* [here, a fort] and so forth, and began to serve him in various ways.

When they had served him for a long time, an enemy came and attacked his fort. [The king] stayed in the temple for twenty-four hours without coming out. His minister ruled as he saw fit over law (*nyāy*) and authority (?, *natya*), while the king devoted himself only to serving [the god]. When the demon came, [the minister] made the announcement [that the enemy had appeared], then sent for the king and told him. The king said, ''I cannot give up serving the god now. If the kingdom is destroyed, I won't object.''

The people said, ''That king is as good as dead. How can we fight the enemy? We need a king, don't we, to protect what comes after us? How can we take the field? We need a king. See if at least his son will come. It will be good for our forces if his son comes. See whether or not the boy will come with us.''

They asked the boy. They told him about the advancing host [of the enemy]. ''I have no misgivings. If the king won't come, then I will.''

''Let's go!'' They placed him on a magnificent seat on an elephant, and they marched against the enemy with beating drums and piping pipes.

[What follows describes the death of the son, the flight of the king to sink Khaṇḍobā in a well, the king's return after the enemy has been ousted, and the final settling of Māḷavḍī.]

The legend of the hare that leads the invading king and the new settlers to the place where the kingdom is to be founded occurs frequently in western India. It is found in stories about the origin of Vijayanagar,[26] and I have referred to it above in the case of a local founding during the Vijayanagar period. The Peśvā Bājirāv I (1720–40) chose the site for the Śanivār palace in Poona when he saw a hare hunting a dog. A similar event is supposed to have led to the founding of a fort (Gulbargā?) by Hassan Gaṅgu, the first ruler of the Bāhmanīs.[27] Hand in hand with the emergence of local princedoms there also grew up new local cults, in which Khaṇḍobā received the greatest dissemination. He gained popularity particularly among the warring lords. Many of the Sardārs and Śiledārs who learned their trade among the Muslims and rose to power under Śivājī and the Peśvās came from pastoral areas. Even when they eventually received a *jāgīr* in another part of western India, their devotion to Khaṇḍobā, their *kulsvāmī,* was concentrated on particular cult places of Khaṇḍobā in the pastoral area. Thus the famous Hoḷkars of Indore were devotees of Khaṇḍobā of Jejurī. As their name indicates, the Hoḷkar

26. R. Sewell, *A Forgotten Empire* (New Delhi, 2nd edition, 1970), pp. 18f.
27. Blumhardt and Kanhere, *Catalogue,* pp. 81f.

family came from Hoḷ, a village near the town of Nirā on the bank of the Nirā River. Khaṇḍojī Vīrkar, a Khuṭekar Dhangar, was a *caugule*[28] in Hoḷ.[29] Later, around 1733, his son received Indore District as a *jāgīr* from the Peśvā Bājī Rāv.

Whereas the Hoḷkars never denied their pastoral origins, the Gāikvāḍs of Barodā are regarded as Marāṭhās, and the word cow (*gāī*) in their name is connected with protecting cows from Muslims.[30] But the name Gāikvāḍ occurs primarily among Gavḷīs,[31] and perhaps the historically correct derivation of the name is from *gāī,* which means "cow," and *kāvaḍ.* A *kāvaḍ* is the carrying pole at both ends of which are found slings for carrying pots of milk or water. In the past such a carrying pole was common among Gavḷīs. A modern wall painting in Kharsuṇḍī portrays as the founder of the Siddha cult a Gavḷī who carries a pole with milk pots hanging from its ends.

The family god of the Gāikvāḍs is the Khaṇḍobā whose shrine is near the village of Nimgāv in Kheḍ Taluka (Poona District). The original Khaṇḍobā is still to be found inside the temple precinct, very close to the newer, Peśvā-style temple. Khaṇḍobā is still a god of the herds here, symbolized by an aniconic, *liṅga*like stone in front of which are placed stone votive figures representing cattle. In Nimgāv too it is believed that the first Gāikvāḍs were Gavḷīs, by occupation if not also by caste.

---

28. A *caugule* was an official, subordinate to the *pāṭīl,* to whom were entrusted the records kept by the *kulkarṇī.*

29. According to Iravati Karvé, *Maharashtra State Gazetteer, Maharashtra—Land and Its People* (Bombay, 1968), p. 20, the Hoḷkars, the famous generals of the Marāṭhās and the rulers of Indore, were Hāṭkars. But a chronicle (*bakhar*) of the Hoḷkar kings (*rājās*) of Indore begins as follows: *mauje hoḷa muruma nīrece kāṃṭhīṃ jejorījavaḷa āhe. tetheṃ khaṇḍojī vīrakara khuṭekara dhanagara caugule rāhata hote.* . . . "The village of Hoḷ is near Jejurī on the bank of the Nirā river. Khaṇḍojī Vīrkar, a Khuṭekar Dhangar, a *caugule,* lived there. . . ." (Blumhardt and Kanhere, *Catalogue,* p. 82, ms. 162).

30. C. A. Kincaid and Rao Bahadur D. B. Parasnis, *A History of the Maratha People,* vol. 2 (Bombay, 1922), pp. 176f.:

> This Pilaji Gaikvad was the founder of the great house of Baroda; and since English historians, as a rule, interpret wrongly the name Gaikvad to mean cowherd, it will not be out of place to narrate here the origin of the family. The word Gaikvad is made up of two Marathi words—"Gai" a cow, and "Kavad" a small door. "Gaikvad" therefore means a "cow's door." The family came to adopt the name in this way. Nandaji, the great-grandfather of Pilaji Gaikvad, was in charge of Bher fort in that part of the Mawal tract which, watered by the Pavana river in the Bhor state, is known as the Pavana Maval. One day a Musulman butcher drove past the fort gates a herd of cows, intending at the close of his journey to convert them into beef. Nandaji, like a virtuous Hindu, rushed out and rescued the cows, which ran for shelter into the fort through a side door or "Kavad." Proud of this meritorious feat, Nandaji assumed the name of "Gaikavad," or cow's door which has since been corrupted into Gaikvad.

31. See above, Text 5.

The famous Marāṭhā family of the Sindias of Gwalior was originally named Śinde. The Śindes too rose to the position of *śiledārs* during the time of the Bāhmanī kings. They are supposed to have been Kuṇbīs originally, and they were called the Peśvās' "slipper-bearers," in allusion to their simple origins.[32] The Śindes held the hereditary office of *pāṭīl* in the village of Kanherkheḍ (Koregāv Taluka, Satara District). Kincaid and Parasnis write, "They became patils or herdsmen of the village of Kanherkheḍ."[33] The *pāṭīl* of a village in the pastoral region was primarily an owner of herds—indeed, owning a herd of cattle was more highly valued than owning land.[34] *Gauḍā* in Kannaḍa is similar in meaning to *pāṭīl*. In Marāṭhī, *gāvḍā* means, among other things, "the *adhikārī* among the *dhangar* people" (Molesworth). Among Kurubas too *gāvḍās* or *gauḍās* are village or caste leaders. Dhangars in the Nirā and Māṇ valleys no longer call themselves Gāvḍās, but they still know that Dhangars who owned cattle used to be called Gāvḍās. The goddess Bāṇāī/Bānubāī came from a Gāvḍā family, and Gāvḍās occur in oral traditions as well:[35]

Text 51

Hemu Gāvḍā's *vāḍā* was on the other side of the Nirā and Bhimā rivers. His wife was Gīrjā Gāvḍī. They had no children. There were only the two of them. In the month of Śimgā, they celebrated Hoḷī. The child was born on the day after Hoḷī, on Dhuḷvaḍī.[36] The child was born in the ashes [of the Hoḷī fire]. Then Hemu Gāvḍā called out, "A child is crying in the Hoḷī fire that was kindled last night." Gīrjā Gāvḍī took *haldī* and *kuṅkum* to sprinkle in the fire.[37] She said, "Oh, goodness me, there really is a child crying. Whose is it?"

Carefully she brought the child, and she wiped it and washed it. "Look, a child has been born to us," she said. "God has brought it to us."

Then came the naming ceremony.[38] What name should be given to him? She said, "He has come from the ashes (*dhuḷ*), so he should be given the name

---

32. Surendra Nath Roy, *History of the Native States of India,* vol. 1, *Gwalior* (Calcutta, 1888), pp. 107–9.

33. Kincaid and Parasnis, *History,* p. 128.

34. In *Jñāneśvarī,* 18.172, cows are referred to as *gāṃvadhaṇa,* "the wealth of the village."

35. The following text comes from Lakḍevāḍī, about ten miles south of Phalṭaṇ (Satara District).

36. Molesworth, *Dictionary:* "The day of throwing dust after burning of the *Hoḷī.* It is the first day after the full moon of Phālgun [February/March]."

37. *Śipāylā,* from *śipṇeṃ,* "the sprinkling and scattering of colored powders or dust towards the close of the festival of *Hoḷī.* The fifth day of the dark half of Phālgun (*raṅgpañcamī*), the day on which the powders, etc., are sprinkled" (Molesworth, *Dictionary*). *Haldī,* or turmeric powder, is bright yellow; *kuṅkum* is bright red.

38. *Bāras* = *barseṃ* or *barsā* = "the ceremony of naming a child on the twelfth day after its birth" (Molesworth, *Dictionary*).

Dhuḷdev.'' At first the god was Ujanī Mankhāl [Ujjainī Mahākāl], but after he was born in the ashes he was given the name Dhuḷdev. . . .

Is it possible that the Śindes too were originally cattle farmers, Gāvḍās? The story of the god Dhuḷdev, whose principal cult is found in Phalṭaṇ (Satara District), but who is also worshiped in Sangli District (at Limbavḍe) and Kolhapur District (north of Paṭṭaṇ Kuḍolī), seems to suggest further connections with the Śindes. The first *bhakta* and *mānkarī* of Dhuḷobā was Kamaḷā Śinde (or Śid, Siddha). His wife Gīrjā came from a Dhangar family, the Wāghmoḍes of Māḷśiras in Sholapur District, who were *pāṭīls* or *sardārs* there. Moreover, Dhuḷobā is supposed to be identical with Ujjainī Mahākāl (Kāḷbhairav) in Mālvā. Around 1735, Ujjain, the site of the most famous temple of Mahākāl, became the headquarters of Rāṇojī Śinde. Marāṭhā saints like Dattanāth Ujjanīkar lived there during the period of Śinde rule.[39]

Besides Khaṇḍobā—and Dhuḷobā, who is similar to him in many respects[40]—Kāḷbhairav was disseminated ever more widely in the forest and pasture region. Thus Kāḷbhairav of Sonārī spread as far as the Karnatak border. In Biḷūr, in Jath Taluka, for instance, Kāḷbhairav of Sonārī has by far eclipsed in importance an impressive Śiva temple in the Hemāḍ-Pant style. In the hall (*sabhāmaṇḍapa*) of this temple, to the right of the entrance, is found what is now the principal cult place, dedicated to Kāḷbhairav. Near a *mūrti* of Kāḷbhairav showing him with a trident, an hourglass drum, and a garland of skulls, there stands an almost lifesize statue of a horseman, which represents Kāḷbhairav as a typical Marāṭhā prince—that is, a *sardār* or *śiledār*. Besides Kāḷbhairav of Biḷūr, Dhuḷobā of Phalṭaṇ and Khaṇḍobā of Jejurī are also represented in this way. In Mhasvaḍ the *mūrti* of Mhasvaḍ-Siddha/Kāḷbhairav wears the typical garb of a Marāṭhā *śiledār,* and every Sunday it is shown mounted on a horse.

Generally Kāḷbhairav was brought to his new cult place by, or first revealed himself to, a member of a pastoralist group. But it is also necessary to ask whether the focal area of my research lost its pastoral character after the period of the Bāhmanī dynasty, under the rule of the Marāṭhās. In this period Khaṇḍobā was above all a god of the warring ''Marāṭhā'' groups—the Marāṭhas in the broadest sense. Drought, famine, and especially war prevented the development of regular agriculture. Under a local ruler, the land could be cultivated, but the more promising source of income was warfare, with its easily gained riches. For that purpose the *śiledār* had to put riders and horses at the king's disposal. Therefore the pastures of the area were more profitable than was agriculture. For the farmers of the pastoral region, cattle were more

39. H. S. Joshi, *Origin and Development of Dattatreya Worship in India* (Baroda, 1965), pp. 128f.

40. *Maharashtra State Gazetteer,* Kolhapur District (Bombay, revised edition, 1960), p. 834.

valuable than was land, which was endangered by war or drought. Cattle could be driven into the forests during a drought, or, when threatened by enemies, they could be hidden in ravines and so forth.

Dādājī Koṇḍev (d. 1647), the regent of Śāhjī and the guru of King Śivājī, is supposed to have striven especially hard to spread agriculture. But it is not surprising that Dādājī Koṇḍev attempted this in the Māvaḷ, rather than to the east of Poona, where the town of Bārāmatī, for example, also belonged to Śivājī's *jāgīr*. The *Gazetteer of Bombay State* conjectures that he did so "either because the māvals, i.e. the western portion of the Poona district, were politically more important or because they had comparatively secure agriculture."[41]

The western part of the districts of Poona, Satara, Kolhapur, and Ahmadnagar was also more densely populated than the eastern part of these districts, and the difference in population density continues today. The contrast between the western and eastern parts of the districts is expressed in the words of T. Ogilvy, who in 1854 wrote about the territory in his *Memoir:*

> The entire territory of Satara is divided into two distinct and very dissimilar parts, by a chain of hills branching off from north to south for fifty or sixty miles nearly to the banks of Krishna near Walwa. The district lying to the west . . . is well peopled with industrious agriculturists, is well cultivated, and productive, and is rendered fertile and salubrious by seasonable showers. The division of the territory to the east of that chain of hills is, though still intersected by spurs, more flat and barren, and it is ill cultivated by a thin, unsettled, and in some degree predatory population. The fall of rain is scanty and precarious, and the climate is hot and insalubrious. These districts yield, however, excellent pastures, which have encouraged the breeding of horses, celebrated among the Marathas, and they maintain numerous flocks and herds.[42]

Ogilvy's words also describe what the British found at the beginning of their rule. When the British—that is, the East India Company—took over the government from the last Peśvā, they also inherited an old problem that had always confronted Indian rulers. There was no shortage of land; rather, there was a shortage of people, whom it was necessary to persuade through wise and just taxation to cultivate the land. "The people are few compared to the quantity of arable land," wrote Mountstuart Elphinstone in his *Report* in 1826;[43] and H. D. Robertson, in his assessment of the captured territories,

---

41. *Gazetteer of Bombay State,* Poona District, p. 49.

42. T. Ogilvy, *Memoir on the Satara Territory,* in *Selections from the Records of the Bombay Government,* no. 41, n.s., R. Hughes Thomas, ed. (Bombay, 1857), pp. 3ff.

43. *Selections of Papers from the Records at the East-India House Relating to the Revenue, Police. . . ,* vol. 4 (London, 1826), p. 178. See also p. 142, on conditions in Khāndeś and in the area south of the Nirā River.

remarked on the achievements of Ṭoḍar Mal and Malik Ambar in the field of agricultural taxation:

> That prince (or rather proprietor), therefore, whose country was better peopled than the country of his neighbours, would be richer than they. Riches give power (especially to sovereigns); and a wise prince who was, or considered himself to be the proprietor of the soil of his kingdom, would readily perceive that his ambition would be best gratified by an indulgent consideration towards (even if he did not share his right of proprietorship) those who laboured on it.[44]

For a long time during the British period, agitation among farmers and a series of robberies carried out by the Rāmośīs under Umājī Nāīk threatened the security of the area.[45] In the nineteenth century, broad stretches of land were still thickly forested. Belgaum was surrounded by thick bamboo forests,[46] and even the area west of Poona (!) was again—probably because of the continuous uncertainty brought on by war—interspersed with jungle inhabited by tigers and panthers. It was a problematic task when in 1836 the jungle began to be cleared for agricultural use.[47]

Even thirty years ago there was still "jungle" on the ranges of hills between Jejurī and Nirā—that is, *māḷrān,* uncultivated land with bushes and bābhūḷ trees. This remained the preserve of nomadic Dhangars and their herds of sheep, while they were increasingly driven out of the valleys and into the ranges of hills. As late as 1935, four thousand truckloads of bābhūḷ trees were carried away from the area around Nirā.

3. The Spread of Agriculture: Historical Evidence from the Nirā and Karhā Valleys

3.1. The Expulsion of the Gavḷīs

In this section I will present some historical evidence from the Karhā and Nirā valleys illustrating the intrusion of agriculture into the forest and pasture region. This development had profound effects, not least of all on religion.

With the start of the monsoon at the beginning of June, the Dhangar camp (*vāḍī*) A returns from its six-to-seven-month stay in the Koṅkaṇ to its mon-

---

44. Ibid., pp. 409f.

45. See A. Mackintosh, *An Account of the Origin and Present Conditions of the Tribe of Ramoossies* (Bombay, 1833) and Ravinder Kumar, *Western India in the Nineteenth Century. A Study in the Social History of Maharastra* (London and Toronto, 1968).

46. *Selections from the Records of Bombay Government,* n.s. (Belgaum, 1857), p. 4.

47. *Gazetteer of the Bombay Presidency,* vol. 18, Poona (Bombay, 1885), part 1, p. 31.

soon camp, five miles east of Jejurī. If the monsoon fails, the pastures dry up and the Dhangars are forced into further wanderings. They pen their herds of sheep on fields belonging to farmers in the Nirā valley, an area protected from drought by the irrigation facilities provided by the so-called Left-Hand Canal of the Nirā River. In a good rainy season the camp has a fixed place, although people remember that the camp has twice been moved a bit farther away from the small village of Nāvḷī. Nāvḷī, which has only in very recent times been connected for most of the year with Nirā and Jejurī by bus, was originally just a small hamlet, which village tradition says grew up out of the jungle near a Muslim *pīr*'s *samādhī* or *dargā* and the site of a Mhasobā cult.[48]

The residents of the village are primarily Kuṇbīs/Marāṭhās surnamed Mhaske. They originally came from Pātharḍī Taluka in Ahmadnagar District. A bit outside the village is a neglected—indeed, practically forgotten—Kanhobā (Kṛṣṇa), the family deity (*kulsvāmī*) of the Mhaskes. The fact that Kanhobā is frequently a god of Gavḷīs/Gollas, and the fact that the name Mhaske (*mhaskyā*) means "a buffalo-grazier or keeper" (Molesworth), suggest that the first settlers followed pastoralist occupations and owned herds of cattle before they turned completely to regular agriculture. I have already alluded to the Mhaske Dhangars, who live today in the Koynā valley, where the pastures in the forests of the Ghāṭs still suffice to maintain herds of cattle. However, all this does not force us to conclude that with the transition to regular agriculture in this area, the Mhaskes of Nāvḷī changed their caste, that they had been Gavḷīs and became Kuṇbī/Marāṭhās instead. In other cases we have seen that farmers immigrating to the pastoral area were called "Gavḷīs" there after their predecessors.[49] But the disappearance of the Gavḷīs does allow us to suppose that some of them became farmers and were absorbed into the Kuṇbī/Marāṭhā caste. The eldest member of camp A was certain that the predecessors of the Hāṭkar Dhangars in this area were Gavḷīs. He remembered clashes between Gavḷīs and Rāmośīs in his youth.

Near the small village of Guḷuñce, between camp A and the town of Nirā, there is a camp that adjoins Jhirāpvāḍī, a small settlement of Marāṭhās. Once when cholera broke out in the Marāṭhā settlement during the rainy season, the Dhangars' camp disappeared. It had been moved two miles away from the settlement. The next year the monsoon failed, and so this group did not return at all to its monsoon camp at Jhirāpvāḍī, but stayed near Vīr, in fields irrigated by the Left-Hand Canal. The principal deity of the camp is Nāīkobā,

---

48. According to the *Śāhū Daptar* (1707–1750), Nāvilī or Nāyevali was an *ināṃ* "granted to the *dargā* of Śāhā Mansūr Pīr, Said Umīndīn Sarphrājkhān Kājī, and the Pīrjāde" (Dīkṣita and Khobrekar, *daptara aṃka* 26, *puḍke* 2, *ināme* [33348, 33602]).

49. See Text 31, above.

a god of the Dhangars who is now worshiped by Marāṭhās as well. Nāīkobā, who can be seen as a deified Dhangar, comes from near Morgāv (see Text 65, below). Of particular interest to us here are the ruins of a large, abandoned Gavḷī settlement, about a mile west of Jhirāpvāḍī, on the foothills of a mountain. From here one has a good view of what are still called the "former pastures," the present-day fields. The three deities of this Gavḷī settlement are still known, and Dhangars who graze their sheep on the hills occasionally worship the deities by smearing them with *śendūr*. They are Lakṣmīāī—the favorite goddess of Gavḷīs and Dhangars who gives wealth in the form of plentiful cattle[50]—Mhasobā, and M(h)asan Buvā.

Buvā is a term frequently used for a *sādhū*. Masan (written *masaṇ;* Sanskrit, *smaśāna*) means "a burning or burying ground for the dead" (Molesworth). Thus Masan Buvā means "the *sādhū* of the burning ground or the cemetery." The term *masaṇ* often refers to ash-besmeared *sādhūs* and Gosāvīs. Here again, then, we have the connection between Gosāvīs and Gavḷīs that occurs so frequently in the region of my research.

Surprisingly, our Masan Buvā is found again about three miles farther west over the chain of hills, in Vālhā. Here Masan Vīr is a god of the Dhangars, especially the *kulsvāmī* of the Madnes. If we recall that the Gavḷīs, who are often also called Gavḷī Dhangars, are supposed once to have formed a single endogamous group with the Hāṭkar Dhangars (Text 35), we see the possibility that the Madnes, who are now regarded as Hāṭkars, were once Gavḷīs. The proud Dhangars of *vāḍī* B, who are surnamed Lakḍe, speak somewhat hesitantly about their marriage alliance with the Madnes, which they entered into because their grandfather was an especially close friend of one of the Madnes. The story of Masan Vīr and the Madnes also illuminates the process of development in the Nirā valley generally:

Text 52

The original holy place of the god Masan Vīr is the village of Karḍāpī in Phalṭaṇ Taluka. Ever since our ancestors came here [to Vālhā], the principal holy place has been here. People with the surname Madne worship Masan Vīr. When they had come here, the devotees (*bhaktas*) collected money and built the temple. The temple has been here for forty or fifty years. Every Sunday, Monday, and Tuesday they give the god *prasād,* and accordingly people receive whatever they wish for (*ichūk goṣṭī astīl tyā icchāpramāṇe hotāt*). In this respect, Masan Vīr is god's holy place, and it has been here for many years. The god is pleased with the people. The original holy place of the god Masan Vīr is Karḍāpī in

---

50. Farmers also call cows, buffalo cows, oxen, and buffalo bulls "Lakṣmī," because they are profitable for agriculture. See Triṃbaka Nārāyaṇa Ātre, *Gāṃva-Gāḍā* (Muṃbai, 3rd edition, 1959), p. 3.

Phalṭaṇ Taluka, and his earlier history (*pūrvīcā tyāncā itihās*) is like this: The god had the form of a Gosāvī. When he was a Gosāvī, he used to watch the cows. And so he first had a liking for the people who used to live in the forest. And so there came into being the devotion (*bhakti*) of the group of Madnes (*Madne kampanī*).

At that time the Madnes owned twelve villages in Phalṭaṇ Taluka. Some of them held the position of *pāṭīl,* and when their numbers had increased they went to other villages. Thus some came here too. And this village has been in existence for forty or fifty years. When we came here, our people lived as they had in the forest. They had sheep and goats, and it was difficult to graze them. So some of the people went to Mahāḍ, Alibāg, and Panvel in Kolaba and Thana districts.[51] They spent the summer there, watched the sheep during the day, penned them at night with farmers, and thus got an income. And they got additional income from the wool. In the rainy season an enormous amount of rain falls in the Koṅkaṇ, and because there is no protection for the sheep, the people used to have to return to the plateau (Deś). And so they became established here in Vālhā. They bought land here. It was dry, barren land (*māḷrān),* and they bought it in order to graze the sheep on it, not in order to farm it. But the Government of India gave orders to produce more grain, and so the people dug wells and laid field walls and made it into farm land, and tilled the dry fields.

This story was narrated by a Madne who is no longer one of the nomadic Dhangars. He can read and write, and he resides permanently in Vālhā. In contrast to the nomadic Dhangars, he wears a "Gandhi cap" rather than a red turban. He speaks of the migrations to the Koṅkaṇ in the past tense, although most Madnes still migrate to the Koṅkaṇ today. Nevertheless, the most recent expansion of agriculture has brought with it, in Vālhā as well as elsewhere, the sight of red-turbaned, nomadic Dhangars plowing their pastures during a good rainy season, often with the assistance of Māḷīs. In addition, the text also seems to provide an example of a group of herdsmen who were driven from the Nirā valley into the hills.

Whether the Madnes were Gavḷī cattle herders or not must remain an open question here. But the text shows us that it was difficult even for herds of sheep to find pastures, let alone herds of cattle. The Gavḷīs disappeared, whether they became farmers or sheep-raising Dhangars.

The famous cult of Someśvar at Karañje, six miles from Nirā, provides a further example of the disappearance of the Gavḷīs. The cult goes back to a founding by Gavḷīs. The brief *Māhātmya*[52] states:

51. In the Koṅkaṇ.

52. Kai. Śrī Ābājīrāva Nāgojīrāva Pavāra (*pāṭīla,* Āmbavaḍe, Ji. [Jilla] Sātārā), *Śrīsomanātha Māhātmya* (*āvṛtti* 15*vi, śake* 1888 [1966]).

Text 53

7. The village of Karañje is holy.
In the past it began as a settlement of Gavḷīs.
Because of *bhakti* Somnāth became self-formed (*svayaṃbhū*)
And stayed here forever.
8. In Bhimthaḍī Taluka,[53]
In Bārāmatī Thāṇā, Poona District,
It lies in the south, two *kos* from the Nirā River.
That is in essence the description of Karañje.
9. At that time there lived in Karañje a Gavḷī.
He was called Mahādū, and he lived with his family.
They were always happy.
He lived with his wife Mālu.
10. Then one day
A yogī came to this village.
Mahādū treated him most respectfully.
He took the Śiva yogī into his house.
11. His parents said to the Śiva yogī,
Our Mahādū has no children.
Show us a solution.
They spoke thus, and beseeched the Śiva yogī.

[Here I summarize the rest of the *Māhātmya:*] The *sādhū* tells Mālu of the importance of Śrī Someśvar of Sorṭī (Saurāṣṭra) in Gujarat, and tells her to worship him every day for twelve years. After twelve years, Somnāth appears in Karañje as a serpent sucking the milk of a *kapila* cow (a black cow). Frightened, Mālu's servant throws an axe at the snake, wounding it on the forehead. Somnāth forgives Mālu and her servant, and promises to appear in the village on the last day of the month of Śrāvaṇ every year. On this day the annual pilgrimage takes place.

Gavḷīs are also considered to have built the temple, which is in the Hemāḍ-Pant style. Here too we again find Gavḷīs connected with the *sādhū,* yogī, or Gosāvī who mediates the cult for them.

The *Māhātmya* was composed in 1911 by a Marāṭhā *pāṭīl* surnamed Pavār, from Khaṭāv Taluka (Satara District).[54] It was probably during this period that the effects of the Left-Hand Canal began to be felt, guaranteeing that regular agriculture not dependent on the monsoon would expand in the area watered by the canal.[55] The Someśvar cult gained new followers. Today the god is

53. Now Bārāmatī Taluka.

54. *Śrīsomanātha Māhātmya,* 280.

55. Work on the Left Hand Canal was begun in 1881, and the canal system was inaugurated in 1885–6. It seems that for various reasons farmers began to use the canal water only at the beginning of the twentieth century. (Information received orally from R. P. Nene, based on a

worshiped especially by rich owners of sugarcane fields watered by the Nirā Canal, but also by farmers of all other kinds and even by residents of Poona and Bombay—a fact to be attributed in large part to the influence of a popular Marāṭhī film about the cult. Hardly any Gavḷīs follow this cult any more, because they have dwindled to a few families, who live in larger places.

Farther east, in Rūī, which is located near Kaḷas, between Bārāmatī and Indāpūr, we find the famous herdsmen's god named Bābīr (see Text 29). He was clearly a god of cattle herders, Gavḷīs. Four earlier cult places are still pointed out, places where the god had been before he settled down permanently at the present site of his temple. This reflects the earlier mobility of the herders, whose camps, and along with them the cult, often moved from one place to another. The priests (*pūjārīs*) of the temple are still Gavḷīs, whereas the devotees (*bhaktas*) are Dhangars—the Dhangar named Thorat, for example, who holds the first right of worship.

A similar development took place on the other side of the Nirā valley. Camp B, in the vicinity of Jāvḷī, near Śiṅgṇāpūr, lies in a region that, according to the oral testimony of the eldest member of the camp, once consisted exclusively of pastures belonging to Gavḷīs. The pastures stretched from the foothills of the "Phalṭaṇ Range" to the road that runs along the Nirā valley, through Phalṭaṇ, Nātepute, and Māḷśiras, to Paṇḍharpūr.

The Siddha of Jāvḷī, near camp B, comes from Mhasvaḍ. The origin of this god is connected not only with Gosāvīs and Gavḷīs, but also with Cāmbhārs (members of the leather-working "caste"). The Cāmbhārs, whose history is obscure, lived not far from Jāvḷī on a hill where the foundation walls of their settlement can still be seen today. Their leader is still respectfully referred to as "king" (Rājā) by the other castes. It is said that the Cāmbhārs were conquered by the Muslims. Perhaps in this place there was a symbiosis of Gavḷīs (the cattle herders) and Cāmbhārs (those who work hides and sell them).

The title "Rājā" reminds us that in the forest and pasture region, many a man—such as the famous Umājī Nāīk—could attain a status and reputation that would have been denied him in the nuclear agricultural region on account of his caste. The strict caste system was dominant in the nuclear agricultural region—in Paiṭhaṇ, for example. In the forest and pasture region there was relative freedom from the caste system. Hence, too, in Maharashtra the *bhakti* movement, which transcends the caste system, was focused on a cult located in the herdsmen's region: in Paṇḍharpūr.[56] The Śiva and Devī cult, which was

---

study of the implementation of the canal in Bārāmatī Taluka.) The Right Hand Canal was completed in 1937–8. In recent years construction was finally also completed on the Vīr dam.

56. Thomas J. Hopkins understands that "the movement probably was urban rather than rural

prevalent here, was overlaid by the milder Kṛṣṇaite Viṭhobā cult, influenced by the Vaiṣṇavas. The characteristics of the "Śaiva" Viṭhobā of the Gavḷīs and Dhangars can nevertheless still be detected in their traditions, although here too the "new" Viṭhobā makes his presence felt.

In Jāvḷī, one new stone sculpture inside the temple precincts depicts a Kānphaṭā Gosāvī; Jogeśvarī is represented on another. There is also here a place called a termite mound where the god revealed himself for the first time. Thus all of the characteristic elements of a cult in the forest and pasture region are at hand.

The Gavḷīs were driven out of the neighborhood of Jāvḷī not too long ago. The eldest of the Dhangars in the *vāḍās* around Jāvḷī remembers the expulsion of the Gavḷīs. The following account comes from a Dhangar who is about thirty years old. It was also given, independently of him, by his father, who is about fifty years old. The father's account agrees with the son's in its essential details. The events related here, which the narrator had heard about from his father and from his grandmother on his father's side, happened in the youth of the narrator's grandfather—that is, around the beginning of the present century:

Text 54

At first Gavḷīs lived here. The Gavḷīs lived where the Lakḍes, Sūḷs, and Devkātes are today. Then the Mendhe [Hāṭkar] Dhangars came here. They said [to the Gavḷīs]: "Let us stay here." The Gavḷīs said, "No, we won't allow you to stay here. If you let your sheep graze here, our cattle will have nothing to eat." In this way their feud began. Afterward they took their dispute to court. The hearings (*tārkhī*) got under way. Bhāgū Lakḍe, Rāmā Sūḷ, and Dhuḍī Devkāte used to go to the hearings, and all of the Gavḷīs would go to the hearings. Then the [three] Dhangars began to say, "Go away from here." [The Gavḷīs] got the land registered in their names in court. All of the Gavḷīs had gone to the hearings. Some of the Dhangars had [stayed behind] here. The Gavḷīs couldn't get back from the hearings. They stayed there.[57] Eight or ten Dhangars got together and went at night to the Gavḷī *vāḍā*. And they destroyed the huts. There were four or five Gavḷīs there, whom they drove away. [The Dhangars] burned their huts. They threw their belongings (*sāmān*) into the river. And they re-

---

and drew its support from members of the depressed urban classes that would be present in sufficient numbers to give the movement stability" ("The Social Teaching of the *Bhāgavata Purāṇa,*" in *Krishna: Myths, Rites and Attitudes,* Milton Singer, ed. [Chicago, 1966], p. 22). Cf. *Maharashtra State Gazetteer,* Maratha Period (Bombay, 1972), p. 234: "The Bhakti movement of the middle ages was a protest against the ritual of Brahminism and the superstition of the masses." Both assessments speak for a relative freedom from the caste system in the forest and pasture region, and for the popular appeal of such pastoral cults as that of the Vaiṣṇavized Kṛṣṇa.

57. Apparently at the Taluka court in Phalṭaṇ.

turned to their own camp (*vastī*). Then the Gavḷīs went away from there. To this day we don't know where they went. From then on Dhangars have lived here.

The reason for the quarrels and for the expulsion of the Gavḷīs was the shortage of pasture land. The intrusion of agriculture reduced the pasture lands and caused them to deteriorate through overgrazing. The following text, which refers to this development, comes from Kheḍbudruk in the Nirā valley (Khaṇḍālā Taluka, Satara District), from a Gurav priest of the goddess Vaḍjāī:

Text 55

Before the village of Kheḍbudruk came into being, there was an estate (*vastī*) of Gavḷīs here. They had cows, buffaloes—animals that give milk. There used to be jungle and pasture land (*kuraṇ*) here. They kept cows and buffaloes. The pastures came to an end. So the Gavḷīs went away, and the Dhangars arrived. Dhangars with the surnames Dhāyguḍe, Ṭhombre, Vhoṭkar, Hāke, and Māṇe came here. Twenty acres make a *cāvar*. There are sixty *cāvars* of land here. The Dhangars had sheep, goats, cows, and buffaloes. They also had oxen. This land belongs to them, and they farm the land (*śetī kartāt*).

3.2 Herdsmen (Dhangars) and Farmers (Kuṇbīs, Marāṭhās, and Māḷīs)

Some Dhangars, like some Gavḷīs, became farmers and began to live in fixed settlements. The Dhangar origin of some of the well-known Marāṭhā families in the Nirā valley is an open secret. But the pastoralist Dhangars were often—because of the frequent failure of the monsoon rain—so used to moving their residence in search of better pastures that they would give way to the immigrant farmers. The story of the Lakḍes, a large exogamous subgroup of the Hāṭkar Dhangars, provides a good example of the relationships between the nomadic herders and the farmers (not only Marāṭhā *jamīndārs,* but also farmers of the Kuṇbī, Marāṭhā, and Māḷī castes).

All the residents of *vāḍī* B are Lakḍes. There are Lakḍes scattered everywhere in the Nirā, Karhā, and Bhimā valleys. The origins of the Lakḍes can be traced as far as the village traditions of Koḷvihire. Koḷvihire is located three miles east of Jejurī and about two miles south of the Karhā River. The beginnings of the village are traced back to Koḷīs. In the fields of the present-day village there are found numerous prehistoric microliths. The Karhā valley is famous for such microliths, which can be found especially near Deuḷgāv-Gāḍa, on the far side of the valley across the river.[58] In prehistoric times, this

58. D. D. Kosambi, *Myth and Reality* (Bombay, 1962), p. 133, and artifacts I myself have found.

area was undoubtedly the residence of tribes, whether Koḷīs or their predecessors.

The oral traditions of the village of Koḷvihire include the famous legend of Vālmīki, who is supposed to have been a Koḷī and a robber before he composed the *Rāmāyaṇa*. The legend is even found in old English writings about the supposed course of the earlier history of the Deccan.[59] The story of Vālmīki as a robber is transposed to many places in India, especially in the Deccan,[60] and it would be a mistake simply to take it as having a historical basis. It could be told about any place, and could enter into local traditions whenever conditions similar to those described in the legend present themselves: a forest or wasteland, a trade or pilgrimage route passing through it, and Koḷīs who threaten this route. All of these conditions are found in the case of Koḷvihire, which in addition was located near the temple of Khaṇḍobā of Jejurī, a Skandalike tutelary deity of the Rāmośīs (robbers).[61] The old road from Poona to Sātārā led past Jejurī, via Vālhā and Nirā, before the new road was constructed farther west, over the steep spurs of the Ghāṭs (Kātraj and Khambāṭkī Ghāṭs). But let us turn to the story from Koḷvihire. It shows how a legend of the great tradition becomes "parochialized" (McKim Marriott). The legend was narrated by an elementary school teacher who comes from the Māḷī caste. It is the common property of the whole village and is also known in the surrounding villages:

Text 56

This village is located in the district named after the home of knowledge, Puṇe [Poona], and in the Taluka named after King Indra's heavenly town, Purandar, and in the territory of the praiseworthy Khaṇḍerāyā [Khaṇḍobā], who lives on one of the spurs of the Sahyādri mountains. The name Koḷvihire came into being in the hoary past (*purāṇik kālāt*) on account of an actual event. And in no respect is this event borrowed from anywhere. This becomes clear as the story is told. The whole story, except for the explanation of the name Koḷvihire, is found in the *Rāmāyaṇ*.[62] Because of this event, then—after people had begun to settle here—this place was given the name Koḷvihire. The author who wrote the *Rāmāyaṇ* in the hoary past, the Ṛṣi Vālmīki, came from Vālhā, near Koḷvihire. His original name was "Vālhyā Koḷī." That led to the name Vālhā.

---

59. *Selections of Papers from the Records of the East India House . . . ,* vol. 4, p. 400.

60. See V. Moeller, *Die Mythologie der vedischen Religion und des Hinduismus* (Stuttgart, 1966), pp. 180f.

61. On the Rāmośīs and Vālmīki, see Syed Siraj ul Hassan, *The Castes and Tribes of H. E. H. The Nizam's Dominions* (Bombay, 1920), s.v. Beḍar. Some minor princely houses in South India claim to be descended from the Vālmīki *gotra,* and the Beḍars understand Vālmīki to be one of their own (B. A. Saletore, *The Wild Tribes in Indian History* [Lahore, 1935], pp. 91, 94, 96).

62. And therefore, in the narrator's view, the story is all the more verified and trustworthy.

Between our village and Vālhā everything was jungle. The whole area was covered with hills, jungle, a valley, trees. Today everything but the hills and the valley has changed. Vālhyā Koḷī had settled here in the jungle with his family. Originally he practiced robbery and killing. The field of his attacks stretched over approximately ten miles. Travelers had to journey over the road leading through the jungle. So it was no trouble for him to attack and rob people who were traveling back and forth. He had a stick that he used to kill people. He was very strong. When he killed someone, he would throw a small stone into a pot. He had stone pots, and he filled seven pots this way. You can still see the shards of these pots on the mountain. He brought home the loot and used it to support his family. The place where his robberies were carried out is now our village.

At first there was a "*vihīr*" (well) here, which was like a water hole. On his daily robbing expeditions, Vālhyā Koḷī naturally became thirsty, and he would drink from the well to his heart's content. And because he always came to the place and a human settlement developed there, the place got the name "Koḷ-Vihīre" on account of this actual event.

Because he killed many people he was burdened with terrible sins. Then he met the *munī* [*muni*] Nārada, [who can travel throughout all] three worlds. Nārada said, "So far you have filled seven pots with stones—do you realize how many people, how many lives (*jīv*), you have killed, and how many sins it has brought about?" In this way he showed him the full extent of his sins. He said, "You alone will be burdened with the crimes you have committed in order to provide for your family, and with the mountain of sins you have thereby built up. You alone will have to bear the painful consequences. Not a single member of your family will have any share in it. Go home and ask. I'll wait here."

He went home, and when he had gotten there, he asked everyone, "This sin has come about. Will any of you share it with me?"

They said, "No, under no circumstances will we have any share in it. You have committed the sin, you must pay for it."

He returned to Nārada, touched his feet, and asked him how to get free from the sin. Nārada said, "If you repeat the name of Rām for twelve years, your burden of sins will disappear."

He took the advice of Nārada *munī* and began to repeat the name of Rām. As he sat there reciting his litany, he had stuck in the ground in front of him the stick he had used to kill people. After twelve years he completed his litany, and leaves broke out on the stick. It is said about this:

Vālmīki repeated the Name;
Leaves broke out on the stick.

When leaves had broken out on the stick, after a long time it grew into a large tree. This tree still stands near our village of Koḷvihire. We call it "pāḍaḷ."[63] It

63. Padrieroot-tree, *Bignonia Chelonoides,* etc. (Molesworth, *Dictionary;* cf. Monier-Williams, *Dictionary,* s.v. *pāṭala*).

blooms every year, but it never bears fruit. How is it that there are no female flowers here? So people are convinced that this must be a divine miracle. There is no doubt about it. The tree is a little ways outside the village. And under this tree the wrestling matches of our [village] festival take place every year. What is special about it is that at the time of these wrestling matches, flowers break out on the tree. And during the wrestling matches they fall of their own accord onto the bodies of the good, gifted wrestlers (*malla*). If people call this something of a miracle, we cannot object.

[Another version adds:] After twelve years, Nārada *munī* came back through this jungle. As he came along, he [continually] heard the cry, "Rām, Rām." When the *munī* looked closely, he saw that a termite mound had grown up.[64] The sound was coming out of it. The stick that [Vālhyā] had had in his hand had turned into a tree. The tree is still there today. The *munī* said, "Get up, Vālhyā." He destroyed the termite mound. Then Vālhyā stood up. The birth of Rām was yet to come. Vālhyā wrote its story, the *Rāmāyaṇ*. Vālhyā became Vālmīki.

[The Māḷī schoolteacher's version continues:] After that the Gavḷīs came. They settled here. At that time there was a forest here. They had cows and buffalo cows. The place where they kept the cows and buffalo cows is still there today. The Gavḷīs became very rich and stayed here for many days. East of Koḷvihire is a stretch of stony heath (*māḷ*) called the "Heath of Father Ram" (*eḍkobā māḷ*). Here the Gavḷīs' ancestors buried seven pots of coins. An enormous cobra watches over these coins. The Gavḷīs wanted to dig up the coins, but because of the enormous cobra they could not. After many days the jungle thinned out, and one day, for one reason or another, the Gavḷīs went away.

After the Gavḷīs had gone away, Dhangars named Lakḍe came here. At that time there were still many fig thistles and pastures here. The Lakḍes had cows and sheep. The cows gave them bulls. Because they had bulls, they tilled the land. They began farming, and they began to graze their sheep. The Gavḷīs were driven away toward Torvevāḍī [today's *vāḍī* A]. It's not known where they went after that. The Lakḍes tilled the land. Still today there is a "Lakḍe Field" in Koḷvihire.

One of the Lakḍes was especially rich. During the period of English rule, rupees were silver. This Lakḍe had an especially large number of them. Because he had buried them, they had turned black. He laid them under the hooves of a buffalo and let the buffalo clean them. Then he threw everything into the wind.[65] With the silver dirt he built a large and beautiful temple, which still exists today. In this temple there are three *mūrtis*. The largest one shows a horseman holding a sword in his hand. The second one shows only a horse. The

64. See V. Moeller, *Mythologie*, pp. 180f.

65. As in winnowing grain—that is, the cleaned coins fell straight to the ground, and the wind blew the dirt, which still had some silver in it, some distance away. There were so many silver coins that he could build a temple with the silver in the dirt.

third one is like the first. Above the temple door there is a yellow stone. This stone commemorates Lakḍe, the Dhangar.

Afterward the Lakḍes brought Bhairavnāth. The *mūrti* is very old. It shows Nāth, Jogeśvarī, and at Jogeśvarī's side a child. Jogeśvarī's hand rests on the child's head. Even the Māruti [Hanumān] comes from the time of the Lakḍes.

Formerly the position of *pāṭīl* also belonged to the Lakḍes. When the Lakḍes were here, the Khaires came from Supe.[66] They began to till the land. Later the Khaires' influence grew. The Khaires took over the position of *pāṭīl* from the Lakḍes.

A long time later, the Lakḍe Dhangars went to [what was later to become] Torvevāḍī, and stayed there for many days. The name of their *vāḍā* was Lakḍevāḍā. From there some of them went past Guḷuñce to the vicinity of Nirā. They acquired land there and built houses. They had sheep from the beginning. Some of them still have land. Some Lakḍes went to Limbūt.

Then the Jhagaḍes [Māḷīs] came from Taḷegāv Ḍhamḍhere,[67] the Khaires from Supe, the Bhosles [Marāṭhās] from Sātārā. Thus people came together from various places, and the village of Koḷvihire came into being. The Lakḍes sold the land to them, then went away. [The Lakḍes] still come from the vicinity of Nirā to make a water offering to the Nāth and to their god[68] and to have *darśan*.

In the following passage, the Māḷī narrator of this "history" of Koḷvihire relates another good example of how immigrants to an area take over a cult:

Text 57

East of Koḷvihire, very close by, is the Heath of Father Ram (*eḍkobācā māḷ*). Earlier there was *māḷrān* there. Our farm (*śet*) is there. At the edge of the field there is a god, a *mūrti* of a human being. In the past, the Lakḍes used to graze their sheep there, because it was a large heath. And after the sheep had grazed, there was one Lakḍe who would always let two rams fight each other. Later this Lakḍe died. After his death the other Lakḍes made a stone *mūrti* for him and placed it there. Thus this field got the name Eḍkobācā Māḷ (the Heath of Father Ram). Our land is there. Because this *mūrti* is in our field, we bring *naivedya* on festival days—a coconut and camphor—and we do *pūjā*. We set up an oil lamp. At threshing time (*dhānya maḷṇīcyā veḷeshī*) we worship the god. We show *naivedya*. We break a coconut, offer camphor, set up an oil lamp. After we have had *darśan*, we come back.

This is an almost classic example of the transition from a cult of herders to a cult of farmers. The takeover of the Mhaskobā cult in Vīr by the Māḷīs, who own the fields where Mhaskobā first appeared, is an essentially similar series

66. The Khaires are Marāṭhās. Khairevāḍī is near Supe, in Bārāmatī Taluka.

67. Śirūr Taluka, Poona District.

68. In the temple built with the silver in the dirt.

of events.[69] As in the case we have just seen, the description of such a cult often comes from the new devotees.

The Lakḍes owned "beautiful" cattle, and this refers above all to Khilārī bulls and oxen. The Lakḍes too disappeared from the neighborhood of today's *vāḍī* A, which had at first been named for them. Many say that they disappeared because of a drought and a shortage of grass. One of their ancestor shrines is still found in *vāḍī* A, and a widow from this once important family still lives there, along with her young son.

After the Lakḍes, a *jamīndār* from Murtī Moḍhve seems to have acquired the pastures and cultivable land around today's *vāḍī* A. The Dhangars who now live in *vāḍī* A first came to Murtī Moḍhve, where they bought land and carried on some farming. "They had sheep and oxen." As so often, quarrels arose between the *jamīndār* and the herders, because the sheep were forever invading his fields. But the quarrel was settled when the Dhangars received 125 acres of pasture land in exchange for 100 acres of cultivable land near Murtī Moḍhve. The pasture land is near the present villages of Nāvḷī and Koḷvihire. Many years later, the *jamīndār* decided to sell some additional pasture land, which the Dhangars had been leasing from him for 200 rupees a year after *vāḍī* A had expanded. With their combined resources, the Dhangars bought the land for 20,000 rupees.

Before the Lakḍes arrived, places like Koḷvihire, Guḷuñce, and Morgāv were certainly already settled; they must have been villages primarily devoted to pastoralism. This brings to mind the hero stones from the Yādava period that are found in these places. Almost all of them depict heroes protecting cattle; in one case (at Guḷuñce), we see on the lowermost relief a panicking cattle herd trampling the hero. Surely the herds, which are depicted with the straight or only slightly curved horns of the Khilārī breed, belonged to the *gāvuṇḍas, gāvḍās,* and *nāyakas,* the *pāṭīls* of the pastoral region, from whom the later Dhangar and Marāṭhā families were descended. These families' names appear in documents from the time of King Śāhū of Sātārā (1709–49). Thus, the Lakḍes[70] are mentioned; the Dhangar family More from Murtī Moḍhve,[71] whose impressive fort (*vāḍā*) is still to be seen today; the Ṭhombres, the Devkā(ṃ)tes, the Tarḍes, and so on; and, last but not least, the family of the Mhānvars or Māhārṇvars, whose descendants can be found in Murtī Moḍhve, in *vāḍī* A, and in the surrounding Dhangar *vāḍīs*.[72] The

69. *Mhaskobā Devācem Caritra,* part 2 (Appendix).

70. Dīkṣita and Khobrekar, *daptara aṃka* 3, *puḍke* 3, *patra kr.* 2868, p. 61.

71. Ibid., *daptara aṃka* 26, *puḍke* 1, 35236, p. 331.

72. Ibid., *daptara aṃka* 3, *puḍke* 2, 2299, 2300, p. 47. In these two documents, officials of King Śāhū in the region (*prānt*) of Wāī are instructed not to demand a toll from Malhārjī Māhārṇvar, who would be moving into the area with his herds, and to allow his four herds of

subject matter of these documents is frequently herds of cattle, sheep, and goats; and the old tradition of cattle-robbing is attested.

There is thus a relative sequence of the following groups in the history of the settlement of this area:

1. Koḷīs or other tribal groups, symbolized by the legend of Vālhyā Koḷī. Today the Koḷīs are a small caste of water-carriers in these villages.

2. Gavḷīs, and villages based primarily on pastoralism, perhaps involving transhumance. The Gavḷīs disappeared or were absorbed as farmers or Dhangars.

3. The Lakḍes, affluent Dhangars with (Khilārī) cattle, who also emigrated or became sheep breeders.

4. *Jamīndārs*—Dhangars, Marāṭhās, and Brahmans—along with the farmer castes of Kuṇbīs/Marāṭhās and Māḷīs, and expanding regular agriculture.

5. The Dhangars of *vāḍī* A, who specialized in raising and selling sheep. Like the Lakḍes, they are Hāṭkar Dhangars.

Some of the Lakḍes went to Nimbūt, near Nirā. The ancestors of the Lakḍes of *vāḍī* B had originally come from Nirā. They were *vatandārs*—that is, they had a hereditary right to the land—around Nimbūt. The Bhairavnāth of Nimbūt is the *kulsvāmī,* the family god, of the Lakḍes, and they are still the first *mānkarīs,* the holders of the first ritual rights, in his temple. The Guravs of the small temple have lists of the names and addresses of Lakḍes who are scattered in all directions. One Lakḍe is supposed to have brought "Bhairavnāth, on a horse, from Kāśī"—that is, from Sonārī in Usmanabad District—or possibly from Koḷvihire. Here also Gosāvīs provide for the mythological background of the cult by telling stories about Bhairav. Today the cult is the focal point of a huge rural festival, which is especially popular because of its bullock-cart races, its bullfights, and its wrestling matches.

At the time of the inauguration of the Left-Hand Canal or later, enterprising Marāṭhās were attracted to the area. The K_____s came originally from a place farther west and thus more likely to be reached by rain. According to the Dhangars, a feud developed between the Marāṭhās and the Dhangars. The Marāṭhās add that the Dhangars had mortgaged their land or sold it to pay for weddings. Whatever the real cause, the Dhangars finally said to the Marāṭhās: "You can eat the land. For the sake of our sheep, we'll move on in search of pastures." Then the Dhangars moved on, and *vāḍī* B came to Jāvḷī. It seems

---

sheep and one herd of cattle to graze freely. Document 2299 is dated in the month of Phālgun, with no mention of the year. It shows us that the wandering or transhumance westward toward the Māvaḷ or the Ghāṭs in the months of March and April had already become necessary in the time of Śāhū. Both of the documents show that the Dhangars had herds of cattle as well as sheep at that time.

that a drought contributed to the Dhangars' decision to give away their land in such an easygoing manner.

With the beginning of the *Pax Britannica* in the middle of the nineteenth century, with the inauguration of the two Nirā canals, and with the intensification of agriculture since 1947, the landscape of the Nirā and Karhā valleys has changed more quickly than ever before.[73] It is clear that many other Dhangars too, like the Lakḍes, did not foresee the extent to which arable land would rise in value more than would land that could be used only as pasture.

3.3 The Transformation of Herdsmen's Gods into Gods of all Castes

At many places it can still be shown that originally Khaṇḍobā was primarily a god of herdsmen.[74] In Jejurī he was first seen by herder youths,[75] and a fairly large proportion of the devotees (*bhaktas*) in Jejurī are members of pastoralist groups. But it was principally through his connection with Bāṇāī that Khaṇḍobā became a god of herdsmen; the history of Mhasobā shows more clearly how a herdsmen's god develops into a god of all castes and a god of established settlements.

In the focal area of my research, village traditions trace back almost all the important cults of Mhasobā/Mhaskobā to an immigrant god of pastoralists. Thus in Hiṃjavḍī in Muḷśī Taluka the god Mhat(∼s)obā first appeared along with Gavḷīs; the Mhat(∼s)obā of Corācī Āḷandī was brought by two Gavḷī brothers named Sāyabā and Māyabā. Sārṇabā of Kharsuṇḍī was apparently a divinized herdsman who healed animals, and who later became equated with Mhasobā. But even Kāḷbhairav, who is originally a Gosāvī from Sonārī, comes mostly to places connected with Mhasobā and the Gavḷīs.

The name Mhasobā probably does not come from the pastoralist groups. Rather, Mhasobā/Mhasāsūr/(Sanskrit) Mahiṣāsura is a name coined from the point of view of sedentary people. The Gavḷī or Dhangar stands outside fixed settlements or at their edges. In the eyes of sedentary people, especially in areas where the caste system is rigidly fixed, he is ritually impure and magically dangerous.[76] Mhasobā, "Father Buffalo," is a dangerous spirit who is

---

73. See also G. D. Sontheimer, "The Dhangars: A Nomadic Pastoral Community in a Developing Agricultural Environment," in *Pastoralists and Nomads in South Asia*, L. S. Leshnik and G. D. Sontheimer, eds. (Wiesbaden, 1975), pp. 139ff.

74. See above, section 2.

75. See chap. 9, n. 7, below.

76. Farmers in the Koṅkaṇ do not accept food from Dhangars. See also *Manusmṛti*, III.166: a shepherd or a buffalo herder should not be invited to a *śrāddha* ceremony. The Rabārīs in Rajasthan are not allowed to live inside villages, because if they did the higher castes might become polluted. The Rabārīs themselves explain this by saying that they are not villagers at all,

associated with herdsmen's buffaloes. He is often the spirit of a cowherd who protects herdsmen's animals for them. The representation of the buffalo as the mount (*vāhana*) of Yama, the god of death, can also perhaps be attributed to the fear of the magical, life-threatening wilderness from which the god comes. Still today in every village in my area of research, a person riding on a buffalo is jokingly called "Yam": an astonishingly close connection between an idea in the high religion and one in the folk religion. To ride on a buffalo is frowned upon by settled farmers, but is common among nomads and pastoralist groups.

The folk etymology of the residents of established settlements generally derives the name Mhasobā/Mhaskobā from *mhasaṇ(~n)/masaṇ(~n)*/(Sanskrit) *smaśāna,* cremation ground.[77] According to a variety of informants, Mhaskobā first appeared at the cremation or burial ground of the village.[78]

As we have seen, the *sādhū* or Gosāvī—or his predecessor, the Kāpālikā—who stays in the *smaśāna* can also be worshiped and deified by Gavḷīs, and can rise to become their family god (*kulsvāmī*).[79] Behind a Mhasobā cult there often lies a deified man who performed miracles—healing cattle, for instance—even in his lifetime. One such cult place is found at the edge of the village of Nājhre, north of Jejurī, on the bank of the Karhā River. Although the god is called not Mhasobā but Sāḷobā,[80] the circumstances are the same as those that lead to the creation of a Mhasobā cult:

Text 58

> At the edge of the village of Nājhre there is a small god place (*devsthān*) for Sāḷobā. Sāḷobā used to be a human being. He gave medicines to animals and got rid of their diseases. He became very famous. After he died, the people set up a *tāndaḷā*[81] for him and began to do worship (*pūjā*). He became a god for people. They offer [that is, sacrifice] sheep to him. They believe that he protects animals. He is especially worshiped in the month of Aśāḍ [Āṣāḍh—June/July].

The pamphlet *Śrīnāth Mhaskobā Devācem̩ Caritra* ("The Biography of God Śrī Nāth Mhaskoba"), which is translated in the Appendix, comes from the village of Vīr. Vīr provides the best example of the founding of the cult of

---

and by pointing out their inherent calling to a wandering existence in the wilderness (S. Westphal-Hellbusch, "Changes in Meaning of Ethnic Names as Exemplified by the Jāt, Rabārī, Bharvad, and Charan in Northwestern India," in Leshnik and Sontheimer, eds., *Pastoralists,* p. 125.

77. As in Vīr, where the written form and pronunciation of "Mhaskobā" tends to deaspiration ("Maskobā"), and so the derivation of the name from *mhais, mhaśā* is forgotten.

78. Cf. Śiva, who lives in the *smaśāna. Brahmāṇḍa Purāṇa,* II.27.79: *smaśāna-vāsin.*

79. See Text 52, above.

80. The etymology of the name is unknown. Perhaps it derives from *sāḷottarī,* horse-doctor (Molesworth, *Dictionary*), or from *sāl,* a tree (Molesworth).

81. See chap. 9, n. 41, below.

a Mhasobā who has migrated into a settlement of sedentary people. According to the oral traditions of Vīr, the arrival of the Dhangars gave the village an especially great uplift. Vīr, which is within the area reached by the southwest monsoon, has fertile farm land, with betel-leaf plantations, orchards, rice, sugarcane, and so on. As many as twelve plow-oxen are required to plow the heavy, black soil. Especially in the pre-British period, wandering cattle breeders or traders such as the Nandīvālās and Bañjārīs provided draft animals not only to the farmers of the nuclear agricultural regions, but also everywhere where warfare or epidemics decimated the cattle herds. Even Hāṭkar Dhangars owned Khilārī cattle at that time, as the octogenarian Marāṭhā *pāṭīl* of Vīr confirms. The biography of the god Mhaskobā speaks of the sheep and cattle (*gureṃ*) owned by Kamaḷā Siddha, the Dhangar who brought Mhaskobā to Vīr.[82]

The most important caste of farmers in Vīr is the Māḷīs, who distinguish themselves by their diligence and skill at agriculture. It seems that the Māḷīs used to get their plow animals primarily from wandering pastoralist groups, and there has certainly long been an economic symbiosis between Māḷīs and Dhangars. In the past, Dhangars used to wander with their herds of sheep and cattle—as they still do today with their herds of sheep—along the banks of the Nirā, where the god Mhaskobā, coming from Mhasvaḍ, appeared for the first time. They would move westward into the Māvaḷ and toward the Koṅkaṇ, returning to the plateau with the beginning of the monsoon. Perhaps it was Dhangars who provided plow oxen in the past, and thus contributed to the prosperity of Vīr.

As is so often the case, however, it is difficult to separate economic and religious factors. Kamaḷā Siddha's capacity for becoming possessed by Mhaskobā, his ability to make prophecies, and his unrestricted devotion to Mhaskobā also contributed to the emergence of the Mhaskobā cult. Dhangars, like others who live in the wilderness, are credited with a talent for prophecy and magic.[83] This is how Kamaḷā Siddha and his descendants, the *siddhas* of Vīr, received a lasting place in the ritual of the Mhaskobā cult. They have a hereditary right to become possessed by the god and to prophesy at the annual pilgrimage festival (*jatrā*). In Vīr today Mhaskobā is much more important and respected than the older Vīreśvar—who has nothing to do with the Birobā/Bireśvar of the Dhangars but is patronized above all by Brahmans. The temple of Vīreśvar is falling into disrepair.

When one asks Dhangars, especially nomadic Dhangars, the test question, "What does Mhaskobā do?" one frequently receives the spontaneous answer,

---

82. *Mhaskobā Devāceṃ Caritra*, part 2 (Appendix).

83. See S. Westphal-Hellbusch, "Changes," p. 126, on the Raikas.

"He protects animals." Then, after some thought, there follows the supplementary information: "He protects people, fields, and animals." Here the informant is remembering Mhasobā's ever-growing function as *kṣetrapāl,* protector of fields, villages, the established settlement, the holy precinct.

Mhasobā of Vīr is equated with Kāḷbhairav, and of course it could be that the Kāḷbhairav cult was already present in the form of a Gosāvī or another holy person before Mhasobā arrived; or, as in many cases, that a Mhasobā cult could have developed into a Kāḷbhairav cult. Finally this becomes a question to which "Mhaskobā/Mhasobā" and "Kāḷbhairav" can sometimes serve equally well as answers.

On the road from Poona to Ahmadnagar there lies the town of Loṇī, which was described by Coats in 1819 and by G. S. Ghurye in 1960.[84] Ghurye writes that Mhasobā, who is especially worshiped by Māḷīs, was first brought from the Koṅkaṇ by Lamāṇīs (that is, Bañjāras). Here too I surmise an economic symbiosis between the Lamāṇīs and the Māḷīs, whether the Lamāṇīs brought rice or provided the Māḷīs with draft animals. This conjecture was confirmed by a local informant at Loṇī, who, when asked what the Lamāṇīs do, related that Lamāṇīs had sold him a draft ox. Ghurye asks why the annual pilgrimage festival for Bhairav referred to by Coats has given way to one for Mhasobā.[85] Inasmuch as the connection between the Kāḷbhairav cult and the cult of Mhasobā is so close that after Mhasobā has arrived in a village he is identified with Kāḷbhairav, it seems likely that the Mhasobā cult simply moved to the foreground, without completely displacing the pilgrimage festival for Bhairav.

Despite having become settled, Mhaskobā preserves many characteristics of his origin in the forest and pasture region, and of his ascetic forest life. Like Skanda as Kumāra and Yogīśvara, he does not allow women to enter the inner sanctum of his temple without special permission.[86] Although, on the other hand, he is married to Yogeśvarī/Jogāī, his resistance to the marriage is also indicated in the oral texts (see, for example, Text 69, below). Perhaps the fact that Mhaskobā's marriage to Yogeśvarī/Jogāī is celebrated anew each year during the pilgrimage festival symbolizes the increasing necessity of reinforcing the union.

Khaṇḍobā, Mhaskobā, and Birobā—as also Murukaṉ, Aiyaṉār, and other south Indian deities of the forest and pasture region who become gods of

---

84. Coats, *Transactions of the Literary Society of Bombay,* vol. 3 (1823), cited in G. S. Ghurye, *After a Century and a Quarter: Lonikand Then and Now* (Bombay, 1960), p. 4.

85. Ghurye, *Century,* p. 40.

86. For example, see *Skanda Purāṇa,* I.2.31.47; *Matsya Purāṇa,* 18.5.3; and Kālidāsa's *Vikramorvaśīyam,* act 4.

established settlements or of all castes—show traces of their earlier affiliation to the wilderness.[87] They are gods who go on military or hunting expeditions, often in the company of *gaṇas, rudras,* or the ghosts of the dead. Such an expedition is often represented in stylized form in the cult: a horse is made ready for the god (Mhasvaḍ-Siddha, Jyotibā of Ratnāgiri) or a hunting expedition is arranged.[88] The cruelty of the Śaiva gods of the wilderness is preserved, albeit in an attenuated form, when they become established in a permanent settlement. The biography of the god Mhaskobā translated in the Appendix shows how unpredictable, even cruel, the god can be when his devotees do not keep their promises, or when they violate the ritual prescriptions. This cruelty can also be seen in folk narratives and legends about the Tamil deity Aiyaṉār.

Thus, like all gods of the forest and pasture region who have become deities of established settlements, Mhaskobā brings together the forest and pasture on the one hand with the established settlement on the other, the tribes of the forest and pasture region with the residents of the established settlement. He marries one wife from a tribe, and another, "pure" wife from a high caste. In Vīr, Bāḷubāī becomes Yogeśvarī/Jogāī. Bāḷubāī comes from the world of the snakes, the underworld, whereas Yogeśvarī is ultimately Durgā/Pārvatī. Thus, in a broader sense, Mhaskobā—like Aiyaṉār, Mallanna, Murukaṉ, Mallikārjuna, and Khaṇḍobā—brings together heaven and earth.

---

87. On the absorption of the forest and tribal deity Bharma/Bharmappa/Brahmā into the Jaina cult in Karnatak (chap. 4, n. 47), see S. Settar, "The Brahmadeva Pillars," *Artibus Asiae,* 33 (1971) 17, 34ff. Bharma is a *kṣetrapāl* who is depicted mounted on a horse, wearing a crown, and holding a sword, a *phala* (fruit), and sometimes an *aṅkuśa* (barbed stick) and a *pāśa* (noose).

88. See 6.3.2; 9.2.

9

The Origin, Structure, and Transformation of the Cults of Birobā, Mhaskobā, and Khaṇḍobā

1. Origin in the World of Nature Spirits

The *Mahāmāyūrī Mantra* mentions Khaṇḍaka as the guardian spirit (*yakṣa*) of Pratiṣṭhāna (Paiṭhaṇ) (*pratiṣṭhāne ca khaṇḍakaḥ*), and Vīra as the guardian spirit of the area around Karahāṭaka (Karhāḍ) (*vīraśca karahāṭake*).[1] The origin of Birobā, Mhaskobā, and Khaṇḍobā is to be found in the *yakṣas* that populate mountains, rivers, and trees, and in spirits having the form of animals. In essence, the history of the three gods is the process by which these spirits connected with the cult of the goddess (*devī*) become identified with gods of the high, literate, and sedentary castes. This process of identification accompanies the expansion of agriculture in the forest and pasture regions, and the spread of Purāṇic ideas.

Because it was with the beginning of English rule that regular agriculture first gained a foothold in the various ecological niches of the forest and pasture regions of India, we can assume that the process of identification began to accelerate at this time. This process has not yet come to an end. Still today, for example, a group of seminomadic Gujars who wander toward Mathurā from the neighborhood of Jaipur name as their god not the famous Viṣṇuite Kṛṣṇa of Braj, but first the goddess Ambā/Bhavānī and then Bālājī—who is not necessarily identical with Kṛṣṇa.[2]

1. Sylvain Lévi, "Le Catalogue Géographique des Yakṣas dans la Mahāmāyūrī," *Journal Asiatique*, 5 (1915) 41.

2. Informal survey conducted near Mathurā. According to Russell and Hiralal, *The Tribes and Castes of the Central Provinces of India* (London, 1916), vol. 2, p. 483, Dhangars in the Central Provinces and Berār worship Bālājī as the younger brother of Rām.

All three gods—Birobā, Mhaskobā, and Khaṇḍobā—can still be found today as lower deities who have hardly grown out of the stage of spirits. Even as late as 1885, the old gazetteer of Poona District says of Mhasobā/ Mhasāsūr/ Mahiṣāsura:

> [He] is perhaps the commonest and most widely feared of the local evil spirits. He lives in an unhewn stone coated with redlead. These stones are all old dwellings of Mhasoba. Some get forgotten. Then sickness falls on the village and the people go to the village guardian and ask him a series of questions which he answers by dropping a betelnut or by some other sign. In the end they find out from the guardian that there is an old neglected dwelling of Mhasoba. The villagers find the stone, cover it with oil and redlead, and kill a goat or a fowl in front of it. Besides to prevent his working mischief Mhasoba is worshipped by men who have a grudge to clear off or a wrong to avenge. They go to Mhasoba, name their enemy, and promise, if he ruins their enemy with sickness, that they will give him a goat or a fowl. So much is he feared that when a man knows that some one whom he has ill-used has arranged to set Mhasoba on him, he makes such amends that the god is not forced to exert his power.[3]

This is a good description of the *original* Mhasobā as he is found above all in the villages and the thick forests of the Māvaḷ. In the view of the villagers, he is terrifying, he lives at the edge of the village, in the forest, and it is difficult to build a roof over his temple. An original, as yet untransformed Mhasobā, anonymous and not yet settled in a temple, "cannot talk"—this according to the statement of a Dhangar.[4] By contrast, the famous Mhaskobā of Vīr, who has risen to become a god, speaks through the Śiṅgāḍe Dhangars or gives signs when he is questioned.[5]

The same gazetteer reports about Birobā:

> [He] is worshipped by Dhangars or Shepherds. He lives in an unhewn stone outside the village. Like Mhasoba he is an unkindly spirit to whom people pray when they are anxious to plague or ruin their enemies.[6]

Khaṇḍobā too is still to be found as a simple stone, shapeless or *liṅgam*-shaped, with votive figures of cattle placed before it. All three gods, but especially Khaṇḍobā, are gods of the mountain or the hill. Because the mountain and the hill are pasture areas, they are the natural abode of herders. In

3. *Gazetteer of the Bombay Presidency,* vol. 18, Poona (Bombay, 1885), part 1, pp. 290–91.

4. See also Molesworth, *Dictionary: mukāmhasobā,* "a reviling term for a person stupidly taciturn or sulkily silent" (s.v. *mukāmaind*).

5. *Kaul lāvṇeṃ:* that is, one places betelnuts or flowers, for instance, on the *mūrti*. If the left betelnut or flower falls down first, this indicates a negative answer; if the right one falls first, the answer is positive.

6. *Gazetteer of the Bombay Presidency,* vol. 18, Poona, part 1, p. 290.

Jejurī, Khaṇḍobā was first seen by herder youths on the mountain.[7] Elsewhere also, the first to experience Khaṇḍobā are herders grazing cattle on the mountain. In most cases, it is a cow that recognizes the god:

Text 59

In the Koṅkaṇ, between the villages of Cilhure, Kusumbaḷ, and Sāle in Māṇgāv Taluka, Kolaba District, there is a mountain. On this mountain there is a temple of Khaṇḍobā. Gavḷīs live in Cilhure. A certain Gavḷī used to graze his cows and buffalo cows on the mountain, and while they were grazing he would cut grass with his sickle. One of the cows would always go to a certain place and stay there to lick a stone. The Gavḷī asked himself, "Why does that cow go there every day? Why does it lick the stone?"

One day as he was cutting grass, he came up close to the cow. He had his sickle, and he hit the stone with the point. And turmeric powder came out of the stone. The more he hit it, the more turmeric powder came out. So he thought, "There must be a god here."

He asked the other people (cf. Text 48), and they decided, "It's Khaṇḍobā."

Later they built a temple for this god and worshiped him. The Gavḷīs' devotion (*bhakti*) for Khaṇḍobā still holds true.

Birobā is a god of the highland pasture (*māḷ*). His temples are usually outside the village, on high ground. In Ārevāḍī he used to live on the hill, but for the sake of one of his devotees—a pregnant woman—he came to the grove near Ārevāḍī. In Karnatak, Birāppā/Bireśvara/Vīrabhadra, the god of the Kurubas, lived "in the forest and not in the village."[8] Again and again we learn that the god comes down from the mountain into the valley. This often expresses a change from pastoralism to regular agriculture in the river valleys. At the same time the god is taken over by other groups.

The Khaṇḍobā in Jejurī lived on the high plateau. But to oblige a devotee who had grown old and could no longer manage the daily climb up to the temple, Khaṇḍobā came down to the newer temple. The Mhat(∼s)obā of Hiṃjavḍī lives alone on a *hill*. His second and later temple is in Vākaḍ, in the *valley*, where he married Jogāī/Yogeśvarī.

If one disregards the later interpretations and additions of the Vaiṣṇavas, the herders' god Kṛṣṇa was also originally a mountain spirit. To this day, the residents of the mountain area around Mathurā affirm that "Govardhan [mountain] is Kṛṣṇa, and Kṛṣṇa is Govardhan."[9] The *Harivaṃśa* expresses this identity when Kṛṣṇa persuades the herdsmen to worship the mountain,

7. G. H. Khare, *Mahārāṣṭrācīṃ cār daivateṃ* (Puṇeṃ, 1958), p. 90 (translation): "One day, when herder youths were sitting in the forest on the high plateau, the god Khaṇḍobā took form there sitting on a horse and armed with a spear, and he sat with them on the woolen blanket."

8. Ya. Ph. Attikoḷla, *Hālumatada Caritra* (Dharvāḍ, 1949), pp. 45ff.

9. Charlotte Vaudeville, "The Govardhan Myth in Northern India," *Indo-Iranian Journal,* 22

and describes mountains as spirits who can change at will into lions and tigers in order to protect the forests.[10] Kṛṣṇa explains to the herders: "Brahmans dedicate mantras to the service of God, farmers dedicate them to the furrow, and herdsmen to the mountains. So let us offer a sacrifice to the mountain."[11] And he continues: "The gods may like to worship Indra, but we should sacrifice to the mountain."[12] The herdsmen arrange a great festival, and through his magic (*māyā*) Kṛṣṇa changes himself into the spirit of the mountain and consumes the sacrificial offerings. He is standing on the mountain as a mountain spirit, and yet he is still visible as Kṛṣṇa. Laughing, he calls out, "I'm full!" At the same time he stands in person among the herdsmen.[13]

Local traditions in Braj, as well as the text *Śri Nāthjī Prākaṭya Vartā* (Manifestations of Śrī Nāth Jī), which is based on them, state that for a long time all that was visible was the god's upraised arm, jutting out of the mountain.[14] This arm was worshiped with offerings of milk. Even cows came secretly and offered milk to it. *Kṛṣṇa's full form became visible only later, through the mediation of a Vaiṣṇava* sādhū.

Vaudeville points out the resemblance of the upraised arm to a snake, and she identifies the mountain spirit with a Nāga deity. According to local traditions, Kṛṣṇa is supposed to have crawled into the mountain. Still today, at the outer end of Govardhan hill, there is a village named "the tail" (*Puchrī*).[15] In the *Mahābhārata,* Govardhan is compared to a termite mound.[16] The termite mound is widely thought of as a favorite abode of snakes.

Everywhere in the focal area of my research there are analogies to this prevaiṣṇava god of herdsmen who lives on the mountain or in a termite mound, often in the form of a snake.[17] Mhaskobā of Vīr lived as a snake in a termite mound on the site of the inner sanctum of the present-day temple,[18] and

(1980). See also Vaudeville, "Braj, Lost and Found," *Indo-Iranian Journal,* 18 (1976) 195–213.

10. *Harivaṃśa, Viṣṇuparva,* 16, 7f.

11. Ibid., 16, 10 and 11, 1. The translation follows that of J. J. Meyer in *Trilogie altindischer Mächte und Feste der Vegetation* (Zurich/Leipzig, 1937), part 3, p. 129.

12. *Harivaṃśa, Viṣṇuparva,* 16, 44.

13. Ibid., 17, 21–25.

14. Cited by Vaudeville, "Govardhan," 6ff.

15. Ibid.

16. *Mahābhārata,* 2.38.9 (critical edition). Cf. the reading in D4 of the apparatus: *saptāhin,* "containing seven serpents."

17. On the affinities among Subramhaṇya, Murukaṉ, Skanda, Aiyappan, Nāgarāj, termite mounds, ant hills, snakes, and *kṣetrapāl,* see also Rā. Ciṃ. Ḍhere, "Subramhaṇya: ek ākalana," in *Ānaṃdavana,* January/February/March, 1974, pp. 20ff.

18. *Mhaskobā Devācem Caritra,* part 2 (Appendix). Molesworth, *Dictionary: peḍ* m., "A

Siddhobā of Jāvḷī, who comes from Mhasvaḍ, first manifested himself in a termite mound.[19] Khaṇḍobā, as we have seen, is most often worshiped in Maharashtra as living on a mountain, although he is also connected with the termite mound and with snakes. But it is primarily Khaṇḍobā's close association with Mallaya/Mailāra in Karnatak that indicates his connection to the termite mound. The Khaṇḍobā of Naḷdurg (Usmanabad District, Maharashtra) came from Ādimailār (Prempur), near Bīdar, in Karnatak. According to local traditions, the Mailāra of Mailār (Ballāri District) originated in a termite mound in which there lived terrifying snakes. A cow belonging to a certain Gomuni used to lactate into the holes of the termite mound. Kapila Muni, who was practicing asceticism at this place, instructed Go Muni to spread the tidings of Mārtaṇḍa Bhairava. Go Muni transformed the termite mound into an image of Mārtaṇḍa Bhairava. The *mūrti* was called *maṇṇāppā* (Sanskrit, *mṛṇmaya) dev* or Mṛṇmaya Mallārī, "Mallārī formed out of earth."[20] In addition, the *Mallārī Māhātmya* states that the *mūrti* of Mārtaṇḍa Bhairava was made out of earth.[21]

Thus, the god lives either on a mountain or in a termite mound. In the following extract from a tape recording, the speaker refers to the god's abode in one breath as a mountain and as a termite mound. The legend is about Sūryabā, Birobā's devotee (*bhakta*). Birobā instructs Sūryabā to worship him, and Sūryabā wanders around searching for the appropriate place to do the worship:

Text 60

Sūryabā Śid took the carrying pole (*kāvaḍ*) with the two baskets holding the *bāvan bīr*,[22] went into the fourteen-part Koṅkaṇ, and got tired of searching. Finally he [left the Koṅkaṇ and] came to Khān-Māṇ-Deś[23] in the Hivar forest. Behind him and in front of him were taraṭī trees; to his left and his right were lalaī trees. To the east was the Candrabhāgā [Bhimā] River; to the west, the Kisnā [Kṛṣṇā] River; to his right, the [Pañc-]Gaṅgā. This place pleased him. On

hillock (esp. as raised by ants) taken possession of by a Cobra de capello. On such a spot a temple is usually erected for the worship of the serpent, i.e., the Nāg or Cobra."

19. See above, 8.3.1.

20. L. S. Kāṭṭi, *Mailāra Kṣetradarśana* (Mailāra, Ballāri District, 1966), p. 6. Ḍhere demonstrates that this is the direction in which to seek the explanation of the name of Maṇi, the "second" demon conquered by Khaṇḍobā: the local name for the temple of Mailāra in Haḍgaḷḷi-Ballāri in Karnatak is "Maṇmailāra Mandir." "Maṇmailāra" or "Maṇṇumailāra" means "the Mailāra formed out of *maṇṇu*." Kannaḍa *maṇṇu* is equivalent to Sanskrit *mṛṇmaya*. See Rā. Ciṃ. Ḍhere, *Khaṃḍobā* (Puṇeṃ, 1961), p. 39.

21. *Mallārī Māhātmya,* 18.14 (Marāṭhī version); 18.9–10 (Sanskrit version).

22. That is, Birobā.

23. The region of the Māṇ valley, and the area around Khānapūr.

the peak of the mountain was a termite mound with three eyes. The god seated himself there, set up flags, and sat there happily on the peak of the mountain. Sūryabā Śid began to worship him. . . .

In another legend Viṭhobā finds Birobā/Birāppā in a termite mound in the form of a snake. Viṭhobā's devotee (*bhakta*), the famous Nāmdev, drew Viṭhobā's attention to the fact that although there were indeed thirty-three crores of *liṅgams* in Paṇḍharpūr, the most important one, Kāśīliṅg Birāppā, was missing. Viṭhobā set out to search for Birāppā:

Text 61

[After many adventures, Viṭhobā (Iṭṭhal) finally took a job as a shepherd with the poorer of two brothers, and increased his employer's herds (cf. Kṛṣṇa as *govardhana,* the "increaser of cattle") in a miraculous fashion.]

Every day Iṭṭhal used to go to the bank of the Varṇā River to graze the sheep. In the village of Sonsaḷī, on the bank of the Varṇā, there was a termite mound with three eyes. Every day he would go to the termite mound and give [the snake] milk to drink, after watering the sheep at the river. And Kāśīliṅg [Birobā/Birāppā] was in this termite mound in the form of a snake. And he drank the milk for twelve years. After twelve years even Kāśīliṅg was in difficulties. "How much trouble Pāṇḍuraṅg Viṭhobā is taking for my sake! He has kept sheep for twelve years. Now I must meet him."

At exactly noon, the snake came out of the termite mound and embraced [Iṭṭhal]. Thus Iṭṭhal and Birāppā, who are said to be a pair of brothers (*joḍice bandhu*), had now met on the bank of the Varṇā. And the two of them left there and rode all around the whole world on horseback. And then where did they come? They came to the vicinity of Kolhāpūr, to Paṭṭaṇ Kuḍolī. . . . [Text 33].

This legend, and the common worship of Viṭṭhal and Birāppā, express the synthesis of two pastoral cults. In the Kannaḍa legends of the Kurubas, Viṭhobā does not come from Paṇḍharpūr; rather, he is a Gavḷī from Karnatak who wears Birobā in the form of a *liṅgam* around his neck.

In mythology and religious imagery, the termite mound originates in the forest and stands in contrast to land used by farmers. It is the seat and place of origin of sheep, which are compared to termites. Farmers believe that termite mounds should not be plowed up—especially not on the Nāgpañcamī day,[24] when snakes are worshiped. In the myths of the Dhangars—particularly of the sedentary Dhangars in Sangli, Sholapur, and Kolhapur districts—the existence of agriculture is presupposed; from the point of view of the Marāṭhā farmers, the origination of sheep demands that the Dhangars, the shepherds,

24. See 7.2. The consequences of plowing up a termite mound are described in *Mhaskobā Devācem Caritra,* part 2 (Appendix).

be created and the fields thus protected from damage.[25] From the point of view of the Dhangars, the termite mound provides not only sheep but also the etiology of the Dhangars' division into Hāṭkars and Khuṭekars, and the explanation of the animals' various colors. The following text was narrated by a Dhangar:

Text 62

A long time ago, Birudev had given the Khuṭekars sheep to graze. Thus from the beginning they had grazed the sheep for many days. Then one day what happened?

One of them had to go to be a guest at a wedding for a few days. He said, "To whom should I entrust the sheep? Who will watch them properly? There isn't anyone."

So before he went to the wedding, he drove the sheep into the holes of a termite mound. He stopped up the holes with thorn bushes and went to the wedding. There was a field near the termite mound, and the owner of the field came to plow it. As he was plowing the field, he struck the termite mound. When he had struck it, the sheep came out like termites. The farmer thought, "What is this coming out?" He set the thorn bushes on fire. Sheep whose wool was badly scorched came out all black. Those that were only somewhat scorched came out splotchy. Some were copper-colored, some brown. Thus they came out in various colors.

Birudev said, "They aren't capable of guarding the sheep." He told this to the Khuṭekars. So he called the other Dhangars, the Hāṭkars, and said to them, "From this day on, the Hāṭkars are to guard the sheep, and the Khuṭekars are to weave blankets out of the wool, to sell the blankets, and thus to provide clothing."

At that the Khuṭekars said, "We have kept watch over the sheep from the beginning, and we will keep watch over them now too."

And they would not give up the sheep. Then the god said, "You stand on this side, and you stand on that side. The ones the sheep follow should guard them." Then they both called to the sheep, and the sheep did not run to the first ones, the Khuṭekars; they ran to the others, the Hāṭkars. So the Hāṭkars began to keep watch over the sheep, and the Khuṭekars began to weave blankets.

Anthills and termite mounds have always been the seat of wealth (sheep) and of gold,[26] even according to the authors of Western classical antiquity.[27] Dhangar mythology tells of a golden box that holds an image of Gaṅgā-

25. *Bhāratīya Saṃskṛtikośa,* Mahādevaśāstrī Jośī, ed. (Puṇeṃ, 1956–1979), volume 4, s.v. Dhangar.

26. See chap. 6, section 2, Version 6.

27. Pauly-Wissowa, *Realencyclopaedie der classischen Altertumswissenschaft,* vol. 1, s.v. "Ameise," p. 1281, 1.

Sūravantī, Birobā's mother. In a playful mood, Śaṅkar conjures up Gaṅgā-Sūravantī from his matted hair (Gaṅgā!), sticks her in a termite mound, and forgets about her. The box is found by two brothers who are plowing; as a punishment for plowing up the termite mound they must serve as herdsmen for twelve years, and during this period their farm falls into ruin. The childless king—as the owner of treasures buried in the earth—claims the box and makes Sūravantī his daughter. But she practices severe asceticism and—without conception—brings Birobā into the world.[28] After trying to kill Sūravantī, the king has Birobā abandoned in the forest.

The legend of the king's daughter who is born in a golden termite mound is widespread. It is also told of Pārvatī. Pārvatī, in the form of a maiden, is pursued by a king and takes refuge in a termite mound.[29] The golden luster of the termite mound is connected with the sun.[30] The luster of Sūravantī or Sūryavatī is like that of the sun:[31]

Text 63

For twelve years she stood on the thorns of a khair tree[32] and worshiped the sun (Sūrya). Then Sūrya created water out of his luster and put it on her eating plate. She drank it. . . .

After the two huntresses Māyavvā and Ekavvā found the child Birobā in the forest, they placed his cradle on the ground. The luster of the sun fell on the cradle. Birobā's luster was still greater than that of the sun:

Text 64

. . . One says to the sun, "Don't rise." To the moon one says, "Don't go down in the Māval." So [bright] was Birobā's golden head of hair. . . .

Khaṇḍoba too is connected with the sun. He is called Mārtaṇḍa Bhairava, and as Mārtaṇḍa, the son of Aditi, he is a sun god.[33] Khaṇḍobā's expedition to the Karhā River at the time of the conjunction of the sun and the moon

---

28. Like Aditi, who undertook the most strict penetential practices and in exchange carried Viṣṇu in her womb (*Mahābhārata,* 3, 134, 19). See V. Moeller, *Die Mythologie der vedischen Religion und des Hinduismus* (Stuttgart, 1966), p. 31.

29. W. T. Elmore, *Dravidian Gods in Modern Hinduism: A Study of the Local and Village Deities of Southern India* (Madras, 1925), pp. 82, 100.

30. The Kharias sacrifice to the sun on an anthill that serves as an altar (William Crooke, *The Popular Religion and Folklore of Northern India* [reprint, New Delhi, 1968], vol. 1, pp. 9f).

31. Cf. *Rāmāyaṇa,* 1, 37, 23.

32. *Mimosa catechu;* Sanskrit, *khadira* (Molesworth, *Dictionary*).

33. See also F. R. Allchin, *Neolithic Cattle-Keepers of South India: A Study of the Deccan Ashmounds* (Cambridge, 1963), p. 10: "The other temple . . . is dedicated to the god Mārtaṇḍeśvara and probably dates from the twelfth to the thirteenth centuries. The shrine contained several icons of Sūrya, probably of similar date."

(Somvatī Amāvāsyā) can also be interpreted as the union of the sun with the moon: Khaṇḍobā is the sun and the river is the moon. The golden turmeric powder with which Khaṇḍobā is equated especially suggests his solar origin. On festival days of Khaṇḍobā in Jejurī (*sonyācī Jejurī*—the golden Jejurī), the devotees sprinkle the demon (*daitya*) Maṇimalla also with so much turmeric powder that he loses his red color and is thus absorbed into Khaṇḍobā not only in name but also in appearance. Sundays are especially holy to Khaṇḍobā, but the *mūrti* of Mhasvaḍ-Siddhobā is seated on a horse and "goes for a ride" on this day as well.

Birobā, Mhaskobā, and Khaṇḍobā are hardly ever still worshiped in the form of a tree; occasionally, however, they live on and in a tree. For instance, in another version of Text 61, Viṭhobā finds Birobā in the form of a snake not in a termite mound but on a palmyra tree.[34] On another occasion Birobā is on an oleander tree,[35] and as a child he is abandoned on a hivar tree[36] in a thick forest. Khaṇḍobā is frequently worshiped with the leaves and twigs of the bel tree.[37] There are sufficient indications that the gods Birobā, Mhaskobā, and Khaṇḍobā are thought of as living in the trunks of trees, or in the lower ends of the trunks. Thus a person possessed by one of the three gods is called *devācī jhāḍ*, "the god's tree." Nevertheless, the tree trunk is primarily, as we have seen, the home of tree goddesses and of ghosts. The following text shows the metamorphosis of a Brahman who is transformed into a pipaḷ tree:

Text 65

The camp (*vāḍā*) of the Ṭakles was there. They had come from far away, in order to graze [their sheep]. In the camp there was a boy whose mother was a widow. When she died, he was without father or mother, and so he had to take work guarding sheep wherever he could find a job. As the camp moved around, it finally came to the forest of Loṇī Bāpkar. Here there lived a Brahman. He had very much land. No one was allowed to enter the land. And so that no one would enter his land, he would sit at home and check in the *pañcāṅg*[38] to find out, "Has anyone come into my field?" If people or animals came into his field, he would use a mantra to kill them.

In the morning, all the [other] shepherds had taken their sheep out of the camp. They had gone in one direction, and the boy had gone in the other. He drove the sheep into the Brahman's fields and climbed a jāmbhūḷ tree[39] to eat jāmbhūḷ fruits.

34. *Borasus flabelliformis* (Molesworth, *Dictionary*).

35. Kanherī = *Nerium odorum* (Molesworth, *Dictionary*). See Text 4.

36. Written *hiṃvar* = *Mimosa tomentosa,* etc.

37. Sanskrit, *bilva; Aegle marmelos.* This tree is especially holy to Śiva.

38. An almanac or astrological calendar.

39. A fruit tree, *Calyptranthes caryophyllifolia* or *jambalana* (Molesworth, *Dictionary*).

The Brahman used to check in his *pañcāṅg* between nine and ten o'clock in the morning, and between four and five o'clock in the afternoon, and at twelve noon, to check, "Is anyone in my field or not?" That day the boy drove the sheep into the fields at twelve noon. The Brahman had taken a bath, sat down, and looked in his *pañcāṅg:* "The boy has climbed the tree, he is eating jāmbhūḷ fruits, and he has driven the sheep into the fields."

The Brahman got angry and pronounced a mantra. When he had pronounced it, the branch on which the boy was sitting broke off. As it fell, a sharp, broken-off branch jutting out from the trunk pierced him in the side. Then he fell to the ground. The sheep came slowly grazing to the camp. Who was there to worry about him? He had no mother and no father. He had been hired for a year to earn his living. Who would search for him now? The Dhangars said, "Where is Naikyā,[40] where has Naikyā gone? Up your mother's. . . ! The sheep have come back, and Naikyā is off somewhere.

The next day they went looking for him. "Where is he, where is he? Where is the boy?" They found out that he had fallen to his death.

At twelve o'clock noon the boy had eaten the jāmbhūḷ fruits and fallen down. At twelve o'clock at night there took place an argument between the Brahman and [the boy's ghost]. [Naikyā said:] "Who are you?"

"I am a Brahman. Who are you?"

"I am Naikyā, one of the Ṭakle boys. I came to graze sheep. Why have you killed me?"

[During the argument] the Brahman used all sorts of mantras, but he had no success with them. Finally the Brahman gave up [the struggle] and asked forgiveness, saying, "Wherever you are, I will be."

When he had said this, the Brahman was struck dead [by the boy].

Now when the Dhangars came to this place, they saw that the boy was dead. They cremated him at the place in Loṇī where the temple stands today. A *tāndaḷ*[41] came out of the earth at this place, and soon afterward there also emerged a pipaḷ tree, which was the Brahman.

Later the Dhangars' camp wandered farther, toward Moghulāī [toward Usmānābād?], and suddenly they experienced many troubles. And he said, "I have died, and no one looks after me." So the Ṭakles came back and built a temple for him. Still today there are some Ṭakles in Kānārvāḍī near Loṇī, and some are in Sāstevāḍī near the town of Nirā. [Naikyā's] relatives on his father's side are the priests (*pūjārīs*). And at the place where they have built the temple, they "play"[42] in large numbers. They slaughter [or sacrifice, *kāptāt*] sheep, and hang the skins on the pipaḷ tree [to dry]. The pipaḷ tree is the Brahman. The pipaḷ tree does not accept any sacrifices of meat. Anyone who climbs a pipaḷ

40. Written Nāīk.

41. Spoken *tāndaḷā,* from *tānduḷ:* a grain of rice, and a stone shaped like one that serves as a *mūrti.*

42. *Kheḷ.* See 7.4, above.

tree should not eat any meat beforehand and should take a bath first. But in Loṇī, Naikyā told the Brahman to allow the skins to be hung [on the tree]. Wherever Naikobā is today, there is also a pipaḷ tree.

2. The *vāhanas*

As an *avatār* of Śiva, Khaṇḍobā has the bull Nandī for his mount (*vāhana*). There is little evidence that Śiva is worshiped in the form of a bull, or that Nandī was or is worshiped independently in Maharashtra, as he is worshiped by Liṅgāyats in Karnatak in the form of Basava.[43] Yet the *Mahāmāyūrī Mantra* does mention as a *yakṣa* the Nandī of Nandīkeśvar, where Nandī is still worshiped today without Śiva. The *Mallārī Māhātmya* describes Śiva/Khaṇḍobā as sitting on a bull in his battle with Maṇimalla. Usually, however, there are one or two horses along with the Nandī in front of a temple of Khaṇḍobā, or in the temple hall (*sabhāmaṇḍapa*). An indication that the bull preceded the horse in the Khaṇḍobā cult is to be found in the *Mallārī Māhātmya* statement that Śiva, mounted on Nandī, accepted the horse from the demon Maṇi at Maṇi's insistence.[44] In another version the vanquished demon Maṇimalla asks permission to remain forever, mounted on his horse, near Śiva/Khaṇḍobā.[45]

43. D. D. Kosambi, *Myth and Reality* (Bombay, 1962), p. 121.

44. *Aśva-ratha-gajātem̐ pāvijem̐* (Marāṭhī version), 13, 59.

45. *Śrīkṣetra Jejurī Māhātmya,* chap. 12, pp. 43f. It is possible that Maṇimalla stands for one of the tribal rulers or deified heroes with whom the Brahmans—the authors of the Māhātmyas about Śiva/Mallārī/Khaṇḍobā—came into contact. *Mallaṉ* means "wrestler" in Tamil, or "great, famous man" (*Dravidian Etymological Dictionary,* 3871). In the villages of Karnatak the wrestler (*malla*) of the village is often a Kuruba (Enthoven, *The Castes and Tribes of the Bombay Presidency* [Bombay, 1920–22], s.v. Kuruba). "Malla" is a common epithet of rulers among the non-Brahmanical dynasties of the Deccan, of Rajasthan and of Nepal. These often came from obscure circumstances—that is, from mountain and forest tribes. Here the etymology of *malla* intersects with that of Tamil *malai* (hill, mountain), Malayalam *male* (mountain, raised land, hill land), Kannaḍa *male,* Koḍagu *male* (thick jungle, cardamum plantation, a jungle on a mountain side), etc. (*Dravidian Etymological Dictionary,* 3882), and Marāṭhī *māḷ*. Cf. Mallaya, 5.3.2, above. Pliny's reference to the Malli, in whose territory is located the mountain Mallus, is well known (VI.21.8–23.11. R. C. Majumdar, *The Classical Accounts of India* [Calcutta, 1960], p. 341). As we have seen, Khaṇḍobā's connections with the tribes are diverse. For the sake of the Brahmans and *ṛṣis,* Khaṇḍobā/Śiva defeats the non-Brahmanical elements of the tribes, symbolized by demons (*daityas* or *rakṣasas*) or ghosts (*bhūts*). That the residents of established settlements still occasionally call the members of nomadic tribes *bhūts* can be seen in Westphal-Hellbusch, "Changes in the Meaning of Ethnic Names as Exemplified by the Jāt, Rabārī, Bharvad, and Charan in Northwestern India," in *Pastoralists and Nomads in South Asia,* L. S. Leshnik and G. D. Sontheimer, eds. (Wiesbaden, 1975), p. 123.

Occasionally the horse itself is worshiped as Khaṇḍobā, as in Canda District,[46] and the horse is especially worshiped among the Bhils.[47] In Jejurī, Khaṇḍobā's horse is worshiped separately on all the major festival days. Here the traditional keepers of Khaṇḍobā's horse are a family of Muslims. Dhangars believe that the horse was hidden in the form of the wind in a mountain cave,[48] before Khaṇḍobā got it in order to ride to Bāṇāī.

Often devotees (*bhaktas*) embody Khaṇḍobā's horse, as at the Somvatī Amāvāsyā festival in Jejurī, when they seem to trot in ecstasy in front of the god's palanquin (*pālkhī*). This is even clearer at Mailār Devaraguḍḍa in Karnatak, where at the time of the Dasarā festival *bhaktas* act like horses and hit themselves with a whip as if they were being ridden by the god.[49] The whole festival on the evening before Dasarā is reminiscent of a hunting expedition. The *bhaktas* light torches, and at the highpoint of the festival the god's bows, each of them about five meters high, are brought out. The eldest Kuruba man climbs up one of the bows and makes prophecies. Other *bhaktas* of the god, the only ones mentioned in the gazetteer,[50] act like his dogs, and thus complete the picture of the god setting out on a hunt. In addition, the god's leather sandals are set up outside the temple, and it is said that the god puts them on to go hunting. The parallel to Murukaṉ is unmistakable.[51]

The great esteem for the horse reached its high point under the Bāhmanīs, under the five Muslim sultanates of the Deccan, and under the Marāṭhās. Large numbers of stone votive figures representing cattle are sometimes to be found standing before a temple of Birobā, Mhaskobā, or Khaṇḍobā. But nowhere in the focal area of my research are there large collections of cultic clay horses such as are found in the tribal areas of central India[52] or in front of

---

46. Information from P. R. Dhamdhere.

47. Syed ul Hassan, *The Castes and Tribes of H. E. H. The Nizam's Dominions* (Bombay, 1920), p. 74: "They reverence the horse and the dog and offer mud horses to Muhammadan saints and Khaṇḍobā." See also J. Haekel, "Kultische Tonpferde in Zentralindien," in *Mitteilungen der Anthropologischen Gesellschaft in Wien*, 92 (1962) 152–56. See also Westphal-Hellbusch, "Die Verehrung von Pferd und Reiter im Nordwesten des indischen Subkontinentes," in *Baessler-Archiv*, n.s., 19 (1971) 1–28.

48. *Bhoyrā*, from *bhuyār:* "A subterraneous cavity, esp. in a hilly region, a cavernous hollow . . . ; a cellar, a vault, a hypogeum, a room under ground" (Molesworth, *Dictionary*).

49. Rā. Ciṃ. Ḍhere refers to the Khaṇḍobā temple of Naḷdurg, where *bhaktas* who become possessed by the god are called "horses" (*vārū*). They hit themselves with a whip made of rope or leather (Ḍhere, *Khaṃḍobā*, p. 140).

50. *Gazetteer of the Bombay Presidency*, volume 20, Dharwar (Bombay, 1884), p. 721.

51. In Paḻani, near Madurai, pilgrims bring leather sandals as an offering to the god Murukaṉ. In *Paripāṭal*, 21, Murukaṉ is described as the god of hunters in the mountains: he rides on an elephant, holds a lance, and wears leather sandals on his feet. In *Paḻanittalapurāṇam*, XX.51, the purpose of the leather sandals is explained as being to protect the god's feet from impurities.

52. Besides the clay horses, Haekel, "Tonpferde," points out the "helmetlike" clay objects

Aiyaṉār's temples in Tamil villages.[53] The large numbers of votive figures of horses, found especially in front of deities who resemble the warlike Bhairav, have been attributed to the rarity value of the horse and to the admiration for it on the part of the tribes and castes ruled by Marāṭhās and Rājputs.[54] In Tamilnadu Aiyaṉār, as the leader of "the wild hunt," commands a cavalry company of ghosts; the village provides the clay horses for their ride so that Aiyaṉār will protect both the village and the fields from enemies.[55]

Khaṇḍobā is accompanied by a dog. This is explained by connecting Khaṇḍobā with Bhairav as Śvāśva ("he who uses a dog as his horse"). Yet the Dhangars are unanimous in stating that the dog came with Bāṇāī.

Birobā and Mhaskobā also have the horse as their principal *vāhana,* as is seen above all in their mythology. A stone horse stands in front of the main temple of Mhaskobā at Vīr; and at Ghoḍe Uḍḍāṇ, Mhaskobā's oldest cult place at Vīr, the imprints of a horse's hoofs are shown in rocks in the river (along with the footprints of elephants). It is here that the god, coming from Mhasvaḍ, is supposed to have landed for the first time with his horse. The god's horse is in the original temple, on the bank of the Nirā River. Birobā has his small, stone horse in front of the temple in Bhāde (Purandar Taluka, Poona District), along with a dog (or a ram?).

In many temples of Birobā, as well as in quite a few temples of Khaṇḍobā, *vāhanas* and votive figures have the form of cows, horses, or rams, whereas the *mūrti* of the god is still without form. Mhaskobā's "*mūrti*" in Vīr is a shapeless stone covered with a thick layer of *śendūr,* from which just the heads of Mhaskobā and Jogeśvarī stand out. Only in Vāśī, near Kolhāpūr, does the stone *mūrti* of Birobā have the faint contours of a warrior with a crown (*mukuṭa*), a sword, and a shield.

All of this evidence taken together seems to indicate that representations of

(*taba*) with doorlike openings, which are called temples. In the pastoral area of Maharashtra—that is, in the more restricted area of my research—this "temple" is clearly similar to a tent modeled in clay, with a smoke hole and bulging seams. It is possible that these tents are remembered much better in the pastoral area than among the tribes of the forest region, where the clay tents were easily modified (or technically misunderstood?). The "tents" are associated with Mhasobā and the Gavḷīs. Mhasobā, the cattle god, gradually becomes the *kṣetrapāl* ("the guardian of the fields"), and his "temple" stands in the middle of a field, at the edge of a field, or at the edge of a village, where he is often identical with Y(∼V)etāl, the lord of ghosts. In this stage the "smoke hole" is often covered with a stone or receives a *śikhar,* a temple dome (which is often removable!). Finally there appears in the "smoke hole" the anthropomorphic head of Mhasobā.

53. A. Höfer, "Aiyanar, der reitende Gott und seine kultischen Tonpferde" (Wien, 1961), manuscript, pp. 5, 33.

54. Haekel, "Tonpferde," p. 160.

55. Höfer, "Aiyanar."

animals preceded the figurative representation of Khaṇḍobā, Mhaskobā, and Birobā.[56]

3. The Emergence of Iconographic Form; Attributes and Cult Objects: The "Fifty-two" *Birudeṃ*

Two images have contributed to Khaṇḍobā and Mhaskobā's taking on of iconographic form. The first is that of Bhairav as it was spread by the Gosāvīs, principally by the Kānphaṭā Gosāvīs. Bhairav is the god who invades the forest, who conquers demons, and who often takes on the defilement arising from Śiva's deeds. Through him a new area becomes a *kṣetra,* and he protects it as Kāḷbhairav, the *kotvāl* of Banaras. The second image derives from the sphere of the *daṇḍanāyakas* or *śiledārs,* local rulers who are dependent on the king, but who often become independent when the central power is weakened. In accord with this image, Bhairav becomes a god endowed with the attributes of a king, who protects the region (as Khaṇḍobā) or the village (as Mhaskobā). This Bhairav helps the king gain victory. He is a god of war, who protects the king and inspires or possesses him to perform feats. But as Aṣṭabhairav, Bhairav is also the village deity who gives the village eightfold protection, in all eight directions (*aṣṭa* means "eight"). Mixed in with the two images are euhemeristic traces of the Hindu king; and some claim to see in Khaṇḍobā an apotheosis of the Yādava king, Rāmacandradeva.

The image of the Gosāvī who penetrates the forest and identifies himself with his god has also surely contributed to the iconography; indeed, one can assume that the iconographic representation of the god had as its model the figure of the Gosāvī who identifies himself with Kāḷbhairav. Thus the god appears as a Gosāvī holding a trident and an hourglass drum, and wearing a garland of the skulls of his enemies. But he also appears as a warrior on horseback holding a shield and a sword, or even just as a horseman with a trident—like Mhat(~s)obā of Hiṃjavḍī. The small metal *mūrtis* of Khaṇḍobā, which are often found in household shrines, depict a horse and rider. The rider holds a sword in his front right hand and a trident (*triśūḷ*) in his back right hand. In his front left hand he holds a shield, and in his back left hand a snake. His front left arm clasps a small female figure who is sitting on his

56. Cf. Russell and Hiralal, vol. 3, p. 163: The Gowārīs, a herding caste in northeastern Maharashtra who are lower in rank than the Ahīrs and Gavḷīs, install a clay horse near an anthill for the divine patron of cattle, Dudhera. According to Russell, their principal worship was of the ancestors.

thigh. Often the horseman is accompanied by a dog. The horseman wears a helmetlike crown (*mukuṭa*) after the fashion of the Hindu kings of Karnatak (or Rājputānā?).

In the three metal double statues in Jejurī depicting Khaṇḍobā and Mhāḷsā, Khaṇḍobā wears the turban of a Marāṭhā or Gavḷī/Dhangar. The turban is changed every day. The stone *mūrti* of Mārtaṇḍa Bhairava in the inner shrine of the temple at Jejurī wears the turban of the Śinde dynasty. One of the three metal *mūrtis* holds a trident in its back right hand, a sword in its front right hand, an hourglass drum (*ḍamaru*) in its back left hand, and in its front left hand a drinking vessel (*paraḷ*), which has the shape of a flat, round tumbler. The *paraḷ* may originally have been a skull (*kapāla*), the drinking vessel of the Kāpālikas, early forerunners of the Gosāvīs. Śiva also holds the *kapāla* in his hand, a fact that led to his not being invited to Dakṣa's sacrifice.[57] Today the worshipers have forgotten this significance, and for them the *paraḷ* is simply a drinking vessel. The two other *mūrtis* of Khaṇḍobā also carry the *kapāla*, and one of them a sword besides, and nothing else. All three *mūrtis* were donated by important Marāṭhā rulers.

Like Khaṇḍobā, Birobā also is often represented in household shrines by a small, metal figure of a mounted horseman. In Paṭṭaṇ Kuḍolī these mounted figures are placed in the temple in front of Viṭṭhal and Birāppā during the pilgrimage festival that takes place between Dasarā and Divāḷī. Viṭṭhal and Birāppā themselves are represented here by two aniconic *piṇḍs*. In contrast to Khaṇḍobā, the mounted figures of Birobā have only two arms, which always hold a sword or a shield in their hands.

It is often said of Birobā that he has laid down his *bāvan birudeṃ* in Ārevāḍī. These are the fifty-two magical cult objects, emblems, and attributes possessed by the god, but also by the Gosāvī or the Dhangar. *V(~b)iruda* is also the "epithet" of a ruler. Thus the Kalacuri king Someśvar Sovideva adopted the *biruda* "Bhujabalamalla," "the strong wrestler."[58] The *Vāksaṃpradāya Kośa* gives a list of the fifty-two *birudeṃ*,[59] many of which also appear in the cult of the three gods—for example, the *mekh-mogarī*, an iron chain made of nails and bits of iron, which is supposed to help against rheumatism, or a kind of club;[60] and the *morcel*, made of bunches of peacock feathers, which often tops a tall pole (*kāṭhī*). The *kāṭhī* is also found as a flagstaff (*niśān*), with a woolen Dhangar blanket as the flag. The *kāṭhī* or

57. *Kālikā Purāṇa*, 16.31.

58. *Maharashtra State Gazetteer*, Ancient Period (Bombay, 1967), p. 351.

59. Ya. Ra. Dāte and Cim. Ga. Karve, eds., *Mahārāṣṭra Vāksaṃpradāya Kośa* (Puṇeṃ, 1942–1947), s.v. *bāvan birudeṃ*.

60. See *Mhaskobā Devāceṃ Caritra*, part 5 and n. 49 (Appendix).

niśān often itself represents the god, and is a weapon that destroys the demon.[61] The yak-tail fly whisk (*cavrī*), *chatras, cakra, śendūr,* and the *korḍā* (whip) also belong to the paraphernalia of the god and the cult, along with the woolen blanket that serves as the seat of the god and of the priest (cf. Text 23), and the bell (*ghaṇṭā*) that the faithful ring as they enter the temple. The Liṅgāyat priest in particular carries the hand bell, and so Liṅgāyats also have the right (*mān*) to ring it during the procession at the temple of Viṭṭhal and Birobā in Paṭṭaṇ Kuḍolī. J. J. Meyer has reported in detail on the magical power of the bell in India.[62] Even mirrors, or the great number of them which are found in most temples of these gods, are not superfluous decoration, but objects which bring good luck and protect against magical harm.[63]

4. Dominion Over Lower Gods and Spirits

Birobā, Mhaskobā, and Khaṇḍobā developed from spirits, *yakṣas, asuras,* or *daityas* into gods, and they are therefore themselves rulers over the troops of spirits ("*kṣudradevatā*"). Thus Khaṇḍobā and Birobā especially are designated *bāvan* (fifty-two) *vīr*—that is, they can take on fifty-two forms of spirits or lower deities. To the *vīrs* belong, for example, not only Mhasāsūr, Bhairav, and the spirit of a dead Māṅg boy (*ceḍā*), but also Narasiṃha, who developed into an *avatār* of Viṣṇu.[64] Mhasāsūr becomes Mhaskobā or Kāḷbhairav, and Kāḷbhairav becomes an important god of Maharashtra, who now himself exerts power over the fifty-two *vīrs*. The fifty-two *vīrs* are not only absorbed by the gods, but are also subject to the priests, who assure themselves of their help through mantras, and occasionally make use of their services for some period.[65]

Among the Dhangars, ideas about the *bāvan vīr* are not distinct—or rather, they are in the process of fading away. They are still the most distinct in the mythology of Birobā, who is referred to as *bāvan vīr*—although the *bāvan vīr* often become confused with the *bāvan birudeṃ* (see section 3, above). In Muḷśī (Muḷśī Taluka, Poona District), ideas about the *bāvan vīr* are still reflected in ritual. Here, during the pilgrimage in the month of Caitra, the

---

61. Cf. *viruda-dhvaja,* a royal banner (Monier-Williams, *Dictionary*). A god's banner often depicts his *vāhana*. Murukaṉ carries the rooster on his banner; Śiva, the bull; Viṣṇu, Garuḍa. See *Tirumurukāṟruppaṭai,* 151 (Garuḍa, white bull) and 220 (rooster). On the worship of Indra in the form of a flagstaff and the power of Indra's tree, see J. J. Meyer, *Trilogie,* part 3, pp. 5, 50.

62. Meyer, *Trilogie,* part 1, pp. 217ff.

63. Ibid., part 1, pp. 220f., n. 1.

64. See Rā. Ciṃ. Ḍhere, *Lokasaṃskṛtīcī Kṣitije* (Puṇeṃ, 1971), pp. 56f.

65. R. E. Enthoven, *The Folklore of Bombay* (Oxford, 1924), pp. 193ff., 203.

bāvan vīr take possession of the Dhangar priest of a small Khaṇḍobā temple. The *bāvan vīr,* who are seen here as a unit, live behind the temple, in the ground:

Text 66

When the *bāvan vīr* come into our bodies, we dig a circular furrow. And in this furrow we build a fire. The god [that is, the Dhangar priest who becomes possessed by the *bāvan vīr,* and who also embodies Khaṇḍobā] sits in the circle.

The god expels other gods [who want to gain power over the *bāvan vīr*—like Jyotibā, for example] by throwing fire at them with his hand. The god sits in the center of the circle of fire for up to two hours. Otherwise he is hidden in the ground. At the time of the festival he comes out and then disappears again into the ground. The *mūrti* of Khaṇḍobā is in the temple. That is, there are two *mūrtis*—one has appeared of its own accord out of the ground, and the other has been installed. The place of the *bāvan vīr* is behind Khaṇḍobā's temple. Vetāḷ is also there.

A Dhangar priest from Paṭṭaṇ Kuḍolī explained why the *bāvan vīr* no longer play a role in the cult of Birobā:

Text 67

All the demons on earth had been killed. Only Gajaliṅg, Reḍeśvar, and Konāsūr were left. In order to kill these three demons, Birudev asked Śaṅkar for the ability to take on fifty-two *avatārs* every day. Earlier the fifty-two *avatārs* had not been necessary in order to kill demons. But to kill these demons they were necessary. . . .

At that time Birobā could take on any form he wanted. Birudev could take on the form of Mahādev, Marutī, Viṣṇu, or Nandī. He could take on many forms, because still more demons arose out of the drops of the demons' blood. When he had killed them, he no longer took on the form of the fifty-two.

The struggle of Birobā, Mhaskobā, and Khaṇḍobā against demons corresponds with the gods' assumption of form and indicates their rise to the ranks of deities close to the Purāṇic pantheon. When the seven sages (*ṛṣis*) are practicing asceticism (*tapas*) on the mountain Maṇicūl, Malla appears and destroys the *āśram,* violates the *ṛṣis'* wives, and ties up several of the *ṛṣis*. Thereupon Śiva arises in the form of Mārtaṇḍa Bhairav, and a battle takes place in the course of which Maṇi and Malla are defeated.[66] Birobā also kills several demons, especially in Karnatak: Gajaliṅg; Reḍeśvar; and Kōn̲āsur, at Kon̲n̲ūr.[67] The descriptions of these battles with demons are notable for a certain uniformity. One favorite motif is that of the drops of blood of the dead demons, which transform themselves into new demons; this motif comes from

66. See the summary of the battle against Maṇimalla in Ḍhere, *Khaṃḍobā,* pp. 3–5.
67. Ya. Ph. Attikoḷḷa, *Hālumatada Caritra,* chap. 13, pp. 45ff.

the myth of Andhaka.[68] The following text sketches one of Birobā's battles, and then changes into an account of the creation of Meṇḍhaka Māyājī:

Text 68

When in those days Birudev lived in Māyavvā's *vāḍā,* there arose a great drought, and the sheep had nothing on which to graze. So he wandered in search of pastures. He went farther and farther. He came to a great sea. And at this sea there were large trees. And he began to cut down these trees.[69] In the trunks there lived great demons who rose up and began to do battle with Birudev. When he killed one demon, a new demon would rise up from the drops of blood of the dead one. And as he fought and fought this way, he felt it as a great burden. And no one was looking after the sheep, so they spread out farther and farther. He had set out alone in search of pastures.

Pārvatī and Śaṅkar flew past [in a sky chariot (*vimān*)]. And Pārvatī said, "God, there is Māyavvā's brother Kāśīliṅg Birāppā. He is exhausted from many battles. There is no one behind or in front of his sheep, to guard them." There was no *pāsāryā.*[70] Śaṅkar and Pārvatī took dirt from their necks and formed a human figure out of it. Then they sprinkled some nectar (*amṛt*) on it and brought it to life.

And they named the figure Māyājī Meṇḍhaka. He was supposed to look after the sheep from behind as the *pāsāryā.* The temple we saw together yesterday in Kirloskarvāḍī is that of Māyāppā or Māyājī.

A *vīr* is thus someone who understands how to provide himself with special yogic abilities. He has the power to subject the fifty-two spirits or deities to himself, or to master the *siddhis,* and he himself becomes a *siddha.* This again places Birobā/Vīrobā close to the Gosāvīs or yogīs. The *siddhas* at the temple of Mhaskobā in Vīr are also occasionally called *vīrs.*[71] They hit themselves with swords in order to force the god to take possession of them. The Kañcavīras at the temple of Mailār at Devaraguḍḍa torture themselves with a series of devices in order to demonstrate to the god their devotion (*bhakti*) and their courage.

Although the name of the god Birobā is thus derived from this conception of his yogic powers, it would be a mistake to explain his name only in terms of the sphere of the yogī. The demon-fighting Birobā is also a hero and a god of war. In this he is like Mhasvaḍ-Siddha and "Nāth" Mhaskobā, who both come from the sphere of the Navnāth sect, or the Kānphaṭā Gosāvīs; in

---

68. See Text 30 and chap. 5, n. 104, above.

69. During the droughts in 1970–73, the common practice was not so much to cut down trees as to defoliate them completely.

70. Two people are needed to drive the sheep during a migration: one (the *mhoryā*) who leads the herd, and another (the *pāsāryā* or *māge jāṇārā*) who keeps the sheep together from behind.

71. *Gazetteer of the Bombay Presidency,* vol. 18, Poona, part 3, p. 464.

addition, he is like Khaṇḍobā, and also like Kāḷbhairav, with whom the three gods Birobā, Mhaskobā, and Khaṇḍobā became identified. In Karnatak especially, the idea of the hero, *vīra,* has also exerted an influence on ideas of Birobā. Still today in Karnatak hero stones (*vīragaḷas*) are worshiped under the name Bīra-(Bire-)deva.[72] In a well-known verse found on hero stones in Karnatak, the yogī and the hero are compared:

> dvāv imau puruṣau loke sūryamaṇḍala bhedinau
> parivrāḍ yogabhuktaśca raṇe cābhimokho hataḥ
> [Mahābhārata, critical edition, apparatus at 5.33.32].

As the yogī breaks through the orb of the sun by means of his yogic abilities, so the hero who dies in battle does the same thing. Battle is therefore a kind of yogic exercise.

The warlike Vīrabhadra has also contributed to the cult and mythology of Birobā/Birāppā. Vīrabhadra is the leader of Śiva's heavenly *gaṇas;* he is especially worshiped by Liṅgāyats. In areas where Vīrabhadra is worshiped he is often equated with Birobā.[73]

5. The Marriage of the God; the Scriptural Definition of the God's "History"

Marriage represents the final stage of the god's incorporation into the circle of the deities of established settlements in areas with regular agriculture. This incorporation also moves him close to the all-India Brahmanical pantheon. At this stage there appears a *Māhātmya* or *Caritra* based on the Purāṇas and ascribed to some one Purāṇa. The marriage of the god of the forest and pasture area moves him out of the ascetic life of the forest, where, according to Brahmanical ideas, only the fourth stage of life is to be spent.

The Kānphaṭā Gosāvīs and their predecessors, the Kālamukhas and Kāpālikas, are originally unacquainted with marriage. The following text explains why the Gosāvī—Kāḷbhairav—must get married:

Text 69

. . . [Demons] were preventing people's *vāḍīs* and *vastis* from growing. So the god began to fight with them, and he killed them all. Before he had killed them, some of the demons stood in the way. Śaṅkar [Kāḷbhairav] said, "Wait a moment."

72. See, for example, Dinkar Desai, *The Mahāmaṇḍaleśvaras under the Cālukyas of Kalyāṇī* (Bombay, 1951), p. 464.

73. Ya. Ph. Attikoḷḷa, *Hālumatada Caritra,* pp. 53–55: legends about the origin of Birāppā, Vīreśvar, or Vīrabhadra—the *ādidev* or *kuladaivata* of the Kurubas.

He went to Pārvatī. Pārvatī said, "The demons won't listen to you this way. Become a bridegroom and get the power of Śakti. Your sword will be granted victory. The demons will die at your hand."

He said, "Why should I get married?"

Pārvatī said, "Even worms, ants, cattle, and birds mate. If you don't get married, this human settlement will not grow."

Thus in Vīr each year Mhaskobā's marriage marks the beginning of the great pilgrimage festival (*jatrā*).[74] Mhaskobā, who originally comes from Sonārī, Mhasvaḍ, and Jāvḷī, is the one of the three gods Khaṇḍobā, Mhaskobā, and Birobā most closely connected with the Gosāvīs and with the mythology of Kāḷbhairav. Dhangars brought Mhaskobā to Vīr; farmers—Kuṇbīs and Māḷīs—took over the cult; and Brahmans celebrate the wedding ceremony. The pastoral god is so well integrated into the areas dominated by agriculture that the Poona gazetteer of 1885, for instance, designates Mhaskobā as "a modern Kunbi-God."[75]

The principal cults of Khaṇḍobā, which differ from one another and compete among themselves, have, in a sense, divided the deeds of the god among them. In Jejurī, Khaṇḍobā defeats the demons; and in Pāl, in Satara District, he marries Mhāḷsā. Śiva took the form of Khaṇḍobā, who defeated the demons with his seven crores of *gaṇas*. Pārvatī took the form of Mhāḷsā.[76] In the case of Birobā, the marriage is a pronounced feature only in the mythology of the Dhangar *farmers* of Sangli District. His connections with his wife, Kāmādevī, are disorganized, and they are overshadowed by her similarity to the old mother goddess (see Text 12). He has remained essentially a god of the forest and pasture land, and his devotees are exclusively Dhangars and Kurubas. Significantly, *nomadic* Dhangars know hardly anything about Birobā's wife, Kāmādevī.

But the myths about Birobā have not found expression in a *pothī,* a "book:" a *Caritra* or *Māhātmya.* This is appropriate for a god who has not yet been fully assimilated into the system of the established settlements. Birobā's myths are alive in the *ovīs* of the Dhangars, and no learned Brahman has brought them to Sanskritized form. Birobā, the only one of the gods to have "studied" and mastered the *bāvan bīrs,* is to take form in Sūravantī's womb at Śaṅkar's request. Birobā's conditions for doing so are as follows:

Text 70

I do not want to be shackled by anything. No line is to be drawn to tell me to stop. I am not to appear in any *giranta* [written *grantha*] or in any *puti* [written *pothī*]. . . .

---

74. On the marriage of Mhaskobā, see *Mhaskobā Devācem Caritra,* part 2 (Appendix).
75. *Gazetteer of the Bombay Presidency,* vol. 18, Poona, part 3, p. 464.
76. *Śrīkṣetra Jejurī Māhātmya,* chap. 12, pp. 43f.

The many illiterate Dhangars sing the history of Birobā. They do not read or recite it out of a book. Indeed, it is even believed that Birobā's significance would diminish if it were not preserved through *oral* traditions and through the all-night performances of *ovīs* recited with religious inspiration.

6. Conclusion

All three gods, Birobā, Mhaskobā, and Khaṇḍobā, have their origin in the forest and pasture region. They are based on a deity who was once found all over South India and who still exists in his original form even today. This is a deity of the forest and the pasture, who appears in the form of a snake, and who lives on the mountain, in the termite mound, and in trees. The original, formless deity of forest tribes and pastoralist groups first took form according to the ideas of these people.

The god is represented as an unhewn stone, which is often found as "self-formed" (*svayaṃbhū*) and to which there is often added a menhir or a *liṅgam*like stone. Later there sometimes follows a *mūrti*. Often the worship of the god in anthropomorphic form is preceded by the worship of his *vāhana*, or at least by the representation of his attributes—spears, flags, or votive figures of animals, for instance. *Sādhūs*, Gosāvīs, Brahmans, and the influence of tribal rulers, rather than destroying the cult, add new layers of imagery. The cult often combines with the manifestations of these figures—with the Gosāvī, for example, who identifies himself with Kāḷbhairav; or with tribal lords, local officials (*daṇḍanāyakas* or *śiledārs*), or central rulers. By emulating the model of the rulers, the Khaṇḍobā cult spread into even the smallest villages. Other forms of representation, deriving from the ideas of groups that once were religiously important in the region—the Gosāvīs, Liṅgāyats, and so forth—diminished in importance, but are still preserved. An essential characteristic of Indian culture makes itself felt: new notions and images, often those belonging to an upwardly mobile dominant group, are taken over without the old ones being given up. Thus original notions are retained in the cults, although they may be reinterpreted: that is, "Brahmanized" or "Kṣatriyaized." There often arise endless "contradictions" between notions about the original deity on the one hand—still found at their purest among the residents of forest and pasture areas and among the lower classes in established settlements—and on the other hand the deity as he has emerged under the influence of the new notions. Thus a Dhangar can believe in the individual identity of his *kulsvāmī* Birobā, but at the same time know that Birobā is only a local or individual manifestation of Śiva, the Mahādev ("Great God") who rules over all. The "contradictions" are also found in the texts: in the identification of Cēyōṉ/Murukaṉ with the north Indian deity Skanda, for instance. Despite many similarities that make the identification plausible—for example, each is a god of fertility, a god of war armed with a lance, and a guardian spirit of trees—Skanda as Kumāra ("the Youthful Boy") and Yogīśvara ("the Lord of Yogīs") avoids women.[77] Women are not allowed to enter his temple. On the other hand, Murukan̲'s connections with his two wives are a pronounced feature, and serve to differentiate him from Skanda.

Khaṇḍobā as Mārtaṇḍa Bhairava, Birobā/Birāppā as Vireśvar/Vīrabhadra, and Mhaskobā thus have many essential traits in common with Murukan̲, Aiyan̲ār, Mallikārjuna, Mallanna, and Mailār. Their development can best be understood by taking into consideration the contrast between the village, the established settlement, on the one hand, and the forest and pasture areas on the other; the change from pastoralism to regular agriculture; and the history and religious ideas of the groups, sects, and castes connected with the cult.

77. See J. J. Meyer, *Trilogie,* part 1, p. 136.

APPENDIX
The Biography of God Śrī Nāth Mhaskobā
(*Śrīnāth Mhaskobā Devācem̩ Caritra,* First Published in 1889)

Part 1. The Origin of Śrī Kāḷbhairav

Once Pārvatī asked Śrī Śaṅkar, "How did Bhairav come into being?"[1]

Śaṅkar replied: "Brahmā and Viṣṇu were pervaded by *yogamāyā,*[2] and so they became proud and began to fight with each other. Viṣṇu said, 'God Brahmā, I am the cause of everything, so *brahman* is in me.'

"Hearing this, Brahmā said, 'And I am the one who created all beings, moving and still, so *brahman* is in me.' And, having said this, Brahmā abused Śrī Viṣṇu terribly. In adverse times, the mind is affected too.

"Anyway, Viṣṇu said, 'Brahmā, don't sing your own praises in front of me. All your sacrifices[3] are useless. Have you forgotten that my essence is the supreme *brahman?* No one is greater than I, and devotees have no secure refuge apart from me.'

"Hearing this, Brahmā got angry and said, 'I created the soul and the Lord (Īśvara), and I am the one who directs the course of the world. So no one at all is greater than I.'

"Anyway, they began to sing their own praises this way. At that point, Nārada Muni's retinue arrived there. Seeing that the two of them were quarreling, he said to them, 'You can't settle anything by sitting here arguing. If both of you go to Badrikāśram,[4] you'll get a decision as to which of you is greater.'

1. The Purāṇas give various versions of the origin of the god Bhairav. See, for example, *Śiva Purāṇa, Śatarudra-saṃhitā,* VIII–IX: *Bhairavāvatāra,* VII.50: Bhairav cuts off Brahmā's left head with the nail of one of the fingers of his left hand. *Liṅga Purāṇa,* 96.49ff.

2. In arguing over whether Viṣṇu or Brahmā is the source of creation and the principle of the eternal, unchanging *brahman,* the gods are under an illusion (*māyā*), because Śiva alone is the creator of life, and he alone is Īśvara.

3. Reading *yajñayāga* for *jñānayoga* or *yajñayoga.*

4. One of the sources of the Ganges, and the location of a famous *āśram* of *ṛṣis.*

"Hearing this, the two of them went to Badrikāśram. There they found Vaśiṣṭha, Vāmadeva, Atrimuni, and many other great, great *ṛṣis* who had practiced asceticism for many eons and had attained the essence of *brahman*. Brahmā and Viṣṇu asked them, 'Which of us is greater?' and [Atri] *ṛṣi* said, 'Neither of you is great. The Vedas are great, but even the Vedas cannot perceive Śiva. Śiva is the one who is truly great.'

"Hearing Atri *ṛṣi* say this, Śrī Viṣṇu got very angry and abused him terribly and said, 'Hey! Why have you given up the essence of Viṣṇu (*viṣṇu-tatva*) this way, and taken to worshiping the essence of Śiva? This shows that you are ignorant.'

"Hearing him say this, Mārkaṇḍeya *ṛṣi* said, 'The Vedas describe *brahman* and also Śiva. Even though there have been many cosmic dissolutions, Śiva is still unchanged. From the Vedas have come the Śāstras and Purāṇas.'

"So Brahmā and Viṣṇu went to the Vedas and asked them, 'In which of us is *brahman* found?'

"The Ṛgveda said, 'Both of you exist because of Śiva's orders. So only Śiva is great.' All four Vedas said the same thing. So Brahmā and Viṣṇu abused them terribly. Then they went to the three-verse Gāyatrī [*mantra*].[5] It too said that Śiva alone is great. So Brahmā and Viṣṇu abused it, saying, 'You are all ignorant.'

"Hearing that they had abused all of them this way, Śrī Śaṅkar became extremely angry, and in his anger he dashed his hand against the ground. Immediately Śrī Bhairav was incarnated out of the ground. He held in his hands a trident and an hourglass drum. Taking on a terrible form this way, he stood before Śrī Śaṅkar with folded hands and said, 'Tell me your command.'

"As soon as he said this, Śaṅkar said, 'God Brahmā and Śrī Viṣṇu have become proud and have offended the gods, the *ṛṣis,* the Vedas, and the three-verse Gāyatrī [*mantra*]. So you must go and pacify the Vedas, the *ṛṣis,* and the Gāyatrī, and cut off the head of anyone who opposes them.'

"On being given this command, Śrī Kāḷbhairav set out with a great roar. He arrived at the place where Brahmā and Viṣṇu were. Brahmā and Viṣṇu asked, 'Who are you, who have come here in this terrible form, and why have you come?'

"When they asked this, he replied, 'I am Kāḷbhairav.'

"Then Śrī Viṣṇu asked, 'Tell us, which of us is greater?'

"Hearing this question, Śrī Kāḷbhairav said, 'The one who can reach the end of my form (*svarūp*) is greater.'

---

5. A verse of the *Ṛgveda* (3.62.10) often personified as a goddess and regarded metaphorically as the mother of the three upper castes. The verse is recited especially at the *upanayana* ceremony.

"When they heard this they said, 'All right.' And Viṣṇu went toward the underworld, and Brahmā went toward the sky.

"In the one direction, as Śrī Mahāviṣṇu went on and on toward the underworld, he got completely exhausted, but he could not reach the end. As he went farther and farther, he met Pātālaskanda.[6] Viṣṇu asked him, 'Who are you, and why are you staying here?'

"When he was asked this question, Pātālaskanda said, 'We have been sitting here practicing asceticism for many eons, but we have not been able to reach the end of Śiva's form (*svarūp*). Don't you fall into pointless pride.' Viṣṇu heard this and accepted it, and he took refuge with Śrī Śaṅkar.

"In the other direction, Brahmā went up and up, but he could not reach the end at all. Then he met a cow (the Kāmadhenū) and a ketakī [tree]; they too said, 'It is difficult to reach the end of this form. Don't wear yourself out pointlessly trying to do so.' But because Brahmā was proud, he brought along the cow and the ketakī to Śri Bhairav to bear false witness that he had reached the end.

"Śrī Bhairav asked, 'Did you reach it?' and Brahmā said, 'Yes, I did reach it, and you ask the cow and the ketakī whether I reached it or not.'

"Hearing this, Bhairav asked the cow and the ketakī, and they too said that he had reached it. When he heard this, Śrī Bhairav got angry and cut off Brahmā's head.[7] To the cow he said, 'Because you bore false witness, your mouth is impure.' And to the ketakī he said, 'Because you bore false witness, you too are impure. Anybody who offers you to Śrī Śaṅkar will be poor for seven lifetimes.' And to this day the kevaḍā [ketakī] flower is not offered to Śaṇkar.

"Anyway, in this way Brahmā was killed. This caused loud mourning in the whole world, and the course of the world came to a stop. Seeing this, Śrī Śaṇkar also came there, and Śaṇkar put the faces of the four Vedas on Brahmā and revived him. And Śaṅkar said to Bhairav, 'You are afflicted with the sin of killing a Brahman. So you should take a human skull in your hands and make a pilgrimage, and you'll be freed from the sin.'

"As soon as he had been given this command, Śrī Bhairav set out from there and traveled around to all holy places (*tīrthas*). Eventually he came to the town of Kāśī [Banaras] on the bank of the Bhāgīrathī [Ganges] River, and stayed there in the Ānanda forest. Then he bathed in the Bhāgīrathī and had *darśan* of Śrī Viśveśvara. Śrī Viśveśvara said, 'You must stay here,' and he gave Śrī Kāḷbhairav the duty of being the guardian (*kotvāl*) of Kāśī."

6. A guardian of the underworld.

7. The story of Kāḷbhairav's destruction of one of the five heads of Brahmā is found combined with local legends, and also occurs in the legends of other Kāḷbhairav temples—at Biḷūr, for example (Jath Taluka, Sangli District).

These days the torments of Yama are not to be found in the holy precincts of Kāśī. For this reason, many holy people go and stay in the town of Kāśī. This same Kāḷbhairav has become incarnated for the sake of his devotees in Sonārī, Jāvḷī, Mhasvaḍ, Borban (Ghoḍe Uḍan), and here in Śrī Kṣetra Vīr on the bank of the Pūrṇagaṅgā.

Those who read or listen to this story of Kāḷbhairav will be freed from all sins, and they will not suffer the torments of Yama. I am writing the story of Kāḷbhairav Mhaskobā as best I can. This is the way it really happened.

(There are four original Siddhas: Mhasvaḍ-Siddha, Vairāg-Siddha, Solāpūr-Siddha, and Sonārī-Siddha. This is an incarnation of only the Siddha of Sonārī.)

Part 2. Why He Became Incarnated in Vīr

In Poona District there is a Taluka whose headquarters is Sāsvaḍ. Six *kos* [about fourteen miles] south of Sāsvaḍ is a famous village named Vīr. North of this village, on the bank of the Pūrṇagaṅgā, is the temple of the god Śrī Maskobā [Mhaskobā]. The population of the village is about 2,715, and the village has plenty of good farm land. There are many Brahmans, Marāṭhās, Māḷīs, Kuṇbīs, and so on, who live in the village. This place is delightful, and the god is very glorious. His origin is as follows:

There was a certain Dhangar named Kamaḷājī who used to take his cattle and wander to a village in Belgaum District named Sonārī, which is a holy place of Bhairav.[8] The [Dhangars'] regular practice is to go and stay wherever their cattle and sheep can find something to graze on. Śrī Bhairav's holy place in that village of Sonārī is very powerful (*jāgṛt*). Kamaḷājī's regular practice was to settle his cattle in the *vāḍā* in the evening, and then to go into the temple, bring water in the palms of his hands to bathe Śrī Bhairav, bring *aṃboṇī* mash[9] and taravaḍ[10] leaves to worship the god, show Śrī Bhairav

---

8. Sonārī is in Usmanabad District, not Belgaum District. But the area between Belgaum and Usmanabad is one where herders stay, and through which they wander. For Kamaḷājī, the devotee of Dhuḷobā, see Text 51, above. Kamaḷājī went to Ujjain every night to worship Kāḷbhairav.

9. Molesworth, *Dictionary—aṃboṇ:* "A mash of grain, bran &c. laid before cows to engage and quiet them during milking: also a fattening mash for cows &c. gen." An earlier edition of "The Biography of God Śrī Nāth Mhaskobā" has *aṃboḷī* instead of *aṃboṇī*. According to Molesworth, *aṃboḷī* is "a preparation of food, —flour soured by exposure to the air and slightly parched upon a girdle (*sic*) or baking-plate."

10. A plant, *Cassia auriculata* or *tora* (Molesworth, *Dictionary*).

11. A food offering. In the temple of Mhaskobā it is vegetarian. Nonvegetarian offerings are shown to the god from outside. *Bhākrī* is a flat bread made of millet flour and water.

naivedya[11] of the *bhākrī* bread he had with him, and then eat the *bhākrī*. He followed this routine for a long time.

I used the term *vāḍā*.[12] A *vāḍā* is a place surrounded by a fence where cattle can be penned without being tied up. Such a place is called a *vāḍā*. Later his *vāḍā* was moved to Borban (Ghoḍe Uḍan) on the bank of the Nirā, because there was plenty of pasture land there. Even after he had come there, Kamaḷājī kept to his routine: in the evening, after settling the cattle in the *vāḍā,* he would close his eyes and meditate on Sonārī, and just by meditating this way he would go to Sonārī; when he had worshiped Śrī Bhairav in the same way as before, and shown the *naivedya* of *bhākrī,* he would eat the *bhākrī,* and at dawn he would return to the place where he had been. This routine too went on for a long time.

At dawn, when the Guravs opened the god's door, they saw that the evening offerings (*pūjā*) had been pushed aside and that *aṃboṇī* mash and taravaḍ leaves had been offered to the god. They decided to see who was coming so late at night, and they arranged to keep watch in turns. The next day when Kamaḷājī arrived, the god said, "Don't you come tomorrow. The Guravs have arranged to keep watch, and if they see you they'll kill you."

Hearing this, Kamaḷājī said, "O God, if I die at your feet, what more do I need? I don't care if they kill me, but I'm not going to give up my regular practice."

That put the god in a very difficult position, and he said, "If I come there for you, that will solve the problem."

Kamaḷājī asked, "How will I know you've come?"

The god said, "Near your place there's a huge, spread-out hivar tree.[13] When fresh leaves sprout on it, you must understand that I have come."

Then Kamaḷājī returned home. The next day he waited all night long for the god to come, but the god never came. Kamaḷājī decided to go to Sonārī the next day and offer his head to the Lord (Nāth). So he kept thinking, "When will sunset come?" and "When can I go?" And with that, a miracle happened. The god came in the form of a huge snake to the place where the cows were grazing, and he went in among the cows. The cows ran every which way, but one barren cow stayed right there. Then Śrī Nāth wound himself around the body of the barren cow, opened his mouths, and began to drink with four of his mouths. Because his fifth mouth was free, he pulled out a root and stood swaying, and a stream of milk began to flow there.

At that point, Kamaḷājī began to wonder why the cows were running away, and he thought, "I wonder if a tiger has come." So he got up from the thick

12. Herders' camp.

13. Sanskrit, *hiṃvara*. *Mimosa* or *Acacia tomentosa* (Molesworth, *Dictionary*).

grass he had been lounging in, and went forward and looked. And he saw that there was a tremendously huge animal drinking from the cow, and that it had wrapped itself around her body. He got very frightened. But then he had the idea, "Śrī Nāth told me he was coming. Might he have come in this form?" So he looked over toward the spread-out hivar tree. Lovely fresh leaves had sprouted on it. Then he felt certain that it must be the god. So he went up close, stood there with folded hands, and said, "O God! O Nāth! Even if you take on an even more terrifying form, I won't be afraid."

Then the god took a form the size of a little finger and came up to Kamaḷājī. Kamaḷājī took the blanket from his shoulders and spread it on the ground for the god to sit on, and the god went there and sat down. Then Kamaḷājī brought Nirā water in the palms of his hands and gave the god a bath, and he milked the barren cow and gave the god the milk to drink. He also showed the god *naivedya* of the *bhākrī* he had with him, and broke his two-day fast.

Later he made a pouch of his blanket and began to keep the god in it. Every day for twelve years he fed him the milk of that cow. Seeing that, someone went and told Kamaḷājī's father, "Your son is keeping a snake, and he has also learned some magic." Hearing this, his father got very worried because his only son had come to such a pass. What would happen if the snake bit him? So he called for Kamaḷājī and asked him, "Have you been keeping a snake?"

Kamaḷājī was very worried. If he said he was keeping a snake, it would be like slandering the god, and if he said he was not, he would be guilty of lying. So without giving his father an answer, he came directly to the *vāḍā* and told the god what had happened. The god said to Kamaḷājī, "Put me into a termite mound somewhere nearby, and come there every day. I'll come out and give you *darśan*." At that time, his *vāḍā* was on Śrī Tukāī's plateau (*māḷ*), east of where the temple is now. Nowadays the god's footprints (*pāḍukās*) are there.

Anyway, later on he found a termite mound, took the god there, and put him into it. And Kamaḷājī bathed as always in the Pūrṇagaṅgā, worshiped the god, fed him the milk of the barren cow, showed him *naivedya* of his *bhākrī,* and then ate it. And when many days had passed this way, his father once again asked Kamaḷājī, "I hear you're keeping a snake."

He answered, "I don't have a snake. Who told you that? Look, here is my blanket." And he shook it out and showed it to his father.

Later his father and mother both died. Kamaḷājī had five sons, who also used to take their cattle and wander around grazing them. At that time, Kamaḷājī was about forty years old. The land where he had put the god into the termite mound was not cultivated, but next to it was land that belonged to Rāūt Māḷī. Rāūt Māḷī took that land next to his, yoked twelve bullocks to a plow, and began to plow the land. Kamaḷājī came and said to him, "You may plow all the rest of the land; just don't plow up that termite mound." But Rāūt Māḷī didn't listen to this, and he plowed all the land. As he plowed up the termite mound, the god became very angry, and the twelve bullocks and the plowmen all died. Only Rāūt Māḷī's nephew, who was surnamed Jamdaḍe, was left alive. He had been leading the plow team. When he saw what had happened, he began to wail loudly. A large crowd gathered there, but no one could figure out what had happened. Then Jamdaḍe said, "There's an old Dhangar who always comes here. He was saying, 'You may plow all the rest of the land, just don't plow up that termite mound.' But we didn't listen, and we plowed up the termite mound. Might that be why this has happened?"

Then some people went to Kamaḷājī and told him what had happened, and they brought him there. And [the god] entered Kamaḷājī's body[14] and began to say, "I am not a ghost. Nothing like that. I am Kāḷbhairav of Sonārī, and I have become incarnated here for the sake of this Kamaḷājī. Even though he told you not to plow up the termite mound, you didn't listen. That caused me a lot of trouble, and that's why this has happened." Hearing this, they all threw themselves on his mercy, and began to pray with folded hands, "O God, if you are truly real (*tujhe jar satva kharem̥ asel tar*), these bullocks and plowmen will all be revived." Then Kamaḷājī took ashes, and as soon as he had sprinkled them on their bodies, they all came to life. Then they were fully convinced.

Later they removed the plow, and as they dug there they found a shapeless self-formed stone (*svayam̥bhū tāndaḷā*).[15] The original place is beneath the god, where the mask (*mukhavaṭā*) is set.[16]

After all this had happened, the god would not leave Kamaḷājī's body, so he went and told his sons all that had happened. Then his sons came there too, and they began to pray, "O Nāth, tell us what you want, and we will do it."

So the god said, "If you want to do what I say, then install me; otherwise don't take me out."

Then the five of them said, "O god, we'll do whatever you command."

Hearing this, the god said, "Cut off the heads of five human beings, and give me a bath in their blood."

They thought, "There are five of us, so if we cut off our heads and bathe the god, that will do it. After we are gone, our father will take care of our children." So they said to the god, "We'll give you our heads, God."

---

14. "The god enters the body." See 7.6, above.

15. A self-originated stone shaped like a grain of rice, which is used as a shapeless *mūrti*. See chap. 9, n. 41.

16. The heads of Mhaskobā and Jogeśvarī stand out from the stone, which, as a *mūrti*, is smeared with red lead (*śendūr*). At the foot of the stone is a silver mask. This covers the original *mūrti*, which is a rounded stone.

But the god said, "I don't want *your* heads, because then who would take care of your wives and children? Instead, bring five unmarried boys and give me *their* heads."

They replied, "The five of us have five sons. We'll give them to you, God."

Then the god said, "You go and ask your wives, and see if they say, 'We are pleased to give our sons.'" So they told their wives everything that had happened, and they too agreed with great pleasure to give their sons. And they said, "If Māmaṃjī[17] has revived humans and animals just by his power (*satva*), through his mercy we will have more sons."

When their wives had said this, the brothers brought their five sons to the god and said, "They are pleased to give them." Then as they were about to cut off their sons' heads, the eldest brother's son ran away. They were setting off to catch him, but the god said, "Just cut off the heads of the sons that are left. What's gone is gone." So they cut off those boys' heads and bathed the god in their blood. And when he saw that they had such devotion, the god was pleased and said, "I am pleased to see your devotion. Ask for anything you want." So the god brought the four boys back to life. The boys said, "Promise us that you will not abandon us as long as the moon and the sun exist."

The god said, "Until the moon and the sun rise in the west, and the Bhimā and the Nirā flow toward the west,[18] I will not abandon you."

Anyway, they established the god this way, with great devotion. And as the god was setting out, the eldest son put his hand to his mouth and blew it like a horn (*śiṅg*); so he got the name Śiṅgāḍe. The second son brought taravaḍ leaves and worshiped the god [with them], so he was given the name Taraḍe. The third son brought a felt blanket (*burṇus*) and tied ropes to it to make an awning for the god, so he was given the name Buraṅgule. The fourth son put his fingers to his lips (*oṭh*) and whistled, so he was given the name Vhoṭkar. And the fifth son simply slapped his buttocks (*ḍhuṅgaṇ*) with his hands, so he got the name Ḍhavāṇ. These are the surnames that their descendants have today.

Anyway, this happened on Sunday, the full-moon day [the 15th] of the bright half of the month of Māgh. The god said to Kamaḷājī, "Hold a festival for me starting on this day for ten days each year. Hold the festival from the bright fifteenth of Māgh until the dark tenth. During those ten days, I will do whatever you tell me to do." Nowadays this is called *bhākaṇūk*.[19]

---

17. Māmaṃjī = Māmājī (maternal uncle). A term of respect for one's father-in-law.

18. Both of these rivers flow from west to east.

19. *Bhākaṇūk* is derived from *bhākṇeṃ*, "to foretell." The usual expression for the prophecy of a Dhangar *devṛṣī* is *vhaīk* or *huīk*. See Prabhākara Māṃḍe, *Lokasāhityāce Aṃtaḥpravāha* (Puṇeṃ, 1975), pp. 188ff.

Now, the land belonged to Rāūt, and his nephew Jamdaḍe had been leading the plow team, so the god gave his promise (*bhāk*) to seven people: to Kamaḷājī's five sons—Śiṅgāḍe, Taraḍe, Buraṅgule, Vhoṭkar, and Ḍhavāṇ—and to Rāūt and Jamdaḍe. And because it was Rāūt's field that the god came out of, Rāūt became a member of the bridegroom's party [at the god's wedding], and he was given the privilege (*mān*) of arranging the god's marriage on the full-moon day, and walking in front of everyone else during the procession. Later Rāūt could no longer do this, so he gave his rights to the Baḍades from the village of Koḍīt; and Jamdaḍe gave [his] to barbers (Nhāvīs) from Wāī.

Anyway, the villagers began to gossip; they learned that the Dhangars had cut off their sons' heads and given them to the god. Then some people went and told the government that this had happened. Then some government officials came there, but it looked to them as if it was goats that had been killed. But to the villagers it looked like boys. Then the officials began to say, "It's goats, but these villagers are making false accusations for no reason." They said this, and they went away. Later, realizing Kamaḷājī's devotion, the people took him for an incarnation of God (Īśvara), and began to call him just Kamaḷājī.

The original word [for someone like Kamaḷājī] in Sanskrit is *siddha;* its vernacular form is *sīd.* Anyway, Kamaḷājī's place is now to the north of the god, near the drum room. And that is where the four boys were killed. This place is called Copāḷā. On the full-moon day of the bright half of the month of Pauṣ, a day that is called Cuḍī Paurṇimā, on the full-moon day of the bright half of Māgh, and on the third and seventh days (*māḷ*) of the Navrātra festival, the god's procession goes to that place. Then the Gurav worships [the boys] and does *āratī* to them with incense, and after that the god's procession returns. This ritual is still performed today.

And the god's original place is at Borban (Ghoḍe Uḍān) on the bank of the Nirā. Here too a small temple has now been built. And in the rocky ground at that place, there are the footprints of elephants, horses, and human beings. And at the place where the god stuck his trident, there is nowadays a stream from which water flows like a trident. Those who want to see for themselves should come and look at this place, and they will be fully convinced. In short, the god became incarnated here for the sake of his devotee. Where there is faith, God is not far away. Because "God is attained through faith." There is a passage in the *Gītā* that says, "I love people in the same way that they surrender themselves to me"[20]—God fulfills a person's wishes in accordance with the way the person loves God. Look: for Pralhād, God took on an

---

20. *Bhagvad Gītā,* 4.11.

incarnation in a pillar.[21] For Dāmājīpant he took the form of an Untouchable and delivered a sack [full of money].[22] He carried off [dead] cattle for Cokhyāmeḷā,[23] and picked vegetables for Sāvtā Mālī.[24] In short, God has taken many incarnations in many places, and has protected his devotees' integrity (*satva*). In the same way, Śrī Kāḷbhairav became incarnated here for the sake of Kamaḷasīd. This is just a small part of all there is to tell about Bhairav.

I used the term Borban (Ghoḍe Uḍān), and I said that the god incarnated himself there. Borban is a place on the bank of the Nirā River about one *kos* [two miles] southeast of Vīr. It is called Laptaḷ's Meadow. The custom is to take the palanquin there on Somvatī and other festival days. Because there was pasture land there, cowherd boys used to take their cattle there to graze. The boys used to see Śrī Nāth as a rider mounted on a black horse, sometimes in the garb of a fakir, sometimes wearing white clothes, so they would get frightened. And even though it would still be daylight, they would come back home with their cattle. Then Śrī Nāth entered Kamaḷasiddha's body and said, "The cowherd boys are frightened of me. Tell them not to be afraid. I am wandering around here night and day in order to protect them, so they should graze their cattle without fear. I won't let them be harmed." Hearing that, the cowherd boys and the adults were fully convinced.

After that some cowherd boys collected stones and built a small temple for Śrī Nāth on the bank of the Nirā, and they installed Śrī Nāth there. They began to go there regularly; they would let their cattle start grazing, and then they would take a bath and worship Śrī Nāth with devotion. They would serve Śrī Nāth until evening; then they would take their cattle and return to the village. Seeing these boys' devotion, other people started going there too. Even a Gurav started going there to do the worship service (*pūjā*).

Around that time, there was a Dhangar in Vīr named Śaṅkarājī Ghuṇe whose regular routine was to take a bath in Vīrcaṇḍ *tīrtha,* take *darśan* of all the gods, and then eat his meal. He too started going to that place. He had two sons, Māljī and Viṭhojī, whom I will tell about later.

---

21. Viṣṇu took the form of Narasiṃha in a pillar in order to prove to Pralhād's father that God is everywhere.

22. Dāmājī Pant was the tax officer of the king of Bīdar in Maṅgaḷveḍhā. During a famine he distributed grain to the hungry populace—or rather, he let them plunder the grain reserves. The king demanded Dāmājī's death. Viṭhobā went to the king in the form of a Mahār Untouchable, bringing sacks of gold as the proceeds of the sale of the grain, if it had been sold.

23. Cokhā Meḷā belonged to the Untouchable caste of the Mahārs, whose traditional duties include removing dead cattle from the village.

24. Sāvtā Māḷī, from the gardener caste, was absorbed in worshiping Viṭhobā. When he reawakened from his worship, he found that Viṭhobā had protected his vegetables from damage, and had already picked them.

Śrīmant Chatrapati Śāhū Mahārāj[25] of Sātārā was an avid hunter. He used to love hunting for tigers. He killed numerous tigers, and he also captured some live tigers and put them into his game preserve (*śikhārkhānā*). And he always had scouts out watching [for game]. One of the scouts came and reported to the king, "there is a huge tiger in Laptaḷ's Meadow on the bank of the Nirā, but nobody can find him." Hearing this, the king told them to get ready for the hunt. And they came there and began searching for the tiger. The undergrowth was dense, and there were thick bushes and huge trees that reached to the sky, so they could find no trace of the tiger anywhere.

The king got tired, and he came to the bank of the Nirā to rest. With him were cavalrymen armed with swords. As the king was sitting there this way, he saw that some cowherd boys had gathered there and were devoutly worshiping a god. The king was very surprised, and he began asking the boys, "Whose boys are you, and what is the name of your god?" When he asked this, the boys answered, fearfully, "Our village is one *kos* from here, and we are the children of Māḷīs. Our god is named Maskobā. We come here to graze our cattle. Our god also responds to vows (*navasās pāvto*)."

When he heard this, the king said, "If your god is truly real (*tumcyā devāce satva kharem̩ asel tar*), he will deliver a live tiger to me; and if this happens, I will understand your god to be truly real and I will make your god my family god (*kulasvāmī*) and I will also provide a regular stipend for your god."

Then the cowherd boys and the Gurav prayed to Śrī Nāth, "O God, if you want to defend your reality (*satva*), do as the king says." Just as they were saying this prayer, a horseman came and reported to the king, "There's a tiger in such-and-such a trap, and it is huge and terrifying."

Then the king ordered, "I will give a grant of a thousand rupees to anyone who brings the tiger here alive; and if he is eaten by the tiger, I will provide for his children and his descendants forever." Although the king had said this, no one had the courage to try. Then, with great daring, one man prepared to go. And shouting, "*cāṅgbhale!*" he entered the trap where the tiger was. And that man got hold of the tiger's ear the way one would grab the ear of a household dog, and, dragging it along, he brought it and put it in front of the king. Seeing this, the horsemen were frightened out of their wits, although they were mounted on their horses. It is upsetting enough even to have to kill a scorpion, but when the king saw the man bring the tiger so easily just by holding its ear, he was astonished, and he was fully convinced of the reality of the god. Afterward they put the tiger into a cage and locked it in with padlocks, and so on. But miraculously, the tiger didn't move at all until it had been put into the cage; as soon as it was put into the cage, it gave a huge and

25. Died in 1849.

terrifying roar and stood up, stretching the way a man does when he gets up from sleep. But because it was locked up, there was nothing it could do. Seeing this, the cowherd boys and the Gurav were delighted, and they began to dance.

Anyway, as promised, the king gave the man a thousand rupees, and he also gave him a shawl, a turban, and other clothes, and he granted him a monthly stipend of two hundred rupees. And the king went into Śrī Nāth's temple and prostrated himself, and he made the god his family god. Śrīmant Chatrapati Śāhū Mahārāj built the inner part [the sanctuary] of the temple that is now in the village and the stone lamp pillar (*dipmāḷ*) near the drum room. And he began to send the god clothes and a sword, and so on, every year; but in recent times that has stopped.

Another miracle occurred on a later occasion. The Mughals came and made a sudden attack. Seeing this, the king did the sixteen rites of worship for Śrī Nāth—pouring water over his hands, washing his feet, and so on[26]—and folded his hands and prayed, "O Nāth, now it is up to you to protect us. There is no one but you." As soon as he had said this, one of the flowers that had been offered to Śrī Nāth fell down from his right side. Understanding this as a favorable answer (*prasād*), the king took the flower and put it in his turban. And without consulting anyone else, he commanded that preparations be made for battle. The miracle was that even though the Mughal army was large and they had a lot of ammunition and other battle supplies, nothing they tried was of any use. The soldiers would fill their muskets, but not even a sound would come from them. So they were overpowered, and they surrendered to King Śāhū, and King Śāhū gained victory.

Many such miracles happened; if I begin to describe them all in detail, this book will come to be very long.

Later a very big pilgrimage festival began to be held every year from the full-moon day of the bright half of the month of Māgh to the tenth day [of the dark half of the month]. And Śrī Nāth's power (*satva*) became famous in village after village. Because the Jamdaḍes of Wāī were also devout, they used to come to the festival every year with poles (*kāṭhīs*) and drums, and the barbers (Nhāvīs) used to come with them to play the drums.

Later the Jamdaḍes stopped coming, but the barbers did not stop coming. Then once, for some reason, the Jamdaḍes came to the god for help, and they began to ask the barbers for the drums, poles, and so on, that they had kept. But the barbers wouldn't give them to them. Then the Jamdaḍes and the

26. *Śoḍaṣopacāreṃ* [*ṣoḍaśopacāreṃ*] *arghyapādyādi*. These are the sixteen acts and objects prescribed for the worship of a god. See the various enumerations in the *Nirṇayasindhu* of Kamalākara Bhaṭṭa (Chowkhambā Sanskrit Series, vol. 52), pp. 1197f.

barbers had a dispute about their hereditary ritual privileges (*mān*). The Jamdaḍes also lived in Wāī. The maternal uncle of the man who had been at the head of the plow team was Rāūt, and the field also belonged to Rāūt, so the Jamdaḍes said, "The god appeared in our field, so we have a greater right (*mān*)," and the Nhāvīs said, "We will not give up our regular practice." To settle this dispute, both sides went to King Śāhū in Sātārā. But this put the king in a difficult position. He thought, "These people's family god is mine too. If I decide they should be treated equally and that makes the god angry, there's no telling what he might do." So the king said to them, "Go to Vīr and get this settled by Śrī Nāth. I can't settle it."

So both sides went to Vīr and asked Śrī Nāth, learning his answer through divination (*prasād lāvaṇeṃ*). The god said, "The privilege goes to the one in whose procession the lame temple servant will dance."[27]

At about that time, in a village near Sāsvaḍ named Koḍīt, there was a great devotee of the Lord (Bhagvat) named Tulājī Baḍade. His story is as follows: The Baḍades were Marāṭhās by caste, and their surname was Bhosle. They used to live in a village near Sātārā called Bhuīñj, but they moved to Koḍīt because they could get an income (*vṛtti*) there, and they just stayed on. Among the Bhosles there was a family with six brothers, Tuḷājī and five others. Their family was well-off, and Tuḷājī was inclined toward God (Īśvara) from the time he was a little boy. He didn't play many kinds of games the way other children do when they're little. Instead he would get together five or ten boys, collect some stones, make one of the stones into a god, bring the fruits of some tree and offer them to it, and loudly shout "*cāṅgbhale!*"[28] Many a time when he was doing this, he wouldn't even come home for two days in a row, and then his family would have to go looking for him and get him. Because he acted this way, they used to call him "Crazy Tuḷyā," but he was firmly devoted to the feet of Śrī Nāth, and he was always thinking of the name of god, and saying, "*cāṅgbhale, cāṅgbhale!*"

When Tuḷājī got a little bigger, his brothers got him married. They thought that after he was married he would take an interest in worldly life, but because Tuḷājī was extremely devout, there was no change at all in his behavior. Then

---

27. That is, a certain devoted temple servant will dance in the procession of one of the devotees, and that devotee will be given the privilege.

28. *Cāṅgbhale* is a cry commonly used by devotees to celebrate Mhaskobā, Khaṇḍobā, and other gods belonging to the Bhairav cycle. Molesworth, *Dictionary,* says: "(*candrabhāla*—Moon-on-forehead. A name of Shiva). The word used in shouting by the worshipers of *Bhairava,* by a body of pilgrims, by the devotees of the *jyotiliṅga,* by a party of hammals, laborers &c., by a number of men making 'a long pull, a strong pull, and a pull all together.' " The word could also be derived from a combination of *cāṅgalā* (Sanskrit, *caṅg*) and *bhala,* both meaning "good" or "fine."

Tuḷājī began to go along with some devout people who came to Vīr every year for Śrī Nāth's festival (*jatrā*). Later Tuḷājī started waiting every night until it was quiet on all sides, then setting out from Koḍīt, coming to Vīr, silently worshiping Śrī Nāth with his whole heart, and then going back to Koḍīt at dawn. He followed this routine for a long time, without anyone else knowing about it.

Tuḷājī had no children. Seeing this, his brothers began to feel very bad, and they began to say, "Our families have grown, but what can be done about Tuḷyā?" When they were thinking this way, a man came and said to Tuḷājī's brothers, "Your Tuḷyā goes somewhere every night. We always notice him."

So they asked Tuḷājī, "Where do you go at night?"

Tuḷājī replied, "I go to god Śrī Nāth Mhaskobā's place at Vīr to have *darśan* of him."

Then they explained to him in many ways that he ought not to go, and they said, "Your worldly life, household, wife, fields, and work are yours alone. You should pay attention to them. What good has ever come of people who have become saints? So you should give up this addiction and pay attention to your worldly life." But no matter what they did, he would not give it up. Then one day his brothers put Tuḷājī into a room and tied him up. They set his wife down near him, locked the door from the outside, and went away.

When this had happened, Tuḷājī was in a very difficult position; silently he called to Śrī Nāth for help: "O all-powerful Lord, friend of the lowly, there is no one but you to get me out of this fix. Look at how they've tied me up. This is interrupting my service of you. What I want is to have your *darśan*."

His wife was a very good woman, devoted to her husband, fully engrossed in serving her husband. She made great efforts to untie the ropes, but to no avail. Then a miracle happened: as soon as Tuḷājī had called to the god for help, the ropes and the padlock broke and fell away of their own accord, and Tuḷājī was free to go. Then he went to Vīr, prostrated himself at Śrī Nāth's feet, folded his hands, and prayed, "O Lord, god of gods, your game (*līlā*) is unfathomable. See, those evil ones tied me up so that I couldn't escape. But now, O God, I want you to come to Koḍīt, and it's up to you to grant my wish."

When he said this, the god replied, "Don't you worry. I have seen your devotion, and I will come to Koḍīt in person." That made Tuḷājī inexpressibly happy. But again the god said, "I will come with you, but you must not look back until we get to the village." Tuḷājī agreed to this, and the god mounted his horse and set out. They went along, and entered the boundary of Koḍīt. At that point, Tuḷājī happened to look back, and as soon as he looked back, the god disappeared. Seeing that, Tuḷājī said, "O God, you've been this kind of fraud from the beginning. You told me you would come, but you haven't come. So now what's the point of my keeping my body?'' Saying this, he gave a loud wail, and just as he was about to give up his life, Śrī Nāth grabbed his hand and said, ''You didn't do as I said, so now I am not going to enter the village.''

Meanwhile, at dawn Tuḷājī's brothers came to see if Tuḷājī had gone or was still there. And when they looked they saw that the padlock was just as they had left it. Then they took off the padlock and looked and saw that Tuḷājī wasn't there. But his wife was sitting there, and they asked her, ''Where did Tuḷājī go?''

She replied, ''He was here until twelve o'clock at night. I don't know what happened later, after I fell asleep. For twelve years it's been like this, and my husband has had nothing to do with me.'' Then they saw that the ropes they had tied him up with had fallen right there with exactly the same knots tied the same way that they had tied them. And when they saw this, they were very amazed. Then they set out to find him, and when they came to the edge of the village they saw Tuḷājī sitting there doing worship. Then they were all convinced of his devotion. And they asked Tuḷājī and he told them everything that had happened.

Then Śrī Nāth was pleased, and he said to Tuḷājī, ''I am pleased. Ask for whatever you want.''

Tuḷājī replied, ''O God, I have no children. I want to have children, and I want to be given some honorary right (*mān*) at your court.'' This is what he asked for. Later Tuḷājī had children, and everyone began to practice devotion to him. Those who had called him ''Crazy Tuḷājī'' started calling him ''Tuḷājī Bovā.''[29] And a small temple was built at the place near the edge of the village where Śrī Nāth had become incarnated, and people began to practice devotion to him, and many began to come to the festival every year.

I was telling about the dispute between the Jamdaḍes and the barbers. The god had settled it by saying that the privilege (*mān*) would go to the one in whose procession the lame servant from the temple would dance, swinging his arms and legs. Accordingly, when all the palanquins, and so on, came to the pilgrimage festival, Tuḷājī's palanquin came too. Then the servant first went into the Jamdaḍes' procession, but it was no use. Then the same thing happened in the barbers' procession. Then he went into Tuḷājī's procession, and people began to say, ''What could happen in that crazy Tuḷājī's procession?'' With that, Tuḷājī remembered what he had earlier asked of the god, and he prayed to the god and said, ''O God, now it's up to you to protect your truth (*satva*).'' When [Tuḷājī] had said this, the servant shouted ''*cāṅg-bhale!*'' and began to dance, swinging his arms and legs freely.

---

29. Bu(~o)vā is a common honorific for a saint.

When Chatrapati Śāhū Mahārāj learned of this in Sātārā, he summoned Tuḷājī to Sātārā. Then the king asked him, "Who are you and what village are you from?"

He replied, "My surname is Bhosle. We originally came from Bhuīñj, but we live in the village of Koḍīt near Sāsvaḍ because we could get a living (*vṛtti*) there. Later we got the surname Baḍade."

Hearing this, the king said, "You belong to our lineage. We have the same family god as you. So you have the greatest privilege (*mān*) of all: your palanquin is to go before all the others. And to you are given the peacock feather brush (*morcel*) and the ocher flag. You are the one who is to light the lamp pillar near the drum room during the pilgrimage festival; no one else has the right to do so." He gave a written order to this effect. And to the barbers he said, "You are to carry your palanquin behind the Baḍades' palanquin." And to this day this is still the custom. In this way Tuḷājī's integrity (*sattva*) became famous among all the people, and the dispute was settled as well. Nowadays Tuḷājī's temple is near the edge of Koḍīt.

At about the same time, there was a Dhangar named Śaṅkarājī Ghuṇe. I mentioned him earlier. He too was a great devotee of God (*bhagvatbhakta*). His occupation was to get wool and weave blankets, and this is how he supported himself. He had two sons, one named Māljī and the other named Viṭhojī. Māljī was a great devotee of God (*bhagvatbhakta*), just like his father. He too would not eat without having first bathed in Vīrcaṇḍ *tīrtha* and worshiped Śrī Nāth. He had followed this practice continuously for twelve years. The workings of karma are certainly strange. For it is said, "God cannot understand the behavior of a woman or the fortune of a man; so how could a human being understand them?" There's no rule about when a man's luck will be on the rise—or perhaps Śrī Nāth just had mercy.

What happened is that one day when Māljī, following his regular routine, had finished his work, meditated on Śrī Nāth, repeated the divine name, and then fallen asleep, Śrī Nāth came and put a philosophers' stone into his hand, then disappeared. Later, when Māljī woke up, he saw a stone in his hand. He looked at it and said to himself, "Somebody must have brought a stone and put it into my hand." Thinking this, he tossed the stone into the weaving pit and went back to sleep, thinking of Śrī Nāth. In the early morning his wife got up and went to sweep around the loom. And as she was sweeping she happened to glance at the weaving pit, and she noticed that the iron ball hanging there as a weight looked different: it had turned yellow. So she went up a bit closer and looked, and she saw that the weight was made of gold. She was astonished, and she went immediately and began to ask her husband, "When did you put up this gold weight?" (Nowadays the weight is said to be worth 125,000 gold one-anna coins.)

When she said this, Māljī was very surprised. "What nonsense is this you're saying?" he said, and began to ask his wife, "Why would poor people like us have gold? And who would make a weight out of gold?"

Then his wife said, "Come on, I'll show you. You see whether or not it's gold," and she took Māljī and brought him up to the loom and showed him. As soon as Māljī saw it, he too was convinced, and he began to wonder to himself, "What miracle is this?" And then he remembered the stone of the night before, and said, "Might that stone have some special power (*guṇ*)?" And he began looking for the stone in the pit. He found the stone in the pit right away. Then he took the stone and touched it to the iron bracelet on his wrist, and that too turned immediately from iron into gold. Then anything he touched it to began turning into gold. So he was very happy and began showing it to anyone and everyone. Then he went to a goldsmith and showed it to him.

The practice of goldsmiths is that when anyone brings a goldsmith something to show him, he first places it on the anvil. Accordingly, the goldsmith placed that stone (the philosophers' stone) on the anvil, and immediately the anvil too turned to gold. Seeing this, the goldsmith thought, "There's some magic in this stone. I had better swallow it." With this thought in mind, he popped the stone into his mouth. When Māljī saw this, he grabbed the goldsmith's throat and thumped him on the neck, and the stone came out. Māljī took it and ran away.

He never showed the stone to anyone again, and because of this he became very prosperous. He built Śrī Nāth's temple, and he built the southern gate of the temple. That cost him 100,000 rupees. And outside the temple, to the east, he built a shrine and a lamp pillar. Then he built a big house with lots of carved wood in it, west of the village, on the bank of the Pūrṇagaṅgā. That cost a good deal too, and besides he built many temples in various places. Thus Māljī became very successful, and he also wrote down a pledge of everything else that he would do in the future.

Eventually he became proud, thinking, "There's no one as wealthy as I am. My house is seven stories high, with lots of carving in it. I will sit in the hall of my palace and watch Śrī Nāth's procession."

When he had become proud this way, the god said, "O you who have become so arrogant, I will throw the stones of your *vāḍā* into the Nirā"—because the god can never tolerate pride. Later that is exactly what happened to Māljī. For fortune (Lakṣmī) is fickle, and doesn't remain forever in any one place. So no one should be proud.

Anyway, once it happened that Śrī Chatrapati Śāhū Mahārāj needed some money. At that time there was a certain Deśastha Brahman in Sātārā named Rāvjī Anagaḷ. He was very rich. The king sent him a message: "I need money, so you must send ten thousand rupees' worth of minted silver two-anna and four-anna coins.'' Rāvjī sent back a message to the king: ''I have numerous minted coins; if the king will inform me which mint he needs, I will send them.'' Hearing this, the king was astonished. ''To think there's a man this rich in my kingdom!'' he said.

At that, someone else said to the king, ''At Vīr, where your family god Śrī Nāth (Maskobā) is, there is a certain Dhangar named Māljī who has no end of wealth.''

When he heard this, the king sent his horsemen to Vīr to get Māljī. They came to Vīr and said to Māljī, ''Śrī Chatrapati Śāhū Mahārāj has summoned you to Sātārā.'' Formerly Mālji had worn a loincloth and a blanket, but since he had been favored by fortune, he wore fine clothes, with a double shawl over his shoulders. In accordance with the king's orders, he went to Sātārā; and he saluted the king and stood there with folded hands. The king asked, ''How wealthy are you?'' and Māljī answered, ''What wealth can we Dhangars have? We earn a living by weaving blankets. Who has counted how much wealth we have? But if your Majesty would like, my brother and I will yoke a harrow and build a road from Sātārā to Vīr, made of diamonds, rubies, and other jewels.''

Hearing this, the king was astonished. ''How did you get so much wealth?'' he said.

Māljī replied, ''I got so much wealth by the grace of Śrī Maskobā.''

The king was pleased, and he gave Māljī a *cāhūr* [about fifty acres] of land as a grant in perpetuity. He gave him the rights of a head district officer (*sardeśmukh*), along with gifts of clothes and so on, and then gave him leave to go. Then Māljī returned to Vīr.

Even though he had received so much wealth, all of his wealth was destroyed because he became proud. If you see his fallen-down building and all that carved woodwork now, you'll be very amazed. Anyway, there's probably no building that beautiful anywhere. Nowadays there are one or two frames from that building left. Their price today would be five hundred rupees each, and when the building was built the frames alone cost a thousand rupees each, and there is lots of beautiful carving on them. The whole building is in ruins.

Māljī built beautiful houses in the village of Śeṃburḍe in the Hoḷkars' kingdom; at Pānevalī, Vaḍgāv, and other places on the banks of the Bhimā in Poona District; and elsewhere as well. He also built a very nice temple of Śrī Viṭhobā on the bank of the Bhimā at Vaḍgāv, and at Pānvale [Pānevalī?] he installed a huge slab, completely set in mortar. It is used just for sorting rupees, gold coins, and so on, and that's the only reason it was put there.

Māljī was buried in the shrine he had built just for himself to the east of Śrī Maskobā's temple. He had said, "Bury me in that shrine."

Presently, in the seventh generation of his descendants, there are two men named Pāṇḍojī and Bāḷkujī. They live in Indore, I understand. Among the grants given by Śrīmant Chatrapati Śāhū Mahārāj, only the *sardeśmukh* rights have diminished, but they still have the *cāhūr* of land granted in perpetuity, and they still have the written order granting it, signed by the king.

Anyway, since becoming incarnated here for the sake of his devotees, Śrī Nāth has increased his devotees' glory. And this is only a small part of what there is to be said about Śrī Nāth. Year after year his festival grew, and there came to be a bazaar as well. Later, when there came to be more and more devotees and they had more and more experiences, some of them gave the god chowries, some gave him ornamented umbrellas, some gave him peacock-feather brushes: they began this way one to give him one thing, and one another. In this way, the festival became magnificent and thronged. And so the festival, which used to last for five days, began to go on for ten days.

Part 3. Description of the Festival

Jatrā [pilgrimage festival] means *yātrā* [Sanskrit for "pilgrimage"]. The reason it is called a *jatrā* is that on the day of a *jatrā* hundreds of [lambs and] kids (*ajāputra*) are killed, so it is called a *jatrā*. The facts about it are that on the twelfth day of the bright half of the month of Māgh, the village officials—the *pāṭīl,* the *kuḷkarṇī*—and other residents of the village gather in the temple and write invitations to Śrī Maskobā's wedding to those who have honorary rights (*mān*) at the wedding. The Ghaḍśī Guravs have the job of delivering the wedding invitations. Accordingly, they take them to Wāī, Koḍīt, and other places. On the fourteenth day the turmeric that is to be applied to the god is brought with great pomp and splendor, to the accompaniment of a band. It comes from the Rāūts, the chief holders of honorary rights. They also send a turban for Śrī Nāth and a blouse and sari for Ādimāyā Śrī Jogeśvarī. These Rāūts live about a mile and a half from Vīr in a hamlet (*vāḍī*) called Rāūtvāḍī. They are Māḷīs by caste. Originally they lived in Vīr, but just as other farmers generally build houses and live wherever their fields are, so the Rāūts too went to live there. Anyway, in the evening, when the turmeric has arrived, everyone gathers together in the temple. Then the Rāūts smear turmeric powder on the god.[30]

30. Before a wedding the hands and feet of the bride and bridegroom are smeared with turmeric powder.

On the full-moon day, the Māḷīs of the village and others get together and paint the temple, and so on. On that day in every household of the village there is a traditional rite called *gaḍagner* [parties in honor of the bride or groom before a wedding]. Except for the Brahmans, people celebrate the festival at night because of their work in the fields. The five kinds[31] of Dhangars named earlier—Śiṅgāḍe, Taraḍe, Buraṅgule, Vhaṭkar, and Ḍhavāṇ—arrive. They wander with their cattle and sheep as far as Khāndeś, Beḷgaum, Dhārvāḍ, and so on, but they have to come to Vīr on the full-moon day.

The Baḍades come and stay in Tuḷājī Baḍade's temple at the edge of Koḍīt on the evening of the fourteenth day of the bright half of Māgh. On the full-moon day of Māgh, they do their traditional rituals, then set out at about noon and arrive at Rāūtvāḍī by evening. Along the way, people from surrounding villages join the palanquin. When they get close to Rāūtvāḍī, the Rāūts go up to the palanquin and take it into the hamlet. Then their wives wave trays of lighted lamps before Śrī Nāth. They eat gruel,[32] boiled grain,[33] sugarcane, and so forth; they take pān leaves, betel nut, and so on; and then the Rāūts lift the palanquin to their shoulders and carry it to the gates of Vīr. This is the tradition to this day.

The palanquin arrives at Vīr in the evening, and from Poona there comes the palanquin of Sakhārāmbovā Pāṇḍhare Māḷī, and from Wāī comes the palanquin of the barber Pāṭaṇe, and another palanquin comes from Supe. And with great enthusiasm thousands of people gather together, bringing drums, poles, one or two more palanquins, and so forth. Then, accompanied by all the residents of the town, the Guravs take incense and go up to the palanquins; and with great ceremony, to the accompaniment of bands, they bring them in.

This is a day of great happiness. In every house a huge crowd of guests gathers. In some places drums are beating, in some places horns are blowing—the crowd becomes a single mass. There's not even room to walk in the streets. Wherever you look there's an enormous crowd of people, and from time to time you hear the cry, "*cāṅgbhale! cāṅgbhale!*" On this day all the residents of the town sweep in front of their doorways, spread cow-dung wash, and draw *rāṅgoḷī* designs with powders of many colors. The women and children in every household get dressed up and make a huge racket getting ready to go to the temple. On the road, clusters of married women can be seen

31. The five branches of Kamaḷa Siddha's descendants belong to the same *jātī* ("caste"), but they should not intermarry, because they have the same *devak* ("totem").

32. *Ambīl.* A curry made of buttermilk (*tāk*) and the flour of five kinds of grain—*nācṇā (Eleusine corocana), jovārī (Holcus sorghum),* rice, wheat, and *uḍīd (Phasaeolus raditatus)*—mixed with garlic, coriander, hot chili pepper, and salt.

33. *Ghugaryā.* A mash made of unground cereal grain.

carrying yellow turmeric powder and bright red *kuṅkum* powder and metal trays with small oil lamps to wave. Children run here and there. In short, this is just a small part of what there is to describe.

Anyway, even though Vīr is a small village, it becomes a veritable city, and there is a crowd like one at a wedding. Māḷīs can be seen hurrying toward the temple with garlands of flowers. When all the palanquins have gathered, the village's palanquin comes too, with great ceremony: there are chowries, decorated parasols, umbrellas, peacock-feather brushes, flags, poles, cloth tubes, and so on; large drums, pipes, horns, wind instruments, trumpets, gongs, small drums, and other musical instruments are playing. Because it is the night of the full moon, there is bright white moonlight, and besides there is the light of torches and lamps, and fireworks are going off. The Gurav walks behind carrying a set of five lamps to wave before the god. To the right of the Gurav walks a Māḷī named Vāgh, and to the left a Māḷī named Ghasāḍe; they hold hands. Behind them goes a member of the Tāndaḷe family of Māḷīs, to massage [the god's] feet. A barber walks along with the palanquin, carrying a hookah.

With such splendor, Śrī Nāth's retinue and all the palanquins go to a place on the bank of the Pūrṇagaṅgā east of the village, where there is an ancient tree. The *siddhas* (*sīds*) I mentioned earlier come there, and the five of them are garlanded according to their honorary rights, and the poles carried by the barbers are garlanded, and along with them the retinue goes to the temple.

Then the village astrologer (*grāmjośī*) and others gather, pronounce the marriage verses (*maṅgaḷāṣṭaka*), and perform the god's marriage. The Rāūts, the chief holders of honorary rights (*mānkarī*), perform the marriage in the evening. Then they put the god's bed, and so on, into the palanquin, and the retinue goes out the southern gate to Kamaḷasiddha, and then on to Tukāī and back through the village to the temple. On the way, near the ''Idlers' Square'' (*rikāmacāvaḍī*), they kill a kid (goat) in the sight of the god, and apply two drops of its blood to the pole being carried by one of the barbers, and to the god's palanquin. Then they go into the temple, and the palanquins are set down in their places.[34] On this day more than two to four thousand people gather. The farmers return to their villages to work in the fields, then gather again from the sixth day of the fortnight on.

Beginning with the first day of the fortnight, there is a procession twice a day: during the second watch—that is, from eleven in the morning to three in the afternoon—and at night from nine until twelve. The procession makes three rounds along the circumambulatory path inside the temple courtyard.

---

34. Each group of devotees bringing a palanquin of the god has its fixed, traditional place during the festival.

And it sets out with great ceremony, with musical instruments—horns, wind instruments, drums, trumpets, and so on—playing, and with umbrellas, chowries, decorated umbrellas, and so on, waving. During the noontime procession, some women pour water on the pavement so that people's feet won't get burned. At both times of day, a big crowd gathers to see the procession. There is a huge crowd of women, men, and children trying to get a place on top of the compound wall.

From the fifth day of the fortnight on, the prophesying (*bhākaṇuk*) begins, and people become possessed and play with swords. "Prophesying" means they say under what constellations during the year rain will fall, how prices will be, where there will be diseases, what will be expensive, where there will be drought, when there will be war and devastation, and so on—and most things actually happen that way. Any of the five *sīds* does this work of prophesying. And when [the god] has entered his body, he takes a sword and, to the sound of the drums, he points the sword at his stomach, bends over, and pushes very hard. He also pushes on his tongue in the same way. Afterward he holds the sword laterally and waves it as if to cut his stomach. Then he takes a deep breath, jumps, and all at once strikes his stomach with the sword. Each time he strikes himself three times.

Numerous people have checked the sword and been convinced that it is real. I will tell about one or two of them, and then I will tell about the bazaar. Once the following miracle happened: A certain Muslim horseman who had come from Śrīmant Chatrapati Śāhū Mahārāj at Sātārā was sitting in the temple to watch the procession. He had a folding sword in his pocket. At that moment a Śiṅgāḍe became possessed and began to play with a sword. And the horseman naturally thought to himself, "What is there to that? They play with a blunt sword. How can it cut them? If they'll play with my sword, then I'll know that the god is true." As soon as the horseman had thought this, the possessed man threw away the sword that was in his hand and stood there. Then he jumped up onto the platform where the horseman was sitting, went up to him, and asked him for the sword. Everyone was amazed to see this. But the horseman got frightened: "If I give him the sword and something untoward happens, what will become of me?" As he thought this, he pulled the sword out of his pocket; the possessed man took the sword from him, jumped down, and began playing with it. As he played, he smashed the sword to bits with his hands and then threw it away. "You've become so proud," he said, "and within a month you will be completely ruined."

Then the horseman descended from the platform, touched the *sīd*'s feet, and said, "You are my mother and father. I acted this way out of ignorance, so forgive all my offenses and give me protection."

With that, another *sīd* became possessed, and they took the horseman and threw him at that *sīd*'s feet. Then the god said, "Your sins have been forgiven. Don't do such a thing again," and gave him leave to go.

Once when the god had come into a certain *sīd*'s body and he was playing with the sword near the tortoise [relief] in front of Śrī Nāth['s temple], the *sīd*'s wife brought food offerings (*naivedya*) to Śrī Nāth. But it was the fourth day of her menstrual period. When the *sīd* saw that she had brought the food offerings anyway, he said, "This evil Cāṇḍāḷaṇī [outcaste woman] has done wrong." And he took a deep breath, struck his stomach with the sword, and cut his body into two pieces. And the woman also died right on the spot.

At the time of the uprising of 1857, when at the command of the government all the subjects' swords were collected, there was also an order to collect the swords in Śrī Nāth's temple at Vīr. But people said, "Those are the god's swords; we won't give them up." When the Māmledār of Sāsvaḍ heard this, he came there in person. And when he was sitting in the road in the area in front of the god['s temple], one of the *sīds* became possessed and shouted, "Are you going to take away my sword? Let's see how you'll take it away." As he said this, he banged his head against the temple; and, even though the whole temple was made of stone, it rumbled so that people began to wonder, "Is it falling down, or what?" But the *sīd* did not even get a bump on his head. And the Māmledār got a pain in his stomach that put him into a state of agony. Then the Māmledār submitted to Śrī Nāth, and asked his pardon, and vowed, "We will leave your weapon alone." Then the pain stopped. Nowadays those who have weapons have licenses from the government for them, but there is no license for the god's sword.

Anyway, there have been many experiences of this sort; to write them all down would make the book too long, so I'll stop here.

Anyway, after circling [the temple] three times, all the palanquins are taken and set down in their places. From the sixth day of the dark half of the month of Māgh, stalls begin to be set up, and many people gather. There are about a hundred or two hundred stalls: there are stalls of sweetmeat sellers, grocers (Vāṇīs),[35] pots-and-pans sellers, bangle sellers, cloth merchants, tassel sellers, stalls for wooden goods, oil sellers, pān [betel leaf roll] sellers, vegetable sellers, perfume sellers, stationery sellers, grain sellers, and contractors,[36] and they are given stalls in different places the way there are different market areas in a town. This is all very beautiful, and besides there are ferris wheels

35. The Mhaskobā cult in Vīr is strongly supported by the local Vāṇīs.

36. The "contractors" rent spaces where they set up tea and food stands for the duration of the festival.

and lots of tents of bangle sellers, and so on. And all the merchants make lots of sales. When you see their stalls on both sides and the crowd of people in the middle, you get the sense of being in a city, and you feel almost as if the shops are always here. People come from as far as twenty or twenty-five miles away. Some buy pots and pans, some buy clothes, some buy fruits and sweetmeats, some buy stationery, knives and scissors, ink, string, pencils, slates, cots, mirrors, and other things. And there is a crowd of women buying bangles in the bangle-sellers' shops. Some people buy fruits, some buy one thing, some another. In this way the merchants make good sales.

On the tenth day of the dark half of Māgh—that is, on the last day—ten or twenty thousand people gather. On every street of the village, on the river-bank, in the temple—wherever you look, there are great crowds of guests in every house. On the last two days, so much red powder (*gulāl*) and coconut kernel is sold that from morning to night those shopkeepers don't get time to take a drink of water. Each of them sells two or three hundred rupees' worth of *gulāl* and coconut, and other goods also sell briskly.

Anyway, on the last day of the festival, when the procession is finished, thousands of goats (kids) are sacrificed. Everywhere one can hear the sound "Baah, baah." This is a bad thing, but nothing can be done about tradition, and it is the gods' work, so I cannot write any more about it.[37] The goats are killed outside the temple, and the food offerings (*naivedya*) are shown from outside. They are not taken into the temple.

On the day after the "tussle" (*mārāmārī*),[38] the festival begins to wind down. People come to the festival from very far away. On the day [of the "tussle," the devotees with] the palanquins, poles, drums, and so on, of the various villages take leave of the god and return to their own villages, but the bazaar continues until the no-moon day. On Śivarātrī [the thirteenth day of the fortnight] the god is washed and worshiped (this is called *pākhāḷaṇī*), and the god's body is annointed with oil to take away his fatigue.

A police station is set up to keep order, and the criminal magistrate (*phaujdār*) of the Taluka also comes, because the merchants bring thousands of rupees' worth of goods, and because there is a great crowd, so that quarrels and so forth can start.

This is the account of the festival.

---

37. The author is also under the influence of the *bhakti* saints and the god Viṭhobā of Paṇḍharpūr, who scorns the consumption of meat.

38. The devotees jostle one another in the temple compound, becoming entirely soaked with red water or covered with red *gulāl* powder.

Part 4. Devotees' Experiences, and the Things the God Likes Best

The glory of devotees is especially great. When one has entrusted oneself to God with singleminded devotion, God is not far away at all; but people's devotion is weak, and so their rewards are slight. Anyway, Umābāīsāheb, from the family of Śrī Ābāsāheb Purandare of Sāsvaḍ, had an ear infection, and her arms and legs were stiff. She tried medicines, and went to many healers (*devṛṣīs*),[39] and so on, but whatever she did, nothing was of any use. Then she and her family learned, "People who were very, very sick have been cured by worshiping Śrī Nāth Maskobā in Vīr, so you should go and worship at Vīr, and you will get better." Having heard this, they came and stayed here, and as soon as she began to worship Śrī Nāth, she was cured of the infection, and her arms and legs loosened up. Then she gave a meal to the god's priests (*pujārīs*), the Guravs and Gosāvīs, to the Ghaḍśīs and to the other servants (hands) of the god, and she also gave donations to some of those people. And she gave money for the god's daily food offerings, for a perpetual lamp, for *bhāṅg*[40] and *gāñjā,*[41] and for anointing him twice a year—that is, when they apply red lead to the god it is called "anointing" (*mājaṇeṃ*). She gave a stipend of ninety rupees a year for all of this. Besides, she used to send the god clothing, and so on, every year. The stipend continued up to the present time, but now it has stopped.

Another example was as follows: Someone from one of the Caugule households here had to go to another village at twelve o'clock at night, so he opened the door to take *darśan* of the god, took *darśan,* and came back. This made the god angry, and a miracle happened: all at once smoke began to come out of the temple. The Guravs woke up and saw the smoke, and when they looked closer they saw that the mattress in the god's (Mahārāj's) bedroom was burning. The bedstead was burning on all four sides, though there was no damage in the center; and the hookah was all disarranged. Then the Guravs put the fire out completely. Until recently the marks of the fire were there, visible on all four sides, [but] then the Caugules had the mattress, and so on, repaired.

The third example is this: There was a tailor (Śimpī) who lived here. His

---

39. See 7.6, above.

40. Hemp, *Cannabis sativa,* and the drink prepared from it.

41. The dried seeds of the hemp plant, and the tobacco prepared from it.

regular routine was to do his service of the god from sunset until the incense ceremony (*dhūpārtī*) took place at nine o'clock at night. Then he would crush *gāñjā,* fill the hookah, leave it there, and go home. This had been his routine for a long time. One day his wife asked him, "Why are you so late getting home? How long must I wait for you?"

He replied, "I have to fill the bowl of the god's hookah. That's why it takes so long."

He explained to her in many ways, but she wouldn't believe him. Then one day she went and hid in the temple. He prepared the bowl as he always did, placed the hookah up [close to the god], and everyone, including the Guravs, closed the door and went out. But the woman did not go out. She stayed inside to see how the god smokes a hookah. This made the god angry, and he dragged the woman, beating her, as far as the tortoise [relief in the temple courtyard]. When the woman began to scream, the Guravs went up to her and started asking her, "What happened?" At that point, she received several more blows. Everyone could hear the sound of the beating, but they couldn't see the god at all. Afterward the Guravs took her away, and she told them everything that had happened. Later that Śimpī's family line died out.

There was a goldsmith there who used to bathe at twelve noon, take the materials for worship (*pūjā*), go and worship Śrī Nāth, and then eat his meal. One day he went a little early to do the worship, and because it was the time for the hookah, the Guravs had given [the god] the hookah and shut the door. At that point, the man came to worship, and the Guravs said, "The door is not to be opened at this time. We'll open the door when it's time to do so." But the man wouldn't listen, and he forced open the door. And he felt as if he had been thumped in the chest with a fist. He took two or three somersaults and fell down motionless near the tortoise. Then the Guravs brought water, and so on, and applied it to his eyes and brought him back to consciousness.

There have been many such experiences. Koṇḍbhaṭ Thiṭe, one of the local Brahmans, also had an experience. He too was completely devoted to the feet of the Lord (Nāth). He was from a poor home; his circumstances were very humble. When the day of the festival came, he worried, "There's no grain in the house, and now four guests will come, so what can I serve them?" This was his worry. And when he thought to himself, "If I go from here to my uncle's house in Haraṇīgāv, I'll be safe," his wife said, "There's a man at such-and-such a place who gives out grain every year; so why don't you go to him and see if you can get something? That would be good."

Every year that man would give people grain. Śrī Nāth went and said to him in a dream, "That Brahman has no food to eat, and you haven't given him any grain." And having said this, Śrī Nāth chastised him greatly, and made him promise, "Tomorrow I will send grain to that Brahman." Then Śrī Nāth disappeared. The next day the farmer (Kuṇbī) hired two men, put loads of grain on their heads, and sent them to Koṇḍbhaṭ in Vīr. But the hired men came by one road, and Koṇḍbhaṭ went by another road, and so they missed each other. Then when he went to the farmer and asked for grain, the farmer told him everything that had happened, and said, "That joker (*jogaḍā*) came at night and beat me until I was exhausted, and the first thing in the morning I hired men to take some grain to you. Why have you made this trip for no reason?" When Koṇḍbhaṭ got home he saw that it was true.

There was a Bhosle [Marāṭhā] in Koḍīt named Bāpū Baḍade. What happened to him was that there was a pile of grain in his field, but he just left it and came to visit the god [here] in Vīr. With that, some Rāmośīs thought to themselves, "If we ask Bāpū for grain, he won't give us any, even though he has it. Today he has gone to Vīr, so this is our chance. We can take it easily." Saying this, they approached the pile of grain, and they saw someone sitting there who looked like Bāpū Baḍade. They were amazed, and they began to say, "With our own eyes we saw Bāpū going to Vīr; so who must this person just like Bāpū be? This is the god's doing," they said, and left. The next day when Bāpū returned from Vīr, he was told what had happened, and he was convinced that Śrī Nāth had protected the pile of grain. And to this day, those people just leave their piles of grain and come [to Vīr], but no one steals a single kernel. This is their experience to this day.

There are many such examples of things that have happened and that continue to happen. I will tell you an example that happened last Navrātra. There is a procession twice a day during Navrātra, just as there is during the month of Māgh. The oil for the torches comes from the village. But instead of giving lamp oil, the village Telī[42] lit the torches with kerosene. The stench of the kerosene reached the god, and the god became extremely angry. And a miracle happened: after the procession and everything was over, the Telī covered himself with a shawl and went to sleep right there, where five or ten people were already asleep. An hour or two later, when one of the men sleeping nearby woke up, he saw that the Telī's shawl was on fire without his being at all aware of it. Then the man woke up the Telī and put out the fire. The next day, during the procession, [the god] entered the body of a *siddha*, and the Telī asked why [the fire] had happened. The god said, "You lit the torches with kerosene yesterday, and that caused me a lot of trouble. That's why this happened." So the Telī stopped using kerosene and began to use lamp oil.

Anyway, if you have faith, God is not far away: this saying is always true. There have been many illustrations of this. Still to this day it happens that if

42. A member of the caste of oil-pressers.

someone[43] who has been badly bitten by a snake is taken into the temple, given a lime to suck, and made to circumambulate Śrī Nāth, he gets better. But that is just for someone who is here. The Dhangars are in Khāndeś, and so on, and if one of them is bitten by a snake or something he goes in the direction of Vīr—that is, toward where Vīr is—and as soon as he takes the name of Śrī Nāth, he is cured. The astonishing thing about those people's devotion is that the women don't have sexual relations with their husbands again until their children are as much as four years old: they wait until their *āhare jatrā*[44] in Vīr, and then go ahead. That's how simply these people love their god.

The other day a man thought that a stick he had found near the temple of Ghoḍe Uḍan was good for holding in his hand [as a walking stick?], so he brought it home. Someone must have offered it to the god. At night when the man was asleep, he suddenly found that he was being beaten. So he began to shout, and people gathered there and began to ask him [what had happened], and he told them the whole story. And the next day he took the stick and put it back in the place where he had found it.

The things that Nāth likes best are *gāñjā, bhāṅg, ghoṭā,*[45] fragrant flowers, red powder (*gulāl*),[46] and coconut.[47] He likes these things very much, because he is an incarnation of Śaṅkar. Among musical instruments, his favorite is the *ḍhol* drum.

I will give a few more examples, and then bring this section to a close. There are some Marāṭhās named Kavaḍe who live in Ghorpaḍī. Because they are related to the Baḍades, they began to attach a peacock-feather brush (*morcel*) to their pole just as the Baḍades do. A dispute developed between the two groups about the hereditary right [to do so]. The Baḍades began saying, "You should not put a peacock-feather brush on your pole," and the Kavaḍes said, "You're the ones who gave us the peacock-feather brush, and now you're saying not to use it. So you must take an oath on the tortoise [relief in the courtyard] in front of Śrī Nāth, and give up the peacock-feather brush." They took a false oath, and gave up the peacock-feather brush. Later the Kavaḍes installed Śrī Nāth in Ghorpaḍī and began to hold a pilgrimage festival there. And they stopped coming to Vīr. And the family line of those who took the false oath has not increased.

Anyway, many people have been cured of serious diseases; many who were

---

43. Reading *kuṇāhī* for the text's *phusāhī*.

44. The first *jatrā* to which the children's parents bring them, when they are presented to the god.

45. Dried hemp leaves, crushed and mixed with water.

46. *Bājrī* (millet) flour dyed red.

47. *Khobreṃ*—pieces of dried coconut. They are mixed with turmeric powder.

blind have begun to see; and childless couples have gotten children, too, after beginning to serve the god. In short, those who have entrusted themselves to him with faith (*bhāv*) have had their desires fulfilled and continue to have them fulfilled.

There are some Deśastha Brahmans who live in Karhāḍ who have him as their family deity, and they too have had many experiences. And they come and stay for two to four months at a time and serve Śrī [Mhaskobā]. Still today there are many very sick people and others who serve in the temple.

Part 5. Who Built the Temple and When, and Present Arrangements

So far we have completed four parts of the account. Now the fifth part is about who built the temple, when, and its present arrangements. Now, there is no indication of who built the temple, or how, but Śrī Chatrapati Śāhū Mahārāj built the inner part of the temple and the lamp pillar near the drum room; and Māljī Śaṅkarjī Ghuṇe built the whole outside part, including his shrine, and also the space for sitting above the southern gate; and people from Paṭaṇe Wāī built the shrine outside the temple in front of the god, the compound wall, and the pavements. And there are stone inscriptions to this effect. These same people built the tortoise [relief in the temple courtyard] also, and the more devoted they became, the higher they built the compound wall. The lamp pillar at the southern gate was built by Limbājī Pāṭīl Dhumāḷ, and one of the lamp pillars at the eastern gate was built by the Hoḷkar government, and the other was built by a man named Limbājī Tāṃbe, surnamed Dhangar, from a village called Jeūr, four miles from here. And the lamp pillar near the shrine was built by the Liṅgāyat Vāṇīs of Vīr. In the inner shrine of the temple is a large horse made of yellow clay, and it too was given by Māljī Ghuṇe, the Dhangar. This is how the temple is arranged.

Now for the present arrangements at the temple. In the morning, before dawn, the god's priests (*pūjārīs*), the Guravs, give the god a bath, prepare *gāñjā*, give him his hookah, and close the doors. When he has been given the hookah, even the Guravs are forbidden to go back inside. At about seven o'clock at night they worship the god once again, and put *prasād* on him. This tells true from false.[48] This really happens to this day, and many people have experienced it. Then there is an incense ceremony (*dhupārtī*), and they prepare the hookah again and place it before him. The god's (Mahārāj's) bedroom is right there. In it there is a bedstead, whose cushions, and so on, have

48. A flower is placed on Mhaskobā's head. If it falls to the left, the assertion is false; if it falls to the right, true.

to be brushed off and straightened; at night, after the god has been given his hookah, no one should go inside. Thus, there is worship (*pūjā*) three times a day, and drums are played three times a day: at five o'clock in the early morning, at eleven o'clock in the late morning, and at six o'clock in the evening.

On Sunday night the god has a procession, and it is very splendid, with drums and horns playing, and with umbrellas, chowries, and so on. On that day there is only one palanquin, the one from the village. It has a hundred or more rupees that people have nailed to it in fulfillment of vows. In addition, there are chowries, umbrellas, decorated parasols, poles, flags, peacock-feather brushes, drums, and so on, which have been offered by devotees in fulfillment of vows. Hanging from the god's door there is a *mekh mogarī,*[49] which was given in fulfillment of a vow, and the god also has a few perpetual lamps.

On a no-moon Monday (Somvatī) there is a very big ceremony. The villagers gather together and go with great splendor, accompanied by a band, behind the retinue of Śrī Nāth Mahārāj Maskobā to Ghoḍe Uḍan, the place which I have told about before. Then the god is bathed in the Nirā, and the villagers also bathe in the Nirā on this auspicious occasion.[50] A small temple has been built here. They circumambulate this temple three times. Then there is a Gondhaḷ[51] and in the evening the palanquin processes back through the village and into the temple. Anyway, there is a big crowd on this day too, and drums and poles from nearby villages also come, as do the pole, and so on, of the chief holders of honorary rights, the Rāūts.

During Navrātra too there is a procession twice a day for nine days, just as there is during the *jatrā* [in the month of Māgh]. And the Navrātra processions are also conducted with great ceremony. After the procession, both times, Kolhāṭaṇīs [female entertainers] sing on the tortoise [relief in the temple courtyard]. The Kolhāṭaṇīs must come for nine days. If they don't come to do this service, they have some bad experience, and they are harmed in some way. Many villagers—Brahmans, Marāṭhās, and so on—stay in the temple for nine days during Navrātra. The rule is that they should not go home for those nine days. On the day of Dasarā [the tenth day], Śrī Nāth's retinue goes to Śrī Tukāī's plateau, to perform, along with the townspeople, the ceremony

49. A *mekh* is a chain made out of pieces of iron and nails—a charm supposed to be effective against rheumatism. *Mogarī,* from Sanskrit *mudgara,* is a kind of club. See Devīsiṃga Vyaṃkaṭasiṃga Cauhāna, *Marāṭhī āṇī Dakhinī Hiṃdī* (Puṇe: Mahārāṣṭra Rāṣṭrabhāṣā Sabhā, 1971), p. 29.

50. The auspicious occasion (*parvakāl*) of Somvatī Amāvāsyā: the conjunction of sun and moon. See 6.3.1, above.

51. A particular type of religious dramatic performance.

of crossing the village boundary. After leaves of the *āpṭā* tree have been worshiped and the other ceremonies have been done there, the retinue processes in the same way from Śrī Vīreśvar's temple through the town, and enters the temple with great ceremony.

Everyone is ready to do his own work, and that is the way things are today. See, even though there's no stipend from the government, the way there is for some institutions, still all the duties are carried out in as well-ordered, regular a fashion as if there were. This will make the god's miraculous power clear to the reader.

In the month of Caitra too there is a considerable festival. There is also one in the month of Śrāvaṇ, and there are festivals in the months of Aśvin and Māgh as well. But the festival in the month of Māgh is the biggest of all. Ten miles from here is the place (*sthān*) of Śrī Khaṇḍobā called Jejurī. There too there are huge festivals in the months of Pauṣ, Mārgaśīrṣa, Māgh, and Caitra, and devotees come here after going to the festival there.

There was a big moneylender in Sātārā who had lent some money to a family. The family ran away with the money. As the moneylender was traveling around searching for the family, he came to Vīr. And he made a vow to Śrī Nāth that if he found the family, he would offer Śrī Nāth a *damaḍī*-worth[52] of camphor. Later he found the family and got back all his money, and then he came to Vīr and had clothes, and so on, made for Śrī Nāth, and gave a meal to all the god's temple servants. And as he proceeded onward, a miracle occurred. When he reached the banyan tree at the resting place outside the village, he suddenly became completely blind in both eyes. He could not see the road ahead of him; but if he looked back, he could see Śrī Nāth's temple. When this had happened, he returned and put *prasād* on the god and asked why this had happened. And the god said, "You forgot your vow to give me a *damaḍī*-worth of camphor; that's why this has happened. Give me my camphor and your eyes will be healed." Then as soon as he brought camphor and lit it, he could see again, and he went to Sātārā. In short, the god cares about even a small vow that is made to him.

Many such experiences keep happening, and this is how things are at present. I too have had several experiences. I'll tell one example from among them, and then ask the readers' leave to bring this section to a close. In 1887 there was a good deal of violence and destruction in Poona, and also in the nearby villages, but here little harm was done. Anyway, because everyone in my family was in Poona, I was worried day and night, and I was especially worried because I didn't even get any letters. Then one day I dreamed that I was sitting in the school and a Brahman wearing a white dhoti and a necklace

52. A quarter paisa, ten or twelve "cowries" (Molesworth, *Dictionary*).

of *rudrākṣa* beads,[53] with ashes smeared all over his body, came and said, "Why are you sitting here worrying this way? Tell me what your problem is." Then I told him the whole story, and he said, "Don't worry. No harm at all will come to your children. Don't you worry. Keep calm. Just bring me some *gāñjā*." When he had said this, I woke up and looked around and saw that I was lying on my bed. Early the next day a letter came saying that they were all right, so I got some *gāñjā* and gave it to Śrī Nāth.

53. Berries of the *Elaeocarpus Ganitrus* (Monier-Williams, *Dictionary*).

BIBLIOGRAPHY

Abhaṃgarāva, Vasudeva Kero. *Śrīpuṃḍalīkastava.* Paṃdharapūra, 1967.

Aiyangar, S. Krishnasvami. *Some Contributions of South India to Indian Culture.* Calcutta, 1942.

Allchin, Bridget and Raymond. *The Birth of Indian Civilization.* Harmondsworth: Penguin, 1968.

Allchin, F. R. *Neolithic Cattle-Keepers of South India. A Study of the Deccan Ashmounds.* Cambridge, 1963.

Ātre, Triṃbaka Nārāyaṇa. *Gāṃva-Gāḍā.* Tṛtīyāvṛtti [3rd printing], Muṃbaī, 1959.

Attikoḷḷa, Yallanagavḍa Ph. *Hālumatada Caritra.* Dharvaḍ, 1949 [in Kannaḍa].

Ayengar, Masti Venkatesa. *Popular Culture in Karnatak.* Bangalore, 1937.

Bābara, Sarojinī, saṃpādikā [editor]. *Eka hotā rājā.* Mahārāṣṭra Rājya Lokasāhitya Mālā, puṣpa 10. Muṃbaī (?), 1964.

———, saṃpādikā [editor]. *Kuladaivata.* Mahārāṣṭra Rājya Lokasāhitya Mālā, puṣpa 19. Muṃbaī, 1974.

Banerjea, Jitendra Nath. *The Development of Hindu Iconography.* Calcutta, 1956.

Basava Purāṇa. Translated by G.Würth. *Journal of the Bombay Branch of the Royal Asiatic Society,* 8 (1864–66) 65–97.

Benson, C. *An Account of the Kurnool District.* Madras, 1889.

Bhāgavata, Ananta Nārāyaṇa. *Umājī Nāīk yācem̱ Caritra.* Puṇeṃ, 1910.

Bhāgavata, Durgā. *Lokasāhityācī Rūparekhā.* Muṃbaī, 1956.

Bhaktavijaya Kathāsāra. Mahipatī Kavikṛta Saṃtacaritre. Āvṛtti 24vī [24th printing], Mumbaī, 1965.

Bhandarkar, Ramakrishna Gopal. *Vaiṣṇavism, Śaivism, and Minor Religious Systems.* Strasbourg, 1913.

Bhāve, V. L. *Mahārāṣṭra Sārasvata,* 2 volumes. Poona, 1925.

Blackburn, Stuart H. "Death and Deification: Folk Cults in Hinduism." *History of Religions,* 24 (1985) 255–74.

Brahmāṇḍa Purāṇa. Bombay: Veṅkaṭeśvara Press, 1913.

Briggs, George Weston. *Gorakhnāth and the Kānphaṭā Yogīs.* Calcutta, 1938 [reprint, Delhi, 1973].

Buchanan, Francis Hamilton. *A Journey from Madras through the Countries of Mysore, Canara and Malabar,* 3 volumes. London, 1807.

Caṅka Ilakkiyam. S. Vaiyapurippillai, ed. 2nd edition, Madras, 1967.

1. Akanāṉūṟu.
2. Aiṅkuṟunūru.
3. Kalittokai.
4. Kuṟuñcippāṭṭu.
5. Kuṟuntokai.
6. Ciṟupāṇāṟṟupaṭai.
7. Tirumurukāṟṟuppaṭai.
8. Naṟṟiṇai.
9. Neṭunalvāṭai.
10. Paṭṭiṉappālai.
11. Patiṟṟuppattu.
12. Paripāṭal.
13. Puṟaṉāṉūṟu.
14. Perumpāṇāṟṟuppaṭai.
15. Porunarāṟṟuppaṭai.
16. Maturaikkāñci.
17. Malaipaṭukaṭām.
18. Mullaippāṭṭu.

Ceṃdavaṇakara, Sadānaṃda. *Tuḷajāpūracī Bhavānī Mātā*. Muṃbaī, 1965.

Chatterjee, Asim Kumar. *The Cult of Skanda-Karttikeya in Ancient India*. Calcutta, 1970.

Chelliah, J. Vijendra. *Pattupattu. Ten Tamil Idylls*. 2nd edition, Madras, 1962.

Cilappatikāram. Kaliyanasuntaraiyer, ed. Madras: Thiyagaraya Vilasam, 1959.

Cox, A. T. *North Arcot*. Revised by H. H. Stuart. *Madras District Gazetteer*. Madras, 1895.

Crole, C. S. *The Chingleput (Late Madras) District. A Manual*. Madras, 1879.

Crooke, William. "Bull-baiting, Bull-racing, Bull-fighting." *Folklore,* 27 (1917) 141–63.

———. *The Popular Religion and Folklore of Northern India,* 2 volumes. 2nd edition, Delhi, 1968.

———. *Tribes and Castes of the North-Western Provinces and Oudh,* 4 volumes. Calcutta, 1968.

Das Gupta, S. *Obscure Religious Cults*. Calcutta, 1969.

Deleury, G. A. *The Cult of Viṭhobā*. Poona, 1960.

Derrett, J. D. M. *The Hoysaḷas. A Medieval Indian Royal Family*. Madras: Oxford University Press, 1957.

Desai, Dinkar. *The Mahāmaṇḍalēśvaras under the Cālukyas of Kalyāṇī*. Bombay: Indian Historical Research Institute, 1951.

Deshpande, Kusumavati. *Marathi Sahitya*. Delhi, 1966.

Devīmāhātmya. Muṃbaī: Nirṇayasāgara Buka Prakāśana, 1966.

Ḍhere, Rā. Ciṃ. *Khaṃḍobā*. Puṇeṃ, 1961.

———. *Lokasaṃskṛtīcī Kṣitije*. Puṇeṃ, 1971.

———. *Marāṭhī Lokasaṃskṛtīce Upāsaka*. Puṇeṃ, 1964.

———. *Śrīnāmadeva Eka Vijayayatrā*. Puṇeṃ, 1970.

______. *Śrīviṭṭhala: Eka Mahāsamanvaya.* Puṇeṃ, 1984.
______. saṃpādaka [editor]. *Gaṃgādhara Kavi Viracita Mārtaṃḍavijaya.* Puṇeṃ, 1974.
______. saṃpādaka [editor]. *Śrīdharasvāmī Nājharekara Viracita Malhāri Māhātmya.* Puṇeṃ, 1975.
Dube, S. C. *Indian Village.* London, 1955.
Dumont, Louis. *Homo Hierarchicus. The Caste System and Its Implications.* Translated by Mark Sainsbury. London, 1970.
Eliade, Mircea. *Myth and Reality.* New York, 1963.
______. *Patterns in Comparative Religion.* Cleveland, 1958.
______. *The Sacred and the Profane.* New York, 1957.
Elphinstone, Mountstuart. *Territories Conquered from the Paishwa. A Report.* Calcutta, 1821; Bombay, 1838; reprint, New Delhi, 1973.
Elwin, Verrier. *Folk-Tales of Mahakoshal.* Oxford, 1944.
______. *The Muria and their Ghotul.* Bombay, 1947.
______. *The Religion of an Indian Tribe.* Oxford, 1955.
Enthoven, R. E. *The Castes and Tribes of the Bombay Presidency,* 3 volumes. Bombay, 1920–1922.
______. *The Folklore of Bombay.* Oxford, 1924.
Fawcett, F. "Festivals of Village Goddesses." *Journal of the Anthropological Society of Bombay,* 2 (1890).
Ferishta's History of the Dekkan, 2 volumes. Translated by Jonathan Scott. London, 1794.
Frazer, Sir J. G. *The Golden Bough.* 2-volume edition, London, 1957.
Ghurye, G. S. *Gods and Men.* Bombay, 1962.
______. *Indian Sadhus.* 2nd edition, Bombay, 1964.
______. *The Mahadev Kolis.* Bombay, 1957.
Gordon, D. H. *The Prehistoric Background to Indian Culture.* Bombay, 1960.
Gune, Vithal Trimbak. *The Judicial Systems of the Marathas.* Poona, 1953.
Gupte, B. A. *Hindu Holidays and Ceremonies.* 2nd, revised edition, Calcutta, 1919.
Hāla. *Gāthāsaptaśatī.* With Gaṅgādhara's Commentary. Kāvyamālā, 21. Bombay: Nirṇaya Sāgara Press, 1889.
Hanumanthiah, V. R. *The History of Shepherds of India.* In 4 parts, fully illustrated. Bangalore, 1958 [in Kannaḍa].
Harper, Edward B., editor. *Religion in South Asia.* Seattle, 1964.
Höfer, A. "Aiyanar, der reitende Gott und seine kultischen Tonpferde." Vienna, 1961 (manuscript).
Hopkins, Edward Washburn. *The Religions of India.* 2nd edition, New Delhi, 1970.
Iyengar, P. T. Srinivasa. *History of the Tamils from the Earliest Times to 600* A.D. Madras, 1929.
Iyer, Ananthakrishna, L. K. *Mysore Tribes and Castes,* 4 volumes. Mysore, 1928–1935.
Jain, Jyotindra. *Bavaji und Devi. Besessenheitskult und Verbrechen in Indien.* Vienna, 1973.
Jettmar, Karl. "Die Entstehung der Reiternomaden." *Saeculum,* 17/1–2 (1966) 1–11.

Jñāneśvarī. Śaṃ. Vā. Dāṃḍekara, ed. Āvṛtti cauthī [4th printing], Puṇeṃ, 1967.
Joshi, Hariprasad Shivprasad. *Origin and Development of Dattatreya Worship in India*. Baroda, 1965.
Jośī, Babūrāva. *Śrīkṣetra Paṃḍharapūra Darśana*. Puṇeṃ, 1960.
Jośī, Mahādevaśāstrī. *Tīrtharūpa Mahārāṣṭra*, 2 parts. Puṇeṃ, 1966.
Jośī, Rāmacaṃdraśāstrī. *Malhārī Māhātmya*. Puṇeṃ, 1970.
Jośī, Śan. Bā. *Marhāṭi Saṃskṛti*. Muṃbaī, 1952.
Kanakasabhai, V. *The Tamils Eighteen Hundred Years Ago*. 2nd edition, Madras, 1956.
Kane, Pandurang Vaman. *History of Dharmaśāstra*, 5 volumes. Poona: Bhandarkar Oriental Research Institute, 1930–62.
Kāraṃḍe, Ya. L. *Suṃbarāna Māṃḍīlaṃ*. Sāṃgalī, 1967.
Karavīramāhātmya. Graṃthakāra: Kai. Dājībā Jośirāva. Kolhāpūra, n.d.
Karve, Iravati. *Maharashtra. Land and Its People*. Bombay, 1968.
Kasturi, N. "The Hero Stones of Mysore." *K. V. Rangasvami Aiyangar Commemoration Volume*. Bangalore, 1940.
Kāṭṭi, L. S. *Mailāra Kṣetradarśana*. Mailāra (Ballāri District), 1966 [in Kannaḍa].
Khāḍe, Bāpūrāva Khaṃḍerāva. *Śrīkṣetra Jejurīmāhātmya*. Puṇeṃ, Śake 1847 [1925].
Khare, Gaṇeś Hari. *Mahārāṣṭrācīṃ Cāra Daivateṃ*. Puṇeṃ, 1958.
———. *Mūrtivijñāna*. Puṇeṃ, 1939.
———. *Śrīviṭhṭhala āṇi Paṃḍharapūra*. Puṇeṃ, 1953.
Kincaid, C. A., and Parasnis, Rao Bahadur D. B. *A History of the Maratha People*. Bombay and Madras: Oxford University Press, vol. 1, 1918; vol. 2, 1922; vol. 3, 1925.
Koppers, W., "Zentralindische Fruchtbarkeitsriten und ihre Beziehungen zur Induskultur." *Geographica Helvetia*, 2/1 (1946) 165–77.
Kosambi, D. D. *Introduction to the Study of Indian History*. Bombay, 1956.
———. *Myth and Reality*. Bombay, 1962.
D. D. Kosambi Commemoration Committee, editors. *Science and Human Progress*. Bombay: Popular Prakashan, 1974.
Kulakarṇī, Sarasvatī Ci. *Śrīkṣetra Paṃḍharapūra Mahātmya*. 2nd edition, Beḷagāva, 1968.
Kulakarṇī, Sītārāma. *Bhāratātīla Ekavīsa Tīrthakṣetre*. Puṇeṃ, 1972.
Kulkarni, Shridhar. *Eknath*. New Delhi, 1966.
Leshnik, Lawrence Saadia, and Sontheimer, Günther-Dietz, eds. *Pastoralists and Nomads in South Asia*. Wiesbaden, 1975.
Līḷācaritra. Vi. Bhi. Kolate, ed. Muṃbaī, 1978.
Līḷācaritra. Uttarārdha, bhāga 2. Śaṃ. Go. Tuḷpuḷe, ed. Nāgpūr and Puṇe, 1967.
Lorenzen, David N. *The Kāpālikas and Kālāmukhas. Two Lost Śaivite Sects*. New Delhi, 1972.
Mackintosh, A. *An Account of the Origin and Present Conditions of the Tribe of Ramoossies*. Bombay, 1833.
Mahābhārata-Khilabhāga Harivaṃśa. Hiṃdī Ṭikāsahita. Gorākhapūra: Gītā Presa, dvitīya saṃskaraṇa [2nd edition], saṃvat 2024.

Malhārī Māhātmya. See Ḍhere, Rā. Ciṃ.

Mālū Tāraṇa Graṃthācā ādhyāyā 32vā sārāṃśa arthāta Koḷyāṃci vaṃśāvaḷi. [Published by] Vasudeva Kerabā Abhaṃgrāva. Dusarī āvṛttī [2nd printing], Paṃḍharapūra, Śake 1890 [1968].

Māṇika-prabhu-kṛta sacitra Malhārī Māhātmya. Āvṛttī 1lī [1st printing], Beḷagāṃva, 1917.

Manu-smṛti. Translated by G. Bühler. Sacred Books of the East, volume 25. Oxford, 1886.

Marriott, McKim, editor. *Village India*. Chicago and London, 1969.

Mārtaṃḍavijaya. See Ḍhere, Rā. Ciṃ.

Mate, M. S. *Temples and Legends of Maharashtra*. 2nd edition, Bombay, 1970.

——, and Kulkarni, G. T., eds. *Studies in Indology and Medieval History*. Professor G. H. Khare Felicitation Volume. Poona, 1974.

Matsya Purāṇa. Ānandāśrama Sanskrit Series, no. 54. Poona, 1907.

Meyer, J. J. *Trilogie altindischer Mächte und Feste der Vegetation*. Zurich/Leipzig, 1937.

Moraes, G. M. *The Kadamba Kula*. Bombay, 1931.

Mūḷastaṃbha Kathāsāra. Āvṛttī 15vī [15th printing], Muṃbaī, 1968.

Murty, M. L. K., and Sontheimer, Günther-Dietz. "Prehistoric Background to Pastoralism in the Southern Deccan in the Light of Oral Traditions and Cults of Some Pastoral Communities." *Anthropos*, 75 (1981) 163–84.

Nandimath, S. C. *A Handbook of Vīraśaivism*. Dharwar, 1942.

Nikitin. *Chozenie za tri morja Afanasija Nikitina 1466–1472* [*Afanasiy Nikitin's journey across the three seas 1466–1472*]. Moscow, 1960 [with translation in English and Hindi].

O'Malley, L. S. S. *Popular Hinduism*. Cambridge, 1935.

Oppert, G. *On the Original Inhabitants of Bharatvarsha or India*. Westminster, 1893.

Pavāra, Ābājīrāva Nāgojīrāva. *Śrīsomanātha Māhātmya*. Āvṛttī 15vī [15th printing], Sātārā, Śake 1888 [1966].

Pillai, J. M. Somasundaran. *Two Thousand Years of Tamil Literature*. Madras, 1959.

Pradhan, M. C., et al. *Anthropology and Archaeology*. Oxford, 1969.

Pradhan, V. G. *Jñāneśvarī*. Translated from the Marāṭhī, 2 volumes. London, 1967.

Prāyāg, K. Bh. *Srīkṣetra Tuḷajāpūra Māhātmya*. Tuḷajāpūra (?), 1969.

Rāmakṛṣṇa Yaśavaṃta. *Sacitra Paṃḍharapūra*. Muṃbaī, 1968.

Ramanujan, A. K., translator. *The Interior Landscape. Love Poems from a Classical Tamil Anthology*. Bloomington and London, 1967.

Ramesan, N. *Temples and Legends of Andhra Pradesh*. Bombay, 1962.

Rao, Gopinath. *Elements of Hindu Iconography*. Madras, 1916.

Rau, W. *Staat und Gesellschaft im alten Indien*. Wiesbaden, 1957.

Rothermund, D. *The Phases of Indian Nationalism*. Bombay, 1970.

Roy, Surendra Nath. *History of the Native States of India*. Volume 1: *Gwalior*. Calcutta, 1888.

Sastri, Nilakanta. *Development of Religion in South India*. Bombay, 1963.

——. *A History of South India*. 3rd edition, Oxford, 1966.

Settar, S., and Sontheimer, G.-D., eds. *Memorial Stones: A Study of Their Origin, Significance and Variety*. Dharwad/New Delhi, 1982.

Sharma, R. S., ed. *Indian Society: Historical Probings*. In Memory of D. D. Kosambi. New Delhi, 1974.

Shulman, David Dean. *Tamil Temple Myths: Sacrifice and Divine Marriage in the South Indian Śaiva Tradition*. Princeton, 1980.

Singer, Milton, ed. *Krishna: Myths, Rites and Attitudes*. Chicago, 1966.

———, ed. *Traditional India: Structure and Change*. Philadelphia, 1969.

Sircar, D. C., ed. *The Śakti Cult and Tārā*. Calcutta, 1967.

Sewell, R. *A Forgotten Empire*. 2nd edition, New Delhi, 1970.

Skanda Purāṇa, 7 volumes. Bombay: Veṅkateśvara Press, 1909–11.

Slater, Gilbert. *The Dravidian Element in Indian Culture*. London, 1924.

Somadeva. *Kathāsaritsāgara*. Bombay: Nirṇaya Sāgara Press, 1889.

Sonnalāpūra [Śolāpūra] yethīla grāma devatā Śrīsiddheśvara caritrābābata . . . Satyadarśana. Śolāpūra, 1964.

Sontheimer, Günther-Dietz. ''Between Ghost and God: A Folk Deity of the Deccan.'' In Alf Hiltebeitel, ed. *Criminal Gods and Demon Devotees*. Albany, forthcoming.

———. ''Bhakti in the Khaṇḍobā Cult.'' In G. H. Schokker, ed. *Proceedings of the Third International Conference on Early Devotional Literature in New Indo-Aryan Languages, Leiden, 1985*. Forthcoming.

———. ''Dasarā at Devaraguḍḍa. Ritual and Play in the Cult of Mailār/Khaṇḍobā.'' *South Asian Digest of Regional Writing*, 10—1981 (1984) 1–28.

———. ''Eine Tempellegende der Dhangars von Mahārāṣṭra.'' In H.Berger, ed. *Mündliche Überlieferungen in Südasien. Fünf Beiträge*. Wiesbaden, 1975, pp. 83–110.

———. ''Folk Deities in the Vijayanagara Empire: Narasiṃha and Mallanna/Mailār.'' In A. Dallapiccola, ed., in collaboration with S. Zingel-Ave Lallemant, *Vijayanagara—City and Empire. New Currents of Research*. Wiesbaden, 1985, pp. 144–58.

———. ''God as the King for All: The Sanskrit Mallāri Māhātmya and Its Context.'' In H. Bakker, ed., *Proceedings of a Workshop at the 7th World Sanskrit Conference, Leiden, 1987*. Forthcoming.

———. ''King Vikram and Kamaḷu Śinde, the Shepherd. Bhakti Episodes from an Oral Epic of the Dhangars of Maharashtra.'' *South Asian Digest of Regional Writing*, 6 (1977) 97–128.

———. ''The Mallāri-Khaṇḍobā Myth as Reflected in Folk Art and Ritual.'' *Anthropos*, 79 (1984) 155–70.

———. ''The Religion of the Dhangar Nomads.'' In Eleanor Zelliot and Maxine Berntsen, eds., *The Experience of Hinduism: Essays on Religion in Maharashtra*. Albany, 1988, pp. 109–30.

———. ''Rudra and Khaṇḍobā: Continuity in Folk Religion.'' In Milton Israel and N. K. Wagle, eds. *Religion and Society in Maharashtra*. Toronto, 1987, pp. 1–31.

———. "Some Incidents in the History of the God Khaṇḍobā." In Marc Gaborieau and Alice Thorner, eds., *Asie du Sud. Traditions et Changements.* Paris, 1978, pp. 111–17.

———. "Some Notes on Biroba, the Dhangar God of Maharashtra." In Professor D. D. Kosambi Commemoration Committee, eds., *Science and Human Progress.* Bombay, 1974.

———. "The *Vana* and the *Kṣetra:* The Tribal Background of Some Famous Cults." In G. C. Tripathi and Hermann Kulke, eds., *Eschmann Memorial Lectures.* Bhubaneswar, 1987, pp. 117–164.

Spate, O. H. K., and Learmonth, A. T. A. *India and Pakistan. A General and Regional Geography.* 3rd edition, London, 1967.

Srinivasan, T. N. *A Hand-Book of South Indian Images.* Tirupati, 1954.

Stokes, H. J. *Selections from the Records of the Bombay Government. An Historical Account of the Belgaum District in the Bombay Presidency.* Bombay, 1870.

Stanley, John M. "Gods, Ghosts, and Possession." In Eleanor Zelliot and Maxine Berntsen, eds., *The Experience of Hinduism: Essays on Religion in Maharashtra.* Albany, 1988, pp. 26–59.

———. "Niṣkāma and Sakāma Bhakti: Pandharpur and Jejuri." In Milton Israel and N. K. Wagle, eds., *Religion and Society in Maharashtra.* Toronto, 1987, pp. 51–67.

———. "Special Time, Special Power: The Fluidity of Power in a Popular Hindu Festival." *Journal of Asian Studies,* 37 (1977) 27–43.

Subbarao, B. *The Personality of India.* 2nd edition, Baroda, 1958.

Syed Siraj ul Hassan. *The Castes and Tribes of H. E. H. The Nizam's Dominions.* Bombay, 1920.

Thaninayagam, Xavier S. *Landscape and Poetry.* 2nd edition, London, 1966.

Thurston, E. *Castes and Tribes of Southern India,* 7 volumes. Madras, 1909.

Tukārāma Gāthā. Prahlāda Narahara Jośī, ed. Muṃbaī, khaṃḍa pahilā [volume 1], 1966; khaṃḍa dusarā [volume 2], 1968; khaṃḍa tisarā [volume 3], 1969.

Underhill, M. M. *The Hindu Religious Year.* Calcutta, 1921.

Vansina, Jan. *Oral Tradition. A Study in Historical Methodology.* Translated by H. M. Wright. London, 1965.

Vaudeville, Charlotte. "Braj, Lost and Found." *Indo-Iranian Journal,* 18 (1976) 195–213.

———. "The Govardhan Myth in Northern India." *Indo-Iranian Journal,* 22 (1980) 1–45.

Verma, O. P. *The Yādavas and Their Times.* Nagpur, 1970.

Wagle, Narendra. *Society at the Time of the Buddha.* Bombay, 1966.

Whitehead, Henry. *The Village Gods of South India.* 2nd edition, Calcutta, 1921.

Wilkins, W. J. *Hindu Mythology. Vedic and Puranic.* 2nd edition, Calcutta and Simla, 1882.

Yazdani, G., ed. *The Early History of the Deccan,* 2 volumes. London, 1960.

Ziegenbalg, B. *Geneaology of South Indian Gods.* Madras, 1869.

Encyclopedias, Dictionaries, Reference Works

Apte, N. G., ed. *Mahārāṣṭra Grāmakośa,* 2 volumes. Poona, 1967.

Bhāratīya Saṃskṛtikośa. Mahādevaśāstrī Jośī, ed., 10 volumes. Puṇeṃ, 1956–79.

Blumhardt, James Fuller, and Kanhere, Sadashiv Govind. *Catalogue of the Marathi Manuscripts in the India Office Library.* Oxford, 1950.

Burrow, T., and Emenau, M. B. *A Dravidian Etymological Dictionary.* Oxford, 1961. Supplement, 1968.

Census of India. Volume 10, *Maharashtra,* part VII-B, *Fairs and Festivals in Maharashtra.* Bombay, 1969.

Census of India 1961. District Census Handbooks.
- Ahmednagar, 1955.
- Jalgaon, 1967.
- Kolaba, 1964.
- Osmanabad, 1966.
- Parbhani, 1965.
- Sangli, 1964.
- Satara, 1963.
- Sholapur, 1967.
- Thana, 1965.

Dāte, Yaśavaṃta Rāmakṛṣṇa, and Karve, Ciṃtāmaṇa Gaṇeśa, eds. *Mahārāṣṭra Vāksaṃpradāya Kośa.* Puṇeṃ, vibhāga pahilā [part 1], 1942; vibhāga dusarā [part 2], 1947.

Dāte, Yaśavaṃta Rāmakṛṣṇa, et al. *Mahārāṣṭra Śabdakośa,* 7 volumes. Puṇeṃ, 1932–38. Supplement, 1950.

Dikshitar, V. R. R. *The Purana Index,* 3 volumes. Madras, 1951.

Dīkṣita, Ma. Gaṃ., and Vi. Go. Khobrekara, eds. *Śāhū Daptarātīla Kāgadapatrāṃcī Varṇanātmaka Sūcī.* Peśve Daptara Abhilekhamālā Varṇanātmaka Sūcī, Khaṃḍa [volume] 1, vibhāga [part] 1, Nāgapūra, 1969; Khaṃḍa 1, vibhāga 2. Vi. Go. Khobrekara, ed. Nāgapūra, 1970.

Dowson, John. *A Classical Dictionary of Hindu Mythology and Religion, Geography, History and Literature.* 10th edition, London, 1961.

Gazetteer of Bombay State. Volume 20, *Poona District.* Revised edition, Bombay, 1954.

Gazetteer of the Bombay Presidency. Bombay.
- Khandesh, 1880.
- Sholapur, 1884.
- Nasik, 1883.
- Satara, 1885.
- Poona, 1885.

Grassmann, Hermann. *Wörterbuch zum Ṛgveda.* 5th printing, Wiesbaden, 1955.

Kittel's Kannaḍa English Dictionary, 4 volumes. Revised and enlarged by Professor M. Mariappa Bhat. Madras, 1968–71.

Madras District Gazetteer. Salem. Madras, 1913.

Maharashtra State Gazetteer. Bombay.
Kolhapur District, 1960.
Satara District, 1963.

Maharashtra State Gazetteer. History. Bombay.
Part 1. *Ancient Period.* 1967.
Part 2. *Medieval Period.* 1972.
Part 3. *Maratha Period.* 1967.

Moeller, Volker. *Die Mythologie der vedischen Religion und des Hinduismus.* Wörterbuch der Mythologie, 4, 1. Stuttgart, 1966.

Molesworth, J. T. *A Dictionary, Marāṭhī and English.* 2nd edition, Bombay, 1857.

Monier-Williams, Monier. *A Sanskrit English Dictionary.* Oxford, 1899; reprint, 1970.

Mysore State Gazetteer. Gulbargā District. Bangalore, 1966.

Prabhudesāī, Pralhāda Kṛṣṇa. *Ādiśaktīce viśvarūpa arthāt Devīkośa.* Puṇeṃ, Khaṃḍa [volume] 1, 1967; Khaṃḍa 2, 1968; Khaṃḍa 3, 1968; Khaṃḍa 4, 1972.

Selections of Papers from the Records at the East-India House Relating to the Revenue, Police. . . . Volume 4, 1826: *Bombay Judicial Selections. Report of the Honourable Mountstuart Elphinstone to the Governor General, dated the 25th October 1899.*

Index

Ābāsāheb Purandare, 231
Ābhīras, 14, 20, 100
Āḍbaṅgīnāth, 95*n*
Ādemmā, 111
adhikārī, 163
Ādigoṇḍa, 110
Adil Shahi kingdom, dynasty, 7, 30. *See also* Bijāpūr
Ādimailār, 106, 159, 189
Ādimāyā, 24, 225. *See also māyā;* Māyā-Śakti; Śakti
Ādināth (Śiva), 95
Ādireḍḍi, 111
Aditi, 192
Agastya, 20
agrahāras, 90
Agriculture, expansion of, 33, 47–48, 147, 151–85, 187, 206
āhare jatrā, 234
Ahīrs, 100, 198*n*. *See also* Ābhīras
Ahmadnagar, 85, 101, 183
Ahmadnagar District, 3, 6, 45, 89, 165, 167
Ahmadnagar kings, sultanate, 83, 155
Ahmadnagar plateau, 7
Ahmadpur Taluka, 6
Aihole, 90, 139*n*
  five hundred Svāmīs of, 90
"Ain-i-Akbari," 124
Aiyaṉār, 17, 183–84, 197
Aiyappan, 188*n*
ajgar. *See* Snakes
akam poetry, 11–12
Ākhāḍ. *See* Āṣāḍh
Aklūj, 96
Akola Taluka, 6
Ālambādī cattle, oxen, 10, 153
Āḷaṇḍī, 96. *See also* Corācī Āḷaṇḍī
Algujdarā, 139, 141
Alibāg, 169
Allchin, F. R., 6, 153
Amaravantī, 49
Ambā, Ambābāī, Ambikā, 40, 72, 185
Ambājogāī, 40
ambīl, 226*n*
aṃboḷī, 210*n*
aṃboṇī mash, 210–11
Āmbyā Koḷī, 73–74
Āmbyācī Jogavā, 40
Amrit Mahal oxen, 10
amṛt (nectar), 55, 59, 117, 202
Anagaḷ, Rāvjī, 223–24
Ananda forest, 209
Ānandakoṇ[ṉ]a, 157
Anantapur District, 8
Ancestor shrines, 125, 136, 138–40, 225
Ancestor worship, 86, 137–41, 198*n*
Āṇḍe Kurubas. *See* Kurubas
Andhaka, 99, 202
Andhra Pradesh, 8–9, 16, 21, 93*n*, 94*n*, 102, 104, 106, 111, 126, 147, 153–54, 157
aṅgāt yeṇeṃ, 78*n*. *See also* Possession
Āñjangāv, 36, 38, 72–73, 113, 123
aṅkuśa, 184*n*
Ankusagari Poligārs, 107
Anthills, 108, 188*n*, 192*n*, 198*n*. *See also* Termite mounds
Ants, 92, 133, 204

Apabhraṃśa, 158
apsaras, apsarases, 4*n,* 36, 71*n*
Āpṭā leaves, 237
āratī, 25, 215. *See also dhūpārtī;* Lamps, oil
Archeological remains, 41, 45, 123. *See also* Microliths, prehistoric; Prehistoric finds
Arcot, 84
  North, 10
  South, 10
Ārevāḍī, 44, 116, 136–37, 153, 187, 199
Arioi, 14
Arya (Candikā), 41*n*
Āṣāḍh (Ākhāḍ, Aśāḍ), 46, 133, 140, 152, 181
Āṣāḍhī Ekādaśī, 133
Āsarās, seven. *See sāt āsarā;* Seven Āsarās
Asceticism, 32, 38*n,* 39, 43, 46, 48, 72*n,* 73, 89–90, 96, 98, 183, 189, 192, 201, 203, 208–9. *See also tapa, tapas, tapaścaryā*
Ascetics, viii, 95, 104. *See also sannyāsīs*
Ashes, 51, 53*n,* 54, 83, 108, 163, 213, 238. *See also vibhūt*
Aśmaka, 20
āśram, āśrama, viii*n,* 201, 207*n*
Assakas, 20
Aṣṭabhairav, 49, 97, 198
Astrologer, 227. *See also* Horoscope; *pañcāṅg*
asur, asuras. See Demons
Āśvin (month), 24*n,* 60, 134, 137, 237
Āśvin Amāvāsyā, 134
āśvinaśuddhapratipadā, 24*n*
Āṭpāḍī, 27, 96, 118*n*
Āṭpāḍī Taluka, 43, 66*n*
Atrafi Balda District, 51
Atri *ṛṣi,* Atrimuni, 208
Attributes, 198–200, 205. *See also specific attributes and cult objects*
Aundh, 33
Aurangabad, 7, 100
Aurangabad District, 7, 45
Auraṅgābād Taluka, 7
Aurangzeb, 74*n,* 83–84, 155, 158
avatār, vii, 24–25, 27, 48, 70, 71*n,* 91, 97, 148, 195, 200–201. *See also* Incarnation
Avatī, 156
Āyars, 14
āycciyar, 14, 17
Bābar family, 152
Bābhūḷ trees, 166
Bābīr, 86, 171
Bābū Ballāḷ, 56, 86–88
Baḍades, 215, 219, 222, 226, 234. *See also* Bāpū Baḍade; Tulājī Baḍade
Badagas, 10
Bādalcī, Bādalcī Baḍdavvā, 40
Badāmī, 21, 40
Baḍdavvā, Bādalcī Baḍdavvā, 40
Badrikāśram, 207–8
Baḍvās, 72, 75
Bag, magical begging (*jhoḷī*), 53–55
bāgāīt (garden land), 59, 158
Bahāl, 41
Bāhmanīs, 19*n,* 83, 155–56, 159, 161, 163–64, 196
Bājirāv I (Peśvā), 161–62
bājrī, 5, 7–8, 94*n,* 151, 234*n.* *See also* Millet
bakhar, 162*n*
Baḷadeva, 92
Bālāghāṭ, 6, 69
Bāḷāī, 50, 58–61, 66. *See also* Bāḷubāī
Balapālapalle, 111–12, 114
Bāḷkujī (Ghuṇe), 225
Ballari District, 8, 189
Bāḷojī Ḍubal, 23–25
Bāluākkā (Bāḷubāī), 67
Bāḷubāī, 31, 45, 58–60, 66–67, 146, 184. *See also* Bāḷāī
Bāḷurāṇi (Bāḷubāī), 59–60
balutedārs, bārā, 70
Bāman (Brahman), 147
"Bamboo Pasture," 36
bāṇa, 160*n.* *See also liṅgams*
Bāṇāī, 47, 50, 58, 60–61, 64, 66–67, 133–34, 155, 163, 180, 196–97. *See also* Bāṇu; Bāṇubāī
Banaras, 27, 73*n,* 96, 198, 209. *See also* Kāśī; Vārāṇasī
Bāṇas, 67
Band, 225–26. *See also* Musical instruments; *specific musical instruments*
Bande Dhangars. *See* Dhangars
Baṅgāl land, 51–52, 54
Bangalore District, 102
baṇij, 153
Bañjāras, Bañjārīs, 153–54, 182–83

Bañjigas, 89
Banners, 90–92, 200*n*. *See also* Flags, Flagstaff
Banśaṅkarī, 40
Bāṇu (Bāṇāī), 66
Bāṇubāī (Bāṇāī), 61–63, 65–66, 163
Banyan tree, 17, 237. *See also* Vaḍ tree
Bāpū Baḍade, 233
Bār Hatti, 126
Bārā Hatkar, 126
Bārāmatī, 36, 96, 104–5, 123, 165, 171
Bārāmatī Taluka, 77, 98, 104, 170*n*, 171*n*, 177*n*
Bārāmatī Thāṇā, 170
bāras, barsā, barseṃ, 163*n*. *See also* Naming ceremony
Barbed stick (*aṅkuśa*), 184*n*
Barbers, 52, 215, 218–19, 221–22, 226–27. *See also* Nhāvīs
barcā, barchī, barcī, barsā, barśī (spear), 124
Bargā, Bargi, Bārgir, Bārgīr Dhangars. *See* Dhangars
Barodā, 162
Bārśī Taluka, 6
Barygaza (Broach), 21
Basava, Basavaṇṇa, 92, 112, 139, 195
Basaveśvara, 111
Bath, bathing, 38–39, 55, 125, 144, 148, 159, 194, 212, 216, 235–36
  of sheep, 36, 64–65
Battle, 71*n*, 195, 201–3. *See also* War, warfare
  as yogic exercise, 203
bāvan (fifty-two) *bīr*, 189, 204
bāvan birudeṃ, 199–200
Bāvan Māvaḷṣ, 83
bāvan vidyā, 51. *See also* Sciences, fifty-two magical
bāvan vīr, 200–202
Bāvari, 20
Bavḍe, 96, 152
Bazaars, 44, 145, 225, 228–30. *See also* Markets; Trade
Beḍar, 84
Beḍars, Beḍas, 84, 103, 174*n*
Beḍsā, 20
Begging bag. *See* Bag, magical begging; *jhoḷī*
Bel tree, 193
Belgaum, 5, 9, 166, 226
Belgaum District, 3, 5, 21, 33, 40, 41*n*, 50*n*, 51, 55, 89, 210
Bells, 200
  hand, 57, 200
Bengal, 9, 51. *See also* Baṅgāl land
Berāḍs, 84, 86*n*
Berar, 124, 126, 155, 185*n*
Berger, H., ix
Betel, betel-leaf, betel nuts, 71*n*, 79*n*, 182, 186, 226. *See also* Pān; *supārī*
bhaḍakhaṃbas, 71*n*. *See also* Hero stones; *vīragaḷas*
Bhāḍalī Budruk, 22
Bhāde, 137, 139, 197
Bhadrakālī, 98–99
Bhagavān (Bhagvat), 28, 78–79
Bhāgīrathī, Bhāgirthī River, 82, 209
Bhāgū Lakḍe, 172
Bhāgubāī, Bhāgulek, 72, 120
Bhagvad Gītā, 215*n*
Bhagvat (Bhagavān), 219
Bhāgvat, Durgā, 47
bhagvatbhaktas, 222. *See also bhaktas*
Bhairav, 32, 42, 49–50, 58–60, 94*n*, 95–98, 179, 183, 197–98, 200, 207–11, 216, 219. *See also* Aṣṭabhairav; Kāḷbhairav
  as a god of war, 198
Bhairavnāth, 25, 59–60, 97, 99, 177, 179
Bhājā, 20, 48*n*
bhākaṇūk, 214, 228. *See also* Prophecy
bhākrī, 61–64, 144, 210*n*, 211–12
bhaktas, 24–25, 30, 72, 85, 92, 113–14, 116, 123, 125*n*, 128, 136–38, 141–42, 164, 168, 171, 180, 189–90, 196. *See also bhagvatbhaktas*; Devotees
bhakti, 36, 38*n*, 43, 48, 70, 71*n*, 72*n*, 73, 89, 136, 141, 145, 149–50, 169–71, 172*n*, 187, 202, 230*n*. *See also* Devotion
  Vaiṣṇava, 70, 71*n*
Bhāldār, 117*n*
Bhaleghol pond, 36
Bhāṃtyās, 98
bhaṇḍār, 36, 61, 73–74, 116, 118–19, 134, 160. *See also haḷaḍ*; Turmeric powder
  with fourteen magical powers (*caudā idyācā bhaṇḍāra*), 118–19
bhaṇḍār house, 32, 53*n*

bhāṅg, 231, 234
Bhaṅgriā, Rāmjī Nāīk, 83
bharāḍ, 96
Bharma, Bharmappa, 50*n,* 184*n*
Bhātgar reservoir, 76
Bhaumāsur, 98
bhāv, 235. *See also* Faith
Bhavānā, 81
Bhavānī, 24, 42, 85, 124, 154, 159, 185
Bher fort, 162*n*
Bhigvān, 96
Bhils, 60*n,* 68, 196
Bhimā River, 5–7, 21, 37, 46, 69, 72, 73*n,* 75, 77, 82, 104, 131, 151–52, 163, 173, 189, 214, 224. *See also* Bhivrā; Candrabhāgā
Bhimāśaṅkar, 69, 96
Bhīmsen, 136*n*
Bhimthaḍī Taluka (Bārāmatī Taluka), 170
Bhir District, 7, 40
Bhivāī, 75–76
/Bhivāyā, Bhivayyā, seven, 36, 75
Bhivrā (Bhimā) River, 82
Bhoīs, 77
Bhokardhan Taluka, 7
Bhoḷā (Śiva), 52–55, 61, 66, 86, 127
/Bhoḷādev, 52
/Bhoḷānāth, 125*n*
Bhor, 49
Bhor state, 162*n*
Bhosles, 105, 177, 219, 222, 233
Bhūgāv, 47, 49
Bhuiñj, 219, 222
"Bhujabalamalla," 199
Bhuleśvar, 125
Bhūm Mahāl, 6
Bhūmi Pūrṇimā, 118
bhutāvaḷ, 136. *See also* Ghosts
bhūts, 143–45, 195*n*. *See also* Ghosts
Bīḍ, 152
Bīdar, 106, 154–55, 159, 189, 216*n*
kingdom of, sultanate, 155
Bihar, 9
Bijāpūr, 7, 22, 30, 74, 122, 126, 128, 138
kings of, sultanate, 7, 22*n,* 30, 155, 158–59
Bijapur District, 90
Bijjala (Cālukya king), 92
Bijjala (Kalacuri king), 21–22, 25, 111
Biḷūr, 58, 60, 97, 164, 209*n*
bīr. *See bāvan bīr*
Bīradeva, 112, 203
Birāppā, 35–37, 40, 43, 50*n,* 106, 113–14, 116–21, 123, 187, 190, 199, 203, 206. *See also* Kāśīliṅg Birāppā
Birdev, 35, 72, 74
Bire Devaru, 108
Biredeva, 203
Bireśvar, Bireśvara, 182, 187
Birjī (Birobā), 77–81
Nārāyaṇ, 79
Birobā, vii, 8*n,* 25–26, 30, 32–33, 40–45, 66–67, 72, 74, 77–83, 104, 106, 116, 120–23, 132–33, 135–39, 141–42, 146–47, 153, 182–83, 185–87, 189–90, 192–93, 196–206
/Birojī, 147
/Birū, 80–81
/Birubā, 135
Births, unusual, 93, 104, 163, 192
biruda. *See bāvan birudeṃ; viruda*
Birudev (Birobā), 191, 201–2
Blankets (woolen), 9, 13–14, 37–38, 62, 74, 103, 106, 109, 115, 121–22, 124, 138, 187*n,* 191, 199–200, 212, 214, 224
/*burṇus,* 214
/*ghoṅgaḍī,* 37*n,* 74*n,* 122, 138
/*jāḍ,* 74*n*
/*kāmbḷī,* 9, 74*n,* 121
Blood, 58, 61, 74*n,* 99, 117–18, 125, 136, 201, 213
of dead demons forming new ones, 99, 201–2
Boatsmen, 69–70, 72–73, 75–76, 78–81
Bombay, 171
Bombay Karnatak, 9
Bomlā, Nāīk Jivājī, 83
Borban, 210–11, 215–16
Bovā, 221*n*
Bows, god's, 196
Brahmā, 50*n,* 55, 89, 184*n,* 207–9
Brahma Rakṣasīs, 111. *See also* Demonesses
brahmacārīs. *See* Celibates
brahman, 207–8
Brahmanism, 172*n*
Brahmanization, 205. *See also* Sanskritization
Brahmans, v–vi, viii, 20, 22–23, 30, 46, 59–60, 65, 71*n,* 72, 75, 88–90, 92, 95,

101, 103, 108–9, 121, 133, 140, 146–50, 159, 179, 182, 188, 193–95, 204–5, 209–10, 223, 226, 232, 236–37. *See also* Baḍvās; Deśastha Brahmans
conceptions of, 17, 181, 203
literature of, 55, 121. *See also* Dharmaśāstra(s); Purāṇas; Sanskrit literature; Vedas
pantheon of, 58–59, 203. *See also* *purāṇic* mythology; Sanskritic deities
superiority of, 89
Brahmapūrī (Karhāḍ), 23–24
Braj, 45, 101, 185, 188
Bṛhaspatī, 48
Briñjārīs, 153
British rule, or period, 83, 85, 97, 113, 155, 165–66, 182. *See also* English, the
Pax Britannica, 180
Broach, 21
Buchanan, Francis Hamilton, 102–4, 106
Buddhist caves, 20, 48*n*
Buddhist monks, viii, 101
Buddhists, 22, 90
Buffalo. *See also mhaśā; reḍā*
as mount of Yama, 181
riding on, 181
Buffalo demon, 32, 56–57. *See also* Mahiṣa; Mahiṣāsura; Mhaiśāsur; Mhaśā
bukkā, 137
Buldhana District, 7
Bullfights, 14
Bulls, 12, 90, 96, 195, 200*n*. *See also* Votive figures
Buraṅgule, 214–15, 226
Burma, 153
burṇus, 214. *See also* Blankets (woolen)
Buttocks, 214
Buvā(s), 32, 168, 221*n*
Byārāḍs, 84, 87

cāhur (measure of land), 224–25
Caitra (month), 33, 44, 46, 67, 75, 78, 133–34, 153, 200, 237
Caitra Pūrṇimā, 133–34
cakra, 200
Cakradhara, 70*n*, 71*n*
Cālukyas, 22–24, 100
of Badāmī, 21–22
of Kalyāṇī, 21–22, 92
Cāmbhārs, 171
Camels, 154
Camp. *See vāḍā, vāḍī; vastī*
Campāṣaṣṭhī, 155
Camphor, 177, 237
Canda District, 196
Caṇḍāla, Cāṇḍāḷaṇī, 89, 229
Candī, 157–58
Candikā, 41*n*
Candrabhāgā (Bhimā) River, 46, 73–74, 82, 189
/Candra, 82
Candūr, 117*n*
cāṅgbhale, 217, 219, 221, 226
Caṅkam literature, vii, 11–19. *See also* Tamil literature, ancient
Cannabasava, 93
Cannavvā, 110–11
capātīs, 64, 67, 133, 136
Caravans. *See* Merchants
Caritras, 203–4
Carrying pole. *See kāvaḍ*
Caste system, 17, 75, 89, 109, 171, 172*n*, 180, 208*n*
Cattle. *See also* Bulls; Cow(s); Oxen; *specific breeds of cattle*
markets, 95, 153–55
theft, 11, 14–15, 25, 70, 71*n*, 84, 87, 101, 103, 152–53, 178–79
and war, 14, 71*n*
caugule, 162. *See also* Deścaugula
Caugules, 120, 231. *See also* Jakāppā Caugule
Cauragaḍh mountain, 67–68
Cauraṅgīnāth, 95*n*
Caves, 20, 48*n*, 196
cavrīs, 200. *See also* Chowries
Ceḍā, 86, 200
Celibates, 50. *See also* Asceticism; Ascetics; *sannyāsīs*
Ceñcūs, 93*n*
Central India, 196
Central Provinces, 185*n*
Cēyōṉ, 16–17, 205
Chandī. *See* Candī
chatras, 200. *See also* Parasols; Umbrellas
Chikbalapūr, 156
China, 153
Chitaldurg District, 102
Chittoor District, 8, 10

Cholas, 14
Cholera, 39, 105, 167
Chowries, 225, 227–28, 236. *See also* *cavrīs*
Chronicles. *See bakhar, kafīyat*
Cikhalavḍī, 152
Cikoḍī Taluka, 50*n*
Cilhure, 187
Cincāle, 31
Cinclī, 32–33, 40–41, 43–44, 128
Cincṇ(~l)īcī Māyavvā, 40
Circumambulation, 227, 236
Citaḷenagar, 61
Clashes, 167. *See also* Disputes; War, warfare
Classical antiquity, Western, 191
Coats, 183
Cobras, 60, 133–34, 176, 189. *See also* Snakes
Cocks, 57, 140. *See also* Roosters
Coconut(s), 24*n*, 35, 76, 79*n*, 80, 82, 119–20, 143, 160, 177, 230, 234
Cokhā Meḷā, Cokhāmeḷā, Cokhyāmeḷā, 71*n*, 216
Copāḷā, 215
Corācī Āḷaṇḍī, 98, 147, 152, 180
Corācī Uṇḍavḍī, 98
Corāmble, Rām, 159
Cotton, 6, 9, 107–9, 111
Cow(s), 18, 31, 42, 45, 90, 93*n*, 96, 102, 123, 134, 162, 168*n*, 169, 173, 176, 209, 210*n*, 211–12. *See also* Kāmadhenū
  barren, 31, 211–12
  black, 87, 170. *See also kapila* cow
  discovering a god, 31, 93*n*, 157, 187, 189, 211–12
  dung, 13, 32, 135, 144, 226
  milk, 30–31, 42–43, 157, 188–89, 210*n*, 211–12
  urine, 143
Cremation ground, 168, 181
Crossroads, 22, 30, 151–52
Crowns (*mukuṭas*), 197, 199
Cuddapah District, 8
Cuḍī Purṇimā, 215
Cumḷīs, 70, 84. *See also* Koḷīs, Malhār
cunā, 137*n*
Curses, 48, 61*n*, 72*n*
Dādājī Koṇḍev, 165
Dahīvāḍī, 22, 159
Dahīvāḍī Taluka, 135*n*
dait, daityas. *See* Demons
dakkhiṇa-patha, 20
Dakṣa, 199
damaḍī, 237
Dāmājī Pant, Dāmājīpant, 216
Daṇḍakāraṇya, 23–24, 31, 48, 98, 158
daṇḍanāyakas, 25, 71*n*, 101, 152, 156, 198, 205
daṇḍvat, 81*n*
dargā, 120, 167
darśan, 46, 177, 209, 212, 216, 220, 231
Dasarā, 67, 72, 78*n*, 118, 133*n*, 134, 140, 154, 196, 199, 236
Dāsaris, 157
Dates, dry (*khārīk*), 79*n*
Dattanāth Ujjanīkar, 164
Ḍauryā Gosāvīs, Ḍavryā Gosāvīs, 96–97
dāvaṇ, 135–36
Deccan, ix, xi, 3, 7, 12, 13*n*, 18, 20, 58, 74*n*, 105*n*, 124, 153, 155–56, 174, 195*n*, 196. *See also* Deś; Plateau
Deforestation, 166
Deleury, G. A., 70
Delhi, kings of, 124
Demonesses, 35, 51, 107–11
Demons, 22–24, 27, 29, 31, 41, 55–58, 84, 91–92, 98–99, 108–9, 145, 189*n*, 193, 195, 198, 200–204. *See also specific demons*
  survival of identities or names of defeated, 26, 32, 76, 83–84, 92, 98–99, 195
Deś, 3, 19, 34, 127, 132, 134–35, 169. *See also* Deccan; Plateau
Deśastha Brahmans, 223, 235
Deścaugula, 23*n*
Deserts, 84–85. *See also pālai;* Wasteland; Wilderness
Deśmukhs, 159
Deuḷgāv-Gāḍa, 173
devak ("totem"), 226*n*
Devana-doḍḍī, 156
Devanahalli, 156
Devaraguḍḍa, 16, 202
  /Mailār, 196
Devgaḍh, 124*n*
Devgāv, 97

Devgiri, 86*n*, 100–101, 151
devīs. See Goddesses
Devkā(ṃ)te(s), 172, 178
  Dhuḍī, 172
Devotees, 24–25, 30, 36, 72, 81*n*, 85, 92–93, 113, 116, 118*n*, 123, 125*n*, 128, 137–39, 141–42, 155, 161, 168, 171, 180, 189–90, 196, 215–16, 218–19, 222, 227*n*, 230*n*, 231. *See also bhaktas*
Devotion, 36, 38*n*, 43, 72*n*, 73, 89, 136, 161, 169, 182, 187, 202, 214–16, 221, 231, 235. *See also bhakti*
devṛṣīs, 138, 140–46, 214*n*, 231
  investiture of (*sthāpaṇuk, ṭhāpaṇuk*), 142–43, 145
devsthān, 181. *See also sthān*
Dhagevāḍī, 81
Ḍhālgāv, 44, 152–53
Dhangar Bābā, 76
Dhangars, vii–x, 4, 23, 27, 29–30, 32–36, 37*n*, 39–41, 43–45, 47, 51, 53, 56, 59–65, 67, 72, 74*n*, 75–77, 79, 84–86, 88, 93, 95, 101, 103, 105–7, 110, 113, 116–18, 120–50, 153, 157, 159, 163–64, 166–73, 176–80, 182, 185*n*, 186, 190–91, 194, 197, 199–201, 204–5, 210, 213, 214*n*, 215–16, 222, 224, 234–35
  Bande, 106, 123
  Bargā, Bargi, Bārgir, Bārgīr, 123–26
  Gavḷī, 122–23, 158, 168
  Hāṭkar, 77, 123–50, 162*n*, 167–68, 172, 179, 182, 191
    Bārā, 126
    etymology of, 125–28
    /Haṭṭikaras, 126–27
  Hāṭkar Khilārī, 131
  Hāṭkar Meṇḍhe, 122
  Hattikaṅkaṇ, 107
  Khāṭīk(s), 123, 133*n*
  Khilārī, 129, 159
  Khilārī Hāṭkar, 127–29
  Meṇḍhe, 122–23, 172
  Meṇḍhe Hāṭkar, 158
  Mhaskar, 122–23, 133*n*
  Mhaske, 4, 101, 122, 167
  Saṇgar, 122, 127
  Śiṅgāḍe, 186. *See also* Śiṅgāḍe family
  Unnikaṅkaṇ, 107
Dhārāśiv, 158
Dharma, 38, 73, 117, 122
Dharmapuri (Salem District), 15
Dharmapurī (Sholapur District), 86
Dharmaśāstra(s), v–vi. *See also smṛtis*
  of Manu, 73*n*, 180*n*
  /science of Dharma, 118*n*
Dhārvāḍ, 9, 226
Dharwar District, 88
Ḍhavāṇs, 214–15, 226
Dhāyguḍe, 173
Ḍhere, Rā. Ciṃ., 189*n*
Dhoṇḍ, 96, 113
Dhoṇḍ Taluka, 77, 113
Dhoti, 144, 145*n*
Dhuḍī Devkāte, 172
Dhuḷe, 100
Dhuḷi Mahāṅkāḷ (Dhuḷobā), 94
Dhulia District, 7, 100
Dhuḷobā, 36, 51, 75–76, 94*n*, 98*n*, 128, 135, 138, 164, 210*n*. *See also* Dhuḷi Mahāṅkāḷ
  /Dhuḷdev, 163–64
Dhuḷvaḍī, 135, 163
Dhumāḷ, Limbājī Pāṭīl, 235
Dhumyā, 61, 63
ḍhuṅgaṇ (buttocks), 214
dhūpārtī, 78, 232, 235. *See also āratī*
Diamonds, 115, 224
Dighañcī, 26, 33
Diṇḍīra forest, 46–47, 70–71
dīpmāḷs, 141*n*, 218
Disputes, 100, 172–73, 178–79, 207, 219–34
Divāḷī, 52, 54–55, 86, 88, 118, 134–35, 199
  /Dipāvaḷī, 133*n*
Divān, 74
Dive Ghāṭ, 113
Divination, 219
Dogs, 103, 157, 161, 196–97, 199, 217
ḍoh. See Water hole
Donakunda, 51
Ḍoṅgarcī Yallavvā, 40
Doorkeeper (*dvārapāl*), 49–50
Dṛḍhaprahāra, 101
Dreams, 87, 142, 237–38
Drought, 4–6, 62, 164–65, 178, 180, 202, 228. *See also* Famines

Drums, 57, 78, 81, 96, 115–18, 120, 142–43, 145, 161, 199, 218, 226–28, 230, 236
  /*ḍamaru,* 96, 199
  /*ḍapha,* 81
  /*ḍaur,* 96
  /*ḍhol,* 81, 234
  hourglass, 96, 164, 198–99, 208
  room for, 215, 222, 235
Dudhāni plant, 53
Dudhera, 198*n*
Dudhgaṅgā River, 7
Dumont, Louis, vi, viii, 147
Durgā, Durgāmahiṣāsuramardinī, 56–58, 184
Durgā Devī famine, 153
dvārapāl. *See* Doorkeeper; Guardian deities
Dvārkā, 47

Ecology, ecological conditions, vii, 3–11, 21, 132, 165, 173, 185. *See also* Deforestation; Drought; Forests; Monsoon; Pastures; Rain; Soil
eḍkobā māḷ, eḍkobācā māḷ, 176–77
Ekavvā, 33, 40, 44–45, 66, 192
Ekāyā, Ekkayā (a goddess), 40, 52
Ekkayya (a shepherd boy), 93
Ekorāma, 93
Eksambe, 40, 41*n,* 50*n*
Elanāgireḍḍi, 111–12, 114–16
Elephants, 12, 25, 90, 161, 196*n,* 197, 215
Ellammā (Yeḷammā), 55, 57
Elphinstone, Mountstuart, 165
Elwin, Verrier, 95
English, the, 84, 162*n,* 174, 176, 185. *See also* British rule
Enthoven, R. E., 69–70, 101, 122–24
Epidemics, 182
Equality, 89
Etāl (Vetāḷ), 37
Etymology, folk, 125–27

Faith, 215, 233, 235 *See also bhāv*
Fakir, 216
Famines, 15, 153, 160, 164, 216*n*. *See also* Drought
"Father temple," 25
Ferrymen. *See* Boatsmen
Festivals, 133–35, 177, 196. *See also jatrās;* Pilgrimage festivals; *specific festivals*
Feuds. *See* Disputes
Fifty-two *avatārs,* 201
Fifty-two *bīr, birudeṃ, vīr.* *See bāvan bīr; bāvan birudeṃ; bāvan vīr*
Fifty-two ghosts, 37*n*
Fifty-two magical cult objects, 199
Fifty-two magical sciences, 51, 54–55
Fifty-two spirits or deities, 202
Fig tree. *See* Banyan tree; Vaḍ tree
Film, Marāṭhī, 171
Fire, 233
  circle of, 201
  sacrifice, 20, 24. *See also hom;* Sacrifice, Brahmanical
Fireworks, 227
Fishermen, 69, 75. *See also* Koḷīs
Fitzgerald, Captain, 124, 126
Flags, 190, 199, 205, 222, 227, 236. *See also* Banners
Flagstaff (*niśān*), 199–200
Fleet, 90
Fly whisks. *See cavrīs,* Chowries
Footprints (*pādukās*), 212
Forest tribes, v–vi, viii, 25, 59, 84, 156, 184, 195*n,* 197*n,* 205. *See also* Tribes; *specific tribes*
Forests, vii–viii, 4, 9–10, 12–14, 16, 21, 23, 26, 31, 34, 42, 44–45, 47–50, 52*n,* 58–62, 70, 83–84, 87, 90, 93, 95, 98, 101–4, 106–9, 114–16, 122, 132–33, 136*n,* 154, 156–58, 164–67, 169, 171–72, 174, 176, 183–87, 190, 192–93, 197*n,* 203–6, 217. *See also* Daṇḍakāraṇya; Diṇḍīra forest; Hivar forest; Jungle; Kātar Bilāgī; Nhāī Rūī; *rān*
  deprivations in (*vanvās*), 52*n*
Forts, 19*n,* 88, 100, 155–57, 162*n,* 178
Fortune, 223–24

gaḍagner, 226
Gahinīnāth, 95*n,* 96
Gāikvāḍ(s), 31, 162
  Nandaji, 162*n*
  Pilaji, 162*n*
Gajaliṅg, 201
gaṇas, 50, 184, 203–4
Gaṇḍakī River, 155*n*
"Gandhi cap," 169
Gaṅgā (Ganges) River, 73*n,* 82, 192, 207*n,* 209. *See also* Māṇ River; Pañcgaṅgā River; Pūrṇagaṅgā

Gaṅgāpur Taluka, 7
Gaṅgā-Sūravantī, 191–92. *See also* Gaṅgā; Sūravantī
gāñjā, 52–55, 231–32, 234–35, 238
Gaoli, 124*n*. *See also* Gavḷīs
Gaṇpatī, 32
garbhārā (inner sanctum), 97, 188, 235
Garden land (*bāgāīt*), 59, 158
Garuḍa, 200*n*
Gāthāsaptaśati, 41
Gauḍās, Gāvḍās, 90–91, 93, 110, 113, 127, 163, 178. *See also* Goṇḍas; Hemu Gāvḍā; Malla Bhaire Gauḍa; Nārubā Gâvḍā; Sanna Bhaire Gauḍa
Gaulas, 100. *See also* Ābhīras
Gautamīputra Satakarṇi, 20*n*
Gavḷī Dhangars. *See* Dhangars
Gavḷīs, 9, 23–27, 29, 31–32, 34, 46–48, 50, 56, 60, 84, 86–88, 95, 98, 100–101, 104–6, 122, 124, 147, 155, 162, 166–73, 176, 179–81, 187, 190, 197, 198*n*, 199
  becoming farmers or shepherds, 147, 167
  expulsion of, 166–73
  Kāsar, 105
  Nagarkar, 101–2
  Vajarkar, 101–2
Gavḷṇīs, 47
Gavḷyāncī Undavḍī, 105
gāvuṇḍas, 84, 152, 178
  /Gāvuṇḍasvāmīs, 90
Gāyatrī *mantra*, 208
Gāykvāḍvāḍī, 116
Ghaḍśī(s), 231
  Guravs, 225
ghaṇṭās. *See* Bells
Ghasāḍes, 227
ghaṭasthāpanā, 24*n*, 134
Ghāṭge(s), 159
  Mahādjī, 159
Ghāṭs, Eastern, 8, 108
Ghāṭs, Western, 3–5, 9, 12, 19–21, 69, 76, 83, 101, 104, 125, 131, 167, 174, 179
Ghoḍe Uḍan, Uḍān, Uḍḍāṇ, 76, 98, 197, 210–11, 215–16, 234, 236
ghoḍyācī jatrā, 154
ghoṅgaḍī. *See* Blankets (woolen)
Ghorpaḍī, 234
Ghosts, 37*n*, 86, 139, 143, 184, 193–94, 195*n*, 197*n*, 213. *See also bhutāvaḷ; bhūts;* Khais
  army of, 136
ghoṭā, 234
ghugaryā, 226*n*
Ghuṇes. *See* Bāḷkujī (Ghuṇe); Māljī (Ghuṇe); Pāndojī (Ghuṇe); Śaṅkarājī Ghuṇe; Viṭhojī (Ghuṇe)
Ghurye, G. S., 183
Ginjee. *See* Candī
Giribuvā, 31–32
Gīrjā (Kamaḷā Śinde's wife), 164
Girjā (Pārvatī), 68
Girjā Gāvḍī, 163
Gītā, 215
Go Muni, Gomuni, 189
Goa, 21
goālā, 9
Godāvarī River, 6–7, 19*n*, 20–21, 69, 126, 153–54
Goddesses (*devīs*), 24*n*, 32, 34–68, 70, 151, 171, 185, 204. *See also specific goddesses*
  of disease and death, 39
  mother, 57, 204
  river, 65, 75
  "seven," 40. *See also* Bhivāī; *sāt āsarā;* Seven Āsarās
  of trees, 34–36, 193
  of water, 4*n*, 36–39, 75–77
Gold, 73–74, 98, 191, 222–24
Golden Age. *See* Satya Age
Golden box, 191–92
Golden hair, 192
Golden hare, 160
Golden Jejurī, 193
Golden sheep, golden ram, 112
Golden termite mound, 192
Goldsmiths, 223, 232
Golkondā, 155
Gollas, 8–10, 51, 93*n*, 102–4, 105*n*, 126, 167
  Kāḍu, 102–4
  Ūru, 102
Goṇḍas (Gauḍas), 110
Gondeśvara temple, 100
Gondhaḷ, 236
Gonds, 124
Gongs, 227
gopālā, 9

Gorakhnāth, 95*n*, 96, 136*n*
Gosāvī-buvā (Giribuvā), 32
Gosāvīs, viii, 27, 32, 37, 42, 44, 49–50, 52, 56, 59, 67, 73, 93, 95–98, 136*n*, 146–47, 157, 168–71, 179–81, 183, 198–99, 202–5, 231. *See also* Dāsaris; Ḍauryā Gosāvīs; Kānphaṭā Gosāvīs; Marāṭhā Gosāvīs; Śinde Gosāvīs
  monastic, 96. *See also* Monasteries
govāḷī, 126
Govardhan, *govardhana*, 187–88, 190
Govārīs, Gowārīs, 9, 198*n*
grāmadevatās, 41
grāmjośī (village astrologer), 227
grantha, giranta, 204
Gruel, 226
Guardian deities, 49–50, 85, 97, 108, 183, 185, 197. *See also* Doorkeeper; *kṣetrapāl*
  regional. *See* Khaṇḍobā
  village, 186, 198
Guardian of the fields, 27, 46. *See also* *kṣetrapāl*
Guardians. *See* Watchmen
Guḍḍāppā, 71*n*
Guḍhī Pāḍvā, 133
"Guest gods," 135, 138
Gujarat, 154, 170
Gujarī-Mahāl, 139*n*
Gujars, 185
gulāl powder, 230, 234
Gulbargā, 161
Gulbargā District, 84, 89
Guḷuñce, 167, 177–78
guṇ (power), 223
Guravs, 23–24, 27, 32, 71*n*, 92, 98, 136, 173, 179, 211, 216–18, 226–27, 231–32, 235. *See also* Ghaḍśī(s)
Gurdi, 126
Guru(s), 89, 91–96, 122
gurubheṭ, 94
Gvālas, 9
Gwalior, 139*n*, 163

Haḍagalli, 16
Haḍgaḷḷi-Ballāri, 189*n*
Haider/Haidar Ali, 10, 107
Hākāyā (Ekavvā), 45
Hākes, 139–40, 173
Hākevāḍī, 139, 141
Hakke family, 34
Hāla, 41
haḷaḍ, haḷdī, 39, 141*n*, 163. *See also* *bhaṇḍār;* Turmeric powder
halemaga, 103
Hālumatada Caritra, 92*n*, 93, 95, 110, 114
hāl-vakkalu-makkalu, 91. *See also* Lineage of milk
Hamlet, 94, 98, 225. *See also* *vāḍā, vāḍī; vastī*
Hamsvaḍ, 35
Hāṇḍe Kurubas. *See* Kurubas
Hansur, 10
Hanumān, 177
Haraṇīgāv, 232
Hares, 160–61
  golden, 160
Harivaṃśa, 187
Hashish. *See* *gāñjā*
Hassan Gaṅgu, 161
haṭ, hāṭ, haṭṭī, 127
Hātakanaṅgale Taluka, 72
hāṭakara cattle, 126
Hāṭkar Dhangars. *See* Dhangars
hāṭa/haṭṭi, haṭṭi, 103, 126, 128. *See also* Bār Hatti
Hattikaṅkaṇ Dhangars, Kurubas. *See* Dhangars; Kurubas
Haṭṭikaras. *See* Dhangars
Havelī Taluka, 4, 40, 98, 116, 147, 152
Head and trunk worshiped separately, 25*n*
Heath. *See* *māḷ*
Heath of Father Ram (*eḍkobā[cā] māḷ*), 176–77
Heggaḍe, 106, 108
Hemāḍ-Pant style, temples, 19*n*, 86, 100, 121, 151–54, 164, 170
Hemādri, Hemāḍ-Pant, Hemāḍī Paṇḍita, 151, 153
Hemu Gāvḍā, 163
Hero stones, 15, 25, 71*n*, 84, 152–53, 178, 203. *See also* Śaiva hero cults; *vīragaḷas*
Heroes, 101, 152, 154, 195*n*, 202–3
Hidimbā, 108
Hierarchy, caste. *See* Caste system
Highway robbers, 15, 155, 174–75. *See also* Robbers
Hill tribes, 16. *See also* Tribes
Hills. *See* Mountain(s)

Himjavḍī, 180, 187, 198
Hindustan, 126
Hingoli, 126
Hirēvūru, 93
Hiryā, 80
Hivar forest, 44, 189
Hivar trees, 142, 193, 211–12
Hoḷ, 162
Holārs, 140, 145
Hoḷī, 128, 134–35, 163. *See also* Śiṃgā
Hoḷkar(s), 161–62, 224, 235
  Tukojī, 83
hom, 24, 143. *See also* Fire, sacrifice
Hookah, 227, 231–32, 235–36
Hopkins, Thomas J., 171*n*
Horns, 157, 214, 227–28, 236
Horoscope, 146*n*. *See also* Astrologer, *pañcāṅg*
Horses, 12, 51, 54–55, 60, 86, 90, 98–99, 113, 124*n,* 154, 164–65, 176, 179, 184, 187*n,* 190, 193, 195–98, 215–17, 220. *See also* Ghoḍe Uḍan; Votive figures
  and horsemen, 164, 176, 199, 216–17, 224, 228–29
Hoysaḷas, 100
Hubli-Dhārvāḍ, 9
huīk. *See* Prophecy
Huljantī, 123, 138
Hultkrantz, A., vii
Hunnūr, 121, 128
Hunters, and hunting, 45, 69, 123–25, 134, 157, 160–61, 184, 196–97, 217
hurḍā, 94
Hyderabad, 8
Hyderabad State, 28
Hyderabad-Karnatak, 84

Ibrahim Adil Śāh, 159
Idaiyans, 10, 157*n*. *See also Iṭaiyaṉ*
Identification of a god, 147–50, 187
"Idlers' Square," 227
Immigrants. *See also* Migration
  taking over the caste name and/or occupation of their predecessors, 105, 167
  taking over a cult, 177
Impurity, 52, 89–90, 114, 133*n,* 144*n,* 180, 196*n,* 198, 209. *See also* Pollution; Purification
ināmdārs, 107
Ināmgāv, 45
Incarnation, 24–25, 27, 216. *See also avatār*
Incense, 226
Indāpūr, 96, 104, 152, 171
Indāpur Taluka, 49*n,* 87, 152
Indarśākā, 31
Indore, 161, 162*n,* 225
Indore District, 162
Indra, 139, 188, 200*n*
  King, 174
Indrasabhā, 139
Indrāyanī River, 50*n*
Inscriptions, 22–23, 93, 100, 151*n,* 235
Integrity (*satva*), 37–38, 216
Intersections. *See* Crossroads
Irānnā, 51
Iriḍige land, 21
Iron Age. *See* Kali Age
Iron chains (*laṅgar*), 134
Irrigation, 4, 6–9, 167, 170–71, 180. *See also* Nirā Canal(s)
iṣṭaliṅga. *See liṅgams*
Īśvar, Īsvar,Īśvara, 52, 207*n,* 215, 219. *See also* Śiva
Iṭaiyaṉ, Iṭaiyars, *iṭaiyar,* 10, 13–14, 157*n*. *See also* Idaiyans
  iṭaicciyar, 14
Iṭhu, 77, 80–82
  /Iṭhubā, 135
  /Iṭubā, 137
Iṭṭhal, 35–37, 40, 72*n,* 74, 106, 113–14, 116–21, 123, 190
Iyer, Anantakrishna, 102–4

jāḍ, 74*n*. *See also* Blankets (woolen)
Jagadekamalla, 21
Jagdambā, 153–54
jāgīr, 161–62, 165
jagīrdārs, 84
jāgṛt deities, holy places, temples, 23, 71*n,* 152, 210
  /*sākṣāt jāgṛt,* 25
Jainas, 22, 50*n,* 90, 92*n,* 101, 121, 154, 184*n*
Jaipur, 185
Jakāppā Caugule, 35–36, 117–18, 120
Jākhābāī, 31
Jākhāī, 31, 32
Jālandharnāth, 95*n*
Jalgaon District, 7

Jamadagni, 55
jāmbhūḷ tree, fruits, 193–94
Jamdaḍes, 213, 215, 218–19, 221
jamīndārs, 178–79
Jāmkheḍ Taluka, 6
Janābāī (Jānāī), 37, 74
Jānāī, 31, 36, 40, 74
Jaṅgamas, 88–89, 94, 108, 110, 122, 146. *See also* Viraktas
  sāmānya, 89
Jānu, Jānubāī, Jānūcandanī (Jānāī), 37–38
Jānyā Sutār, 35–36
Jasmine, 13, 34
Jath, 33, 58
Jath plateau, 7
Jath Taluka, 5, 33, 58, 60, 164, 209*n*
jātī ("caste"), 226*n*
jatrās, 26, 44, 75–76, 135, 141, 154, 182, 204, 220, 225, 234*n,* 236. *See also* *āhare jatrā;* Pilgrimage festivals
Jāts, 124*n*
Jāvkāī, 49
Jāvḷī, 39, 97, 122, 131, 171–72, 179, 189, 204, 210
Jejurī, 40, 60, 61*n,* 67, 76*n,* 85, 96, 98, 125, 131, 136, 141*n,* 145, 161, 162*n,* 164, 166–67, 173–74, 180–81, 187, 193, 196, 199, 204, 237
Jeūr, 133*n,* 147, 235
jhāḍ, devācī, 193. *See also* Possession
Jhagaḍes, 177
Jhare, 27
Jhirāpvāḍī, 127, 167–68
jhoḷī (magical begging bag), 53, 55
jivant dev. See jāgṛt deities
Jñāneśvar, 47, 96
Jñāneśvarī, 163*n*
Jogaḍā, 59, 233
Jogāī (Jogeśvarī), 27, 31–32, 50, 56, 60, 183–84, 187
Jogavā (Jogeśvarī), Āmbyācī, 40
Jogayya, 93
Jogeśvarī, 27–29, 40, 49, 58–60, 99, 146, 172, 177, 197, 213. *See also* Jogāī; Jogubāī; Yogeśvarī
  Ādimāyā Śrī, 225
  Ambā, 28
Jogī (*yogī*), 59
Jogubāī (Jogeśvarī), 27, 56, 58–59
jondhaḷā, 94
jovārī, 7–8, 226*n*
Juglahs, 85
Jungle, viii, 8, 49, 69, 98, 109, 158, 160, 166–67, 173, 175–76, 195*n. See also* Forests
Junjappa, Jinjuppa, 103–4
Junnar, 20
Junnar Taluka, 4, 47
Jyotibā, 184, 201
jyotiliṅga, jyotirliṅg, 96, 219*n. See also* *specific jyotiliṅgas*

Kaḍak Lakṣmī, 39, 57
Kāḍu Gollas, Kurubas. *See* Gollas, Kurubas
kafīyat, 157
Kāgal, 35
Kaikāḍīs, 121
Kailās, Kailāsa, 80, 111–12, 114
Kāḷā Pīparyā pool, 43
Kalacuris, 21–22, 25, 111, 199
Kāḷambā, 35
Kālamukhas, 203
Kaḷas, 87, 171
Kāḷāsura, the demon Kāḷ, 24, 26
Kāḷavā (Kāḷubāī), Sirsaṅgīcī, 40
Kāḷbhairav, 23–27, 31–32, 50–60, 96–99, 164, 180, 183, 198, 200, 203–5, 207–10, 213, 216. *See also* Bhairav
  /Kālabhairava, 94
  /Kāḷbhairī, 53–54
  Mhaskobā, 210
Kālī, Kālikā, 40, 57
Kali Age, 38, 45, 74–75
  /Iron Age, 149
Kalīśā, 116–18, 121
kallākkōvalar, kōvalar, 13–14
Kallāṭaṉār, 15
Kalleśvar (Kalīśā), 116*n,* 121
Kāḷubāī, 40, 48–49
Kalyāṇa, Kalyāṇapaṭṇam, 111–12, 114–16
Kalyāṇī, 21–22, 92
Kāmābāī, Kāmādevī, 44–45, 204
Kāmadhenū, 209
Kamaḷā Śinde (Śid, Siddha), 128, 164
Kamaḷājī (Kamaḷā Siddha, Kamaḷasīd, Kamaḷasiddha), 136, 182, 210–16, 227
Kamaḷākara Bhaṭṭa, 218*n*
Kāmbaḷeśvar, 36, 75–76
kāmbḷī. See Blankets (woolen)
Kānadās, 126

Kanāī, 40
Kanakāmā, 44
Kanarese kings, 89
Kānārvāḍī, 194
Kāṉavar, 12
Kañcavīras, 202
Kāñcīpuram, 156
Kandārī, 92*n*, 97–98
Kandāsura, Kanda, 92*n*, 98
Kanherkheḍ, 163
Kanhobā, 167
Kanīphnāth, 95*n*
Kānphaṭā Gosāvīs, 27, 95, 97, 172, 198, 202–3
kaṇyaghugryā, 140
kapāla, 199
Kāpālikās, 181, 199, 203
Kapila muni, 189
kapila cow, Kapilī (black cow), 87, 170
Kāpus, 108–9, 111–12
Karahāṭaka (Karhāḍ), 20*n*, 185
Kārande, 97
Karañje, 169–70
Karavīr, Karavīra, 20*n*, 42*n*. *See also* Kolhāpūr
Karavīr Taluka, 152
Karḍāpī, 168
Karhā River, 7, 21, 49*n*, 50, 75, 82, 85, 125, 131, 151, 166, 173, 180–81, 192
Karhāḍ, 19*n*, 20–21, 23–25, 41, 185, 235
Karhāḍ Taluka, 33, 121
Karhāṭa (Karhāḍ), 21
Karjat Taluka, 6
Kārle, 20
Karma, 222
Karmāḷā, 97
Karmāḷā Taluka, 6
Karnatak, v, 3, 5–6, 8–9, 16, 21, 40, 44, 47, 50*n*, 60, 84, 88, 90–91, 93, 94*n*, 102, 103*n*, 104, 106–7, 109, 112, 119, 121, 147, 152*n*, 153–54, 164, 184*n*, 187, 189–90, 195–96, 199, 201, 203
Kārttik (month), 24, 46, 88
Kārttikeya, 17, 41*n*
Karvé, Iravati, x, 162*n*
Kāsāīs, 123
Kāsar Gavḷīs. *See* Gavḷīs
Kāsārambolī, 49–50
Kāsegāv, 74
Kāśī, 27, 30, 51, 54, 73*n*, 82, 99, 209–10. *See also* Banaras, Vārāṇasī
"Kāśī" (Sonārī), 179
Kāśīliṅg Birāppā, 42, 44, 190, 202
Kāśīviśvanāth, 25. *See also* Viśvanāth, Viśveśvara
Kātar Bilāgī, forest of, 42
Kāṭecīvāḍī, 136, 141–42
Kathanna, 51
kāṭhīs, 199–200, 218. *See also* Poles
Kātkarīs, 86
Kātraj Ghāṭ, 174
Kauṇḍiṇya *ṛṣi*, 121
kāvaḍ, 32, 162, 189
Kavaḍes, 234
Kāvēri River, 15–16
Kavlapūr, 41
Kerala, 58
Ketakī tree, 209
Kevaḍā (ketakī) flower, 209
Khair tree, 192
Khaires, 177
Khairevāḍī, 177*n*
Khais, 143–44
Khambāṭkī Ghāṭ, 174
Khānapūr (Mailārpūr, Pember, Prempūr), 155
Khānapūr (Sangli District), 189*n*
Khānapūr plateau, 7
Khānapur Taluka, 5, 27, 30, 122, 128, 152
Khaṇḍaka (Khaṇḍobā), 185
Khaṇḍāḷa Mahāl, 137, 159*n*
Khaṇḍāḷā Taluka, 34, 173
Khandālī, 26
Khāṇḍerājurī, 86*n*
Khaṇḍerāyā (Khaṇḍobā), 174
Khāndeś, 8, 86, 100, 126, 165*n*, 226, 234
Khandesh, East, 7
Khandesh, West, 7
Khaṇḍobā, vii, 16, 26, 47, 58, 60–67, 70, 76*n*, 77, 84–85, 88, 91–92, 98, 106, 109, 116, 124–25, 132–36, 138, 154–55, 159, 161–62, 164, 174, 180, 183–87, 189, 192–93, 195–201, 203–6, 219*n*, 237
  connected with the sun, 125, 192–93. *See also* Mārtaṇḍa Bhairava
  as a god of war, 125
  as territorial guardian of Maharashtra, 125, 198

Khaṇḍojī Vīrkar, 162
Khān-Māṇ Deś, 118, 189
Kharaspiṇḍī, 31
Khare, G. H., 23*n*
Kharias, 192*n*
khārīk (dry date), 79*n*
Kharsuṇḍī, 22, 29–34, 43, 56, 58, 97, 162, 180
Kharsuṇḍī-Śīd, 31, 58
kharvas, 30–31
Khaṭāv, 159
Khaṭāv Taluka, 5, 33, 151, 170
Khaṭāvkars, 117*n*
Khāṭīks, 123, 133*n*. *See also* Dhangars; Muslim(s)
Kheḍ Taluka, 47, 162
Kheḍbudruk, 34, 173
kheḷ, 78*n,* 137–38, 140, 142–45, 194*n*
Khilārī cattle, 33, 104, 127–29, 178–79, 182
Khilārī Dhangars. *See* Dhangars
Khilubā (Khilu Rājā, Khilubā *bhakta,* Khilurājā), 36–39, 42, 72–75, 113–14, 123
Khuldābād Mahāl, 7
Khuṭekar Dhangars. *See* Dhangars
Kiklī, 152
Killing (of people), 175, 193–94, 213. *See also* Sacrifice, human
  of a Brahman, 209
Kincaid, C. A., 163
Kingship, vi
Kirloskarvāḍī, 202
Kisnā (Kṛṣṇā) River, 77–80, 82–83, 189
  /Kisnā Bāī, 80
Koḍi-Mañcenahalli, 157
Koḍīt, 215, 219–20, 222, 225–26, 233
Kolaba District, 21, 169, 187
Kolar, Kolār, 9, 156
Kolāras, 139*n*
Kole, 33
Kolhāpūr, 9, 20–21, 24, 32, 40–41, 72, 91–92, 106–7, 113, 116, 152, 190, 197. *See also* Karavīr
  Mahārājā of, 113
Kolhapur District, 3, 5, 33, 42, 72, 164–65, 190
Kolhāpūrcī Ambikā, 40
Kolhāṭaṇīs, 236
Koḷīs, 35–36, 69–84, 95, 156, 173–74, 179. *See also* Vālhyā Koḷī
  assimilation of, 83
  connection with Birobā, 77–83
  Mahādev, 69–70, 75
  Malhār, 69–70, 84
  Son, 69
  traditional Indian policy toward, 83
kōlkar, 103
Kolvadī (Paṭṭan Kuḍolī), 73
Koḷvihire, 61, 173–79
  /Koḷ-Vihīre, 175
Kōn̲, Kōn̲ān̲, 157*n*
Konars, 157*n*
Konāsūr, 201
Koṇḍanpūr, 40, 56
Koṇḍbhaṭ Thiṭe, Koṇḍbhaṭ, 232–33
Koṇḍev, Dādājī, 165
Koṅkaṇ, the, 3, 19, 21, 34, 51, 69, 86, 96, 104–5, 126–28, 132, 134–38, 140, 142, 153, 166, 169, 180*n,* 182–83, 187, 189
  fourteen-part, 189
Kon̲n̲ūr, 201
korḍā (whip), 200
Koregāv Mūḷ, Koregāv-Muḷā, 19*n,* 152
Koregāv Taluka, 5, 163
Korkūs, 68
Kor̲r̲avai, 18, 85
Kosala, 20
Kosambi, D. D., vi, x, 4*n,* 20*n,* 26, 45, 67, 72, 76*n,* 77*n*
Kota, 90*n*
Koṭeśvar, 24
kotvāl, 198, 209
kōvalar (kallākkōvalar), 13–14
Koynā River, 4, 82, 122, 167
Kṛṣṇa, 17, 45–46, 71, 104, 167, 172*n,* 185, 187–88, 190
Kṛṣṇā (Krishna) River, 5, 7–8, 21, 24, 165, 189. *See also* Kisnā River
Kṛṣṇadevarāyā, 157
Kṛṣṇaite Viṭhobā, 172. *See also* Vaiṣṇava Viṭhobā
Kṛṣṇarāja I, 19*n*
Kṛttikās, 17, 41*n*
"Kṣatriyaization," vi, 205
kṣetra, viii, 95, 107, 145, 198
kṣetrapāl, 27, 183, 184*n,* 188*n,* 197*n*

kṣudradevatā, 200
Kuḍuvakkaligas, 94, 113*n*
kuḷkarṇī, 162*n,* 225
kuḷsvāmīs (family gods), 135–36, 138, 141, 143, 161, 167–68, 179, 181, 205, 217
Kumāra, 183, 206. *See also* Skanda
Kuṇbīs, 69, 95, 104–5, 124, 163, 167, 173, 179, 204, 210, 233
Kuṇḍal, 120, 122*n,* 148
kuṅkum, 45, 115, 137*n,* 163, 227
kuraṇ, 173. *See also* Pasture(s)
kuravai dance, 14, 17
Kuṟavars, 12, 16, 106
Kurbattyavva, Kurubattyavva, 60, 106
kuṟiñci (mountain landscape), 12, 14–17
Kurkhumb, 49*n*
Kurnool, 111
Kurnool District, 8, 93*n,* 111
Kurubas, 9–10, 40, 41*n,* 43, 50*n,* 60, 88, 91, 93, 105–16, 121–22, 187, 190, 195–96, 203*n,* 204
  Āṇḍe/Hāṇḍe, 107, 121
  etymology of, 106
  Hattikaṅkaṇ, 9, 107–13
  Kāḍu, 106, 108
  Oḍeru, 122
  Uṇṇikaṅkaṇ, 9, 107–13
  Ūru, 106–7
  vaḍaḍ (Oḍeru?), 122
Kurumas, 9, 109
  unni (wool), 109
Kurundvāḍ-Śiroḷ, 5
Kurvinal, 51
Kuśāṇā reliefs, 20
Kusumbal, 187

Lāds, 153
Lakade, Sakharam B., x
Lakḍe(s), 136, 168, 172–73, 176–80
  Bhāgū, 172
  Dhangars, 177
  Field, 176
Lakḍevāḍī, 163*n*
Lakṣmaṇ, 103
Lakṣmī, 39–40, 46, 141, 168*n,* 223. *See also* Kaḍak Lakṣmī; Mahālakṣmī
Lakṣmīāī, 39, 57, 168
Lalaī trees, 189
Lamāṇīs, 153, 183
Lambāḍīs, 153
Lamp pillars, 222–23, 235. *See also dīpmāḷs*
Lamps, oil, 177
  waving trays of, 226–27. *See also āratī*
Landscapes, five, in Caṅkam literature, vii, 11–19
  deities of, 16–18
laṅgar (iron chain), 134
laṅgoṭī, 145. *See also* Loincloth
Laṅkā, 85
Lapis lazuli stones, 115
Laptaḷ's Meadow, 216–17
Laṭṭalūra (Lāṭūr), 21
Lāṭūr, 21, 154
Lāṭūr Taluka, 6
Lāṭyā, 73–74
Left Hand Canal. *See* Nirā Canal(s)
līlā, līḷā, 71*n,* 119, 220
Limbā Koḷī, Limbā Bābā, 78–82
Limbājī Pāṭīl Dhumāḷ, 235
Limbājī Tāmbe (Dhangar), 235
Liṃbavḍe, 43, 66*n,* 164
Limbgāv, 77–78
Limbūt (Nimbūt?), 177
Limbyā, 145
Limbyā Koḷī, 73–74
Lineage of milk (*hāl-vakkalu-makkalu*), 91, 94, 110
liṅgams, liṅgas, 23*n,* 31, 71*n,* 88–89, 92*n,* 93, 112, 114–15, 121–22, 139, 142, 160*n,* 162, 186, 190, 205. *See also bāṇa; jyotiliṅga;* Kāśīliṅg Birāppa
  /iṣṭaliṅga, 91
Liṇgāyat(s), 22, 30, 35, 67, 88–95, 107, 110, 112, 114–17, 121–22, 137, 146–47, 195, 200, 203, 205
  artisan castes, 121
  carpenters, 35
  merchants, 153
  priests, viii, 88–90, 146, 200. *See also* Jaṅgamas
  pūrva-ācāryas, 93
  saints, 107
  Tirāḷes, 121
  Vāṇīs, 88, 91, 235. *See also* Vāṇīs
Liṅguśā Pāṭīl, 117–20
Lions, 188
Lohatīrtha, 99
Loincloth, 145*n,* 224. *See also laṅgoṭī*

Loṇī, 194–95
Loṇī (Lonikand), 183
Loṇī Bāpkar, forest of, 193
Loṭevāḍī, 26, 32, 57

Macchindarnāth, Macchindranāth, 95*n*, 96
Mackintosh, Captain A., 69, 84–85
madār (Muslim gravestone), 120, 135
Māḍhā Taluka, 72, 73*n*, 113, 123
Mādharīputra Īśvarasena, 100
Madhya Pradesh, 67, 139*n*
Madnes, 168–69
Madurai, 196*n*
māge jāṇārā, 202*n*
māge[ṃ] mhaṇāre, 77*n*
Māgh (month), 41, 46, 67, 134, 145–46, 214–15, 218, 225–26, 229–30, 233, 236–37
Māgh Pūrṇimā, 134
Magic, magical, 182, 188. *See also* Miracles
  bag. *See* Bag, magical begging (*jhoḷī*)
  cult objects, fifty-two, 199
  danger, 180–81, 200, 212. *See also* Witchcraft
  healing, 103
  powers, 42–43, 51, 115, 146
  tricks, 119
  words. *See mantras*
Mahābaḷeśvar (place), 3, 92*n*
Mahābaḷeśvar (Śiva), 92*n*
Mahābaḷeśvar Mahāl, 92*n*
Mahābaḷi, 92*n*
Mahābhārata, 188
Mahāḍ, 169
Mahādev, 70, 75, 78*n*, 86*n*, 94, 105, 125*n*, 132, 201, 205. *See also* Śaṅkar; Śiva
Mahādev Koḷīs. *See* Koḷīs
Mahādev mountains, 3, 69
Mahādū (Gavḷī), 170
Mahādū, Mahādyā, 144. *See also* Mhānvars
Mahākāl, 51–52, 164
Mahākālī, 43
Mahāl, 159
Mahālakṣmī, 40
M(ah)āldār, 117*n*. *See also* Somā Mahāldār
Mahāmāyūrī Mantra, 185, 195
Mahānubhāv sect, 70*n*, 71*n*
mahā-purusha, 157
Mahārāj (god), 28, 149, 231, 235
Māhārṇvar(s) (Mhānvars), 178
  Malhārjī, 178*n*
Mahārs, 84, 121, 216*n*
Māhātmyas, 195*n*, 203–4. *See also specific Māhātmyas*
Mahiṣa (Mahiṣāsura), 58
Mahiṣāsura, 23, 26, 37, 56–57, 180, 186. *See also* Buffalo demon; Mahiṣa; Mhaiśāsur; Mhaśā
Mahiṣavāḍā (Mhasvaḍ), 23
Māhud, 26, 33, 96
Māhulī (Sangli District), 152
Māhulī (Satara District), 151
Maidān, 9
Mailār (god), Mailāra, 16, 60, 106, 109, 154–55, 189, 202, 206
Mailār (place), 189
Mailār Devaraguḍḍa, 196
Mailārpūr, 155
mājaṇeṃ, 231
Makar Saṅkrānt, 134
māḷ, 5, 7, 116, 123, 125, 154, 176, 187, 195*n*, 212
  eḍkobā(cā), 176–77
māḷ (day of the Navrātra festival), 215
Māḷāī, 31, 40
Ma̱ḷavars, 14–15, 18
Māḷavḍī, 158–61
Māḷegāv, 155
Malhār, Malhārī (Khaṇḍobā), 70, 77, 91
  /–Khaṇḍobā, 70
Malhār Koḷīs. *See* Koḷīs
Malik Ambar, 166
Māḷīs, 5, 23, 34, 84, 132, 169, 173–74, 176–77, 179, 182–83, 204, 210, 212–13, 217, 225–27. *See also* Sakhārāmbovā Pāṇḍhare Māḷī; Sāvtā Māḷī
Māḷjī (Ghuṇe), 216, 222–25, 235
Malla (demon), 91–92, 201. *See also* Maṇi
Malla (rulers' epithet), 195*n*
Malla Bhaire Gauḍa, 156–57
Mallanna, 16, 106, 109, 184, 206
Mallāppā, 91
Mallārī (Khaṇḍobā), 91–92, 98, 195*n*
Mallārī Māhātmya, 91, 189, 195
mallas (wrestlers), 176, 195*n*. *See also* Wrestling matches
Mallaya, Mallayya, 91–93, 154, 189
Malleś, 91

Malli, 195*n*
Mallikārjuna, 16, 72, 93*n*, 115, 184, 206
Mallināth, 91
Mallus, 195*n*
Malnāḍ, 9, 106
māḷrān, 166, 169, 177. *See also rān*
Māḷśiras, 164, 171
Māḷśiras Taluka, 26, 61, 86, 151–52
Mālu, 170
Malu Gavḷaṇ, 87
Mālū Tāraṇa Graṃtha, 70
Mālvā, 94*n*, 164
Māḷvāḍī (Māḷavḍī), 159
Māmaṃjī, 214
Māmledār, 229
mān, 34, 36, 75, 85, 117, 146, 200, 215, 219, 221–22, 225. *See also* Right of worship, honorary
mānkarīs, 121, 128, 164, 179, 225, 227
Māṇ River, 7, 21–24, 84, 118*n*, 122, 128, 131, 158–59, 163, 189*n*
Māṇ Taluka, 5, 75, 122
Māṇdeś, 7, 84, 118
Māṇḍhardev, 40, 48
Māṇe family, 30, 124*n*, 173
maṅgaḷāṣṭaka verses, 60, 146, 227
Maṅgaḷavāḍ (Maṅgaḷveḍhā), 21
Maṅgaḷveḍhā, 21–22, 27, 71*n*, 105, 216*n*
Maṅgaḷveḍhā Taluka, 57*n*, 121, 123, 128, 138
Māṇgāv Taluka, 187
Mango trees, and boughs, 15, 63, 133
Māṅgobā, 30
Maṅgrāvaḷ Pāṭīl, 47
Māṅgs, 84, 86, 121, 200
Maṇi (demon), 91–92, 189*n*, 195, 201
  etymology of, 189*n*
  Maṇimalla, 193, 195
Maṇicul mountain, 201
Maṇmailāra, Maṇmailāra Mandir, 189*n*
maṇṇāppā dev, 189
Maṇṇumailāra, 189*n*
mansab, 159
mantras, 66, 188, 193–94, 200. *See also* Gāyatrī *mantra*
mārāmārī, 230
Marāṭhā Gosāvīs, 96
Marāṭhās, 23, 42, 48, 69, 104–5, 121, 123–24, 137, 139, 152–53, 155, 157–59, 162–65, 167–68, 170, 173, 177–79, 182, 190, 196–97, 199, 210, 219, 233–34, 236
Marāṭhī, development of, 151
Marāṭhvāḍā, 105, 154
Maravḍe, 57*n*
Mārgaśīrṣa (month), 33, 154–55, 237
Margosa tree, 18
Mariāī, Marīāī, Marībāī, Marīmāī, 27–28, 30, 34, 39–40, 57, 141
Marīammā, 25*n*. *See also* Yeḷammā
Mārkaṇḍeya *ṛṣi*, 208
Markets, 90, 97, 127, 229. *See also* Bazaars; Cattle, markets; Merchants; Trade
Marriage, weddings, v, 27–29, 56, 58–68, 89*n*, 90, 92, 93*n*, 96, 99, 108–11, 122–23, 132, 135, 141, 146, 168, 179, 183, 191, 203–4, 215, 219, 225, 227
  by abduction, 60
  child, 89
  and extramarital relations, 107
  gandharva, 60
  and *haḷdī* day, 141
  hypogamous (*pratiloma*), 109
  inter–, 112, 128
  rakṣasa, 60
  and unmarried boys, 214
  and widow remarriage, 89
Marriott, McKim, 174
Mārtaṇḍa Bhairava, 60, 189, 192, 199, 201, 206. *See also* Khaṇḍobā; Sun; Sūrya
  /Mārtaṇḍa, 125
Mārtaṇḍeśvara, 192*n*
Maruḷa, Māruḷasiddha, 93–94, 111
marutam (river valley), 15
Māruti, 177, 201
Masā, Masāī (Mhasā, Mhasāī), 30, 34, 45–47
  /Masādevī, 46
masaṇ(~n)/mhasaṇ(~n) (smaśāna), 168, 181
Masan Buvā, Masan Vīr, 168
Maśāsur (Mahiṣāsura), 37
Masi Reddi, 108
Mask (*mukhavṭā*), 104, 213
Maskobā (Mhaskobā), 181*n*, 210, 217, 224–25
  Śrī Nāth, 231
Masur, 121
Mate, M. S., 46, 139*n*
Mathurā, 45, 101, 185, 187

Mātṛkās, 99
mauṇḍ (measure of weight), 111
Māvaḷ, the, 4, 20, 34, 40, 47, 49–50, 56, 62–63, 83, 145, 153, 157, 160, 162*n*, 165, 179*n*, 182, 186, 192
  Pavana, 162*n*
Māvaḷ Taluka, 35, 47
mavaḷā-devī, māvalyā, 4*n*, 30
māyā (illusion), 207*n*
māyā (magic), 188
Māyā (policeman), 80
Māyabā, 147, 180
Māyājī, Māyājī Meṇḍhaka, 147, 202
Māyakkā, 43
Māyaṇī, 33, 151
Māyāppā, 202
Māyārāṇī, 44
Māyā-Śakti, 24. *See also* Ādimāyā
Māyavvā, 33, 40–44, 66, 128, 192, 202
Māyī, 107
Māyōṉ, 16–17
mekh-mogarī, 199, 236
Memorial stones, 71*n*, 138–39. *See also* Ancestor shrines; Hero stones; *satī* stones; *vīragaḷas*
Meṇḍhaka Māyājī (Māyājī), 202
Meṇḍhe Dhangars. *See* Dhangars
Menstruation, 82, 144*n*, 229
Merchants, 15, 26, 39, 73–74, 85, 88–92, 96–97, 153–54, 229–30. *See also* Liṅgāyat(s), Vāṇīs; Trade; Vāṇīs; Vīra-Baṇañjas
  as bankers, 96–97
  caravans of, 88, 154
  cattle, 154. *See also* Cattle, markets
Meyer, J. J., viii, 200
Mhaiman Gaḍ, 87
Mhaiśāsur, 23, 27. *See also* Buffalo demon; Mahiṣāsura; Mhaśā
Mhākavvā (Māyavvā), 66–67
Mhākāyā, Mhākkayā, 40, 45, 52
Mhākubāī, 41, 43–45
Mhāliṅgrāyā Māḷāppā, 8*n*, 43, 123, 138
Mhāḷsā, 47, 60, 67, 91–92, 204
Mhāluṅg, 152
Mhaṅkāḷ, 51. *See also* Dhuḷi Mahāṅkāḷ; Ujanī Maṅkhāḷ
Mhānvars, 136, 139–42, 178
  various, 139–42
Mhaśā, 23, 27. *See also* Buffalo demon; Mahiṣāsura; Mhaiśāsur
mhaśā (male buffalo), 104
Mhāsā, Mhasāī, 30, 32, 34, 43–47
Mhasāīcīvāḍī, 30, 32, 43–44, 67
Mhasan Buvā. *See* Masan Buvā
Mhasāsūr (Mahiṣāsura), 180, 186, 200
Mhaskar/Mhaske Dhangars. *See* Dhangars
Mhaske(s) (surname), 167
Mhaske, K. B., 23*n*
Mhaskobā, vii, ix, 33, 51, 55–59, 76*n*, 85, 96, 132, 135–36, 143, 145–47, 177, 180–86, 188, 193, 196–98, 200–206, 210, 213*n*, 219*n*, 220, 235
Mhasobā, 26–27, 32, 46, 50, 56–57, 85, 104, 141, 167–68, 180–83, 186, 197*n*. *See also mukāmhasobā*
Mhasobāvāḍī, 104
Mhasojī Gavḷī, 23–24
Mhasvaḍ, 22-27, 29–34, 39–40, 42–44, 50, 67, 89–90, 92*n*, 97, 105, 118*n*, 124*n*, 135, 143, 145, 151, 164, 171, 182, 189, 197, 204, 210
Mhasvaḍ-Śid, Mhasvaḍśid, Mhasvaḍ-Siddha, Mhasvaḍ-Siddhobā, 23–26, 51, 92*n*, 135, 164, 184, 193, 202, 210. *See also* Nāth; Siddhanāth; Siddheśvara; Siddhobā
Mhat(~s)obā, 180, 187, 198
Mhātyrāī, 76*n*
Mhāyā, 71*n*
mhoryā, 202*n*
Microliths, prehistoric, 123, 173
Migration and transhumance, 14, 40, 51, 72, 78*n*, 86, 90, 96, 103–5, 107, 112–13, 126–27, 132, 134, 137–39, 144*n*, 158, 169, 171, 179. *See also* Nomadic life; Nomads
  routes, 72, 90, 113, 138
Military campaigns, expeditions, 30, 158, 184. *See also* War, warfare
Military leaders, 107
Militiamen, 106
Milk, 91, 94, 104–5, 108, 110, 144, 149–50, 173, 188, 190. *See also* Cow(s); Lineage of milk
Millet, 5, 9, 12–13, 19, 21, 151. *See also bājrī; jondhaḷā; jovārī*
Mīnīnāth, 95*n*

Miracles, 176, 181, 211, 218, 220, 223, 228, 231–35, 237. *See also* Magic
and miraculous power, 237
Miraj, 73–74, 91–92
Miraj Taluka, 86*n*, 152
mirdhā, mirdhin, 61*n*
Mirrors, 200, 230
Moghulaī, 194
mola (measure of land), 110
Mominabad, 40
Monasteries
Buddhist, 20, 48*n*
Gosāvīs', 27, 32*n*, 96
Liṅgāyat, 89
Mondays, 26, 64, 125, 134, 168, 236. *See also* Somvatī Amāvāsyā
Monsoon, vii, 3–7, 19, 21, 32, 59, 72, 82*n*, 85–86, 101, 113, 125, 127, 131–32, 138–39, 166–67, 170, 173, 182. *See also* Rain
"break of the," 125
camp, 125, 127, 139, 166–67
Moon, 66, 75, 125, 192–93, 214, 227, 230, 236*n*
Morasu Vakkaligas, 156
morcel, 199, 222, 234. *See also* Peacock feather(s)
More family, 178
Morgāv, 168, 178
Mountain(s). *See also specific mountain ranges*
and hills, vii, 3, 7, 12–13, 16–17, 31, 51, 69, 78, 91–92, 125, 128, 131–32, 154, 165, 168, 186–90, 195*n*, 196, 201, 205
spirits, 92, 185–87
tribes, 12. *See also* Tribes; *specific tribes*
Mounts, 92, 104, 181. *See also vāhanas*
Mhasobā's, 104
Yama's, 181
mṛṇmaya dev, Mṛṇmaya Mallārī, 189
Muḍḍāppā, 110
Muḍḍavvā, 110
Muddaya, 94
Muddugoṇḍa, 93
Muḍhal, 135
Mughals, 74, 155, 157, 159, 218
Muhammad Śāh, 19*n*
mukāmhasobā, 186*n*
mukhavṭā, 104, 213
mukuṭas, 197, 199
Mūlā River (tributary of the Bhimā), 7
Muḷā River (tributary of the Godāvarī), 20
Mulaka land, 20
mullai (pastureland), 13–17
Muḷśī, 200
Muḷśī Taluka, 47, 180, 200
Munnimodakamānu, 111–12
murheṃ, 4
Mūrti Moḍhve, 152, 178
mūrtis, 23, 25, 42, 46, 50, 125, 140, 164, 176–77, 186*n*, 189, 193, 194*n*, 197–99, 201, 205, 213*n*
Murukaṉ, 16–18, 91, 106, 183–84, 188*n*, 196, 200*n*, 205–6
Musical instruments, 115, 227–28, 234. *See also* Band; Drums; Gongs; Horns
Muskets, 218. *See also* Rifles
Muski, 126
Muslim(s), 36, 120–21, 123, 133*n*, 135, 138, 153, 155, 161–62, 167, 171, 196, 228
gravestone (*madār*), 120, 135
Khāṭīks, 123
saints, 120–21, 196*n*. *See also dargā; pīrs*
Mutes, 93–94, 186
Muṭhā River, 7
Mutrāya, 104
Muttala plant, 110
Mysore, 9–10, 102, 154, 156–57
Mythology, *purāṇic*. *See purāṇic* mythology

Nāgābāī, 37–38
Nāgāī, 40
nāgalok, 112
Nāgambā, 92
Nagar (Ahmadnagar), 101
Nāgarāj, 60, 188*n*
Nagarkar Gavḷīs. *See* Gavḷīs
Nāgas, Nāgs, 28, 45, 59–60, 188, 189*n*. *See also* Snakes
Nāgobā, 25, 27, 30
Nāgpañcamī, 133–34, 190
Nāgpūr, 19–20
Nagpur District, 7
Nāgrāj. *See* Nāgarāj
Nāīkobā, 167–68, 195. *See also* Naikyā
Nāīk(s), 83, 156–57
Jivājī Bomlā, 83
of Phalṭaṇ, 158. *See also* Nimbāḷkar(s)

Nāīk(s) (*continued*)
  Rāmjī, Bhangria, 83
  Umājī, 85, 166, 171
  Vijayaranga, 157
nāīks (nāyakas), 156
Naikyā (Nāīk), 194–95. *See also* Naikobā
naivedya, 64–65, 67, 119–20, 133, 177, 210–12, 229–30. *See also nived*
Nājhre, 181
nakṣatra name (*nāvras*), 146–47
Naḷdurg, 106, 159, 189, 196
Nāmdev, 139, 190. *See also* Nemdev
Naming ceremony, 163. *See also bāras, barsā, barseṃ*
Nandāī Pāṭlīn, 47
Nandaji Gaikavad, 162*n*
Nāndeḍ, 154
Nanded District, 123
Nandī, 86, 92, 111–12, 114, 127, 195, 201
Nandīkeśvar, 195
Nandīkoṭkūr Taluka, 93*n*
Nandīvālās, 103, 152, 182
Nañjarājas of Mysore, 156
Nappiṉṉai, 17
Nārada, Nārada Muni, 175–76, 207
Nāraḷī Purṇimā, Nāraḷya-Puṇav, 82
Narasiṃha, 37, 200, 216*n*
Narayā Tarāḷe, Narī Tarāḷ, 35–36
Nārāyaṇ
  Birjī, 79
  Śeśnārāyaṇ, 28
Narbadā River, 75
Narsing (Narasiṃha), 37
Nārubā Gāvḍā, Nāru Gāvḍā, 35–36, 117
Nāsik, 19, 21, 41, 96, 100
Nasik District, 69
Nāsik Taluka, 96
Nātepute, 96, 171
Nāth, 23, 25, 27, 59, 177, 202, 211–13, 218, 232, 234. *See also* Mhaskobā; Mhasvaḍ-Śid; Śaṅkar; Siddhanāth; Siddheśvara; Śidobā; Śiva
  /"Nāth" Mhaskobā, Śrī Nāth, Śrī Nāth Mahārāj Maskobā, Śrī Nāth Maskobā, Śrī Nāth Mhaskobā, 202, 211–12, 216–27, 229, 231–34, 236–38
  /Nāth sect, Nine Nāths, 93, 95–96, 202
  names of the Nine, 95*n*
Nāthjī Prākaṭya Vartā, Śrī, 188
navas, 31, 76, 120, 141, 217. *See also* Vows
Nāvḷī, 167, 178
  /Nāvilī, Nāyevali, 167*n*
Navnāth sect. *See* Nāth
nāvrās. See nakṣatra name
Navrātra, 24, 134, 215, 233, 236
Nāyabā Gavḷī, 31–32
nāyakas, 107, 152, 156, 178
Nectar. *See amṛt*
Neem tree, 18
Nelkarañje, 31
Nemdev (Nāmdev), 71*n*
Nepal, 153, 195*n*
Neṭiyōṉ, 17
Neṭumāl, 17
Nevāsā, 41, 45
neytal, 12. *See also* Seashore
Nhāī Rūī, forest of, 87
Nhāvīs, 215, 218–19. *See also* Barbers
Nīlalocanā, 92
Nilamma, 108
Nilgiris, 10, 12, 106
Nimbāḷik, 158
Nimbāḷkar(s), 97
  Rāja Naik, Rāv Nāīk, 22, 158
  Rājās of Vaḍgāv, 158
Nimbāvḍe, 128
Nimbūt (Limbūt?), 179
Nimgāv, 162
Nimḷāk, 158
Nirā (town), 140, 162, 166–67, 169, 174, 177, 179, 194
Nirā Canal(s), 171, 180
  Left Hand, 167, 170, 179
  Right Hand, 171*n*
Nirā River, 5, 21–22, 34, 51–52, 75, 82, 122–23, 128, 131–32, 158, 162–63, 165*n*, 166–71, 173, 180, 182, 197, 211, 214–17, 223, 236
Nirṇayasindhu, 218*n*
niśān (flagstaff), 199–200
nived, 133–34, 136–38, 140. *See also naivedya*
  /*nivad,* 119
Nivṛttināth, 96
Nizam, 124
Nomadic life, 107, 129, 132. *See also* Migration and transhumance

Nomads, 8, 39, 45, 85, 125, 131–47, 166, 169, 181–82, 185, 204. *See also* Migration and transhumance
Non-Brahmanical dynasties, tribal elements, 195*n*
Nonvegetarian offerings, 210*n*. *See also* Sacrifice, animal
Noose (*pāśa*), 184*n*
Nuclear agricultural regions, 20–22, 90, 151, 153–54, 156, 171, 182
 and centers, 155

Oḍeru, 122
Ogilvy, T., 165
Oleander tree, 193
Oral traditions, v–vi, viii, xi, 45, 47, 127, 154, 174, 182, 205. *See also ovīs*
ovīs, viii, 29, 45, 61–67, 77–83, 86–88, 127, 204–5
 performance of, 77
Oxen, 102, 154, 158, 173. *See also* Cattle; *specific types of oxen*

pāḍā, pāḍī, 126
pāḍal (tree), 175
Paḍalkars, 135
Padmā, 51
Padma, Padmākhya, 108
Padmagoṇḍa, 110–11
Padmākṣī, 109
Padmaṇṇa, 107–8
 Undala, 108–9
Padmāvatī, 47–49, 50*n*
Padmiṇī (Padubāī), 47, 50
Padubāī, 45, 47–50, 72*n*, 120
pādukās, 212
pāhuṇā dev. *See* "Guest gods"
Paiṭhaṇ, 20–21, 70, 171, 185
Paiṭhaṇ Taluka, 7
pākhāḷaṇī, 230
Pāl, 155, 204
Pālāī, 155
pālai (desert region), 15, 18, 85
Pal̲an̲i, 196*n*
Palani hills, 12
Palanquin(s), 85, 125, 216, 221–22, 226–27, 229–30, 236. *See also pālkhi*
 processions, 215, 219*n*, 221, 227–28, 236
Paḷas, palāśa tree, 52, 108
Paḷayaṭṭhāṇa (Phalṭaṇ), 21
Pālī canon, 20, 101
pālkhī, 45, 117*n*, 120, 125, 196. *See also* Palanquin(s)
palli, 70
Palmyra tree, 87–88, 193
Pān, 29, 52, 141, 226, 229. *See also* Betel
Pānbharīs, 70
pañcāṅg, 193–94. *See also* Astrologer; Horoscope
Pañcgaṅgā River, [Pañc-]Gaṅgā, 7, 189
Pañcmāḍhi, 67
Pāṇḍaraṅgapallī (Paṇḍharpūr), 70
Paṇḍharpūr, 21–22, 24, 26–27, 30, 37, 45–48, 70–74, 90, 105, 137, 139, 147, 151, 171, 190, 230*n*
Paṇḍita, 93
Pāṇḍojī (Ghuṇe), 225
Pāṇḍuraṅg Viṭhobā, 190. *See also* Viṭhobā
Pānevalī, 224
paṅga, 32
Pānvale (Pānevalī?), 224
Panvel, 169
paraḷ, 199
Parameśvara, 74
Parasnis, Rao Bahadur D. B., 163
Parasols, 227, 236. *See also chatras;* Umbrellas
Paraśurām, Paraśurāma, 25*n*, 55–56
Pārbatī (Pārvatī), 48–50
Parbhani District, 7, 123, 126
Pareṇḍā, 73*n*
Pareṇḍā Taluka, 6, 97
"Parochialization," 174
Parvatāppā, 71*n*
Pārvatī, 17, 45, 48, 49*n*, 50, 52, 67–68, 91, 94, 110–12, 139*n*, 184, 192, 202, 204, 207
pāśa, 184*n*
pāsāryā, 202
Pasture(s), pastureland, and pastoral regions, vii, 4–6, 13–15, 26, 30, 59–60, 86*n*, 87–88, 95, 101–2, 104–7, 113, 115–19, 123, 132, 136*n*, 144, 153–54, 156–59, 161, 164–69, 171–73, 176, 178–80, 183–86, 197*n*, 202–6, 211, 216. *See also kuraṇ; māḷ; mullai*
pāṭāl, 27. *See also* Underworld
Pātālaskanda, 209

Pāṭaṇ Taluka, 33
Paṭaṇe Wāī, 235
Pāthardī Taluka, 6, 167
pāṭīls, 97, 163–64, 169–70, 177–78, 182, 225
Paṭṭaṇ Kuḍolī, 35–38, 40, 47, 72–75, 106–7, 113, 116, 117*n*, 120, 123, 138, 164, 190, 199–201
/Kaḍulī, Kaḍulī Paṭṭaṇ, 35, 116–20
pattemane, 103
Paunā, Pavana River, 35, 50*n*, 162*n*
Pauṣ (month), 33, 215, 237
Pavārs, 22*n*, 158, 170
Pax Britannica, 180
Peacock feather(s), peacock feather brushes, 199, 225, 227, 234, 236. *See also* *morcel*
Peṃber, 155
Pennagaram, 10
Periplus, 21
Peśvā(s), 22, 23*n*, 83, 161, 163, 165
Bājī Rāv, Bājirāv I, 161–62
"slipper bearers" of, 163
style of architecture, 152, 162
peṭh, 157. *See also* Trade, centers of
Phālgun (month), 26, 128, 134, 163*n*
Phalṭaṇ, 21–22, 36, 51, 75–76, 97, 98*n*, 158, 163*n*, 164, 171, 172*n*
Phalṭaṇ range, 7, 131, 171
Phalṭaṇ Taluka, 5, 39, 75, 86, 122, 168–69
Pharaṇḍe land, 73
phaujdār, 230
Philosophers' stone, 222–23
Phiraṅgāī, 49*n*
Phirkāy, 49
Pidirāj, king, 51
Pilaji Gaikvad. *See* Gāikvāḍ(s)
Pilgrimage festivals, 33–34, 36, 39, 46, 72, 78*n*, 86, 90, 95–96, 106, 117*n*, 118, 120–21, 127, 135, 141, 145, 154–55, 170, 179, 182–83, 200, 204, 216, 218, 220–22, 225–30, 237. *See also* *jatrās*; Somvatī Amāvāsyā
Pilgrimage routes, 72, 97, 174
Pilgrimages, pilgrims, 78, 209
Pilīv, 33
piṇḍ, *piṇḍī*, 23–24, 30, 199
piṅglyā prophecy, 74
Pipaḷ trees, 43*n*, 118–19, 193–95
pīrs, 121, 167
Plaques, stamped silver, 138
Plateau (Deś), 69, 105, 125, 128, 169. *See also* Deccan
Pliny, 195*n*
Poison, 28–29, 59
Poles, 227, 230, 234, 236. *See also* *kāṭhīs*; *kāvaḍ*
Poli, 126
poḷīs. *See* *puraṇpoḷīs*
Pollution, 89, 180*n*. *See also* Impurity; Purification
Ponds, 15, 37, 54, 114
Pool (*ḍoh*). *See* Water hole
Poona, x, xiii, 3–4, 19–20, 49, 70, 85, 96, 152, 156, 158, 161, 165–66, 171, 174, 183, 226, 237
Poona District, ix, 3–5, 33, 40, 47, 49, 51, 56, 61*n*, 77, 95*n*, 98, 104, 113, 116, 125, 127, 133*n*, 147, 152, 162, 165, 170, 177*n*, 186, 197, 200, 210, 224
Population density, 165
Possession, 57–58, 78*n*, 116, 140, 142–46, 182, 193, 196, 213, 228–29. *See also* *aṅgāt yeṇeṃ*; *jhāḍ*, *devācī*
pothī, *puti*, 121, 204
potrāj, Pot-Razu, *poṭṭurāju*, 57–58
Power(s). *See* *guṇ*; Magic; Miracles; Śakti; *sattva*; *siddhis*
Pracaṇḍāsur, 98
pradhān, 28
Pralhād, 215, 216*n*
prasād, 168, 218–19, 235, 237
Pratiṣṭhāna (Paiṭhaṇ), 20–21, 185
Precipitation. *See* Drought; Monsoon; Rain
Prehistoric finds, 76*n*. *See also* Archaeological remains; Microliths, prehistoric
Prempūr, 155, 189
Privilege, ritual. *See* *mān*; Right of worship, honorary
Processions. *See* Palanquin(s); *pālkhī*
Prophecy, 182, 196, 214*n*, 228
Ptolemy, 14, 19*n*
Puchrī, 188
puḍhārīs, 117–19
pūjā, 54, 75, 177, 181, 211, 216, 232, 236
sixteen rites of worship in, 218
pūjārīs, 24–25, 27, 40–41, 117*n*, 120, 171, 231, 235
Pūnaka Viṣaya (Poona), 19*n*

Puṇḍalik, 46, 72
Puṇe, Puṇeṃ (Poona), 174
puṟam poetry, 11
Purāṇas, 20, 49, 58, 67, 100, 110, 118*n*, 203, 207*n*, 208. *See also purāṇic* ideas, *purāṇic* mythology
Purandar hills, 7
Purandar Taluka, 4, 51, 56, 61, 95*n*, 113, 125, 127, 133*n*, 139, 147, 152, 174, 197, 210
Purandares, 231. *See also* Ābāsāheb Purandare; Umābāīsāheb (Purandare)
purāṇic ideas, 185
purāṇic mythology, viii, 23, 55–58, 67–68, 99, 181*n*, 199, 201–2. *See also* Purāṇas; *specific deities*
purāṇik kāl (the hoary past), 174
puraṇpoḷīs (poḷīs), 67, 133–34, 140
Purification, 125. *See also* Impurity; Pollution
Pūrṇagaṅgā, 210, 212, 223, 227
Pūrvamīmāṃsāsūtras, vi
Pusegāv, 33

Quarrels. *See* Disputes

Rabārīs, 124*n*, 180*n*
rabi crops, 7
Rādhā, 46
Rafts, children floated on, 76
Rai doab, 8
Raicur, 7
Raicur District, 89
Rain, 3–8, 78–79, 165, 179, 228. *See also* Drought; Monsoon
/rainy season, 101, 167, 169
Rājārāma (Śivājī's son), 158
Rajasthan, 124*n*, 154, 180*n*, 195*n*
Rājāvaḷ Pond, 37
Rājputāna, 199
Rājputs, 197
Rājurī plateau, 7
Rākh, 140
Rakhu, Rakhumāī, 45–46
rakṣak. *See* Guardian deities
rakṣasa, rakṣasī. *See* Demonesses; Demons
"Rām, Rām" (greeting), 117, 176
Rām, Rāma, 48–49, 84–85, 175–76, 185*n*
Rām Corāmble, 159
Rāmacandradeva Yādava, 151, 198
Rāmāyaṇ, *Rāmāyaṇa*, 174, 176
Rāmośīs, 84–88, 166–67, 174, 233
etymology of, 84–85
Ramuppa, 103
rān, 84, 87. *See also* Forests; *māḷrān*
rāṅgoḷī designs, 226
Rāṇojī Śinde, 164
rānvāsī, 84
Rashin Circle, 6
Rāṣṭrakuṭas, 19*n*, 21
Ratnāgiri (Jyotibā), 184
Ratnagiri District, 21
Ratnāṅgī, 109
Rāūt, Rāūt Māḷī, Rāūts, 212–13, 215, 219, 225–27, 236
Rāūtvāḍī, 225–26
Rāv Govinda, 100
Rāvaḷ mountain, 75
Rāvaṇ, 49
Rāvjī Anagaḷ, 223–24
Rāyalasīma, 8, 67, 107
Rāygoṇḍa (Liṅgāyat Pāṭīl), 121
Red lead, 24*n*, 50, 76*n*, 136, 141, 186, 231. *See also śendūr*
reḍā (male buffalo), 104
Reḍḍis, 112–13
Reḍeśvar, 41, 201
regur soil, 7
Reṇukā, 25*n*, 55. *See also* Yeḷammā
Revaṇa, Revaṇa Siddha, Revaṇa Siddheśvar, Revaṇasiddha, Revaṇasiddheśvar, 93–94, 107, 110, 114–15
Ṛgveda, 71*n*, 101, 208
Rice, vii, 3–4, 8–9, 12–13, 15, 19, 48, 56, 65, 76, 94, 96, 105, 132, 144, 153–54, 182–83, 194*n*, 213*n*, 226*n*
Rickwalldar, 85
Rifles, 113. *See also* Muskets
Right Hand Canal. *See* Nirā Canal(s)
Right of worship, honorary, 34, 36, 72*n*, 75, 146, 171, 179, 200, 221, 225, 227, 236. *See also mān*
rikāmacāvaḍī, 227
Robbers, 83–88, 98, 103, 155, 166, 174–75. *See also* Cattle, theft; Highway robbers
Robertson, H. D., 165
Rohā, 145
Rome, 20
Roosters, 200*n*. *See also* Cocks

Ropes from twelve cots, 43
Routes. *See* Pilgrimage routes; Trade routes
ṛṣis, 55, 91–92, 121, 195*n*, 201, 207*n*, 208. *See also devṛṣīs; specific ṛṣis*
Ruben, vi
Rubies, 224
Rudra, *rudras*, 90, 184
rudrākṣa beads, 238
Rūī, 120, 171
Rukmiṇī, 45–47, 71
Russell and Hiralal, 95

sabhāmaṇḍapa, 97, 164, 195
Sacrifice, animal, 67, 104, 135–38, 140, 143, 146, 186, 188, 215, 225, 227, 230. *See also* Nonvegetarian offerings
 of cocks, 137
 dāvaṇ, 135–36
 of a fowl, 186
 of goats, 136–37, 186
 of rams, 67, 135–36
 of sheep, 65, 114, 117–18, 135–38, 181, 194
  of a pregnant, 146
Sacrifice, Brahmanical, 20, 103*n*, 207. *See also* Fire, sacrifice; *hom*
 Dakṣa's, 199
Sacrifice, human, 136, 213–15
Sadāśiva (Śiva), 93–94, 110
sādhūs, 68, 73*n*, 95, 168, 170, 181, 188, 205. *See also* Ascetics; Gosāvīs; *yogīs*
Śāh Jahān, 83, 156
Śāhjī, 165
Śāhū of Sātārā, king, 159, 178, 179*n*, 217–18, 222–25, 228
Sahyādri mountains, 4*n*, 131, 174
Śaiva deity(ies), 72, 137, 147, 184
 Viṭhobā as a, 137, 147, 172
Śaiva Gosāvīs, viii. *See also* Gosāvīs
Śaiva hero cults, 71*n*. *See also* Hero stones; Heroes; *vīragaḷas*
Śaka era, 70*n*
Sakhārāmbovā Pāṇḍhare Māḷī, 226
Śakti, 50, 204
Sāle, 187
Salem District, 10, 15, 107
 North, 153
śāligrāmas, 155
Śālivāhana, king, 70
Sāḷobā, 181
śāluṇkhā, 160
samādhī (state), 76
samādhīs (graves), 32, 71*n*, 167
Sambhā [Śambhu] (Śiva), 80
sampādnī, saṃpādaṇī, saṃpādaṇūk, 77*n*
Saṃvadattī. *See* Saundattī
Sanctum. *See garbhārā*
Sandals, leather, 196
sandhyā, 148
Saṅgamner Taluka, 6
Saṇgar Dhangars. *See* Dhangars
Sāṅglī, 104
Sangli District, 3, 5, 27, 33, 41, 43, 58, 60, 66, 86*n*, 89, 120, 122, 128–29, 136, 148, 152, 164, 190, 204, 209*n*
Sāṅgolā, 26, 33, 97, 105
Sāṅgolā Taluka, 6, 96
Śanivār palace, 161
Śaṅkar, 23–24, 27–29, 31–32, 42, 45, 48–49, 86, 98, 192, 201–4, 208–9, 234. *See also* Mahādev; Śiva
Śaṅkarājī Ghuṇe, 216, 222
Sanna Bhaire Gauḍa, 156
sannyāsīs, 27, 90. *See also* Ascetics
Sanskrit culture, 60
Sanskrit literature, v, vii–viii, 100. *See also* Brahmans, literature of; Dharmaśāstras; Purāṇas; Śāstras; *smṛtis*
Sanskritic deities, 57–58, 83–84. *See also* Brahmans, pantheon of; *purāṇic* mythology
Sanskritization, vi, 147, 204. *See also* Brahmanization
Sardārs, 158, 161, 164
sardeśmukhs, 22*n*, 158–59, 224–25
Sārṇabā, 31–32, 180
Sarpaṭīnāth, 95*n*
Sāstevāḍī, 194
Śāstras, 208. *See also* Dharmaśāstra(s); *smṛtis*
Sāsvaḍ, 49–50, 96, 113, 210, 219, 222, 229, 231
 basin, 7
sāt āsarā, sātī āsarās, 4*n*, 30, 36. *See also* Seven Āsarās
Sātārā, 19, 22, 26, 40, 85, 159, 174, 177–78, 217, 219, 222–24, 228, 237
Satara District, 3, 5, 21, 33–34, 39–40, 43, 48*n*, 75, 77, 86, 89, 121–22, 124, 129, 135*n*, 137, 151–52, 155, 159*n*,

163–65, 170, 173, 204
Sātavāhanas, 4*n,* 20, 41, 70*n,* 100
satī stones, 139
Sāṭpuḍā plateau, 9
Saturdays, 26
sattva, satva, 37, 74*n,* 213–14, 216–18, 221–22. *See also* Integrity
Saṭvāī, 56*n*
Satya Age, 37–39, 45, 73–75, 120
/Golden Age, 148–50
Saundattī, 32, 40, 51, 55
Saurāṣṭra, 170
Sāvantvāḍī, 21
sāvkārs, 73. *See also* Merchants
Sāvtā Māḷī, 216
Sāyabā, 147, 180
Sāyājī (Tayājī), 147
Sciences, fifty-two magical (*bāvan vidyā*), 51, 54–55
Scorpions, 37
Seashore (*neytal*), vii, 12
Sects, extra-Brahmanical, 22. *See also* Buddhists; Jainas; Liṅgāyat(s); Mahānubhāv sect
Śeṃburḍe, 224
śendūr, 47, 50, 76, 136, 141, 168, 197, 200, 213*n*. *See also* Red lead
Serpents. *See* Snakes
Service castes, twelve (*bārā balutedārs*), 70, 85
Śeṣ, Śeś, Śeṣanārāyaṇa, Śeśnārāyan, Śeṣnārāyaṇ, 27–29, 59
Settlement, in valleys, of people from hills, 47, 187
Seven Āsarās, 37–39, 42–43. *See also sāt āsarā*
Seven Bhivāyā, Bhivayyā. *See* Bhivāī
Seven sisters, 40, 55. *See also* Bhivāī; *sāt āsarā;* Seven Āsarās
Seven Veḷvand-women, 76
Shaman, 142
Sheep
bathing of. *See* Bath, bathing
origin of, 67, 107–8, 110, 112, 133, 191
penning of, in farmers' fields, 88, 113, 128, 132, 167
sacrifice of. *See* Sacrifice, animal
Shields, 197–99
Sholapur District, 3, 6, 27, 33, 57*n,* 61, 70, 71*n,* 72, 73*n,* 86, 89, 96, 106, 113, 121, 123, 126, 128–29, 138, 151–52, 164, 190
Shrines, portable, 39, 42–43
Siddarāmayya, 91, 93–94
Siddavvā, 111
Siddha(s), 27, 29, 94, 95, 107, 162, 164, 171, 210. *See also* Kāḷbhairav; Kamaḷā Śinde; Sonārsiddha
Siddhanāth, 23–25, 27–30, 32, 89*n*. *See also* Mhasvaḍ-Śid; Nāth; Siddheśvara; Śiddhobā
Siddhapuruṣa, 31
Siddharām, 94
siddhas, 37, 116, 146, 182, 202, 215, 227, 233. *See also sīds,* Śids, *śīds*
Siddheśvar (of Śolāpūr), 94–95
Siddheśvar Kurolī, 135*n,* 137
Siddheśvara, 23. *See also* Mhasvaḍ-Śid; Nāth; Siddhanāth; Śiddhobā
siddhis, 43, 95, 146, 202
Siddhobā, Śidobā, 23, 143, 145, 189. *See also* Mhasvaḍ-Śid; Nāth; Siddhanāth; Siddheśvara
Śidojī, 25
sīds, Śids, *śīds,* 78*n,* 116, 146, 164, 215, 227–28. *See also* Kamalā Śinde; Kamaḷājī; *siddhas;* Sūryabā
Khilubā the Śid, 37–38
śikhar (dome), 25
śikhārkhānā, 217
Śilāhāras, 21
śīledārs, 30, 124*n,* 161, 163–64, 198, 205
Silloḍ Taluka, 7
Silver coins, 176, 224
Śiṃgā, 128, 134, 163. *See also* Hoḷī
Śimpīs, 117*n,* 121, 231–32
Śinde(s), 163–64, 199. *See also* Kamaḷā Śinde
Rāṇojī, 164
Śinde Gosāvīs, 96
Sindias, 163
śiṅg. *See* Horns
Śiṅgāḍe Dhangars, 186
Śiṅgāḍe family, 214–15, 226, 229
Śiṅgṇāpūr, 75, 78*n,* 86*n,* 105, 131–32, 171
Sinnar, 100
Sirsaṅgī, Sirsaṅgīcī Kāḷavā, 40
Sirūr Taluka, 4, 177*n*
Śirval, 33
Sītā, 48–49

Śiva, vii, 17, 27, 50, 52, 55–58, 68, 70, 75, 86–87, 89–96, 99*n*, 108, 110–12, 114–15, 116*n*, 127–28, 139, 151–52, 160*n*, 164, 171, 181, 193*n*, 195, 198–99, 200*n*, 201, 203–5, 208–9, 219*n*. *See also* Bhoḷā; Īśvar; Mahādev; Śaṅkar
pañcamukha of, 93
yogī, 170
Śivājī (Marāṭhā king), 42, 124, 136*n*, 155, 157–59, 161, 165
Śivājī Ḍubal, 24–25
Śivarātrī, 230
Śivpurī, 139*n*
Skanda, 17, 41*n*, 45, 85, 155, 174, 183, 188, 205–6
Skull (*kapālā*), 199
Sky chariot (*vimān*), 202
smaśāna, 168, 181
smṛtis, 60*n*. *See also* Dharmaśāstra(s)
/*Manusmṛti*, 73, 180*n*
Snakes, snake deities, 27–29, 35*n*, 45, 47, 50, 103, 108, 112, 170, 184, 188, 189*n*, 190, 193, 205, 211, 234. *See also* Cobras; Nāgas; Nāgobā; Śeṣ
Soil, vii, 4–5, 7, 33, 157, 166, 182. *See also regur* soil
Śolāpūr, 6, 19, 22, 94–95, 113, 153
Solāpūr-Siddha, 210
Somā Mahāldār, 117–19
Somanātha Māhātmya, Śrī, 169–70
Someśvar, 169–71
Śrī, of Sorṭī, 170
Someśvar Sovideva (Kalacuri king), 199
Somnāth, 170
Somvatī Amāvāsyā, 85, 125, 134, 192–93, 196, 216, 236
Son Koḷīs. *See* Koḷīs
Sonār, Rāmacandra Udavanta, 70
Sonārī, 23, 27, 30–32, 42, 96–99, 164, 179–80, 204, 210–11, 213
Sonārsiddha (Siddha of Sonārī, Sonārī-Siddha), 27, 97, 210
Songīr fort, 100
Sonnaligī, 94
Sonsaḷī, 190
Sonyādaitya, 23
Śorāpūr, 84
Sorṭī (Saurāṣṭra), 170
Spate, O. H. K., 6–7
Spears, 16, 124–25, 138, 187*n*, 205
/bear-spear, 124
/lance, 206
Spirits, nature, 185–87
śraddhā (desire), 141
śrāddha, 180*n*
Śrāvaṇ (month), 26, 82*n*, 125, 133, 170, 237
Śrī Vaiṣṇavas, 103
Śrīgonda Taluka, 6
Śrīśailam, Śrīśaila, 16, 93–94, 111, 115
Stein, Burton, 20*n*, 156
sthān, 237. *See also devsthān*
sthāpaṇuk. *See thāpaṇuk*
Subedar of the Deccan (Nizam), 124
Subramaṇyan̲, Subramhaṇya, 17, 188*n*
Sudrasain [Sudarśan] Bhagavān, 79
Sugarcane, 7, 9, 15, 171, 182, 226
Suggaladēvē, Suggalādevī, 93–94
Sūḷ(s), 172
Rāmā, 172
Sultān Tipū, 157
Sultanates of the Deccan, five, 155–56, 196
Sultānpūr (Paṇḍharpūr), 74*n*
Sumālinī, 108
Sun, 66, 74*n*, 75, 125, 192–93, 214, 236*n*. *See also* Mārtaṇḍa Bhairava; Sūrya
Sunandā, 108
Sundays, 164, 168, 193, 214, 236
supārī, 79*n*. *See also* Betel
Supe, 49, 177, 226
Sūravantī, Sūravantī Bāī, 104, 134, 192, 204. *See also* Gaṅgā-Sūravantī; Sūryavatī
Sūrdī, 58
Sūrya, 192. *See also* Mārtaṇḍa Bhairava; Sun
Sūryabā, Sūryabā Śid, 116, 136, 189–90
Sūryavatī, 192
Sutār(s), 121
Jānyā, 35–36
Suttanipāta, 20
Suvarṇapurī (Sonārī), 99
Suvarṇāsur, the demon Suvarṇa, 98–99
Śvāśva, 197. *See also* Bhairav
svayaṃbhū images of deities, 31, 170, 205, 213
Swords, 42, 124, 145, 176, 184*n*, 197–99, 202, 217–18, 228–29
Śivājī's ("Bhavānī"), 42, 124

Syed Siraj ul Hassan, 8, 9*n*, 51, 101, 105, 109, 123–24

Tagara. *See* Ter
Tailors. *See* Śimpīs
Takaṭūr, 15
Ṭakayā (Tukāī), 52
Ṭakles, 193–94
Taḷegāv Ḍhamḍhere, 177
Tāṃbe, Limbājī (Dhangar), 235
Tamil deities, 184
Tamil literature, ancient, vii, 15. *See also* Caṅkam literature
Tamilnadu, 10, 14, 57–58, 197
Tammāpura, 110
tāndaḷ, tāndaḷā, 181, 194, 213
Tāndaḷe family, 227
Tanjore, 15
tapa (twelve years), 42
tapa, tapas, tapaścaryā, 32, 38*n*, 39, 42, 46, 48, 72*n*, 73, 95, 98, 201. *See also* Asceticism
Taptī River, 7
Taraḍe, Tarḍes, 178, 214–15, 226
Taraṭī trees, 160, 189
Tārgāv, 40
Tarvaḍ (taravaḍ) leaves, tree, 160, 210–11, 214
Tāsgāv Taluka, 120, 122*n*, 136, 148
Taxation of land, 83, 156, 165–66. *See also* Tolls
Tayājī (Sāyājī), 147
Telaṅgaṇa, 51, 57, 102, 109, 112
  plateau, 8
Telīs, 233
Ter, 21, 41
Termite mounds, 93*n*, 95, 111, 133–34, 157, 172, 176, 188–93, 205, 212
Terracotta shrines (usually for Mhasobā), 26–27, 196–97*n*
Teyvayānai, 16
Thana District, 21, 169
thāpaṇuk (investiture of a *devṛṣī*), 143, 145
Theūr, 76*n*
Thieves. *See* Cattle, theft; Corācī Āḷaṇḍī; Corācī Uṇḍavḍī; Highway robbers; Robbers
Thiṭe, Koṇḍbhaṭ, 232–33
Ṭhombres, 173, 178
Ṭhombrevāḍī, 77
Thorats, 171
Three and a half, as significant number, 119–20, 123, 133*n*
Tigers, 103, 166, 188, 211, 217. *See also* Vāghjāī, Vāghobā, Vāghyās
tiṇai, 11
Tipū Sultān, 157
Tirāḷes, 121
tīrthas, viii, 47, 97–98, 209. *See also* Vīrcand *tīrtha*
Tirumāl, 17
Ṭodar Māl, 83, 166
Todas, 10
Tolls, 178*n*. *See also* Taxation
Toran pasture, 36, 116
Tortoise relief in temple courtyard, 232, 234–36
Torvevāḍī, 176–77
"Totem" (*devak*), 226*n*
Trade, 20–22, 96–97, 127, 151–55, 183. *See also* Bazaars; Cattle, markets; Markets; Merchants
  centers of, 21, 95, 97, 153, 157–58
Trade routes, 6, 20–21, 90, 97, 151, 154–55, 174
  intersections of. *See* Crossroads
Traikuṭakas, 21
Transformation of a cult of herders into a cult of farmers, or of all castes, ix, 17, 71*n*, 177, 180–85, 197*n*, 204–5
Transhumance. *See* Migration; Nomadic life; Nomads
Treasure, buried, 176, 192
Tribes, 18, 147, 174, 179, 195*n*. *See also* Forest tribes; Hill tribes; Mountain(s); *specific tribes*
Tribal system, 103
Trident (*triśūl*), 29, 53–55, 96, 99, 164, 198–99, 208, 215
Trimbak, Trimbakeśvar, Tryambakeśvar, 69, 96
Tripurasundarī, 58
Tristapitha, 157
triśūl, trisūl, 29, 96, 198. *See also* Trident
Trustworthiness. *See sattva*
Tryambakeśvar, 69. *See also* Trimbak
Tubes, cloth, 227
Tuesdays, 168
Tukāī, 40, 42, 48, 52, 56–58, 99, 227
  plateau of Śrī, 212, 227, 236

Tukārām, 43
Tukavvā (Tukāī), Tuḷjāpūrcī Tukavvā, 40
Tulājī Baḍade (Crazy Tuḷyā, Tuḷājī, Tuḷājī Bovā, Tuḷyā), 219–22, 226
Tuḷjābāī, 48. *See also* Bhavānī
Tuḷjāpūr, 24, 32, 40, 42, 85, 99, 154
Tuḷjāpūr Taluka, 6
Tuḷjāpūrcī Tukavvā, 40. *See also* Bhavānī
Tuḷśī birdāvan [*vṛndāvan*] bush, 87–88
Tumkur, 9
Tumkur District, 102
Tuṅgabhadrā dam, 6, 8
Tuṅgabhadrā River, 5–6, 8
Turbans, 61–63, 65, 124*n*, 125, 199, 218
  red, 125, 131, 169
Turmeric powder, 35–36, 39, 53*n*, 61–64, 66, 73, 115–16, 118, 138, 141*n*, 160, 163*n*, 187, 193, 225, 227, 234*n*. *See also bhaṇḍār; haḷaḍ*
Twelve families, *vāḍās, vāḍīs,* villages, 61, 126–28, 169

Udgīr, 155
Udgīr Taluka, 6
udyāpan (installation ceremony), 25
Ujanī Maṅkhāl, Ujanī Mhaṅkāl, Ujjanī Mahākāḷ, Ujjainī Mahākāl, 52, 94*n*, 164
Ujjain, Ujjayanī, 51–52, 94*n*, 164, 210*n*
Ujjanīkar, Dattanāth, 164
Umābāīsāheb (Purandare), 231
Umājī Nāīk, 85, 166, 171
Umāmaheśvara pose, 139*n*
Umbar trees, 52, 55
Umbrellas, 142, 225, 227–28, 236. *See also chatras;* Parasols
Umyā, 61, 63
Undala Padmanna, 108–9
Undavḍī. *See* Corācī Uṇḍavḍī; Gavlyāncī Undavḍī
Underworld, 27–28, 59–60, 112, 184, 209. *See also nāgalok; pātāḷ*
Unnikaṅkaṇ Dhangars, Kurubas. *See* Dhangars; Kurubas
Untouchables, 89, 216. *See also specific Untouchable groups*
upanayana, 208*n*
Uprising of 1857, 229
Ūru Gollas, Kurubas. *See* Gollas; Kurubas

Usmānābād, 194
Usmanabad District, 3, 6, 21, 23, 27, 40, 73*n*, 97, 106, 154, 158–59, 179, 189, 210*n*
Usmānābād Taluka, 6–7
Utensils emerging from water (in the past), 76

Vaḍ tree, 34, 120, 158. *See also* Banyan tree
vāḍā (fort), 161, 178
vāḍā, vāḍī (sheep pen, pastoralists' camp, hamlet), 25, 39, 60–66, 86, 117*n*, 126–28, 131–39, 141–42, 146–47, 159, 161, 163, 166–68, 171–73, 177–79, 193, 202–3, 210–12, 223, 225
vaḍaḍ, 122
Vaḍapurī, 152
Vaḍgāv, 224
Vaḍgāv Nimbāḷkar, 158
vāḍī. See vāḍā, vāḍī
Vaḍjāī, 34, 173
Vadūj, 33
vāghāṃṭī, vāghāṭī bush, 87
Vāghjāī, 49–50
Vāghobā, 50*n*, 85
Vāghs, 227
Vāghyās, 124–25
vāhanas, 181, 195–98, 200*n*, 205. *See also* Mounts
vaidūrya, 115
Vaijāpūr Taluka, 7
Vaingaṅgā basin, 9
Vairāg-Siddha, 210
Vaiṣṇava *bhakti. See bhakti*
Vaiṣṇava Gosāvīs, viii. *See also* Gosāvīs
Vaiṣṇava Viṭhobā, 71*n*, 137, 172
Vaiṣṇava(s), 172
  and prevaiṣṇava god, 188
  sādhu, 188
Vaiṣṇavized Kṛṣṇa, 172
Vajarkar Gavḷīs. *See* Gavḷīs
vajra, 115. *See also* Diamonds
Vākaḷ, 37
Vākāṭakas, 21
Vakkaligas, 19*n*, 108, 112–13, 156
  Morasu, 156
Vālaṇḍ (Veḷvand), 76
Vālhā, 95*n*, 168–69, 174–75

Vālhyā Koḷī, 174–76, 179
Vaḷḷi, 16–17, 106
Vālmīki, Ṛṣi Vālmīki, 174–76
  gotra, 174*n*
Vaḷunj, 50
Vāmadeva, 208
vana, vanam, viii, 107. *See also* Forests
vaṇij, 153
Vāṇīs, 26, 30. *See also* Liṅgāyat(s)
Vanśrī, 60
vanvās, 52*n*
varaippu, 13
Vārāṇasī, 27. *See also* Banaras, Kāśī
Vārkarī sect, 137
Varṇā River, 116, 128, 190
Varṣapratipadā, 133*n*. *See also* Guḍhī Pāḍvā
vārū ("horses"), 196*n*
Vāśī, 113, 197
Vaśiṣṭha, 208
vastī, 24, 98, 159, 173, 203. *See also* Hamlet; *vāḍā, vāḍī*
Vāsudeva, 17
vatandārs, 179
Vaṭeśvar, 158
Vaudeville, Charlotte, 188
Vedas, 89, 118*n*, 208–9. *See also* Ṛgveda
Vegetarian(s), vegetarian offerings, vegetarianism, 67, 85, 89, 114, 121–22, 133–37, 194, 210*n*, 230*n*
vēlaṉ, 16
Veḷāpūr, 96, 151–52
Veḷvand, 76
Vetāḷ, 37, 85, 99, 197*n*, 201
vhaīk. *See* Prophecy
Vhoṭkars, Vhaṭkars, 173, 214–15, 226
vibhūt, 51, 53*n*. *See also* Ashes
Vidarbha, 19–20
vidyā, bāvan, 51
vidyās, fourteen, 118
  listed, 118*n*
Vīhe, 33
vihīr (well), 175
Vijayanagar, Vijayanagara, 113, 155–57, 161
Vijayaranga Nāīk, 157
vimān, 202
Vinayāditya I, 22
Vīr (place), ix, 33, 51–52, 55–57, 59, 67, 76*n*, 95*n*, 97, 116, 135–36, 143, 145–46, 167, 177, 181*n*, 182–84, 186, 188, 197, 202, 204, 210, 216, 219–20, 224–27, 229, 231, 233–35, 237
  Śrī Kṣetra, 210
Vīr dam, 75, 171*n*
Vīr Malhār, 42–43
Vīr Velhāl, 42–43
Vīra, 20, 185
Vīra Viṭhṭhala Cakravarti (Viṭhobā), 71*n*
Vīra-Baṇañjas, 90–92, 153
Vīra-Banañju-dharaṇa, 90
Vīrabhadra, 57, 91, 187, 203, 206
vīragaḷas, vīrgaḷs, 71*n*, 84, 152, 203. *See also* Hero stones; Memorial stones
Viraktas, 89–90. *See also* Jaṅgamas
Vīraśaivas, 94*n*. *See also* Liṅgāyat(s)
Vīrcand *tīrtha,* 216, 222
Vīreśa, 108
Vīreśvar, 182, 203*n*, 206, 237
Vīrkar, Khaṇḍojī, 162
Vīrobā, 202. *See also* Birobā
vīrs, vīras, 121, 200, 202–3. *See also bāvan vīr;* Kañcavīras; Masan Buvā, Masan Vīr
viruda, 199–200. *See also bāvan birudeṃ*
Viṣṇu, 17, 89, 103, 147–50, 155*n*, 192*n*, 200–201, 207–9
  /Mahāviṣṇu, 209
  /Viśṇu Mahārāj, 149
Viṣṇuvardhana Vīra Ballāladeva, 100
Viśva, 93
Viśvanāth, Viśveśvara, 27, 209. *See also* Kāśīviśvanāth
Viṭhobā, 45–48, 70, 71*n*, 72*n*, 74*n*, 77, 106, 137, 147, 151, 172, 190, 193, 216*n*, 224, 230*n*. *See also* Iṭṭhal; Pāṇḍuraṅg Viṭhobā; Viṭṭhal
Viṭhojī (Ghuṇe), 216, 222
Viṭhṭhala (Viṭhobā), 71*n*
Viṭṭhal, 47, 72, 74, 78, 151, 199–200. *See also* Iṭṭhal; Viṭhobā
Votive figures, 31, 44, 47, 50*n*, 67, 123, 141*n*, 162, 186, 196–97, 205
  of animals, 67, 205
  of bulls, 31
  of cattle, 50*n*, 123, 162, 186, 196
  of cows, 31, 141*n*, 197
  of deities, 44, 47
  of horses, 196–97, 198*n*

Votive figures (*continued*)
of rams, 197
of sheep, 141*n*
Vows, 31, 76, 120, 124, 141, 217, 236–37. *See also navas*
vraja, 101
vṛtti, 219, 222

Wāghmoḍes, 113, 164
Wāī, 178*n,* 215, 218–19, 225–26
Wāī Taluka, 40, 48*n,* 152
Walwa, 165
War, warfare, 11, 14, 71*n,* 124, 155, 164–66, 182, 198, 202, 206, 228. *See also* Battle; Cattle, theft; Military campaigns
Wardha, 124
Warriors, 18, 22, 69, 83, 125, 156, 164, 197–98
Wasteland, vii, 98, 174. *See also* Deserts; Forests; *pālai;* Wilderness
Watchmen, 70, 85, 126
Water hole (*ḍoh*), 36, 43, 75
Water offerings, 177
Wealth, 39, 90, 153, 166, 168, 176, 191, 222–24. *See also* Gold; Silver coins
Weddings. *See* Marriage
Wheat, 32, 79*n,* 133, 226*n*
Whips, 57–58, 200
Whitehead, Henry, 57
Wilderness, 27, 181–82, 184. *See also* Deserts; Forests; Wasteland
Wind, 54, 196
Bhoḷā's, 54
Witchcraft, 34, 186. *See also* Magic
Wives, gods with two, 16–17, 58–60, 67, 184
Wool, 9, 107–9, 111, 114, 169, 191, 222. *See also* Blankets (woolen)
Wrestling matches, wrestlers, 176, 179, 195*n,* 199. *See also mallas*

Yādava(s), 10, 22, 86*n,* 100–101, 151, 155–56, 198
period, 71*n,* 151–55, 178
yajamān, yejamāna, 103
yakṣas, 20*n,* 45, 185, 195, 200
yakṣī, 31
Yalammā, Yalammāī, Yallamma, Yallammāī, 27–29, 33, 40, 55. *See also* Yeḷammā
Yallavvā (Yeḷammā), Ḍoṅgarcī Yallavvā, 40
Yalu Gavḷan, Yelu, Yeḷu Gavḷan, Yelu Gavḷaṇ, 56, 86–88, 127
Yam, Yama, 181, 210
Yamajī, 23–25
Yamunā River, 82, 101
Yantra, 24*n*
yātrā, 225. *See also* Pilgrimages, pilgrims
Yeḍyā Khilubā (Khilubā), 72, 74
Yekavvā (Ekavvā), 44
Yeḷammā, Yeḷammāī, Yellammāī, 25*n,* 27, 32, 34, 39–40, 42, 50–57, 106. *See also* Ellammā; Marīammā; Reṇukā; Yalammā; Yallavvā
Yeḷmakkaḷtāī, 35–36, 55
Yeḷubāī, 56
Yerlā River, 7
yeśkars, 70
Yetāḷ (Vetāḷ), 37, 197*n*
yogamāyā, 207. *See also māyā*
Yogeśvarī, 28, 31–32, 50, 56, 58, 67, 183–84, 187. *See also* Jogāī; Jogeśvarī; Jogubāī
Yogiṇīs, sixty-four, 42, 99
yogīs, 59, 170, 202–3, 206. *See also* Gosāvīs; *sādhūs*
Śiva, 170
Yogīśvara, 183, 206. *See also* Skanda
yonī, 160*n*